THE ORIGIN AND GROWTH
OF RELIGION

THE
ORIGIN AND GROWTH
OF RELIGION
FACTS AND THEORIES

BY

W. SCHMIDT
PROFESSOR IN THE UNIVERSITY OF VIENNA

TRANSLATED FROM THE ORIGINAL GERMAN BY
H. J. ROSE
PROFESSOR OF GREEK IN THE UNIVERSITY OF ST. ANDREWS

NEW YORK
COOPER SQUARE
PUBLISHERS, INC.
1972

128359

Originally Published, 1931
Published 1971 by Cooper Square Publishers, Inc.
59 Fourth Avenue, New York, N. Y. 10003
International Standard Book No. 0-8154-0408-5
Library of Congress Catalog Card No. 74-184909

Printed in the United States of America

AUTHOR'S PREFACE

WHEN the second edition of my *Ursprung der Gottesidee*, Vol. I, appeared, a friendly critic expressed the opinion that that work, if only because of its great size, could not be used as a manual of the comparative history of religion. He was perfectly right, both for the reason he gave and because the various parts of the subject are there handled at full length, as they needs must be, since it was necessary to engage in extensive controversies in a work intended to clear away much that was out of date and to open new roads.

But the need for such a manual, giving a brief review of all that is essential for an understanding of the subject as it is to-day, has long been keenly felt. I have myself often regretted the lack of it in my own lectures. So, after long waiting, I have plucked up courage and found time to write such a manual myself, using the notes of a year's lectures which I have delivered both in the University of Vienna and at the Missionary Training College at St. Gabriel. The result is the work which I now offer to a wider public under the title of *The Origin and Growth of Religion : Facts and Theories*. I am not without hopes that by its conciseness and brevity, the systematic arrangement of the whole, the ready comprehensibility of its details, the typographical arrangement and sundry other features, it will serve the purpose of a handbook. I have therefore given a tolerably full bibliography, in hopes that teachers who make it the basis of their lectures and students who, while attending such lectures, found their private reading upon it may be enabled to penetrate further into the problems discussed.

It will be quickly seen that this manual is founded on my larger work, dealing with the Origin of the Idea of God, of which the first two volumes have already appeared and the third is in the press. However, apart from the introduction of wholly new sections, I have arranged the entire material in a totally different manner.

I have indeed worked out in this treatise an idea which is merely suggested in my *Ursprung*, Vol. I, ed. 2, p. 795, namely that the various schools of Comparative Religion and their respective theories follow one another in a succession just the reverse of that in which the religions themselves have appeared in the course of history. For details of this, see below, p. 9 *sqq*. Thus my book has the advantage of giving at once a history of the subject itself, an account of the various theories, movements and schools, and a brief account of religions in the historical order of their appearance.

This involves a further advantage, particularly important for a manual. A good part of the controversial matter contained in *Ursprung* has been omitted here, because the theories and schools involved are put each in its proper place, and thus their positive contribution in particular is set in the right light and evaluated accordingly. I think this will be instructive and encouraging, especially for the beginners who may use this handbook ; since they will learn that no theory has been put forth wholly in vain, but that each one, when put in its proper place, has had an important contribution to make to the development of the history of religion. This contribution, both in its positive content and in its limitations, becomes clear once it is given its right position in the history of subject. I have myself found much satisfaction and delight in following this new way, because it has enabled me to give a more positive estimate of the services rendered by many a deserving fellow-worker, and thus to evaluate them aright.

But it is not only the arrangement of the material that has been fundamentally altered ; the scope has also been considerably enlarged, so as to give a description in proper proportions of the whole subject. The first section (Introduction, History of the Subject, Dissemination) is entirely new ; for the third chapter I have been able to make use especially of Father Pinard de la Boullaye's fundamental work *L'Etude comparée des religions*, Vol I. (*Son histoire dans le monde occidental*), Paris 1922 (ed. 1), 1929 (ed. 3). In the second section separate chapters are devoted to a more thorough discussion of nature-myths, fetishism and manism. A new chapter (IX) has been added, dealing with totemism, and another (XI) on the sky-god. In Part V, Chapters XV, XVI and XVII, dealing with the high god of primitive culture, are wholly new, and give a foretaste of Vols. III and IV of *Ursprung*, which have not yet appeared. Despite this enlargement of the scope, the size of the book is decidedly less than that of even one volume of the larger work ; which shows clearly that the character of a handbook has been kept in view, and the material consequently limited to what is really essential and only the outlines of the historical development given.

Despite the great multiplicity of topics dealt with in the present work, one has been left out entirely, although perhaps many who are drawn to it would wish it to be included. I have described the history of religion only in so far as it can be done by means of purely natural knowledge and the methods of historical ethnology. Wherever the question of the oldest form of religion is treated, my intention has been to speak only of the religions of those peoples who, according to the results of such investigation, are seen to be ethnologically the oldest. That religion existed and had developed even before them is implied in the fact that these peoples, though ethnologically the oldest, do not belong to a wholly uniform culture. To throw light on this subject, working from different principles and by differing methods, is the business of other branches of knowledge, philosophy and theology, which the present work does not touch. But I think that both in my *Ursprung* and in this book not a little useful preparatory work is done for the benefit of those studies also.

I would express my hearty thanks to Professors Andres, of Bonn, and Moock, of Lippstadt, for helping me to read the proofs [of the German edition] and for many useful suggestions.

W. SCHMIDT

St. Gabriel, Mödling, near Vienna
   Whitsuntide, 1930

TRANSLATOR'S PREFACE

THE translator wishes it to be understood, in the first place, that his office has been to render Father Schmidt's work into English, without implying thereby acceptance of his theories. The name of Father Schmidt is known wherever Anthropology and Comparative Religion are studied ; his learning and industry are as familiar as his name. These facts are quite enough to warrant the introduction of his own short statement of his views to the English-speaking public, especially as he accompanies it with a review of the whole history of the subject, remarkable alike for its completeness and its brevity.

In the English version, a few short additions have been made, mostly in the form of footnotes. These may be readily distinguished from the text by their being enclosed in square brackets [ ], and, in the case of notes, by the use of an asterisk instead of a figure to refer to them. They consist of corrections and supplements on small points of detail.

Throughout, the word 'culture' is used in the sense of German *Kultur*, which it translates. That is, it signifies any way of life distinctively human, however far removed from civilization or refinement. When the word 'civilization' is used, it renders the German *Hochkultur*. As explained later, 'culture' is also used in a number of passages to render *Kulturkreis*, literally 'culture-circle', a word the meaning of which is sufficiently explained in Chapter XIV, Sect. 1. 'Primitive culture,' 'primitive religions' etc., signify here and in the original, not the absolutely earliest forms but those belonging to the earliest known peoples, those still in the food-gathering stage.

I have to thank Dr. R. R. Marett for valuable suggestions with regard to terminology, and Mrs. C. B. Lewis for help in revising the translation.

H. J. ROSE

St. Andrews
June, 1930

ix

CONTENTS

PART III
THE TWENTIETH CENTURY

PART IV

THE SUPREME SKY-GOD IN THE NINETEENTH AND
TWENTIETH CENTURIES

PART V

THE METHODOLOGICAL BASIS. CONTENT OF THE PRIMITIVE BELIEF IN HIGH GODS

THE ORIGIN AND GROWTH OF RELIGION

PART I

INTRODUCTION, HISTORICAL AND PRELIMINARY REMARKS

CHAPTER I

THE COMPARATIVE HISTORY OF RELIGION, ITS NATURE, AIM, AND METHODS

THERE can hardly be a more fascinating object of investigation than the history of religion. Perhaps also there cannot be a more difficult one. For, as we nowadays realize more and more clearly, this history is most intimately connected with the beginnings of human culture, and with the further development of that culture in general.

The science which has this subject for its province came into existence as such towards the end of the last century but one. The entire nineteenth century, during which our science first began to expand, was really not favourable to it in the various currents of thought both of its former and of its latter half. But it might be supposed that our own century is in a position to steer the bark into a quiet middle channel, after it has so often wandered to right or left from its course, and so, without waste of time and energy, to bring it to its desired haven.

1. DEFINITION OF 'HISTORY OF RELIGION'

The very definition which we must now set forth will show how much more lucid we can now be both in positive determinations and in negative distinctions. We are to deal with an introduction to the comparative history of religion. Two things must be defined : our subject, religion, and the form in which we handle this subject, comparative history.

(*a*) Religion may be defined both subjectively and objectively. Subjectively, it is the knowledge and consciousness of dependence upon one or more transcendental, personal Powers, to which man stands in a reciprocal relation. Objectively, it is the sum of the outward actions in which it is expressed and made manifest, as prayer, sacrifice, sacraments, liturgy, ascetic practices, ethical prescriptions, and so on.[1]

And now the words ' personal Powers ' call for explanation. It is of course possible to feel oneself dependent upon impersonal powers, but it is not possible to enter into reciprocal relations with them, since they cannot answer from their side. Consequently, it makes no difference whether it is a material force, as for example the vast and mighty universe, or some inexorable law thereof. Both are dumb and unresponsive to the human personality. Hence also primitive Buddhism, inasmuch as it recognizes no personal gods, cannot be considered as a religion, but only as a philosophy. Later Buddhism indeed, and Buddhism everywhere that it has become a popular religion, has included in its wide-reaching system innumerable personal deities, brought in by a thousand back doors.

(*b*) It is not merely *a* religion, or the religion of particular peoples, with which we are concerned ; we are to make a comparison of all religions, one with another. It is a pity that we cannot express this by a single word, as for instance the German word ' Völkerkunde ' differentiates itself from ' Volkskunde ' a description of any single people. Even in German it would hardly be possible to bring into use any such term as *religionenkunde*, ' science of religions ', or *religionengeschichte*, ' history of religions ', in distinction to *religionskunde, religionsgeschichte*, which are used to mean respectively the science and the history of religion in general, but might also signify the knowledge or history of a particular religion.*

---

[1] H. Pinard de la Boullaye, *L'étude comparée des religions*, Vol. II (ed. 3, Paris 1929), pp. 2–10 ; S. A. Cook, in Hastings, *Enc. Rel. Eth.*, art. Religion (Vol. XI, p. 662 *sq.*).

* [I have translated the above paragraph freely, as the terminological difficulties in English are quite different. Our phrases ' history of religion ', ' science of religion ' are unambiguous ; but we lack the convenient substantives *religionskunde, religionsgeschichte*, and the corresponding adjectives. Hence the difficulty of rendering, e.g. *vergleichende Religionsgeschichte*, literally ' comparative religion-history ' or *religionsgeschichtliche Lehre*, ' religious-historical teaching '.]

The object of this comparison is, firstly, to understand the peculiarities of each individual religion by the very fact of contrasting it with others, and secondly, to attain to a synoptic grouping of religions and religious phenomena, in other words to a typology of religion.   But we will not rest content with a mere static typology, which claims no more than to review the facts as they were and are.   This is rather the business of the psychology of religion.   We endeavour to grasp all that is characteristic of each religion, and thus also we can comprehend the influences which have affected it and the results which it has produced.   We comprehend religions in their capacity as cause and effect of other things ; but also we include the other cultural factors which have played this same part of cause and effect to religions.   We plunge into the flowing stream of events ; our subject is the comparative history of religion, and thus, and only thus, do we grasp the full reality of religion.

(c) We speak of the comparative *history* of religion.   This is the final differentia of our science.   It aims at setting forth the issue and the course of religious facts ; it therefore does not rest content with a typological juxtaposition of them.   Nor is it satisfied with a merely outward sequence, but tries to investigate the causal nexus of action and reaction between the facts.   That is to say, it tries to attain to an inward understanding of the outward course of events, to pragmatic history.

Our science is thus clearly differentiated from the other members of the group dealing with religion, and as clearly marked as belonging to this group.   The other sciences which are to be classed with it are the psychology and the philosophy of religion.   That we are now able to differentiate the history of religion clearly from these sister sciences is one of the most important advances that our subject has made, and therefore we must speak of it somewhat more fully.

2. RELATION OF OUR SUBJECT TO THE PSYCHOLOGY OF RELIGION

The psychology of religion is concerned with those religious happenings which take place and forces which exist within the human soul.   Now these inner experiences are of the very essence of religion ; outward forms and observances are of themselves lifeless and not real religion at all.   Hence the historian of religion, while he describes the outward course of events, must also to a certain extent include the inward life. This he can do in part by means of a quite natural knowledge of the soul, not formally scientific ; but in part also he will gratefully use the results of scientific psychological study. The psychology of religion thus will be one of the principal ancillary sciences to the historian of the subject, and he will neglect it as his peril.

An American writer on religious psychology, James H. Leuba,[2] defines the objects of the two sciences very justly as follows :

'As to the psychologist, he may regard his task as completed when he has pointed out the several *possible* origins of the god-ideas, the characteristics of each, and the nature of the *general* causes which determine the dominance of particular gods.' A little earlier he writes : 'It is for the anthropologist and the historian (I should prefer to say "the anthropologist who has been trained in the history of culture ") to discover what in any *particular* case has *actually* happened . . . and to determine the origin or origins of any *particular* god.'

It is then the duty of the psychologist to define simply the general psychological possibilities, not the actual series of historical events.[3]

G. Wobbermin [4] seems also to agree with him, although he holds that we are in danger of 'falling into the vicious circle of "no psychology of religion without history" (Wundt), but on the other hand "no history of religion without psychology" '. This circle, he goes on to say, cannot be wholly got rid of, and 'a method, rightly so styled, of the psychology of religion' is to be obtained only by definitely elevating it to a methodological principle. The viciousness of this alleged circle surely can be got rid of simply by engaging in historical and psychological work, each at its own proper time ; first historical investigation aided by psychology, and then psychology aided by history.[5]

[2] *A Psychological Study of Religion, its Origin, Function and Future* (New York, 1912), p. 99. The italics are mine. [Throughout this book Father Schmidt gives nearly all the passages quoted in German. With one or two small exceptions, the original, if English, has been copied by the translator ; if in any other language, such as French, a new translation from the original has been made.]
[3] Cf. W. Schmidt, *Ursprung der Gottesidee* (second ed.), Vol. I, p. 636.
[4] In his article, *Die Frage nach den Anfängen der Religion in religionspsychologischer Beleuchtung (Zeitschrift für angewandte Theologie, IX, 1915, p. 346 sq.).*
[5] W. Schmidt, *op. cit.*, p. 630.

The misuse which the Evolutionist school of the science of religion made, in the last generation, of psychology,—its own popular psychology,—consists in this. They imagined that certain psychological states follow on one another of necessity ; and that consequently, if one of them were known, the historical sequence of the rest could be determined therefrom, without any historical investigation. To this misuse they added a second. They explained this necessary sequence, the progressive evolution of these psychological states, by a certain judgement of values which they regularly made. According to this, the lower, the more bestial and ugly, must also be the older ; the better in each case was the higher, and therefore the later, stage of development.

3. RELATION TO THE PHILOSOPHY OF RELIGION

As the modern comparative history avoids unnecessary dabbling in psychology and is to be distinguished from the psychology of religion, so also it carefully abstains from passing judgement on the value and truth of the particular religions. It is thus sharply differentiated from the philosophy of religion. The latter may judge, from the standpoint of its own philosophy, which can hardly be separated from some general view of the universe, what truth and what value for the conduct of life the various religions and their elements possess. The history of religion, as such, abstains from any such judgements, and is careful that any which may unconsciously be made shall not influence the comprehension and exposition of the facts.

The question whether in this connexion a wholly uninfluenced exposition is possible is answered in the negative at the present day by intelligent men of all opinions. They have learned to recognize that absolute freedom from preconceived ideas is beyond any man's power. Here and there only the amusing simplicity of some reactionary imagines that an unprejudiced view of the science of religion is the privilege of the unbeliever. To all such, a French student of religion, Father H. Pinard de la Boullaye, makes the following sound remarks : [6]

' If we speak of an instinctive and spontaneous tendency (sc., to judge in accordance with one's own religious convictions), that seems an undeniable fact ; but we often forget to complete this platitude.

[6] H. Pinard, L'étude comparée des religions, Vol. II (Paris, 1929), pp. 37–8.

'The fundamental cause of such an inclination is, that when religion is in question the soul hazards all it has. It risks, we may say, everything on the truth of the conclusions to which it has been led ; the rational dignity of its own conduct, the gain or loss of the rewards in a future life, in short all that makes existence worth while, that existence which it controls for a few moments. Now the religious man is not the only one who runs this risk. The irreligious man also hazards all he has, neither more nor less than the religious, on this same inevitable question of the sense of life. He has a different ideal, it is true ; but, for him as for the believer, that ideal is the hidden mainspring of his conduct, the one good which makes him ready to take the trouble of living at all. . . . The interests involved are, we may say, mutually opposed for the two types of men ; but they are equal. The same thoughts, which are outside the range of our critical powers, trouble men's souls from one direction or the other ; and the non-religious, or definitely irreligious psychologist must defend himself against them, no less than the religious.'

It is then the duty alike of the believing and of the unbelieving investigator not to let their views of the universe, their philosophy and their resultant judgements as to truth and value, in any way influence their setting forth of the historical facts. And an investigator who seeks honestly for objective truth will be especially grateful for the frank criticism of one who holds different views from his own, because that can expose his own unavoidable weaknesses to him, and so forward his advance towards the whole truth, better than a friend's could.

But it is just in the investigation of the history of religion that a believing student of the subject has an advantage which his colleague who thinks otherwise can hardly equal. If religion is essentially of the inner life, it follows that it can be truly grasped only from within. But beyond a doubt, this can be better done by one in whose own inward consciousness an experience of religion plays a part. There is but too much danger that the other will talk of religion as a blind man might of colours, or one totally devoid of ear, of a beautiful musical composition.[7] Renan perceived this ; he however believed that a still better investigator was one who had formerly been religious and had since abandoned his creed. This cannot be allowed. Renan commits himself thereby to the most emphatic expression of a judgement concerning truth, and so forfeits all claim to objectivity.

[7] Schmidt, *op. cit.*, p. 712.

The Belgian savant, Count Goblet d'Alviella, has suggested the following division and nomenclature of the stages of our subject : [8] Hierography, or the introductory critical description of the facts and their geographical extension ; Hierology, which proceeds to group these facts, to establish their chronological sequence, and, where possible, to go back to their origin ; Hierosophy, which judges of the truth, value and metaphysical character of religions. H. Pinard likewise accepts this division and the terminology.[9] There is a great deal to be said for both, but there are two disadvantages attached. Firstly, no distinction is made between the history and the psychology of religion ; secondly, the word ' religion ', which is fully naturalized and can hardly be done away with, is dropped in favour of the wholly new ἱερός. If we could tolerate the composition of Latin *religio* with Greek *-γραφία*, *-λογία*, *-σοφία*, we should get such formations as ' religiography ', ' religiology ', ' religiosophy ', which would have to contend with ' religionography ', ' religionology ', ' religionosophy ', like ' missiology ' and ' missionology '. Hardly any of these words would gain acceptance, particularly in German, which possesses the serviceable words *religionshistorie, religionspsychologie,* and *religionsphilosophie.*

---

[8] *Transactions of the Third International Congress for the History of Religion,* Oxford, 1908, Vol. III, p. 365 *sqq.* ; also in his work entitled *Croyances, rites, institutions* (Paris, 1911), the three volumes of which have each one of the above terms as its title.   Cf. *Anthropos,* Vol. VIII (1913), p. 268 *sq.*

[9] Pinard, *op. cit.,* II, p. 14 *sqq.,* 54 *sqq.*

CHAPTER II

OUTLINE HISTORY OF THE SUBJECT

1. THE SUCCESSION OF RELIGIONS AND OF CULTURES

THE fact that ethnology in general is at present in a stage of transition makes its unwelcome presence felt in the history of religion in particular. In the whole domain of ethnology, the old Evolutionary school is bankrupt. The lovely long single lines of development which it used to construct so readily have been shattered and overthrown by the criticism of the new historical tendencies. Already, in the fields of ergology, sociology and economics, the historians of culture in particular have set about, not only clearing away the remnants of Evolutionism, but raising new and more solid structures. But the subject of religion, and in general of the non-material culture of man, has at most got so far that it can here and there make a beginning with these new constructions.

In these circumstances it would not be a cheering or encouraging task at the present day to write a history of religion ; for the ruins of the former Evolutionist system would have first to be produced, and more ruins piled up by further criticism. The sight of such wholesale destruction might make the researcher tremble lest the building which he would fain rear by his positive results should one day prove to be but another link in the long chain of the errors in the history of religion which have passed over the world. To set forth the results of the history of religion would not therefore be an attractive task to-day.

However, it is not quite so bad as all that. The ethnological study of the history of culture has gone so far in the departments of ergology, sociology and economics as to establish the existence of a series of culture-horizons, within which the development of human culture has taken place ; and an easily intelligible conspectus of these can be given, as will be done later (see p. 240 *sqq.*).

Now it is a remarkable fact that this historical succession of religions is reflected, and can be observed in a concrete form, in the successive theories of the history of religion which have been put forward in the last few decades, only the order being reversed. But again, it is not so surprising. Indeed, it is very natural that the latest religions, those peculiar to the latest cultures, were also the first to be comprehensible ; for they were the best preserved, and also to some extent the most widely distributed. The less recent, the earlier that they are, the less they show and the more they are obscured by those which, being later, are better preserved. Can we wonder then that the first theories on the subject turned their attention to those religions which belonged to the latest and widest spread stratum of mankind ? Can we wonder that each of these theories in turn, so long as it saw only this form of religion, declared it the first form, the origin of religion in general, until it was dethroned by another theory, based on religions and peoples more recently noticed, which had hitherto lain further back ?

This retirement and dethronement can come to an end, of course, only when it can be guaranteed that behind the last form of religion and the last people of the moment there are no more to be looked for, because all have been discovered and the earth has disclosed her last hiding-place. As a matter of fact, we have nearly attained this consummation, and therefore we can, by objective means, set forth that form of religion which is really the oldest, because it is the last, that we can reach ; and our final task will consist of the attempt to determine how far this form of religion which is the last within our reach is removed from the absolute origin of religion, and how much of that origin it has retained.

2. ·THE SUCCESSION OF THEORIES

(a) Before beginning to treat of the series of hypotheses concerning the history of religion, and likewise of the successive religions themselves, we will briefly examine the long period during which much was said and written concerning religion, and some comparisons made, but no such thing as the history of religion, properly so called, as yet existed. I mean the Greek and Roman times, the early days of Christianity, the Middle Ages, and the Age of Discovery. In all this time, the history, psychology and philosophy of religion, as we now call them, were not differentiated. The motive of these investigations, moreover, was purely practical ; it was the desire to uphold, modify, or entirely to overthrow the particular religion existing at the time and in the country concerned.

(b) When the history of religion proper took shape as a real science, which occurred at the end of the eighteenth and the beginning of the nineteenth century, it did so in connexion with the Indogermanic group of languages and peoples, which was then becoming known and was large enough to provide abundant material for comparison, and yet not so large as to be lost in a mass of details. But all these peoples belonged to the high or at least the middle culture [i.e., were civilized or barbarian, not savage] ; consequently they belonged to the latest strata of development, the tertiary or secondary cultures. A characteristic of these is a wide development of nature-myths having a religious direction. And as a matter of fact, the first theory of the history of religion which was constructed was the theory of nature-myths. According to this, the source of religion and its earliest form was the nature-myth, especially the star-myth ; and these myths were generally given a symbolic explanation.

(c) But in the first half of the nineteenth century the savage races of Africa, Oceania and America were brought within the purview of Europe ; and in proportion as this occurred, their religions attracted scientific attention. Even in the eighteenth century, one of the grossest and therefore most conspicuous of these peoples' cults, namely fetish-worship, was made the foundation of a theory, by de Brosses, in 1760. This theory was taken up again in the middle of the nineteenth century (1851 and the following years) by A. Comte, and was further developed by (Sir) J. Lubbock [afterwards Lord Avebury]. It found easy and ready acceptance, especially in popular scientific circles. This cult belongs to the later stratum of savagery, the secondary cultures.

(d) The same applies to the worship of ancestors, or manism, although its roots go back to the primary cultures, particularly the two patrilineal forms, totemism and pastoral nomadism. On this Herbert Spencer (from 1876 on) founded his ghost-theory, which long held the field, especially among philosophers and sociologists.

(e) But now the long and deep array of the lower agriculturalists, the horticultural peoples,* disclosed itself. These

* [See L. H. Dudley Buxton, *Primitive Labour* (Methuen 1924), p. 46. 'A convenient division . . . has been generally adopted by the German ethnologists. The terms they use are " Hackbau " and

savages belong to the latest primary culture-horizon, matrilineal horticulture. Among them belief in and worship of souls is to be found in the most manifold forms, and E. B. Tylor (1872 and following years) used it as the basis of a comprehensive theory of Animism, the first theory of the history of religion which was thoroughly worked out and shaped from all sides. Consequently, it had the most important results, and lorded it over almost all the scientific world until the beginning of the present century.

(f) In consequence of the progressive decipherment of Babylonian and Assyrian cuneiform inscriptions and Egyptian hieroglyphics after the middle of the nineteenth century, the religions of these two highly civilized peoples, both of which belong to the tertiary culture, became more and more imposingly prominent. They were manifestly composed of nature-myths, star-myths in particular. Hence at the end of the nineteenth century a new school of astral- and nature-mythologists was formed, in opposition to the animists.

(g) Behind the matrilineal horticulturalists, and now and then between them, appeared at last those higher hunting tribes of the primary culture among whom occur the strange phenomena of totemism (descent from and relationship to certain species of animals, and a religious respect for those animals). In this it seemed that a new and older form of religion had been found. A theory on these lines was first put forward by Robertson Smith in and after 1885. The progressively widening range of (Sir) J. G. Frazer's collections made it clear that totemism is not a religion nor the source of one, but a sociological system with a set of ideas to correspond.

(h) But among these totemistic peoples Frazer discovered a vast assemblage of beliefs and practices which he declared to be the fore-runner of religion, namely magic. The wide-reaching importance of magic was perceived with still more profundity and comprehensiveness by an American scholar, J. H. King, in 1892, and he also considered it the source of religion. But his work attracted no notice, and it was not

" Ackerbau ". . . . The divisions correspond roughly to our words horticulture and agriculture—the latter depends essentially on the use of domestic animals, the former on man's labour alone. That the division is not a mutually exclusive one is shown by the fact that most peoples who cultivate fields with their animals also cultivate gardens.' Throughout this book I render *hackbau, hackbauer,* by ' horticulture ', ' horticulturalist ', in accordance with Mr. Buxton's suggestion.]

till the beginning of the twentieth century that there sprang up, at almost the same time in Germany, England, France and America, a reaction against animism. A stage of religion earlier than animism, namely preanimism, was postulated, and supposed to be identical either with magic or with a yet undifferentiated mixture of magic and religion. Thus, in and after 1895, R. R. Marett, Hewitt in 1902, K. Th. Preuss in 1904 and later, A. Vierkandt in 1907 and E. S. Hartland in 1908, but most of all the French sociological school of Durkheim, set about developing this theory. The leaders of the French school were at first H. Hubert and M. Mauss, in and after 1904, then, from 1912 on, Durkheim himself. In their opinion, totemism and magic combined, in the Central Australian form, are the origin of religion.

Later, certain Protestant students of the psychology of religion endeavoured by a more extensive introduction of psychological considerations to support the view that a mixture of religion and magic, as yet undifferentiated, is the first stage in man's religious development. Among these are Archbishop N. Söderblom, in 1916 ; also G. Wobbermin in and after 1915. K. Beth, in 1914 and later, and R. Otto, in and after 1917, endeavour to penetrate to an earlier stage still, one which was neither religion nor magic. However, no such stage can be ethnologically shown to exist, nor be assigned to any culture-horizon.

(i) Even in the older school of nature-mythologists, one sovran figure stood out among all the various personifications of natural phenomena, in the Indo-European peoples. This was the sky-god. He was conspicuous also among the Hamitic and Semitic pastoral races, and still more among the Ural-Altaic pastoral nomads, being in fact the predominant figure in the religion of the primary culture of the cattle-breeding nomads of the vast steppes. This phenomenon had been noticed by Schelling, and, among the nature-mythologists, by Max Müller for a time ; but the invasion of materialistic Evolutionism destroyed its interest, and only theologians set any store by it.

(j) All the theories we have mentioned, with the exception of a few supporters of the first, that of nature-myths, were under the sway of progressivist Evolutionism, that is to say, they assumed that religion began with lower forms, and explained all its higher manifestations, especially monotheism, as the latest in time, the products of a long process of development. At about the same time that the reaction set in against the animistic theory, which had hitherto been supreme, that is towards the end of the nineteenth century, Andrew Lang, a former pupil of Tylor, turned his attention to certain high gods found among very primitive peoples.   These figures were regarded as creators, as the foundation and bulwark of the moral code, as kind and good.   They were acknowledged and adored as ' fathers ' ;   and being found among exceedingly primitive peoples, they could not, for that very reason, be the products of a long process of development.   Lang's work on the subject, *The Making of Religion*, was received at first with general opposition, and then with still more general silence.

3.   THE SUCCESSION OF METHODS

One of the reasons why Lang's investigations did not carry conviction was this.   He had indeed, by his recognition of the ancient Supreme Being, existing even among very low savages, destroyed one of the fundamental propositions of Evolutionism.   But having brought this fact into prominence, he did not himself use any stable method to confirm it permanently.   It is therefore incumbent upon us, having now considered the various successive theories, to cast a glance at the methods by the help of which they arrived at their results.

(*a*) The oldest school, that of the nature-mythologists, followed a historical method in the narrower sense of the word.   That is, it rested upon the ancient written documents of the various peoples in question, nearly all of whom were acquainted with writing.   If these scholars were affected by Evolution at all, it was not the materialistic theory of Darwin, but Hegelian idealism.   The later school of astral mythology was already much more influenced by the theory of Evolution.

(*b*) All the other theories, however, came into being after the outbreak of materialism and Darwinism, and their work was all done on the lines of Evolutionist natural science.   This puts all that is low and simple at the beginning, all that is higher and of worth being regarded only as the product of a longer or shorter process of development.   This they found it easier to do, because the principal objects of their study were savages who had not yet made the acquaintance of any sort of writing by which to date the monuments of their culture.   Hence the question of earlier and later, of the chronological sequence of religions and forms of religion, which must be settled before the causal interaction of the facts can be exactly determined, could be answered only by help of the Evolutionist method, which is really no method at all, as we shall see later.

(c) An end was put to this unhappy state of affairs, which governed the whole of ethnology, by the school of cultural history, headed by Ratzel (1886 and after), Frobenius (1898), Gräbner and Ankerman (1905), to which the present author joined himself not long after. This school is able to lift even the unwritten monuments of culture out of the featureless plane where they lay side by side, and to arrange them one behind another in a sequence extending far back. Thus it can fix objectively their arrangement in time and distinguish cause and effect. Further details of this method will be given in the proper place. I applied this method, which then was far from perfect, to the Pygmy peoples in my work entitled *Die Stellung der Pygmäenvölker in der Entwicklungsgeschichte der Menschen,** 1910. Soon after, I made a better use of it in the case of the South-East Australians, in Vol. I of my *Ursprung der Gottesidee.*† In this, the primitive high gods which Lang had been the first to value aright were set in their proper methodological perspective and thus made of permanent value.

(d) This is not one of the many transitory theories which, when their time comes, are replaced by others ; it is not one of the many errors, but a permanent conquest, an entire and therefore an enduring truth. Of this we may be fully confident, for by the methods of the history of culture we can establish two connected propositions, firstly, that these high gods are found among, and only among, the peoples ethnologically oldest, and secondly, that all these ethnologically oldest peoples have such gods. But the earth is now so thoroughly explored that only a few peoples, in the interior of Africa, the Philippines and New Guinea, are still to be discovered ; and it is not probable that they will produce any essential change in our present picture of the peoples of the world.

So, if we cast our eyes over the history of our subject, we obtain a miniature of the comparative history of religion itself, but in the reverse order. The sequence of the theories and of the religions they are founded upon, as they come one

* [' The Position of the Pygmy Peoples in the History of Human Development.']
† [' The Origin of the Idea of God.']

after another into prominence, is exactly the reverse of the order in which those religions were actually and historically developed.

In order to understand all the factors which have influenced theories concerning the history of religion, and have, in particular, so often prevented their authors from rightly understanding and appreciating the different religions brought to their notice, we must proceed to examine the different movements of thought which, in the two halves of the nineteenth century, swung in almost diametrically opposite directions, and at last, in the twentieth century, show signs of coming to rest in the middle.

4. THE SUCCESSION OF ATTITUDES

(a) The first half of the nineteenth century was directly influenced by the reaction against the French Revolution. This reaction took the form of traditionalism and idealism in theology and philosophy, of romanticism in literature, and of aristocracy and absolutism in social and political thought. Hence the nascent history of religion retained in its turn a conservative and religious spirit, which was expressed in the recognition of the supreme position of the sky-god, and on the other hand in the symbolical and mystical exposition of the nature-myths. The defect which made itself felt was the too great value set in the ideal, and the insufficient allowance for the material factor, in religious development as elsewhere. Narrowness in one direction, over-stress in the other, led about the middle of the century to a fresh outbreak of political revolution and to an intellectual *volte-face*, the former in nearly all, the latter in all the countries of Europe.

(b) So it came about that the second half of the nineteenth century was marked by the intrusion, first of Liberalism, then of Socialism, both more or less associated with materialism, which, in both these movements, turned with ever-increasing strength against religion and tradition. This materialism was strengthened by a doctrine of progressive Evolution, the fruit of Darwinism in natural science, which was opposed to the idealistic Evolutionism of Hegel, this having already appeared in the preceding epoch. Its significance for the methods of the history of religion has already been dealt with. As regards the spirit in which the inquiries were conducted, it meant an increasing inability to grasp the deeper essence of religion, to give due value to its higher forms, and a tendency to over-estimate the outward elements and underestimate, or entirely neglect, the spirit. All things considered, this meant that the historical study of religion suffered almost more than it had done in the previous period.

(c) As the twentieth century dawned, a negative and a positive movement began. For the first, the insufficiency and failure of materialism grew ever clearer, and the abandonment of it more pronounced. For the second, the recognition of the unique character of spirit and of its freedom made increasing progress, and this resulted in a deeper and more ready insight into the nature of religion ; more attention was paid to its importance for the whole of civilized life. A historical, in opposition to a purely scientific, spirit and interest grew stronger, for the limitations of natural science become daily more obvious. Hence also the boundaries of purely inward evolution grow clearer, and the importance of the historical factor more visible. History, by being separated from philosophy, gains considerably in serenity and objectivity. There is dawning the day of critical realism, which strives to comprehend the whole of reality, to preserve mind and matter alike, and is preserved by its critical character from exaggerations in one direction or the other.

CHAPTER III

THE PRECURSORS OF THE COMPARATIVE METHOD

1. GENERAL SURVEY

ALTHOUGH the comparative and historical study of religion did not come into being as a science until the end of the eighteenth century and the beginning of the nineteenth, the comparative study of religions is many centuries older than this, and a feeling for criticism and chronology is to be found still earlier.

For the first beginnings of such studies we must look to Greece, in which country, despite a relatively narrow religious horizon, they attained a vigorous development. In this as in other things the Romans were the heirs of Greece, but despite the much wider religious horizon which opened for them, they did not make any notable additions. The clash between paganism and Christianity brought fresh attractions and more inspiration to the subject, and a new force appeared, the Christian philosophers and apologists. As a pagan riposte to the Christian attack, Neo-Platonism appeared. The victory of Christianity brought with it a diminution of interest in the multifarious religions of heathendom.

Not long after came the flood of Islamic conquests. Islam itself made no contribution to the scientific and comparative study of religion; it overran a great part of the Christian countries and thereby deprived most of them of their areas of contact with the pagan faiths. As a result, the interest in such matters is greatly lessened throughout the Middle Ages. At last came the Age of Discoveries, which all at once let in the incalculable wealth of religions belonging to high Asiatic and American civilizations and the bewildering multitude of savage peoples. This rapidly aroused an interest which at first expressed itself in numerous descriptions of various cults, then in more or less scientific investigations thereof. This lasted through the Humanistic period and the Reformation,

17

till in the course of the eighteenth century our science slowly came to birth.

The beginnings of a brief historical survey of this whole period have been made by E. Hardy, *Zur Geschichte der vergleichenden Religionsforschung*, in *Archiv für Religionswissenschaft*, Vol. IV (1901), pp. 45–66 and 97–135. For a fuller account, see J. Réville, *Phases successives de l'histoire des religions*, Paris, 1909. Full treatment of the medieval and subsequent periods in O. Gruppe, *Geschichte der klassischen Mythologie und Religionsgeschichte während des Mittelalters im Abendlande und während der Neuzeit*, a supplementary volume to W. H. Roscher, *Ausführliches Lexikon der griechischen und römischen Mythologie*, published by Teubner, Leipzig, in 1921. The whole subject is treated in great detail and with complete bibliography by H. Pinard de la Boullaye, *L'étude comparée des religions*, Vol. I, ed. 3 (*Son histoire dans le monde occidental*), Paris, 1929.

2. THE GREEKS AND ROMANS

The Greeks and Romans had material for the comparison of religions with one another in the surviving remains of Cretan, Pelasgian, Thracian, Etruscan, and other pre-Hellenic and pre-Roman cults.*   This was supplemented by the knowledge of the religions of Asia Minor, Egypt, Babylon, Persia, and South Russia gained by travellers such as Hekataios of Miletos in the fifth century B.C., and especially by Herodotos in the same century.   A third increase in knowledge was brought by the triumphant advance of Alexander the Great to India, which bore fruit in such works as that of Berosos on Babylon, of Megasthenes on India, Hekataios of Abdera on the Hyperboreans, and Manetho on Egypt.

Pinard [1] divides the Greek activity in the study of religions into three periods : (*a*) the mythological and poetic, in which, under Homer and Hesiod, a naïve collecting of myths took place ; (*b*) the philosophic, marked by reflection and discussion of the truth or falsehood of religion ; and (*c*) the pragmatic, when criticism and scepticism appear.

In the second of these periods the Ionian philosophers, such as Thales and Herakleitos, explained the fundamental elements of the myths as natural forces, while Pythagoras, Xenophanes,

---

* [This is inexact.   Etruscan and Thracian religion did not merely survive into the classical epoch but continued in full vigour, the former during the greater part of it, the latter down to the end of paganism. By Pelasgian religion the author seems to mean the pre-Hellenic cults of the Greek mainland.]

[1] *Op. cit.*, pp. 3 *sqq.*

Empedokles, and later Demokritos, Plato and Aristotle, assailed the myths, sometimes with great vehemence, and upheld the claims of a higher and purer religion, whose nature differed with the philosophical standpoint of each writer. Plato and Aristotle, and before them Anaxagoras, postulate a governing intelligence as the beginning of all things, and both teach degeneration, assuming that religion was formerly higher and purer.

In the third period, the religious and moral collapse led to critical scepticism and to confining attention to the $\pi\varrho\tilde{\alpha}\gamma\mu\alpha$, that is, to daily life. Of the two systems which now came into being, Epicureanism and Stoicism, the former did next to nothing for the comparative study of religion. Stoicism, with its greater interest in morality, asceticism and discipline, was more interested in religion and tried to elevate it to a higher form out of the chaos of myths. According to the Stoics, the active principle of the world is the Logos, the subtle fire which everywhere orders motion. They taught polyonymy, that is, that the various names of the gods are but different titles of the One God; and here an excessive use of allegory helped out their interpretations.

In particular, Apollodoros of Athens used this method in the twenty-four books of his work $\pi\varepsilon\varrho\grave{\iota}$ $\theta\varepsilon\tilde{\omega}\nu$ (middle of the second century B.C.). Later (330–260) came Euhemeros, the founder of Euhemerism, the theory that the gods were prominent men of old days. Polybios (about 210 to about 125 B.C.) and Strabo (about 66 B.C. to about A.D. 25) showed a more critical spirit in their historical investigations, by which they endeavoured to determine the historical content of the myths. Palaiphatos (middle of the second century B.C.) held that many gods owed their existence to mythological corruptions of names, *numina nomina*.

At last the general scepticism threatened to turn into the Academic doctrine of Plato's followers, who would pronounce decisively on nothing whatever. But the Academic Antiochos of Askalon (124/7 to about 69 B.C.) turned against it, and opposed scepticism with ecclecticism, a 'rejuvenated dogmatism' greatly influenced by Stoic views.

Antiochos' followers included two Romans, Varro, who in the forty books of his *Antiquitates Romanae* was principally concerned with collecting the material facts of Roman religion, and Cicero, whose treatise *De natura deorum* introduces representatives of the different philosophical schools.

This ecclecticism could but be advanced by the invasion

of the foreign cults of the East, those of Kybele, Isis, Ba'al, Mithra and others, which appeared in Rome from the second century A.D. onwards.* The problems relating to religion and its scientific study which arose out of these manifold forms are solved by the Neo-Pythagoreans, Plutarch, Maximus of Tyre and Celsus, by supposing the inferior gods and daimones to be created by the Supreme Deity, while the Stoics, Seneca, Epiktetos and Marcus Aurelius, suppose them to be His emanations. Both parties arrived at their results by allegorical interpretation of ritual and mythology, and this also made it possible in actual life to take part in as many cults as one pleased, and to feel more or less benevolently tolerant of all religions.

3. CHRISTIANITY

In the sharpest opposition to this wide-reaching theoretical syncretism and practical tolerance arose the absolute monotheism of the new faith, Christianity, and its uncompromising claim to sole validity. In the first period, up to about the end of the second century, its apologists turn their weapons not so much against paganism as against the Jews and Gnosticism, a syncretistic system combining Christian, Jewish and pagan elements. They are headed by Justin Martyr, whose influence is to be found in nearly all the others (Tatian, Irenaeus and Hippolytos), though Theophilos of Antioch is more independent. All of them make the demons largely responsible for the origin of pagan polytheism. With the exception of Theophilos and perhaps Tatian they follow the apocryphal Book of Enoch in supposing these demons to be the offspring of the intercourse between the sons of God and the daughters of men, the former being explained as fallen angels (see Genesis vi. 2 *sqq.*). They derive a number of the good points of paganism from plagiarism or borrowing from Judaism, while others are credited to the λόγοι σπερματικοὶ scattered in every soul. The imperfections of Judaism in doctrine, morals and cult they ascribe to the ' condescension ' of God, Who temporarily allowed that which is imperfect to subsist. Irenaeus, one of the latest writers of this period, derives from this a regularly ascending series of progressive revelation, which must naturally begin with the imperfect. None the less he, like all other teachers of this period, stoutly maintains the absolute transcendence of Christianity, by

* [They were known much earlier than this, although their importance in the West was not so great.]

reason of which it surpasses all other religions in the universality and precision of its monotheism and the uncompromising purity of its moral code.

In the second period the contest between the Christian writers and the champions of paganism begins. The latter had at first, from indifference or contempt, simply ignored infant Christianity, but now its growing power troubled them. Both sides of the controversy are of interest to the student of the history of religion among others, and it is from this point of view that we now mention it.

A Neo-Pythagorean, Celsus, in a work entitled ἀληθὴς λόγος (' In defence of Truth '), brought against Christianity a long series of charges whose sharpness and concreteness show that he was thoroughly acquainted with it. The sophist Philostratos, at the request of the Empress Julia Domna, consort of Septimius Severus (193–211) composed a tendencious romance on the life of the world-renowned sage Apollonios of Tyana. In this, although Christianity is not mentioned, the hero is portrayed as a miracle-worker and a pattern of pagan piety, and numerous coincidences with events in the life of Christ are introduced.*

On the Christian side there was then arrayed a group of Africans,† consisting of Minucius Felix, Tertullian, and Cyprian, joined later by Arnobius, Lactantius and Firmicus Maternus, and an Alexandrian group consisting of Clement and Origen. We may call the former practical realists, the latter speculative idealists.

The African group holds to the two theses of the first period, namely the origin of the demons from the intercourse of the fallen angels with the daughters of men and the theory of borrowing ; at the same time, however, they lay more emphasis on the universal human appeal of the fundamental tenets of their faith. The doctrines of condescension and of progressive revelation are scarcely mentioned again in their works. Numerous details of pagan cult are preserved to us only through their polemical writings.

The Alexandrian group is far more learned and original. It is well versed in secular philosophy and writes in a spirit of broad conciliation, which often takes it outside the bounds of orthodoxy. The thesis of the adulterous angels (*angeli fornicatores*) disappears

* [The theory that Philostratos had either the life of Christ or Christianity in view, although it has been long current, appears to the translator unfounded.]

† [That is, inhabitants of the Roman province of Africa, which was then the centre of a considerable literary culture, mostly Latin. All these men, so far as is known, were of European descent, not negroes nor Berbers.]

in both writers, and Origen also drops the theory of borrowing, while Clement develops it further with great erudition. Origen lays great stress on the inner significance of an outward cult-act, which according to him determines its value.

4. MANICHAEISM, NEO-PLATONISM AND CHRISTIAN OPPOSITION THERETO

Though to outward seeming the combat between Christianity and paganism was so unequal, the former had, by the middle of the third century, continued to gain ground both in outward semblance and in inward reality. The result was that paganism began to assimilate itself to it in doctrine, cult and ethics. In their struggle with Christianity, the Emperors encouraged this movement, in order to give paganism a greater advantage.

From this state of affairs two new religions arose about the middle of the third century, one in the East, but extending its influence into the West, the other in the West, but also invading the East. The former was Manichaeism, the latter Neo-Platonism.

(*a*) Manichaeism was founded by Mani or Manes (died 277). It is a mixture of elements Zoroastrian, Buddhist, Babylonian, Gnostic and Christian ; the last are especially numerous in its outward ceremonial and its organization. It teaches the ancient Persian doctrine of the struggle between light and darkness. To decide this, Christ, Whose throne is in the sun, became in outward appearance man, and suffered. Manichaeism spread in the West especially in North Africa, where Augustine, who had formerly been a Manichee himself, fought it stoutly. To him we owe most of our information about Manichaeism, and his testimony has been brilliantly verified by the excavations made in Eastern Turkestan by Grünwedel, von Le Coq and Sir Aurel Stein. In these, original Manichaean manuscripts were found, which proved how wide an extension Manichaeism had achieved in Central Asia among the Turko-Mongolian races, as far east as China. In the West it appeared to approach nearer and nearer to Christianity, but it went on in secret and appeared again in the Middle Ages in the Cathari, Albigensians, and Bogomilists.

(*b*) The second, and far more formidable, religion was Neo-Platonism. Its founder was Plotinos * (204–270), who did

* [Plotinos was not strictly the founder of Neo-Platonism ; but he was the creator of its fully developed doctrine, incomparably its greatest teacher, and ranks among the foremost minds of antiquity, of which he is the last great pagan philosopher.]

not engage in any polemic against Christianity.   In his view,
God is the One, the Beautiful and the Good, Who is above all
definition.   From Him all things that exist emanate in ever-
increasing degrees of remoteness, but always retaining some
trace of divinity.   By means of virtue, the soul must free
itself from every trace of the sensual, in order to return to
God.   Plotinos taught that, besides intellectual apprehension
of God, He might be known through an inward experience.
Prayer, sacrifice and ritual have an inner magical potency
to bring men into connexion with God and the gods.   Plotinos
did not reject polytheism, but worked it into his system by
means of allegorizing and universal tolerance.

His pupil Porphyry (from about 233 to about 305) turned the
whole doctrine against Christianity in a spirit of deadly hatred.
So also did Iamblichos (about 280–330), the Emperor Julian the
Apostate (331–363), Libanios (314 to about 395) and others.   Iamblichos occupied himself with the theory of ecstasy, of sacrifice
and of divination, in other words individual mysticism.   Julian
put the imperial power at the service of the new doctrine, whence
one more persecution of the Christians came about.

The refined philosophy, purified ethics, and ravishing
mysticism of the new religion was spread over the old mythologies and cults, and seemed to have provided paganism
with new and undreamed of forces.   But they were not truly
living forces ; they did not penetrate the mass of the people
and could indeed retard the dying out of paganism, but not
prevent it.   Neo-Platonism is interesting for our purposes
owing to its fully systematized doctrine and its importance
for religious experience and mysticism.

(c) Its Christian opponents had meanwhile increased greatly
in numbers and importance.   In the East, the Alexandrian
school was continued by Athanasios (died 373) and Cyril of
Alexandria (died 444), and a new school arose at Antioch,
represented by John Chrysostom and Theodoros (died 457/8),
another in Cappadocia, including Basil the Great (died 379),
his brother Gregory of Nyssa (died 394) and his friend Gregory
Nazianzen (died 389/390).   Besides these we must include
Eusebios of Caesarea (died about 340) and Epiphanios (died
403).   In the West, there were Ambrosius (died 397), Jerome
(died 420) and Augustine (died 430).   The theories of the
angeli fornicatores and of borrowing vanish.   Allegorism and
universal toleration were vehemently opposed, for their
weaknesses were clearly perceived.   In opposition to the Neo-
Platonic emanations, emphasis was laid on the essential and

unbridgeable difference between Creator and created, even angels and saints. The doctrine of the condescension of God was widely applied, and with it a doctrine of elementary religious concepts. In history, Julius Africanus, Eusebios of Caesarea and Augustine introduced chronology, and the last-named especially employed it in support of a profound philosophy of religion. At the same time Eusebios, Gregory Nazianzen, Theodoret and Augustine continued to develop more strongly the doctrine of a development of religion, which, they taught, had taken two forms. In paganism, there had been degeneration, a descent from purer and more simple beginnings to forms outwardly more splendid but inwardly more debased. On the other hand, revealed religion had risen from simpler and more childish elements to ever deeper and higher forms. Gregory Nazianzen emphasized the slowness of the upward development and its temporary adaptation to lower stages of human progress, and Theodoret and Augustine compare the growth of peoples and of mankind in general to that of the individual from childhood to full maturity. Augustine brings all these ideas together in his great work *De ciuitate Dei*, a profound combination of the history of religion and that of civilization, philosophy of history and philosophy of religion, which had far-reaching importance for the whole of the Middle Ages.

5. THE MIDDLE AGES

(a) In the Middle Ages the horizon was considerably narrowed as regards the number of religions known and the consequent possibility of comparing them. Roman and Greek paganism with their Eastern ingredients were gone, and were known only in a fragmentary way from the writings of the Fathers. East and South, the outlook upon the heathen nations was blocked by the fanatically monotheistic religion of Muhummed, and even that was for a long time known but imperfectly.

Hence the only pagan religions known were those of the Germanic North and the Slavonic and Ugro-Finnish East, as these peoples were progressively converted to Christianity. But they were known only fragmentarily, because they belonged to peoples who had no writing and no high civilization, and also because the early Middle Ages were too much taken up with the almost material cares of their own development to be ripe for an interest in such matters.

Nevertheless, we have some information concerning these religions from the acts of councils and from penitentiaries, also in certain descriptions by missionaries or by men of miscellaneous learning. Thus there is the chronicle of the monk Regino of Prüm (907–967), the work *De situ Daniae* of Canon Adam of Bremen, who died in 1076, the chronicle of Kadlubek, Bishop of Cracow, 1206–1218, and the *Chronicon Slauorum* of a country priest, Helmold, of Lübeck, who died in 1270. But none of these works aroused any further inquiry.

(*b*) Later, Islam itself and also Judaism came on the scene, for as their intellectual influence extended to Christian Europe, a more lively interest in both these religions was aroused. Both Islam and Judaism had had to pass through crucial periods of thought within themselves, arising from the antagonism between Platonism and Neo-Platonism of a mystic tendency and Aristotelianism with its intellectualist leanings, which philosophies both religions had absorbed. As far as Islam was concerned, Ibn Roshd (1126–1198 ; the ' Averroes ' of medieval writers) settled the controversy in favour of Aristotelianism. But he sharpened its intellectualism into rationalism, keeping a good deal of Neo-Platonism in the process and rationalizing its mysticism also. But he also shattered the foundations of Islam by his symbolistic doctrine, which left the dogmas standing only as symbols of philosophic truths, and by his relativity, which declared that all religions, if they accorded with philosophy, were equally good.

The principal work of Maimonides, or Rabbi Moses ben Maimon, 1135–1204, the greatest Jewish philosopher and theologian of the Middle Ages, was the *Moré Nebúchim* (' Guide of wanderers ' ; quoted by the Schoolmen as *Doctor perplexorum*). He was also an Aristotelian, and adopted Averroes' interpretation of Aristotle. He dissented from him, however, inasmuch as he insisted strongly on the freedom of God to create and to work miracles. He also rejected his relativity, holding Moses to be the greatest guide, to whom no other could be compared. The gaps and shortcomings of the Jewish code he explained by the law of development [progressive revelation] and the condescension of God. He also opposed the excesses of allegorical interpretation, and laid down fixed rules for its use.

(*c*) The teaching of Averroes found a follower in the Christian West also. This was Siger of Brabant, whose doctrine was rejected by the University of Paris for that reason. It was successfully refuted by William of Auvergne, Alexander Hales, and above all, Thomas Aquinas (1225/7–1274) in his *Summa theologica* and also in his *Summa contra gentiles*, the latter work being especially directed against Islam. All these used purely philosophical and theological arguments ; but Vincent de Beauvais, Roger Bacon and Raymund Lully followed the more positive method of direct reference to the various religions. In this connexion the early Christian doctrines were in some measure taken up again and enlarged, except the theories of borrowing and of development. On the other hand, Thomas Aquinas, in opposing the agnosticism of Averroes and Maimonides, developed the doctrine that the being of God must not be understood *uniuoce*, for this is anthropomorphism, nor *aequiuoce*, which leads to agnosticism, but *analoge*, that is, by following the direction of our thought, but with omission of all limitations.*

The defence was successful not only in repulsing the attack of Averroism on Western Christendom but also in combining Aristotelianism with Platonism, which had hitherto been the stronger, owing to the influence of Augustine. Hence was created a philosophy whose foundations went deep and whose importance for the science of religion, among other things, was great, if only because of the clearer ideas and calmer intellectualism which it brought into recognition.

Simultaneously with this struggle between the philosophies of Christianity and Islam in Europe, the door was opened in the East. The great missionary expeditions of the Franciscans and Dominicans brought to Europe new and astonishing information concerning the wholly unknown races and faiths of Tartary, China and India. Hence attention and a keen desire to learn more were aroused.

We may mention the following: Giovanni di Piano Carpini, 1245 ; Wilhelm Ruysbroek, or Rubruk, 1249–53,—these two travelled through Central Asia to Mongolia ; Oderico da Pordenone (1104–1330), who made his way to China through Asia Minor, Persia, India, and the Sunda Islands, and came back to Europe by way of Mongolia and Tibet ; Giovanni di Marignola (1338), who travelled via Central Asia to Pekin and came back through India, Ceylon, and Ormuz.

It was this desire that led Europe to strive and search for a direct route to these countries by sea, and this search brought on the great epoch of discovery.

* [A good account of this is given by Pinard, *L'étude comparée*, Vol. I, p. 137 (ed. 3).]

6. THE AGE OF DISCOVERY

The fifteenth, sixteenth and seventeenth centuries saw tremendous events, both in Europe and out of it, which produced a total change in men's view of the world about them and in their own reaction to it. The outer events were the discovery of Africa, Southern and Eastern Asia, America and Oceania ; those in Europe itself, the Revival of Letters and the Reformation.

(*a*) The Revival of Letters was the first in time of these events. The recovery of the ancient paganism of Greece and Rome from its own sources led immediately to all the ancient controversies of the classical authors concerning religion becoming known again. Especial interest was taken in the interpretation of mythology. For the very reason that the Renaissance valued the classical paganism above all else in the world, it was not till later that it began to take an interest in the new peoples and religions made known by the geographical discoveries.

I mention here, as the first work, Boccaccio περὶ γενεαλογίας *deorum libri xv* (written 1375, first printed in Bâle, 1532) ; also G. Pictorius, *Theologia mythologica* (Freiburg in Breisgau 1532) and others by the same author ; A. Sardi, *De moribus et ritibus gentium* (Venice, 1557) ; Natalis Comes (Noel Conti), *Mythologiae siue explicationum fabulae libri x* (Venice, 1551). There are many other authors ; see Pinard, *op. cit.*, Vol. I (ed. 3), p. 146 *seq.*

The high-water mark of the Revival of Letters, from the point of view of our subject, was the attempt to equate or combine classical philosophy, particularly Platonism, and a profoundly idealized classical religion with Christianity.

The principal representatives of this movement were F. Patrizi, *Noua de uniuersis philosophia*, Ferrariae 1591 and following years, and still more R. Cudworth in his great work, *The True Intellectual System of the Universe*, London 1678 and following years. The latter in particular was opposed by the Lutheran theologian J. L. Mosheim in his work, *Systema intellectuale huius uniuersi*, Jena, 1733, whose great learning and sober criticism put these exaggerations in their proper place. Of him Pinard says (*op. cit.*, p. 164), ' His moderation and prudence assure him a place, perhaps the foremost, among the best critics of that period '.

(*b*) The Reformation and Counter-Reformation were of importance for the history of religion both formally and materially. Formally, because the controversies between the two parties resulted in an elucidation of many concepts important for the scientific study of religion, and encouraged critical and comparative investigation, in particular of Christian antiquities. Materially, because they widened the field of the subject by the study of Hebrew and other Semitic languages.

But progress was unfortunately hindered by the view of the Bible as literally inspired and the consequent over-valuation of Hebrew as the supposed original speech of mankind. This idea was prevalent throughout this period, among Catholic as well as Protestant writers, for instance the Jesuit Athanasius Kircher, who in his learned work, *Oedipus Aegyptiacus* (Rome, 1652-4), dealt with all the religions of the world, but unmethodically and uncritically. John Selden's *De dis Syris syntagmata duo* (Leipzig, 1672) has a more modest scope and more critical sense.

The Protestant doctrine of the total depravity of human nature as a result of original sin lent new strength to the theory that all that was good in pagan religion must necessarily have been borrowed from the Jews.

This was the view of Gerhard Voss (1577-1649), Samuel Bochart (1599-1667), and Hugo Grotius (1583-1645), but it was shared by the Catholic bishop Huetius or Huet, a pupil of Bochart, in his influential work *Demonstratio euangelica*, Paris, 1690. This widespread opinion was opposed by an Anglican, Dr. John Spencer, in his famous work *De legibus Hebraeorum ritualibus earumque rationibus*, 1685, who embraced and developed with much learning the old doctrine of the condescension of God. Of this book Robertson Smith says (though with some exaggeration, as Pinard, *op. cit.*, p. 180, remarks), that ' it may justly be said to have laid the foundations of the science of Comparative Religion '.[2] A Jesuit, P. Lescalopier, took the same line in his work *Humanitas theologica*, Paris, 1660, in which also he made use of the newly-discovered religions. So also did the learned Benedictine abbot, Dom Calmet (1672-1757), in his exegetical works, and likewise A. Maichin in his *Théologie païenne*, 1657, which is a formal sketch of comparative theology.

An unfortunate result followed upon the Reformation in this respect, that with Europe divided by it into two camps, the discovery of the new regions of the earth was not properly and quickly completed, either geographically or intellectually. The Protestant maritime nations, England and Holland, ceaselessly interfered with the Catholic countries, Portugal, Spain and France, and, to the great harm of Europe, the natives were drawn into the jealousies and colonial wars of both sides. All this was very bad for missionary activity also,

[2] *Lectures on the Religion of the Semites*, new ed., London, 1907, p. vi.

and consequently for the scientific understanding of these peoples and their religions. The Protestant peoples were behindhand in this respect for some time for another reason, namely that they had no missions for two hundred years, and when they did, began timidly with the efforts of a few small pietistic sects such as the Moravian Brethren. Thus the first great harvest of information on ethnography and the science of religion from the discovery of the new portions of the globe was reaped almost exclusively by the Catholic missions.

(c) The great discoveries of the new continents widened the domain of our subject immeasurably, owing to the addition of the religions of the civilized peoples in Eastern and Southern Asia and in Central and South America ; but especially by the knowledge of the savages of Africa, America and Oceania. These last made a real and wide-reaching comparative history of religion possible for the first time. Some time must necessarily pass at first before the novelty of these cults, often quite unheard of, could be grasped and the vast wealth of information which poured in could be collected and stored. Then it was that precious material was heaped up, which the history of religion will never at any time be able to dispense with, especially as since then a number of the religions in question have disappeared from the earth, either by the peoples and races to which they belonged dying out or by their conversion to Christianity.

As regards the reports of the missionaries, which in the nature of the case were for the most part monographs on individual countries or tribes, it is enough for the present to refer to the history of ethnology.[3]

A work worthy of special mention is the *Historia universal de Nueva España*, by the Franciscan missionary Bernardino Ribeira de Sahagun (1500–90). Addressing himself to the priests and nobles of ancient Mexico, he obtained from them by exact inquiries an account of the entire ancient religion of the country, including festivals, rites, laws and hymns, all told in detail in the original language and illustrated with pictures and drawings. But, as his work aroused no interest and got no encouragement from his superiors, clerical or lay, his precious manuscript was lost until, in 1830, Lord Kingsborough found it in Spain and published it. In like manner the work of a secular priest, Cristobal de Molinos

[3] See W. Schmidt and W. Koppers, *Völker und Kulturen* (Regensburg, 1924), p. 14 *sqq.* ; Pinard, *op. cit.*, p. 193 *sqq.* ; Hardy, *op. cit.*, p. 97 *sqq.*

(1520–84), was published only in 1873, by Markham, under the title *Report on the Fables and Rites of the Incas*. One savage people was described in classical Latin by an Austrian Jesuit, Father M. Dobrizhoffer, in his book *Historia de Abiponibus equestri bellicosaque Paraguariae natione*, Vienna, 1783–84. The reports of the Jesuit missionaries are collected in *Relations de la Nouvelle-France* and *Lettres édifiantes* ; on these, see Father de Rochemonteix, *Les Jésuites et la Nouvelle-France au XVIIe siècle*, Paris, 1859 and following years.

PART II
THE NINETEENTH CENTURY

CHAPTER IV
NATURE-MYTHS

1. THEORY OF NATURE-MYTHS

(a) THE END OF THE EIGHTEENTH CENTURY

THE spirit of the second half of the eighteenth century was by no means such as to lead up to a school concerned essentially with peoples of the middle and higher culture, as was to be characteristic of the school of nature-mythologists. Its scientific interests were preoccupied rather with savages, who had indeed been the subject of Lafitau's fundamental work. This feeling was so strong that it produced two works anticipating a movement which was not to come into being till the last third of the nineteenth century, when the nature-mythologists had had their day.

The first of these is Ch. de Brosses, *Du culte des dieux fétiches ou parallèle de l'ancienne religion de l'Egypte avec la religion actuelle de la Nigritie*, Paris, 1760. He supposed that fetishism, to which he gave a broad and vague meaning, had sprung from fear, and Sabeism or astrolatry [star-worship] from admiring wonder. These were the original religious states of all peoples, with the exception of the Hebrews ; whether or not this last reservation was made simply with an eye on the censorship, is unknown.

The second, a work of much learning and keen critical sense, is N. S. Bergier, *L'origine des dieux du paganisme*, Paris, 1767. Bergier was the pioneer of the animistic school, for he taught that both fetishism and astrolatry had grown out of a childish state of mind which supposed everything full of genies or spirits. As the psychological cause of religion he named not only fear and wonder, but held that the entire range of the emotions found vent in religion, and also the rational impulse to find a cause, and practical considerations.

(b) THE PHILOSOPHY OF RELIGION IN THE FIRST HALF OF THE NINETEENTH CENTURY

The French Revolution and the Napoleonic Wars which followed weakened or destroyed missions and cut communications with the colonies. Hence, in France especially, all scientific activity was difficult, and the getting in of fresh ethnological material was nowhere easy. In consequence, the forming of theories, mostly speculative, concerning the development of peoples and the history of religion, was of course encouraged. An epoch of such theories started first in Germany, to which country France had now to cede for a time the supremacy she had hitherto enjoyed in these branches of learning. It delayed for a while longer the forming of a history of religion on a real and objective basis. Another influence was the reaction against the eighteenth-century encyclopædism and rationalism and the spirit of the French Revolution, which filled the atmosphere of European thought throughout the first decades of the nineteenth century. Characteristically, this took different forms in Protestant Germany and England on the one hand, Catholic Germany, France and Italy on the other.

(a) *Philosophy of Religion in Protestantism*

The whole development of German idealistic philosophy, which now began in Protestantism, was concerned with assuring religion against all attacks in the intellectual sphere by relegating it to that of morality, as Lessing, Kant and Fichte did, or to that of personal feeling, as was done by Herder, Jacobi, Schelling, Schleiermacher and Fries. In addition, Kant declared that the reality of the outer world was beyond the grasp of the reason, that it was ' phenomenal ' only ; and from this Fichte and still more emphatically Hegel deduced the consequence that only the ego was real, that is the spirit, in which alone God exists. Lessing in his *Göttliche Erziehung der Menscheit,** 1780, and Herder in his *Ideen zur Philosophie der Geschichte der Menscheit,†* Riga and Leipzig, 1789–90, had taught that man had risen to higher and higher levels in religion, but always under the influence of a personal, extra-

* ['Divine education of Mankind.']
† ['Ideas for a Philosophy of Human History.']

mundane God. For Hegel, the history of religion was the story of how the God in the soul rose to higher self-consciousness. From this point of view, Hegel made out the sequence of the development of religions.[1]

A. NATURAL RELIGIONS

1. Immediate natural religion (i.e., of sentient and spontaneous knowledge) ; Magic.
2. The religion of the consciousness divided within itself (by distinction between the true Self and spontaneous consciousness) :
(a) the religion of measure (China).
(b) the religion of imagination (Brahmanism).
(c) the religion of Being in itself (Buddhism).
3. Religions which form the transition to the sphere of free subjectivity.
(a) the religion of the Good and of Light (Parseeism).
(b) the religion of Pain (Syria).
(c) the religion of the Enigma (Egypt).

B. RELIGIONS OF THE SPIRITUAL INDIVIDUALITY OR FREE SUBJECTIVITY

(a) The Religion of the Exalted (Judaism).
(b) The Religion of Beauty (Greece).
(c) The Religion of Finality or Fate (Rome).

This series, with its unbelievable omission of Islam and Christianity,* is really no more than a succession of the religions of civilized peoples, for it lumps together all the rich variety of savage religions under the single heading of ' Magic '. Taken as a whole, it does indeed possess a certain grandeur, but is the very pattern of *a priori*, speculative, wholly unhistorical, one might almost say anti-historical treatment of religion. It is amazing that it could have been constructed in the very period in which the real history of religion came into being.

(β) Philosophy of Religion in Catholic Circles

In Catholic Europe a movement began which hoped to insure religion against the attacks of rationalism by declaring that religious truths were not a product of the intellect, but had been given to man by God in a primaeval revelation, simultaneously with the primaeval language. These had

---

[1] Pinard, *op. cit.*, p. 264, following A. Véra's French translation of Hegel's *Philosophie der Religion*, Paris, 1876, Vol. II, p. 9 *sqq.*
* [The latter is included in Hegel's theory as the Religion of Absolute Finality, comprehending all the rest ; Véra, *ibid.*, p. 18, note 2.]

then been handed down by tradition—hence the name 'traditionalism' for this movement.

This idea is already found in *Le Génie du Christianisme*, published in 1802 by Chateaubriand, who had once been a follower of Rousseau and Voltaire, after his conversion. His expression of it, however, leaned to the poetical. Joseph de Maistre also upheld this view in his *Soirées de Saint-Petersbourg*, posthumously published at Lyons in 1821. It was developed and given a systematic foundation by Vicomte de Bonald (1754-1840) in his *Législation primitive*. Similar theories were held by A. Bonnetty (*Annales de philosophie chrétiennes*, 1830 and following years), and G. C. Ubaghs (1809-75) of the University of Louvain. It is pushed to its utmost extreme by F. de Lammenais in his brilliant *Essai sur l'indifférence en matière de religion*, Paris, 1817-23.

Thus, among Protestants and Catholics alike, an extreme distrust of the reason in matters of religion had sprung up, directly opposed to the eighteenth-century rationalism, which tried all religions alike by its touchstone of 'good sense'. Protestantism naturally took refuge in the subjective feelings of the individual ; the Catholic movement just described, in the objective force of tradition. However, official Catholic theology rejected both views as early as 1834, and insisted on the possibility of religious knowledge won by the reason as well as by revelation, and on the necessity of rational proofs of the natural foundations of religion. This doctrine was explicitly approved at the Vatican Council of 1870.

Nevertheless, during those first decades of the nineteenth century the above tendencies still found expression in the attempts of numerous writers who were affected by them to find traces of the ancient primitive revelation in the religions of pagan peoples.

Out of a great number we name here only the following : A. de Nicolas, *Études philosophiques sur le Christianisme*, Paris, 1843-45 ; J. Brunnati, *Dissertazioni bibliche*, Milan, 1838 ; F. Lüken, *Die Traditionen des Menschengeschlechtes*, Münster, 1856 ; same author, *Die Stiftungsurkunde des Menschengeschlechtes, oder die mosaische Schöpfungsheschichte erläutert und bestätigt durch die Sagen der Völker*, Freiburg im Breisgau, 1876 and following years ; Fr. Hettinger, *Apologie des Christentums*, Freiburg im Breisgau, 1863-7. The incomplete and doubtful material which these writers often employed, their ignorance of scientific ethnology and linguistics —which did not then exist—and their lack of any certain method, prevented their arriving at conclusions of permanent value. On particular points, however, they sometimes made interesting demonstrations, and at any rate, interest in foreign peoples and religions was decidedly advanced.

(c) The Symbolists and the Foundation of the
Historical Method by K. Otfried Müller

(a) *The Symbolists. Friedrich Creuzer*

At this time there was working in Germany a body of
scholars endowed with more learning and method, but also
under the influence of the two movements just described.
Their centre was the University of Tübingen, and they are
known as the Symbolists, from the title of their founder,
Friedrich Creuzer's, chief work, *Symbolik und Mythologie der
alten Völker, besonders der Griechen*, Leipzig, 1810–12.* According to them, the development of religion began with ' psychic
paganism ', that is, the personifying of and attributing of
soul to the forces of nature—a germ of the animistic theory.
Or rather—here the influence of Schelling made itself felt—
it was ' anthropomorphic pantheism ', by which man felt
himself one with nature. From this feeling of unity came
language wholly filled with symbolic expressions ; and from
this spontaneous symbolism arose in turn a conscious one, to
meet the need of expressing, within the limits of language
and art, the illimitability of God, which they recognized as
they developed further. This was especially the duty of the
priesthood, in their instruction of the laity. This was the
period of the creation of myths. The pastoral peoples with
their coarser understanding had known only the exoteric
meaning of these symbols, but the more refined religion of the
agriculturalists had fostered the esoteric meaning in their
secret rites. The better representatives of Neo-Platonism,
such as Plotinos, Porphyry and Proclus, had comprehended
the significance of these mysteries, which had many points
of contact with Christianity.

Creuzer's work was translated into French from the second edition,
and remodelled by J. S. Guigniaut, Paris, 1819–29, and appeared
as such under the title of *Religions de l'antiquité*, Paris, 1825–
51. To the same movement belong J. Jos. von Görres, *Mythen-
geschichte der alten Welt*, Heidelberg, 1810; F. J. Mone, *Geschichte
des Heidentums im nördlichen Europa*, 1822–23 ; Uvarov, *Essai sur
les mystères d'Eleusis*, St. Petersburg, 1812 and 1815; J. B. Braun,
*Naturgeschichte der Sage, Rückführung aller religiösen Ideen, Sagen,
Systeme auf ihren gemeinsamen Stammbaum und ihre letzte Wurzel*,
Munich, 1864–5 ; D. A. Chwolson, *Die Ssabier und der Ssabismus*,
Petersburg, 1856 ; C. C. Baehr, *Symbolik des mosaischen Kultes*,

* [' The Symbolism and Mythology of the Peoples of Antiquity,
with special reference to the Greeks.']

Heidelberg, 1837-9; F. C. Movers, *Die Phönizier*, Bonn, 1841-56; F. Lajard, *Recherches sur le culte de Vénus*, Paris, 1837, and other works; and many more authors. F. Ch. Baur also much resembles Creuzer in his *Symbolik und Mythologie oder die Naturreligionen des Altertums*, Stuttgart, 1824-5.

Owing to his attitude of active sympathy with religion and mysticism, Creuzer was denounced by E. Voss as a ' Jesuit agent in disguise ', and violently attacked by him in the Jena *Allgemeine Literaturzeitung* for 1821, pp. 162-217, and in his *Antisymbolik*, Stuttgart, 1824. There is more moderation in the tone of Chr. A. Lobeck's attack in his *Aglaophamus siue de theologiae mysticae Graecorum causis*, Königsberg, 1828. K. H. W. Voelcker was more profound and at the same time did positive, constructive work in the criticism contained in his *Mythologie des japetischen Geschlechtes*, Giessen, 1824. Still more comprehensive was Karl Otfried Müller's criticism in his *Prolegomena zu einer wissenschaftlichen Mythologie,** Göttingen, 1825. This last work laid the foundations of a more strictly historical understanding of religion.

(β) Otfried Müller

O. Müller was still dependent upon the philosophy of his time to some extent, for he treats the ' universal feeling for the divine ' as the beginning of religion, and explains that ' it is not reflection on the phenomena of nature, but the need of the human heart, that contains the living kernel of religion '. This need was, according to him, satisfied among the Greeks by a plurality of superior beings, while monotheism is the fruit of a later development. See his *Kleine Schriften*, Vol. II, p. 86 *sqq.*

But he at once turns to history when he adds that every people, every race, has expressed this universal feeling after its own fashion, in a ' national ' or ' tribal legend '. These legends are the most plausible explanations of events known to all. The reality, i.e. the happening itself, and the ideal, in other words the subjective portrayal of it, are one and the same for naïve myth-making thought ; consequently, in order to understand the myths of any people at any given time it is necessary to be deeply versed in their mentality. The most necessary preliminary condition is to determine the age of a particular myth ; and this determination is arrived at in a fashion wholly positive, from the dates of our authorities, the nature of the variants and details of the story, and by

* [' Introduction to a scientific mythology.']

comparison with dates historically fixed. He believed he was able to prove that the oldest myths are a residuum of the prehistoric migrations, and are therefore of a markedly historical character. Simple, rude local legends and variants of myths are of the greatest importance in determining the place and time when a myth originated.

The meaning of the myths, when thus traced back to their origin, is to be grasped by ' intuition ', that is, by one's ability to enter into the mental processes of the time and place in question, and also by ' combination ', or methodical comparison with similar myths and their variants. He distinguished between religion and mythology ; according to him, the latter is of later origin, and marks already a beginning of syncretism and philosophizing.

Müller confined his attention to Greece and adopted a policy of ' wait and see ', even of rejection, so far as Greek mythology was concerned, towards Indo-Germanic studies, which indeed were then far from being complete. But his pupils led the way to the philological school of nature-mythologists.

We may especially mention J. A. Hartung, *Die Religion der Römer*, Erlangen, 1836, and *Die Religion und Mythologie der Griechen*, Leipzig, 1865–73 ; L. Preller, *Römische Mythologie*, Berlin, 1858 ; C. Eckermann, *Lehrbuch der Religionsgeschichte und Mythologie der vorzüglichsten Völker des Altertums nach der Anordnung K.O. Müllers*, Halle, 1845–9 ; C. Schwenck, *Die Mythologie der asiatischen Völker der Ägypter, Griechen, Römer, Germanen und Slaven*, Frankfort, 1843–5, seven vols. Max Müller also, the chief representative of the nature-myth school, called himself a continuator of K. O. Müller.

(d) THE NATURE-MYTH SCHOOL

Thus, in the domains of general philosophy and of formal methodology, the way was slowly being paved for the school of nature-myths. Meanwhile, the requisite material and content were being got ready by the discovery and investigation of the Indo-Germanic languages by Father Coeurdoux, 1767, Sir William Jones, 1788, F. von Schlegel, 1808, F. Bopp, 1816 and following years, F. Pott, 1833 and following years, and others.

The leading place which Germany had won here in the scientific philological study of languages made itself felt in the sphere of comparative religion also, when these studies had come to their maturity. Now for the first time, students of comparative religion had before them a definitely bounded field to investigate, the Indo-Germanic peoples, and the first school of historians of religion began to appear. Its pioneer was Adalbert Kuhn, and his chief work was *Die Herabkunft des Feuers und des Göttertranks,** Berlin, 1859, besides his essay *Über Entwicklungsstufen der Mythenbildung,*† in the Transactions of the Berlin Academy of Sciences, 1873, also published separately in 1874. Another work, *Mythologische Studien*, was published, after his death, at Gütersloh in 1886.

The same tendencies are found in the work of W. Schwartz, *Der Ursprung der Mythologie, dargelegt an griechischen und lateinischen Sagen*, Berlin, 1860 ; F. H. Windischmann, *Über den Sonnenkultus der Aryer*, Munich, 1846, and *Ursagen der arischen Völker*, Munich, 1853 ; W. H. Roscher, *Studien zur vergleichenden Mythologie der Griechen und Römer*, Leipzig, 1873–5 ; .E. H. Meyer, *Indogermanische Mythen*, Berlin, 1883–7 ; M. Bréal, *Hercule et Cacus, étude de mythologie comparée*, Paris, 1863 ; N. D. Fustel de Coulanges, *La cité antique*, Paris, 1864 (the seventeenth edition appeared in 1900) ; H. d'Arbois de Jubainville, *La Mythologie grecque et l'histoire de l'Europe occidentale*, Paris, 1878 ; Ch. Ploix, *La nature des dieux, études de mythologie grécolatine*, Paris, 1888.

This school unanimously agreed that the figures of mythology, and hence those of religion, were personifications of natural objects, especially of the principal heavenly bodies, but also of meteorological phenomena. Max Müller, to whom we shall return later, and M. Bréal held that all mythology consisted of sun-myths, and that its only subject was the rising, setting and activities of the sun. Ch. Ploix taught that the sky in its various forms was the principal subject of myths. A. Kuhn declared for rain, storms, and thunder and lightning as mythological themes. While Regnaud and Renel in later works (1892–6) held that fire was the principal Indo-Germanic material for myths, an outsider, P. W. Forchhammer, was of opinion that it was water (see his *Hellenica*, Berlin, 1837 [Vol. I alone published] ; *Daduchos*, Kiel, 1876 ; *Prolegomena zur Mythologie*, Kiel, 1891).

A very favourite method of interpreting myths was to explain the names of gods, which of necessity often led to mistaken results, for the laws of phonetics were still but imperfectly worked out. Such identifications as those of Varuna with Uranos, Erinys with Saranyâs, Hermes and Saramêyas, Kentauroi and Gandharvas, are in our days

* [' The Origin of Fire and of the Drink of the Gods.']
† [' On Stages of Development in the Construction of Myths.']

either rejected entirely or regarded as very uncertain. A particularly characteristic example of this method, and one which raises questions still not fully answered, is the comparison of Greek θεός and Latin *deus*.[2] On the other hand, one equation has stood the test, that of the names of the principal gods, Ζεύς (genetive Διός), Iuppiter, Ziu, and Tyr, all connected with Sanskrit Dyauspitar and derived from the common root DIV, to shine ; compare also Lithuanian *dēwas*, Old Icelandic *dia*, Gaulish *dévo*, Old Prussian *deiws*. From this follows the original existence of an ancient supreme sky-god among the primitive Indo-Europeans. Another defect of this school was its too exclusive use of philological evidence and insufficient comparison of other monuments, such as the material objects used in cult. Hence it was but imperfectly able to deal with the pre-Indo-Germanic religions and gods, which had already been combined with the Indo-Germanic in various ways when they appeared in the myths.

Their treatment of the great natural objects and phenomena as the main themes of mythology was quite justifiable, for these really are prominent among peoples of the higher and middle cultures, such as the Indo-Europeans were. The curious thing is that the moon-myths, which are really very numerous, were at that time almost wholly overlooked. The fact that in those days Indo-Germanic religion was often represented as the oldest form of religion is psychologically intelligible ; it was due to the joy of discovery. The mistake was soon corrected by the other schools of the history of religion which followed, stage by stage.

(e) The Works and Theories of Max Müller

One of the oldest, and also one of the longest-lived representatives of this school, and at the same time its most successful apostle and popularizer, was Friederich Max Müller. A son of Wilhelm Müller, the German poet, he studied in Paris and passed the whole of his learned career as a Sanskritist and a student of religion in England, mostly at Oxford. In the course of his life he put forth a tolerably long series of hypotheses which for a time were influential, and in consequence he has been given the honourable appellation of ' the Founder of Comparative Religion '.

[2] It seems to have been lately established again by Prof. Bartoli of Turin, a pupil of Ascoli, who had always held to it. See his article, *La Monogenesi di ΘΕΟΣ e DEUS*, in *Rivista di Filologia e d'Istruzione classica*, N.S. VI (1928), pp. 108–17.

As early as 1856 he published his *Essay on Comparative Mythology*, which he republished, along with other pieces, in *Chips from a German Workshop*, London, 1867–75. Next came his *Introduction to the Science of Religion*, in 1873. In the year 1878 he delivered his Hibbert Lectures *On the Origin and Growth of Religion, as illustrated by the Religion of India*, Oxford, 1878 ; a German version appeared in 1881 with the title *Vorlesungen über den Ursprung und die Entwicklung der Religion*. These lectures found such favour and such wide publicity that towards the end of his life (1888–92) he was chosen lecturer several years in succession on Lord Gifford's foundation, and was able to deliver the following courses : *Natural Religion*, London, 1889 ; *Physical Religion*, London, 1891 ; *Anthropological Religion*, London, 1892 ; *Theosophy or Psychological Religion*, London, 1893.* A little before his death in 1900 he published another work, a collection entitled *Contributions to the Science of Mythology*, London, 1897. To the very end of his life he continued to work at the publication of the series *Sacred Books of the East*, a monumental collection of most valuable documents for the history of religion.

Max Müller traces the origin of mythology to a ' disease of language ' consisting in a ' redundancy ' thereof. The existence of many names for one object (polyonymy) and of the same name for several objects (homonymy) produced, according to him, a confusion of names, resulting in the combination of several gods into one and the separation of one into many : *nomina numina*. Particularly, the endings denoting grammatical gender led to personifying the gods. He did not recognize a primitive revelation from without, but at first would still admit an indefinite revelation from within at the beginning of man's religious development. This consisted in the effect of the Infinite upon the human soul. Later, however, he dropped this or gave it a materialistic shape. The beginning of the idea of Deity was neither monotheism nor polytheism, but henotheism or kathenotheism, that attitude by reason of which the particular god present to the religious consciousness at any given moment is treated and invoked as the only one. In his later Gifford lectures he leaned more and more to Positivism. He distinguished three kinds of cult-objects, namely (1) things which could be grasped, such as stones and shells ; (2) or partly grasped, as trees, rivers, and mountains ; (3) or not at all, as the sky, the sun and stars. The older poets had addressed their hymns not to the first of these classes, but to the other two, and these were praised as active, living and luminous. The first class

* [A new edition appeared in 1895.]

developed into fetishes, the second into gods, the third into greater gods, and above these the Infinite was vaguely conceived as existing. This was ' physical religion '. From the social relationships of mankind, the cult of parents and ancestors, who constituted another infinite series, ' anthropological religion ' had developed, which had risen to the worship of God the Father and Creator, and elsewhere to that of the archetypal man, the Son of God. But man has an infinity in himself also, his consciousness or ego ; from this is produced ' theosophical or psychological religion '. The self was in Christian philosophy called the Holy Ghost,

' who should however return to that for which he was originally meant, the spirit which joins all that is holy in man to the Holiest, the Infinite behind the veil of the ego, who brings unity and coherence to the purely phenomenal self '.

All three religions together, the physical, the anthropological and the psychical, make up ' natural religion '. By way of criticism, we must observe that these theories contain too much speculation and too little history or sound philology. The derivation of mythology from gender-endings will not hold, for mythology is to be found also among peoples whose languages have no genders. Kathenotheism, a clever device for avoiding the decision between monotheism and polytheism, is an isolated phenomenon, and late even in the higher civilizations.

Müller outlived his own reputation, and before he died, saw the almost complete collapse of the school of nature-mythologists before the attacks of its opponents, especially the animistic school led by Tylor and Lang.

2. NATURE-MYTHS IN THE RELIGIONS OF INDO-EUROPEAN PEOPLES

(a) INTRODUCTORY

If we now wish briefly to pass in review the religions on the examination of which the school of nature-mythologists was founded, that is the religions of the Indo-European peoples, we must keep one fact clearly in mind. That is that we now know these religions decidedly better than did those first founders of the school in question, both as regards the number and quality of the documents at our disposal, and in respect of the advance made in the examination thereof. This very advance which scientific study has made since those days has made it clear that these religions are after all not so largely a matter of nature-myths as they no doubt seemed to be then. That they are not is a consequence of the fact, which has come to be more and more clearly recognized since that time, that the culture of the Indo-European peoples was neither simple nor primary. It was a compound, even a complex one, and this was already in some measure true before they set out on their migrations to the various countries with whose previously existing cultures and religions they blended their own. Let us remember, for instance, that at all events the European branch of the family must have been acquainted, not only with cattle-breeding, but, even at that date, with the rudiments of agriculture.

None the less it remains true that nature-myths played an important, indeed often a dominant part in the religion of these peoples. And even where other religious elements entered, they are still connected with processes or objects in nature which form the subject of myths, and they derive their outward form from these. For instance, the cult of ancestors and of the dead generally is found closely connected with moon-myths. Even so spiritual an element as the moral aspect of religion is here closely connected with belief in and worship of a god of the sky or of fire. So we really are still able to use Indo-Germanic religion as a good example of a religion of nature-myths. In accordance with the scheme of the present work, this single chapter can of course give but a rough general sketch of these nature-myths, especially as we are obliged to include in our survey the religions of a whole great family of peoples.

Here I depend generally upon Leopold von Schroeder's classical work, *Arische Religion*, Vols. I and II, Leipzig, 1914 and 1916. It is certainly one of the best accounts of this vast subject as a whole—there are not many such. It must however be admitted that it has one defect : the too early death which robbed science of the author prevented the completion of the projected third volume. According to Schroeder's theory of the nature and origin of religion, its roots are three : firstly, the Supreme Being, whose tendency is rational and moral ; this is the subject of Vol. I ; secondly, the worship of nature, treated in Vol. II ; thirdly, the cult of souls, which was to have been dealt with in Vol. III. The lack of this volume is a serious loss to science in general, certainly ; but for our purposes it matters less, because he meant to deal in that part of his work with the animistic cult of souls, which does not interest us for the moment, but will be separately treated in a later chapter.

(b) The Supreme Being

We must include the Supreme Being in our discussion for two reasons. Firstly, because he forms an essential part of these religions ; secondly, because, while properly speaking he stands outside and above the nature-myths, yet he is more deeply entangled in them, in the cults of the Indo-European peoples, than von Schroeder was willing to allow. Undoubtedly one of von Schroeder's chief merits is that he has worked out in a convincing manner the existence of a moral Supreme Being among these peoples. His demonstration is far stronger than any that the first founders of the nature-myth school gave or could give, and his polemic against the blank negations of O. Gruppe and the scepticism of Bremer is also successful.

He lays it down that the word *deiwo*, ' god ' is connected with the general root DIV, ' shine ' as its strengthened form, with addition of the suffix *o* or *a*, which appears in the ' strong ' cases, nominative, vocative and accusative ; thus, nom. Ζεύς, which = *Djeus, but gen. Διός = *divs.* His proof that a supreme sky-god is meant here depends on the fact that this word has remained in various languages, although the word for the sky itself is quite different. This sky-god is called Father, as we see from Sanskrit *Dyauspitar*, Greek Ζεὺς πατήρ, Latin *Juppiter*, Scythian Ζεὺς Παππαῖος, Thrako-Phrygian Ζεὺς Παππῷος.

In India,[3] the older name of the sky-god Dyauspitar is Dyaus Asura (= Lord of Heaven). In the Vedic age Varuna supplants him, and bears the title of *rajan*, or king. His name is derived from the root VAR, to cover, in his capacity of god of the firmament of heaven, particular the starry night-sky. ' In his whole nature, in the exalted dignity and majesty of his appearance, in his attributes as creator, orderer, upholder and governor of the world, in his spotless purity and cleanness, in the holy anger with which he judges and punishes the wicked, in his grace and mercy towards the penitent '—in all this, says Schroeder,[4] he appears as a real Supreme Being, nearly allied to the Ahuramazda of the ancient Persian religion. He is connected with him likewise by two quite specific resemblances. Firstly, he is always coupled with Mitra or Mithra ; secondly, seven celestial gods of light are in especially close attendance upon him. In India

---

[3] L. v. Schroeder, *op. cit.*, I, p. 315 *sqq.*
[4] *Ibid.*, p. 325 *sqq.*

these are the Âdityas, ' those who are not bound (by guilt) ' ; in Persia they are called the Amesha Çpeñtas.

The connexion of Varuna with Mitra[5] is so close in India that in one and the same hymn the sun is called the eye of Varuna and the eye of Mitra, as if the two were but one god, one person. Von Schroeder refuses to see a sun-god in Mitra ; he is a moral deity, as is appropriate to his name, ' the Friend ' ; he is god of fidelity in friendship and alliance. In Persia, in accordance with the warlike character of their religion, he is a warrior-god who takes bloody vengeance for breaches of faith. The Indian Mitra never was and never became a sun-god ; the Persian Mithra did, but only in post-Avestan times, in which, as Sol Inuictus, he played a leading part in his own mysteries. But originally, Mitra was nothing but the separate hypostatization of a particular attribute of the Supreme Being, as the guardian of fidelity, of friendship and contracts.

The Âdityas again have no nature-myth behind them.[6] Their number, seven, may be a piece of Babylonian influence, as in the religion of that country the seven planets are the chief gods. But in the character of the Âdityas we can see no trace of anything astral ; their number may according to von Schroeder have been in earlier times nine, which is native Aryan. They are the guardians of the sacred order of the universe and of mankind, and they watch over it day and night. They again may be hypostatizations of what were originally functions of the Supreme Being. This is particularly obvious in the case of Parjanya, god of thunder and rain-storm ; von Schroeder, neatly settling the problem attaching to the seventh Âditya, who has no name, puts him in this position. He also is called ' our lord and father ', like Dyauspitar and (once only) Varuna. The Âdityas have this in common with Mitra, who is one of their number, Varuna and Dyauspitar, that no myths of a discreditable character are told of them ; they are thus outside of and above mythology.

Among the Persians,[7] in consequence of Zarathustra's reform, mythology is quite neglected, and the Supreme Being, Ahura Mazda, elevated far above all other beings. Even the Amesha Çpeñtas are reduced by this reformation to pale phantoms ; they remain, it is true, near Ahura Mazda, but Zarathustra gave their functions back to him again.

[5] L. v. Schroeder, *op. cit.*, I, p. 367 *sqq.*
[6] *Ibid.*, pp. 354 *sqq.*, 384–438.   [7] *Ibid.*, p. 441 *sqq.*

The figure of the Greeks' Supreme Being, Zeus, has gone furthest in the direction of anthropomorphism.[8] However, we must distinguish between the later and unrestrained poetical myths and the ritual forms; also, we must allow for the blending with Zeus of gods from non-Indo-Germanic peoples. Even so, he remains the guardian of order, the first and greatest ruler and king, father and begetter of gods and men, superior to all, god of the sky and storms. He is so emphatically the last that here among the Greeks, as also among the Romans, no separate thunder-god was developed. Faintly in the background there stands also the figure of Uranos, an old sky-god, with his wife Gaia, the earth. His connexion with Zeus is not clear.

Among the Italians,[9] Iuppiter is in still greater measure the upholder of moral and civic order. As Optimus Maximus, he is the highest embodiment of all power, goodness and glory.* He too is the only god of storm and rain. He is so essentially 'father' that this title is permanently incorporated in his name.

Among the Teutons,[10] the old sky-god is driven into the background by Odhin or Wodan, a being of different origin, and only fragments of his personality are to be found in obscure places in the Germanic area, and at obscure times. Thus we have the ancient Norse Týr, the Anglo-Saxon Tiu, Old High German Zio or Ziu; the last was uninterruptedly worshipped by the Suebi. He is, generally speaking, a war-god, hence Tuesday, Tiu's day, *dies Martis*, O. H. G. Ziestac, Old Norse Týs-dago, Anglo-Saxon Thusday. He appears in Friesland and Lower Saxony as Mars Thingsas, president of the folk-moot; from his name comes mod. Germ. *Dienstag*, Tuesday. In Heligoland he is Fosete, the wise judge of gods and men; among the Baiuvari (modern Bavaria), Ere or Erech, that is 'the kindly', 'the gentle'; hence *Ertag* or *Erchtag*, the local name for Tuesday. In Scandinavia, we find the old sky-god Freyr, 'the lord'.

Our knowledge of Keltic religion is much more fragmentary still.[11] But we do find a supreme war-god, who is nevertheless also called Loucetius, or 'shining', Rîgisamos, 'royal', Albiorix, 'lord of the world', and Camulus, 'sky'. Beside him there is Iuppiter Optimus Maximus Tanaros, whose name

[8] *Ibid.*, p. 445 *sqq.*   [9] *Ibid.*, p. 467 *sqq.*
* [The titles mean in reality that the Juppiter worshipped on the Capitol in Rome was better and greater than any other Juppiter.]
[10] *Ibid.*, p. 483 *sqq.*   [11] *Ibid.*, p. 524 *sqq.*

has also the form Taranus, a god of thunder, who certainly took a high position, if not the highest.

Among the Lithuanians, Diwas (in Lettish, Deews) is ' God ' in general, the father of the sun and of the sons and daughters of God, which in Lettish are also addressed under the form of affectionate speech, *deewins* (God's son). Diwas appears also as Diveriks, ' king of the gods '. Beside the god of light stands Perkunas or Perkuns, god of thunder and perhaps also of oaths.[12]

The Slavs had a thunder-god and oath-god, Perun, who seems to have been identified entirely with the chief god, Bog. Wolos, god of cattle and game, is also probably no more than a hypostasis of Bog.[13]

The distribution of this sky- and storm-god over the whole Indo-European area makes it certain that he existed also in primitive times, and originated then. This is the more certain because, according to a fine discovery of von Schroeder,[14] the grouping of the forms into which he develops coincides exactly with an important division of the Indo-European languages. This is the division into *centum* and *śatem* tongues, that is, those which retain the original *k(w)* in the word for ' hundred ' and those which change it into *ś* ; the former occupy the western and the latter the eastern part of the whole linguistic area. Corresponding to this, then, is the distinction in the field of religion between (*a*) an eastern group in which the god Bhaga, Boga or Bog is characterized as rich, kind and generous ; to this belongs the Indian Bhaga, the Bactrian and Persian Bagha or Baga, the Phrygian Zeus Bagaios, and the Slavonic Bog(ŭ) ; (*b*) a western group, which worships the Supreme Being as a god of war and as the president of the council and the national assembly ; to this group belong the warlike, state-forming peoples, namely Germans, Kelts, Romans and Greeks.

But this division is not an irreconcilable cleavage, for (*a*) the warlike and violent attributes are not wholly wanting in the east ; (*b*), those of gentleness and kindness are also to be found in the west.

(c) NATURE-MYTHS

(a) *The Earth*

Even the Supreme Being and the gods connected with him have so to speak a flavour of nature-myths about them here ;

---

[12] L. v. Schroeder, *op. cit.*, I, p. 526 *sqq.*
[13] *Ibid.*, p. 534 *sqq.*   [14] *Ibid.*, p. 566 *sqq.*

for they are gods (*a*) of the calm, peaceful bright sky in its daily and nightly aspects, and (*b*) of the stormy sky, covered with clouds, slashed across with lightning, and echoing with thunder. But another relation smacks yet more of nature-myths. This is the position of this great Indo-Germanic sky-god, at so many points of the whole area, as husband of the earth-goddess whom his embrace fertilizes with rain. This union is so commonly found that it must go back to the times of the primitive Aryans. Thus, in India, Dyauspitar and Parjanya are united to Pṛithivi; in Greece, Uranos with Gaia; in Germany, Njördhr with Nerthus and Fjörgynn with Frigg. Von Schroeder finds such a conjunction 'most natural'. We can no longer say so to-day, now that we know (*a*) that the Supreme Being of primitive culture has no earth-consort, or any consort at all, and (*b*) that the idea of the earth as the fertile mother of all living things is not earlier than the matrilineal culture, which produced it, and is a nature-myth pure and simple. As the earth is not otherwise particularly prominent in Indo-European religion (the most noteworthy earth-goddess is perhaps the Teutonic Nerthus, Hertha, or whatever she may be called), she probably is not to be considered a primitive Aryan deity, but a composite figure, due to crossing with one of the pre-Aryan peoples of matrilineal agriculturists.

(β) *The Sun*

There is no doubt that the sun, in myth and cult alike, is primitive Aryan; his shining figure is so manifest that many students of our subject in the older period imagined him the most important mythological factor.

Among the Indians,[15] Sûrya (= Greek Helios, Latin Sol, Gothic *sauil*, Slavonic *solnce* etc.) is the sun personified. He drives in a chariot drawn by seven shining horses across the heavens, and is the sentinel, the 'eye' of Mitra and Varuna. Another sun-god, who likewise is a god of the order of the universe, is Savitar, who drives over the sky drawn by two golden steeds; another again is Pûshan, at the same time god of flocks and herds, who climbs up the firmament on a pair of mountain goats. Vishnu, 'the efficacious', also called Hari, 'the yellow', who measures the extent of heaven in three great strides (rising, zenith and setting), is not very prominent till later ages; the same is true of Shiva. He is past a doubt the sun-god of the Dravidians, who has forced

[15] *Ibid., op. cit.*, Vol. II, p. 6 *sqq.*

his way into the Aryan Olympus ; his avatars, or trans-
formations into various beasts, remind us of Dravidian
totemism. Sûryâ, the eternally charming daughter of the
sun, who is desired in marriage, is considered a female solar
deity ; another is Ushas, the sun rising in the glow of dawn,
as von Schroeder explains her.

Among the Iranians the reform of Zarathustra crushed this
thriving mythology of the sun, although he is still occasionally
invoked and styled ' eye of Ahuramazda '. Mithra certainly
was not a sun-god.[16]

In Greece [17] the resplendent and vigorous Helios, driving
across the vault of heaven with his team of snow-white horses,
is the exact counterpart of the Indian Sûryá ; he also is called
the all-seeing ' eye of Zeus ' ; he is supposed to hear oaths.
Apollo, whom learned poetry later made into a sun-god, was
originally a god simply of light and fire. The story of the
Argonauts and the Golden Fleece is a Greek sun-myth, as
is also the legend of the Apples of the Hesperides. The
goddess Eos, the ' rosy-fingered ', corresponds to the Indian
Ushas.

In Rome we find Sol [18] the charioteer, patron of the circus-
races, the discoverer of everything hidden, corresponding to
Sûryâ and Helios. In Janus von Schroeder finds another
sun-god, who opens the door (of heaven) in the morning and
closes it at night, like Savitar in India ; he is also called
Matutinus pater. As his feminine counterpart we have Mater
Matuta, goddess of the dawning light and of birth ; Aurora
is a later poetic invention.*

Among the Teutons [19] we find in Scandinavia the goddess
Sôl, whose car is drawn by two horses, Ârvakrr (Early Awaken-
ing) and Alsvidhr (Allknowing), led by a wolf, who in mythology is a solar beast, and followed by another. We must
also mention the rising sun at the beginning of spring, the
Anglo-Saxon Eostre, probably Austrô in primitive Teutonic,
after whom April was called Eostur-month and from whose

---

[16] Schroeder, *op. cit.*, Vol. II, p. 19 *sqq.*
[17] *Ibid.*, p. 21 *sqq.*   [18] *Ibid.*, p. 27 *sqq.*
* [Many of von Schroeder's theories are here quite out of keeping
with modern results in Greek and Roman religion. For instance,
Apollo has nothing directly to do with either light or fire ; the story
of the Argonauts contains no elements of sun-myth at all, nor does
that of the Hesperides ; Sol as ' patron of circus-races ' is not native
Italian ; the theory concerning Janus is an old fallacy ; Matuta may
or may not be a dawn-goddess.]
[19] *Ibid.*, p. 35 *sqq.*

name that of Easter is derived. The sun is one eye of Odhin ;
the other he gave as a pledge to Mimir and never got it back ;
this is the reflection of the sun in water.

I omit the traces of solar mythology to be found among the
Slavs,[20] and more clearly among the Lithuanians and Letts,[21]
and can give only a brief mention of the customs connected
with sun-myths.[22] These include leading about the sun in
the shape of a wheel on a carriage drawn by horses ; the
imitation of the supposed jumping, dancing and swinging of
the sun at the beginning of spring or at the solstices (a piece
of magic to help the sun move) ; greeting the sun in the
morning ; bonfires on Midsummer Day and Shortest Day ;
games with wheels ; discus-throwing ; foot-races and horse-
races ; shooting at targets ; games at ball ; vegetation magic
and fertility-customs at the solar festivals ; sacrifices on these
occasions. In all these practices it is clear how powerful and
many-sided is the influence exercised by sun-cult in the life
of the Indo-European peoples.*

Von Schroeder, following Mannhardt, considers the ' sacred
marriage ' also to be a heritage from primitive Aryan times.
This consists in the wedding of the sun with the sun-maiden
or the moon, and is celebrated as the pattern of all earthly
marriages. The morning and evening stars appear as suitors,
and he would explain in this manner the two Açvins of Indian
mythology, the Greek Dioskuroi and the Lettish ' sons of
God '. In this connexion also come Hera and Juno as the
consorts of Zeus and Juppiter.

(γ) The Moon

In comparison with the 458 pages in which von Schroeder
sets forth to his readers the riches of Aryan solar mythology,
the bare seven which he devotes to the moon make but
a poor showing.[23] They confirm throughout, however, the
statement I have already made concerning the remarkable
neglect of moon-myths by the nature-myth school. This
neglect has indeed been made good, but not by members of
that school ; the correction came, as we shall see below,
from the school of astral mythologists who take Babylon as
their starting-point, and from ethnological investigations, and
so does not appear till later. If I may anticipate, I would

[20] *Ibid.*, p. 39 *sqq.*   [21] *Ibid.*, p. 45 *sqq.*   [22] *Ibid.*, pp. 38–391.
* [Several of these customs are doubtfully solar and others certainly
not solar at all.]
[23] *Ibid.*, p. 459 *sqq.*

mention here that even von Schroeder is not without traces of these later influences. These are especially noticeable in the last sixteen pages of his second volume, in which there appears a section with the title *Was the Aryan sun-cult preceded by an older cult of the moon ?* [24] in which the veteran scholar makes some interesting concessions.

For a long while he had rejected the lunar theories of Hüsing and Schultz, and still more the pan-lunar hypothesis of Siecke. But apparently constant dropping had worn away the stone. However, this was not fully apparent till the publication of his admirable article *Die Wurzeln der Sage vom heiligen Graal,** in the *Transactions of the Imperial Academy of Sciences at Vienna*, departments of history and philology, 1911. Here, following A. Hillebrandt, *Vedische Mythologie*, Vol. I (Breslau, 1891), he was himself obliged to admit what an important part the moon has played in Aryan myths as the vessel containing the water of life, or some intoxicating drink. But for this, he would have allotted to the moon but three short pages of his great work ; now he adds four more, simply to deal with the significance of the moon as the vessel containing the drink of immortality. Thus he comes to the admission ' We may thus consider it after all probable that besides the sun, the moon also in primitive Aryan times was honoured, although to what extent, is not easy to determine '.

Indeed at the very end of the volume, in the section already mentioned, he makes many corrections of his earlier statements about the sun, and now holds the attribution to the moon to be more probable and more primitive. This applies to the custom of swinging, the ideas of the loaf, the vessel, the Easter hare, the island, the fish and others ; all these he explains as more readily intelligible by reference to the changing aspect of the moon than to the immutable shape of the sun.†

It must also be added that he explains such figures as Diana, Artemis, Aphrodite, Rudra or Shiva, Dionysos, Hermes, Odhin, which the school of astral mythologists make out to be lunar figures, as gods of souls, leaders of departed spirits. These he intended to treat of in the third volume of his work,

---

[24] Schroeder, *op. cit.*, Vol. II, p. 659 *sqq.*
* [' The Origins of the Legend of the Holy Grail ', in *Sitzungsberichte der k. Akad. der Wiss. in Wien. Philol.-Hist. Klasse.*]
† [The connexion of any of the above objects in myth or ritual with any celestial phenomenon whatever is more than doubtful.]

which he was never able to finish. In it he would, no doubt, have recognized their true origin in lunar mythology.*

(d) FIRE

Among the Indo-European peoples we find three kinds of holy fire : that on the altar, that used in rites of aversion, or apotropaic ceremonies, and that in the house.[25] Von Schroeder does not believe that the first of these is primitive Aryan, for he holds that in those days sacrifices were not yet burned. He admits, however, that in later times the altar-fire won the dominant position among certain individual peoples. Thus among the Indians,[26] the sacrificial fire, Agni, is the messenger who brings men into relation with the deity ; he is likewise himself the sacrificing priest. But he is also very prominent as the hearth-fire, also as guardian of the herds and as a protective and apotropaic fire. He has three origins, one on earth, from two parents (two pieces of wood, one male, the *ficus religiosa* [or tulsi], the other female, the *acacia Sama* ; these are rubbed one against the other), one in the air, the thunderclouds, and one in heaven, the sun.

The cult of fire is still more conspicuous among the Iranians,[27] as the fire of the altar, of the hearth, and in rites of aversion. It was, as W. Geiger says,[28] in the eyes of the believer in Ahura-Mazda,

'the holiest and purest element, the radiance of Ahura-Mazda, his highest deity. For him, it is the symbol of moral purity and a powerful agent for the expulsion of demons.'

Omens were obtained from the behaviour of the fire. There were holy places for it, where it was always kept alight. Probably the house of every petty chieftain and every elder of the community, certainly that of every family, must have on its hearth a fire which was never put out and was kept up by the head of the house in person.

Among the Greeks,[29] von Schroeder supposes Apollo to have been originally a god of light and fire, honoured in the three-legged fire-pot (the tripod) and therefore also a giver of oracles, as in Persia. He is also protector of the hearth-fire and thus of the family, and of cities and colonies ; further,

---

* [Save for theories ancient and modern, none of these deities has any connexion with the moon.]

[25] Von Schroeder, *op. cit.*, Vol. II, p. 472 *sqq.*
[26] *Ibid.*, p. 475 *sqq.* [27] *Ibid.*, p. 489 *sqq.*
[28] *Ostiranische Kultur*, p. 253.
[29] Schroeder, *op. cit.*, Vol. II, p. 497 *sqq.*

he is the protector of flocks and herds.   Hephaistos is rather
god of material fire and of the forge.   Hestia is accounted
a fire-goddess, particularly of the hearth-fire ; she also guards
the fire of the community and of the city, and before and after
all sacrifices, an offering is made to her.

In the last two figures it is evident how much the Greeks and
Romans had in common.[30]   In Rome the god of fire is
Vulcan, god of the smithy and of destroying fire ; but he is
also connected with the fire of the household and of the state-
hearth.   The last two are more under the guardianship
of Vesta, whom the Vestal Virgins had to serve in keeping up
the holy fire of the community and the state.*

Among the Teutons,[31] the enigmatic double figure of Loki
belongs to this class.   He is nearer Vulcan than Agni-Apollo,
and takes a peculiar tone from his character of a crafty
deceiver ; Sophus Bugge would explain this by supposing
that he has been influenced by the Christian figure of Lucifer.

Among the Slavs, Lithuanians and Letts, we do indeed hear
of holy fires but not of actual fire-gods.[32]

Von Schroeder holds [33] that for the primitive Aryan period
we must distinguish between the cult of the hearth and that
of fire as a natural force and of a male fire-god.   The hearth-
fire became a recipient of cult for sociological reasons ; it
was regarded as a superior being, to which offerings of food
were presented ; it was respectfully tended and ceremonially
honoured, especially at a marriage, when a new hearth was
to be lit.   The cult of fire as a great natural force, on the
other hand, seems hardly separable from that of the sun ;
consequently sun-festivals and life-festivals were also fire-
festivals, and in other respects the cult included sun and
fire as well.   The ceremonial kindling of the new fire by
rubbing sticks together took place especially at solstitial
festivals.

(e) THE THUNDER-GOD

The thunderstorm, that impressive natural phenomenon,
with its flashes, its peals, and its bursts of rain, was brought
unchanged into immediate relation with the Supreme Being.

---

[30] Schroeder, *op. cit.*, Vol. II, p. 534 *sqq.*

* [The reader should note that Apollo's tripod is not necessarily
an instrument for supporting a pot, but was used as a stand for all
manner of objects ; that Hephaistos is not originally a Greek, or an
Indo-European god ; and that Vulcan has no connexion with the
smithy-fire or the hearth, at any rate in his native Italian cult.]

[31] *Ibid.*, p. 546 *sqq.*   [32] *Ibid.*, p. 579 *sqq.*   [33] *Ibid.*, p. 582 *sqq.*

Both in its beneficent and in his destructive aspect it was felt to be one of his most outstanding functions; and in the case of the Greek Zeus and the Roman Juppiter no change took place here.[34] In India, however, there appeared and won permanent standing a hypostasis of the Supreme Being, Parjanya, although he never attained any great importance. Corresponding to him among the Teutons is the faded figure of the Scandinavian god Fjörgynn. The reason why neither of these remained long an important deity was that both among the Indian and the Teutons a more robust thunder-god of their own became prominent; of him we shall speak shortly. On the other hand, Perun among the Slavs, Perkunas among the Lithuanians, and Pehrkons among the Letts remained more important, sometimes appearing alongside the sky-god, sometimes identified with him.

The Teutons [35] developed a thunder-god of their own, in the shape of the German Dunar or Thunar, who must have been a leading deity in that country, since Thursday (*Donnerstag*) is named after him, and his Scandinavian counterpart Thôrr (originally Thonraz), concerning whom we are better informed. He has a red beard, the shaking of which causes storms. In his hand he carries the 'Crusher', a hammer or club, which he hurls and which comes back again to him. He rides in a car drawn by two goats, Tanngnjöst and Tanngrîsnir, *i.e.*, Teeth-grinder and Teeth-gnasher; the rolling of this causes thunder. He has gigantic strength, and is a monstrous eater and a sturdy drinker of mead. The oak and the stag-beetle are sacred to him; Thursday was his holy day, and on it there was often no work, especially no spinning done. He became the favourite of the peasants and drove the old sky-god into the background. In his turn he was later put in the shade by Odhin, who to all appearances was the god of the Viking nobility.

In nearly all these characteristics he resembles the Indian deity Indra.[36] He too has a fair beard, and hurls a thunderbolt, shaped like a St. Andrew's cross, which comes back to him. His chariot is drawn by roan horses, two, twenty, or a thousand in number. Like Thôrr, he is a notable trencherman and a mighty drinker, consuming incredible quantities of soma. He is the champion of gods and men, soon becomes popular, and casts even Varuna into the shade.

Von Schroeder derives both these figures from old thunder-giants, whom he supposes to have been originally helpers of

[34] *Ibid.*, p. 599 *sqq.*   [35] *Ibid.*, p. 608 *sqq.*   [36] *Ibid.*, p. 691 *sqq.*

the sky-god in making thunder-storms, like the Lettish Perkuns' five or nine sons, or Zeus' three Kyklopes. In his article *Herakles und Indra*, in the *Denkschriften der Akademie der Wissenschaften in Wien* * von Schroeder supposes Herakles also to have been an old god of thunder, of the same type as Thôrr and Indra.

(*f*) GODS OF THE DEAD AND DEIFIED ANCESTORS

Von Schroeder had intended to handle this subject in his third volume, which he never lived to finish. Among such gods are the Indian Shiva, also Yama and Yami, the Teuton Wodan or Odhin, and the Slavonic Triglav and Svantovit. We shall learn more of this kind of gods and other super-human beings in treating of the animistic theory. As they have for the most part some connexion with moon-myths, to know them will complete our understanding of the wide-reaching importance of nature-myths among Indo-European peoples.

* ['Memorials of the Viennese Academy of Sciences.' Unfortunately for von Schroeder's theory Herakles' name makes it clear that he cannot originally have been a god at all, but a man, real or imaginary. See L. R. Farnell, *Greek Herocults*, p. 99.]

CHAPTER V

FETISHISM

1. THEORIES OF FETISHISM

(a) THE WHIRLIGIG OF TIME

THE exaggerations and over-stressings which gradually came over the movements prevailing in the opening decades of the nineteenth century resulted in their collapse by about the middle of it. Idealistic philosophy was exaggerated till it explained away reality in brilliant but facile *a priori* propositions, or even denied it altogether. Traditionalism went too far, in that it denied the activities of the reason. Conservatism fossilized in its endeavour to preserve what had once and for all broken down, and in many cases was only galvanized into a semblance of life. All such tendencies were fatally weakened, both by reason of their own absurdity and also by the reappearance of those subterranean revolutionary forces which had existed at the end of the eighteenth century and had been merely repressed, not crushed.

Their weakness resulted in utter collapse, especially as two new and powerful forces arose which, by a coincidence in the time of their appearance, were caught up almost entirely by this undercurrent of revolution. One of these was the increasingly brilliant discoveries and inventions in the realms of pure and applied natural science, and the other, the progress made in revealing the history and prehistory of mankind. The latter process was hastened by the fact that, now Europe had once more come into contact with the countries beyond her borders, voyages of discovery both geographical and ethnological began again in Africa, Oceania and America, thus giving an increasingly full and clear view of the mass of savage peoples which lies behind the middle and higher cultures.

This whole tendency, spreading as it did with growing strength, first appeared, rather shamefacedly, in the sphere

of philosophy, under the name of Positivism. However, it
soon gained confidence and proclaimed itself openly as Materialism, which was destined to influence, if not to dominate, the
whole intellectual life of Europe for decades to come.

Its results were of course felt in the history of religion, and
all the more strongly as the school of nature-mythologists,
whose work lay among the civilized and semi-civilized peoples
of the past, was divorced from present reality, particularly as
it looked so much to books and written documents to show
it the past. Thus a great part of the newly-awakened interests were lost on it, and forced to turn to new theories
which seemed more in keeping with the spirit and movement
of the age.

The year 1859 saw the new development in full bloom. At
that date the French Academy at last recognized the prehistoric
discoveries made by their countryman, Boucher de Perthes,
in the valley of the Somme, for what they were. In England, a geological authority, Sir Charles Lyell, had already
supported them against Cuvier. Thus was revealed a new
chapter of human history, hitherto concealed under the ground,
and its revelations extended to far-distant millennia. These
thousands and tens of thousands of years seemed immediately
to stretch out to hundreds of thousands when, in the same
year, Charles Darwin published his work, *The Origin of Species
by Natural Selection*, which laid human history open far back
into stages before man appeared. Still in the same year new
horizons in the history of mankind were revealed by the extensive treatise of Th. Waitz, *Anthropologie der Naturvölker,**
and in the first work of A. Bastian, *Der Mensch in der
Geschichte* [1].† The idea of development, which had been
pushed to the furthest extreme, especially by Hegel, in the
department of idealistic philosophy, now gained a very different vigour and force when brought into contact with solid
and visible facts. Thus it won complete mastery, and Evolutionism was born.

(b) Fetishistic Theories

(a) A. Comte and Positivism

The connexion between the new movements and the end
of the eighteenth century is nowhere so clear as in the theory

* [' Savage Anthropology.']   † [' Man's Position in History.']
[1] Yet another product of this year was the book of Karl Marx, *Zur
Kritik der politischen Ökonomik* (' Critique of Political Economy ',) which

of the history of religion developed by A. Comte in accordance with the spirit of his Positivist philosophy. He believed he had discovered a sociological law, that the development of man passed through three stages, the theological or fictive, the metaphysical or abstract, and the positive or scientific. In the first stage, the universe was explained as a result of the activities of personal beings ; in the second, it was made to depend on abstract forces ; in the third, inquiry was confined to establishing the succession and interrelations of experimental facts without troubling about the question of the Absolute. For the whole attention of man must now be turned upon the positive, that is to say, the precise, actual and relative. The first or theological stage was again subdivided into three, namely, fetishism, polytheism and monotheism.[2] Here he manifestly follows Ch. de Brosses' *Du culte des dieux fétiches* (Paris, 1760), for which see p. 31.

But while the latter author had alleged only that fetishism was one of the sources of religion and placed star-worship alongside it as another, Comte gave the word ' fetish ' so wide a significance as to embrace even the heavenly bodies ; indeed, he expressly talks of the sun, moon and earth as ' the great fetishes '. According to him, fetishism is the worship of nature in the strictest sense of the word. It is a religion which addresses itself to all natural objects as such, without thinking of them as inhabited by a spirit. In the festival calendar of his new Positivist religion, he actually devotes a whole month to fetishism, with feast-days of the animals, the sun, the moon and fire. It is not, in his theory, till the second phase of religious development that these things are personified or animated, that is, provided with indwelling spirits ; in this manner a plurality of gods, polytheism, arose, and from that, after a long process of development, came at length the third stage, monotheism.

This theory, which forms a part of a still wider synthesis, dealing with the whole history of the human mind and not only of religion, explicitly involved progressive Evolutionism. It thus corresponded to the tendencies and needs of the day,

brought the idea of development into dominance in the sphere of economics. At the same time the discovery of spectrum analysis was made by Kirchoff and Bunsen, thus enabling it to be applied to the farthest recesses of the stellar systems.

[2] A. Comte, *Cours de philosophie positive* (6 vols., Paris, 1830–42), LI Leçon. Cf. also his *Système de philosophie positive ou traité de sociologie instituant la religion de l'humanité*, 4 vols., Paris, 1851–4.

and so was warmly welcomed, particularly in the wider sociological circles. Among scientists in the stricter sense, however, it was not so widely spread. Its over-simplified and
schematized ' triplicity ' was too thin, and as a matter of fact
was sadly lacking in support from positive data, especially
those relating to savage peoples.

(β) Sir J. Lubbock and Ethnology

Twenty years later an attempt was made to get rid of
both the defects attaching to Comte's theory, in the work
of (Sir) John Lubbock (afterwards Lord Avebury), *The Origin
of Civilization and the Primitive Condition of Man*, London,
1870.

Ethnology had indeed accumulated in the meantime an
increasingly rich store of material from the savage races, and
Lubbock made copious use thereof. These more abundant
data were of themselves enough to break through the narrow
limits of Comte's system, and Lubbock, enlarging it at top
and bottom, arrived at the following series of stages in religious
development : Atheism, or total absence of religion ; Fetishism ; Totemism, or the worship of Nature ; Shamanism ;
Anthropomorphism, or Idolatry ; God as Creator of the
Universe, and union of religion with ethics. This long and
detailed series became the model of many others, evolutionary
like itself, which during the following decades undertook to re-
place real history, especially in the field of the science of religion.

On the other hand, Lubbock found no supporters for the
individual steps of his series. The examples of peoples with
no religion which he had collected, in order to get a stage
earlier yet than fetishism, were shown to be incorrect by the
criticism which followed upon his work, beginning with Ross-
koff, *Das Religionswesen der rohesten Naturvölker,** Leipzig,
1880, and with which all ethnologists of any standing agreed.
Modern ethnology has therefore dropped the category of peoples
without religion. Not long ago it had been reduced to one
example, the Kubu of Sumatra, and the work of van Dongen
and Father Schebesta struck even that off the list. W. Tess-
mann recently made a last attempt to find ' men without a
god 't in the Indians of the Ucayali, but this has been emphatically rejected by ethnological criticism.

Comte did not succeed in winning important disciples for

---

* [' The Religious Life of the Lowest Savages.']

† [This is the title of his work, in German *Menschen ohne Gott*,
Stuttgart, 1928.]

his theory of the science of religion ; still less did Lubbock, for F. Schultze, with his work *Der Fetischismus* (Berlin, 1871), certainly cannot be reckoned as such. Lord Avebury, as he became in 1900, was, however, stubborn enough to announce in 1911, two years before his death, when so many other theories had already come and gone, his unwavering adherence to his hypotheses, in *Marriage, Totemism and Religion, an Answer to Critics* (London, 1911). He met, however, with but little success.

2. FETISHISTIC RELIGION

Both Comte's conception of fetishism and that of Lubbock depart very widely indeed from their point of origin, to which de Brosses had still remained faithful. The term ' fetish ' comes from the Portuguese *feitiço*, Lat. *facticius*, and is defined to mean ' sortilège, maléfice, enchantement, charme ', in short, magic or an amulet. It was used by the Portuguese in their dealings with the negroes of West Africa to denote certain inanimate objects, as teeth, claws, tails, feathers, horns, shells, sticks, pieces of iron, rags of clothing, heaps of clay stuck with nails, and many other such, to which the negroes addressed themselves with prayers and sacrifices, or with a certain reverence, to obtain help of some kind. But the negroes protest vehemently against the idea that they revere the material object itself.

Major A. Glyn Leonard, in his work *The Lower Niger and its Tribes*, comes, after a rather long discussion of the common misuse of the word ' fetish ', to the following conclusion (p. 297) :

' In practically every case, irrespective of the form or exterior of the emblem, the adoration is not paid to the object or element itself, but to the object or element as being the symbol containing and representing the ancestral deities of households, communities, and tribes.'

Much the same expressions are used by P. Amaury Talbot, for many years British Resident in Nigeria, in his work *The Peoples of Southern Nigeria* (four vols., Oxford, 1926), Vol. II, pp. 20–1 :

' True fetishism, in which the object of worship is not symbolic but is worshipped for itself and not as connected with, or representing, a deity or spirit, is absent from this country.'

But above all, there is not a single religion, even in West Africa, the stronghold of fetishism, which consists of fetishism wholly or even principally. Fetishism never forms the main integral element of the religion, but is generally a mere incidental phenomenon, almost as it were a cast-off from it, a separate part of little account. Invariably we find here in the centre of the cult the adoration, by prayer and sacrifice, with other ceremonies, of a supreme sky-god, whose wife is the Earth, with a numerous progeny of earth-gods. Next in strength to him is the cult of the ancestral ghosts and of departed kings and chiefs, which often finds expression in hecatombs of human victims. Both the earth-gods and the ancestors may reside, not only in real images, but in those formless objects which are commonly called fetishes.

See the comprehensive account of Schneider, in *Die Religion der afrikanischen Naturvölker*, Münster, Westphalia, 1891, pp. 28–47, 113–35, 169–232 ; and the descriptions of particular districts in J. Spieth, *Die Ewe-Stämme*, Berlin, 1906, pp. 66–93, 414–548, 638–86, 710–24, 786–916 ; A. Glyn Leonard, *The Lower Niger and its Tribes*, London, 1906, pp. 79–504 ; P. Amaury Talbot, *op. cit.*, Vol. II, pp. 1–351 ; C. K. Meek, *The Northern Tribes of Nigeria*, Oxford, 1925, Vol. II, pp. 1–131 ; D. Westermann, *Gottesvorstellungen in Oberguinea*, in *Africa*, Vol. I (1928), pp. 189–209 ; A. B. Ellis, *The Tshi-speaking Peoples of the Gold Coast of West Africa*, London, 1887, p. 189 *sqq.*

Under these circumstances it is evident that, since fetishism nowhere exists in a pure state, it is ethnologically quite unjustifiable to place it, as an independent stage, at the first beginnings of religious development. But there is also another objection to so doing. Where fetishism really does exist, it is not among races in the lowest or the middle stage of savagery, but among peoples whose savage state has developed into a higher culture, those whom we commonly call half-civilized. Such are the West African negroes in Upper Guinea, the Polynesians, the Dravidians of South India, and a number of prairie peoples in the southern part of North America, who are in the agricultural stage, as the Pueblo, the Maskogi tribes, and such Algonkin and Sioux tribes as make use of the various sorts of medicine bags. All of these belong more or less to the secondary cultures, generally having free father-right.* They are therefore only a little way behind the middle and high cultures of the Indo-Europeans.

* [By ' free ' father-right or mother-right is meant a system under which descent is counted through the father only, or the mother only as the case may be, but no exogamous clans or phratries, totemic or other, with their restrictions on the choice of a partner, exist.]

CHAPTER VI

MANISM, OR GHOST-WORSHIP

1. HERBERT SPENCER'S GHOST-THEORY

IF we wished to keep a strict chronological order, we should be obliged to describe Tylor's theory of Animism next. But I prefer to take Spencer's ghost-theory first, for one thing because its origins are older, for another because Tylor's theory had a deeper and more lasting influence on the succeeding epoch, to which therefore we can more conveniently pass from it.

Herbert Spencer developed the science of Sociology, which Auguste Comte had founded, with more breadth and better method ; especially, he founded it on a more comprehensive set of ethnological data ; and his theory of religion is even more sociological in its nature than Comte's fetishism had been. The latter has in reality but little that is specifically sociological, but walks half in the old ways of metaphysics, half in the new paths of science. It was Herbert Spencer who made an important sociological element, the departed members of the community, carry the weight of his theory.

How important he thought this theory is clear from the fact that it stands at the beginning of his sociological system, as set forth in his *Principles of Sociology* (London, Vol. I, 1876 ; Vol. II, 1882 ; Vol. III, 1896). After developing, in the first nineteen chapters of his first volume, his ideas concerning the primitive thoughts of mankind on life, death, resurrection, souls, spirits, the other world, and the cult of ghosts, he sums the matter up in the twentieth chapter as follows : [1]

' (1) Taking the aggregate of the human peoples—tribes, societies, nations—we find that nearly all of them, if not literally all, have a belief, vague and wavering or settled and distinct, in a reviving other-self of the dead man. (2) Within this class of peoples, almost

[1] Spencer, *op. cit.*, Vol. I, pp. 322–3. The numbers in brackets are mine (W. Schmidt).

coextensive with the whole, we find a class not quite so large, by the members of which the other-self of the dead man, definitely believed in, is supposed to exist for a considerable period after death. (3) Nearly as numerous is the class of peoples included in this, who show us ghost-propitiation, not only at the funeral, but for a subsequent interval. (4) Then comes a narrower class contained in the last—the more settled and advanced peoples who, along with the developed belief in a ghost that permanently exists, show us a persistent ancestor-worship. (5) Again, somewhat further restricted, though by no means small, we have a class of peoples whose worship of distinguished ancestors begins to subordinate that of the undistinguished. (6) And eventually, the subordination growing decided, becomes more marked where the ancestors were the leaders of conquering races.'

In the following chapters he is at pains to show that the other forms of religion are themselves developed out of ancestor-worship (Chap. XXI, Idol-worship and Fetish-worship ; XXII, Animal-worship ; XXIII, Plant-worship ; XXIV, Nature-worship), till in Chapter XXV he derives deities themselves, properly so-called, from this source. At the end of this chapter he reaches the conclusion of the whole matter in these terms :

' Behind the supernatural being of this order, as behind supernatural beings of all other orders, we thus find that there has in every case been a human personality.
' Anything that transcends the ordinary, a savage thinks of as supernatural or divine : the remarkable man among the rest. This remarkable man may be simply the remotest ancestor remembered as the founder of the tribe ; he may be a chief famed for strength and bravery ; he may be a medicine-man of great repute ; he may be an inventor of something new ; and then, instead of being a member of the tribe, he may be a superior stranger bringing arts and knowledge ; or he may be one of a superior race gaining predominance by conquest. Being at first one or the other of these, regarded with awe during his life, he is regarded with increased awe after his death ; and the propitiation of his ghost, becoming greater than the propitiation of ghosts which are less feared, develops into an established worship.
' There is no exception then. Using the phrase ancestor-worship in its broadest sense as comprehending all worship of the dead, be they of the same blood or not, we reach the conclusion that ancestor-worship is the root of every religion ' (*op. cit.*, p. 440).

The wide-reaching effects of this theory are largely due to its position as an organic part of an imposing sociological system, which in turn is a part of a more comprehensive philosophical system. The fundamental tenet of this philosophy was the incomprehensibility of the ultimate cause of things (the Unknowable), and it led, so gradually as to be unobserved, from belief to unbelief by way of scepticism. Moreover, it put, for the first time, the idea of Evolution in its new, concrete form, a view upheld by Spencer seven years before Darwin, as is shown by his article *The Development Hypothesis*, in the *Leader* for March 20, 1852. This idea it works out in the most comprehensive manner. Consequently, both in philosophical circles and among students of the growing science of Sociology, the theory was widely welcomed. But historians of religion itself, and ethnologists also, were not much in favour of it, because the idea of development, once the starting-point was assumed, was worked out too ruthlessly. Moreover, the documentation was hopelessly inexact. Neither title, date, or page of the works quoted is ever given, because, to cite the reason adduced by Spencer himself, to look at such notes is ' a waste of energy and time ' ! Andrew Lang also accuses him of getting his documentation done ' by proxy ', through the agency of helpers whose instructions were to look for facts in support of his theory. The result of course was that data of a contrary kind were simply omitted.

2. ANCESTORS AND THEIR WORSHIP IN THE VARIOUS
CULTURES

(*a*) THE VARIOUS FORMS OF ANCESTORS

Herbert Spencer's theory is the most comprehensive and radical application of Euhemerism that the science of religion has hitherto seen. It cannot be denied that, with its abundant, though shaky and uncertain documentation, it passes in review and includes practically all the various kinds of ancestors. But, although Spencer did not shut his eyes to the possibility of partial degeneration ; although he did not imagine all savages of to-day to be unaltered survivals of older phases of development ; yet in fact progressive Evolutionism was his only criterion for determining the order of the separate forms of ancestor-worship. Not the faintest disposition is shown to settle the chronology of these forms by genuinely historical methods.

We will now proceed to set forth the position of ancestor-worship in the different religions, arranged in the objectively determined order which the succession of the individual culture-complexes allows us to discover, thanks to the historical method of studying human civilization. We shall see that we have here an utterly different picture from that painted by Spencer. Especially, it will be seen that there is not a single religion which consists of ancestor-worship alone ; that this is never more than one element of religion. Then we shall be able, above all, to determine what the relation of ancestor-worship to the other elements really is.

(a) Ancestors in Primitive Cultures

(i) In the great majority of peoples belonging to the primitive cultures, the typical figure which we find is that of the Supreme Being, who has neither wife nor family. Under him and created by him are the primal pair from whom the tribe is descended. We find this form among the Pygmies of Central Africa, the South-East Australians, the inhabitants of North Central California, the primitive Algonkins, and, to a certain extent, the Koryaks and the Ainu. In South-East Australia the primal pair takes the form of two sex-totems, generally birds and for the most part small ones, one, representing the First Father, for all the men, the other, the First Mother, for all the women. These play a prominent part in the initiation of the youths, in which the initiands are made like the tribal ancestors, and hence into full-blown members of the tribe ; also in the introductory ceremonial of marriage, in which they are empowered to carry on the tribe. The relation of the survivors to the dead is, again, frequently rather one of love than of fear. Among other proofs of this, we see that the remains of the body, the skull and parts of the bones, are kept and carried about for months by the relations, especially the widow, as dear memorials, for instance, among the Andamanese and the Kurnai of South-East Australia. It is true that the camp is often deserted, for instance, by the African and Asiatic Pygmies, when a death takes place ; but this is due not so much to fear of the dead as of the Supreme Being, who often sends early death as a punishment,—this is, e.g., the belief of the Tierra del Fuegians, —and whom they therefore try to avoid. The most widely distributed form of sepulture is burial in the earth ; cremation is found only exceptionally.

(ii) So much for the two earliest, or primitive cultures, the central, represented by the Pygmy and Pygmoid races, or southern, consisting of the South-East Australians and Tierra del Fuegians. Ancestors are differently conceived in the so-called boomerang-culture, which in both Australia and Africa follows upon the earliest stage, or more probably results from a crossing of it with one of the later primary cultures, the matrilineal and agrarian.   Here we no longer find a pair of tribal ancestors, but a single figure, the First Father.   He is the first man. ˉBeing at once the first mortal and also risen from the dead, he is equated with the moon, which wanes and disappears, but also is seen again new.   He is symbolized under the form of the moon, and also of lunar animals, which live in the earth and come forth from it again, such as hares, rabbits, porcupines, jaguars, coyotes ; or which shed their skin, as snakes and lizards.   He appears under these shapes particularly at the initiation of the young people, which at this stage is secret and confined entirely to boys. Often, perhaps generally, in these cultures, he is no longer subordinate to the Supreme Being but has coalesced with him into a single figure, so as to assume his high attributes. He thus appears at once in the capacity of chief god and creator and in that of tribal father, and receives in his own person the combined cult of both.   This again is the stage at which idols are first used in worship ; rough images are made of this First Father of the community ; they are especially used at initiation ceremonies, when they are first shown the young men ; they likewise become images of gods.   Among these figures are Daramulun, the god of the Yuin and neighbouring tribes in South-East Australia ; Heitsi-Eibib among the Hottentots ; and the Old Man among the Blackfeet.   These figures are often characterized by a legend that they have a wounded or a withered knee.   This is an expression of the fact that the moon, which is their symbol, wanes more and more after the full.   Here again we find no cult of the individual dead.   The method of burial may be the so-called niche-grave, a pit dug in the ground with a side chamber in it.

(β) Ancestors in Primary Cultures

Conditions are entirely changed in the so-called primary culture-complexes, which come next in order.   In these, man passes to a higher economic stage and begins to exploit Nature herself.   In all the three states of culture which fall within this division, we now observe a remarkable change ; it is no longer only the primal pair, or the First Father, who receives worship, but a greater or smaller number of other dead ancestors, or even other dead persons.

(i) In the patrilineal culture of the cattle-breeding nomads, which, so far as this point is concerned, is best known from the Mongol and Turkoman peoples of Northern Asia, the father of the race, Erlik, sometimes has acquired the same cult as the Supreme Being—compare the boomerang-culture— while sometimes he appears as the representative of the evil principle, a kind of devil. In the latter case his cult is apparently connected with sorcery. But among these warlike races, not only is the memory of departed heroes celebrated in epic ballads of considerable extent, but these heroes also receive separate worship under many different forms. Here we see ancestor-worship passing into hero-cult. The ordinary dead are buried under barrows of earth, either above or but little under the ground-level ; sepulchral chambers or so-called mortuary chapels are built above the bodies of the rich and distinguished.

(ii) The patrilineal totemistic culture of the higher hunting peoples is to be found in South and East Australia, New Guinea, the Moluccas, the southern portion of Hither * India, large parts of Africa, North-Western and North-Eastern America, and parts of South America. Here the number of those ancestors who are in receipt of worship greatly increases. Besides the First Father, who is here identified with the sun and symbolized by solar animals, as the lion, the wolf, the eagle, the hawk and the falcon, a sort of cult is given to the ancestors of each totemic clan, who are either the totem-animals regarded as ancestors, or human forebears or founders of the clan, or both at once. The chief magician has also a kind of cult, expressed mostly in a special burial ceremony. But also the ordinary dead are often identified with the solar First Father, and so win immortality, as was the case in the Egyptian cult of Osiris. In this case they also receive a kind of worship, expressed in their funeral rites, in which drying on a tree-platform or some other kind of mummifying plays a part, and is in-tended to assure immortality for the dead man, body and all.

(iii) The worship of ancestors is still more extended, even becoming a cult of the dead in general, in the exogamous matrilineal culture of the lower agriculturalists, the ' horti-cultural ' peoples. Here, instead of the father of the race, we have its mother, as might be expected from the economic and sociological predominance of women which finds expres-

* [Hither India (*Vorderindien*) is India proper : Farther India (*Hinterindien*) is Assam, Burma, Annam, Tonkin and Siam.]

sion in mother-right. She is identified with the moon, conceived as a female, or with Mother Earth, and bears two sons, who are the tribal culture-heroes and represent the full moon and the dark of the moon respectively. By way of reaction against the privileged position of the women, the men found secret societies among themselves, in which the worship of ghosts and the honouring of individual male ancestors are especially practised, in the form of skull-worship and masked dances. Here the peculiar effect of animism appears and results in the development of a cult of the dead in general. The dead often receive a double burial, a temporary one until the flesh has left the skeleton, and then the disinterring and preservation of the skull, alone or with other bones. In the later, non-exogamous, form of mother-right, head-hunting is engaged in, to get the skulls, or the hands, feet and other parts, of strangers, which are used chiefly in magical rites of fertility.

(iv) The worship of ancestors and of the dead extends yet more widely in the secondary and tertiary cultures, which arise from the crossing of the primary cultures either with each other or with the primitive culture. If the patrilineal, totemistic culture of the higher hunting peoples crosses with the matrilineal culture of the lower agriculturalists, a combination takes place between the totemic ancestors of the former and the ghosts of the latter. This gives a still greater impetus to the cult of the dead. A cross of pastoral nomads with matrilineal agriculturalists, or totemistic hunters, or both at once, leads to a division of society into classes, one above another. The pastoral people form the aristocracy, their chiefs the royal houses, and the latter develop the cult of ancestors more and more decidedly into a cult of departed chiefs and kings, especially as their position even in life amounts to deification.

(b) The Various Forms of Ancestor-Worship

Having thus arranged the various forms of ancestors in a purely objective series, we will now proceed to do the same for the different forms of their cult, corresponding to the different cultures.

(a) Worship of Ancestors in Primitive Cultures

In dealing with primitive cultures we cannot speak of any fixed forms of the cult of ancestors, which itself is a feeble thing enough. For in these cultures ceremonialism has not yet made itself felt in this or any other department. Possibly the offering of first-fruits, the only kind of sacrifice known at this stage, may here and there be presented, not to the Supreme Being, as it usually is, but to the tribal ancestors or the First Father, who acts as the Supreme Being's intermediary. In some Semang Pygmy tribes who have a sacrifice, not of first-fruits, but of their own blood, offered when great storms occur, the blood is presented, as a preliminary, to the Earth-Goddess, and then finally to Kari, the Supreme Being. The former ceremony is clearly due to matrilineal influence. The practice of laying on the graves of the dead, food, drink, or their own weapons and tools, is not universal but only sporadic among this people ; it is quite inconsistent with the much more general custom of abandoning the hut and camp entirely when a death occurs. Where it does occur (and this is true far into the beginnings of primary culture) such tendance of the dead has nothing religious about it, but is merely the continuation after death of the customary duties of social life. This conclusion has been reached independently of each other by such prominent investigators as Professor Nieuwen-huis, for the Indonesian peoples of the East Indian Archipelago (see *Internationales Archiv für Ethnographie*, Vol. XXIII, 1915, p. 83) and Dr. Ankermann, for the people of Africa (see his article *Totenkult und Seelenglaube bei afrikanischen Völkern* * in the *Zeitschrift für Ethnologie*, 1918, p. 137). A definitely religious cult of ancestors, including sacrifices and prayers, is however found among the Ainu, who are under decided matrilineal influence.

(β) *Worship of Ancestors in Primary Cultures*

In the primary cultures, the funeral ceremonies are generally of increasing richness and elaboration. Offerings of food and drink continue to be laid on the grave for some considerable time ; the entire property of the deceased may be laid in his grave or on his pyre ; such offerings are commonly broken, burned or otherwise destroyed, and so made into ' ghosts '. In later times the offerings may include beasts, slaves, even wives, who are laid, living or dead, in the grave. All these, and likewise rites of atonement and sacrifices performed at the tomb, tend at this stage to become more frequent and more liberal. They appear to have found especially strong

* [' The Cult of the Dead and the Belief in the Soul among African Peoples.']

development among the pastoral nomads of Asia and the palæoasiatic peoples. The object of the cult which at this stage is directed to the dead is, above all, to prevent their return and guard against their evil influences. This is the reason for such things as the breaking of the bones of the dead, the binding or tying into a bundle of the body, and the weighting of the grave with large stones. In the totemistic tribes the cult of totemic ancestors results, or so it would seem, in lessening the fear of the dead in general ; the latter also have a share in the functions which the former exercise for the general benefit. In matrilineal cultures, on the other hand, the souls of dead sorcerers or shamans are especially dreaded and all manner of rites employed to quiet them. So it is with the Northern Asiatic peoples and many Indian races, to whom shamanism has penetrated from Tibet and other matrilineal regions. Generally, the souls of those who have died a violent death are especially feared ; for instance, suicides, persons eaten by wild beasts, those drowned or struck by lightning, and women who have died in childbed.

A particular form of the cult of ancestors and of the dead is necromancy, that is to say divination and the getting of oracles from the departed, by sleeping on their graves, carrying out certain rites with their bones, or making sacrifice to them. Such necromancy is to be found in various parts of Africa, as among the Yorubas, the Kikuyu, and in South Africa, also in Australia, Melanesia and Indonesia (the Dyaks), Lappland, among the classical Greeks and in Babylonia.

In the primitive cultures (except the boomerang-culture, which in any case marks a transition to matrilineal agriculture), it is rare to find sacrifice among the rites by which the cult of ancestors expresses itself, when addressed to the First Father. Such sacrifices, on the other hand, are prominent and numerous in the primary cultures, and particularly among the pastoral nomads and the matrilineal agriculturalists.

(i) Among the former, the First Father receives also bloodless offerings of first-fruits, a sacrifice in its nature appropriate only to the Supreme Being ; but his offerings are usually bloody, and, as we shall see, are an importation from matrilineal culture. This is true of the Yakuts, the Altai, the Burjats and Mongols, and most emphatically of the Ugro-Finns, whose entire religious activities are often absorbed by ancestor-worship. See M. A. Czaplicka, *Aboriginal Siberia*, Oxford, 1914, p. 277 *sqq*. Similar conditions to those prevailing among the Ugro-Finnish peoples are likewise to be found in some of the pastoral races of Africa, such as the Hottentots, Kaffirs, and Bechuana, and a part of the Nilotic tribes. Here the cult of the tribal ancestor, who is often at the same time the hero from whom the royal house is descended, has so far thrown that of the Supreme Being into the shade that the latter no longer receives any sacrifice, or does so only on rare occasions and in great emergencies.   See the present author's *Ethnologische Bemerkungen zu theologischen Opfertheorien*,* St. Gabriel-Mödling, 1923, p. 23 *sqq*.   In North and East Africa, a decided tendency to ancestor-worship properly so called is found throughout the Bantu and Hamitic races. Other districts to which the same applies are Madagascar and, in the South Seas, the Solomon Islands, Fiji, and Polynesia.   Where these peoples are agricultural, their ancestors are often presented with the offering of the first-fruits of their fields.   Genuine ancestor-worship is rare throughout America ; the best instance of its occurrence is in Peru, where it takes the form of cult of the dead in general, together with deification of the Incas after death.

(ii) In the matrilineal cultures there developed alongside of offerings of food to the departed, bloody sacrifices as well. Probably these were originally made to the mother of the tribe, the Old Woman of the Moon, and likewise to Mother Earth, in order continually to reinforce the fertility of the soil with blood, as nearly as possible still living.   To these sacrifices belong the tearing out of the heart, liver or lungs from the living bodies of both human and other victims ; the presentation to the deity of the still quivering organs ; the cutting off of toes and fingers ;   the piercing with arrows of the victims, who are bound in prescribed positions to trees or scaffolds ;   while the torture and sacrifice of prisoners taken in war or on head-hunting raids must largely be included here. Such customs are found among the matrilineal races of Indonesia, Farther India, Tibet (from which country they have made their way northwards into the pastoral peoples of Central Asia), also in North America among the tribes around the Great Lakes and in the south-west, and, moreover, among the ancient Aztecs of Mexico, see the author's *Ethnologische Bemerkungen*, p. 34 *sqq*.

(iii) In totemistic culture, sacrifice nowhere reaches any noteworthy development (see Schmidt, *op. cit.*, p. 31 *sqq*.) ; hence it is no wonder that it does not appear in connexion with their worship of ancestors.   The idea of magic, depending

*['Ethnological remarks on Theological theories of Sacrifice.']

on human self-confidence, finds its most vigorous development in this culture, and prevents sacrifice, which is the offspring of self-renunciation. Its place is taken by certain magical rites which renew the union with the totemic ancestors, so as to continue to share in their living power.

(γ) *In Secondary and Tertiary Cultures*

In the secondary and tertiary cultures, the initial stage of civilization, we find a high development of ancestor-worship especially among the Iranians, Indians, Chinese, Japanese, and many European Indo-Germanic peoples, besides the Polynesians, Peruvians and Ugro-Finns, who have already been mentioned. It takes all four forms : cult of the father of the race, of the father of the family, hero-cult and worship of kings. But here again the departed spirits are almost always a step lower than the gods properly so called, although the First Father here and there wins his way into their ranks, for example Yama in India.

3. CRITICISM OF THE GHOST-THEORY

(*a*) After all that has already been said about the nature, origin and growth of the worship of ancestors, it seems no longer worth while to give here a formal refutation of Spencer's theory. Its falsity is shown by the mere fact that ancestor-worship is very feebly developed in the oldest cultures, while a monotheistic religion is already clearly and unmistakably to be found there. But in addition, the numerous nature-deities cannot possibly be all explained as originally ancestral figures, especially as the natives themselves usually distinguish clearly between the two ; see, for the New Hebrides and Fiji, Bishop H. Codrington, *The Melanesians*, Oxford, 1891 [for instance, p. 121]. It is also unfortunate for Spencer's theory that the highest development of ancestor-worship does not come till the most recent times, and that even then the ancestors almost always remain clearly differentiated from the gods and inferior to them. Even in later times, ancestor-worship has by no means a universal distribution, see p. 68 *sqq. supra*. But such distribution is what we should expect if it were really of such fundamental importance.

(*b*) The same considerations dispose of the attempt to derive sacrifice from the gifts laid on the graves of ancestors and of the dead in general as food for them. It has already been pointed out that in primitive cultures such gifts are still quite rare, while the offering of first-fruits is already to be found among most Pygmy and Arctic peoples. But this is meant simply as an act of homage, and is not an offering of food. This is not to deny that this offering to the dead did make its way later even into religion proper, with the result that the number of sacrifices in religious cult was greatly increased. Thus we find bloody sacrifices of human or other victims originating in the later matrilineal culture, and appearing in many religions of civilized races.

(c) A similar effect of ancestor-worship on religion, and one in reality of still greater importance, is that to it is due the use of images of gods, and representations of the objects of worship in general. In this connexion we find images and figures, not merely of the father of the race, as in the boomerang-culture, but also of the individual dead, erected at first at the grave, but also in temples. The Pygmies were essentially inartistic and had no images, religious or other ; here, and for a great while in the later cultures also, especially that of the pastoral nomads, the law was very strictly observed that no likeness of the Supreme Being might be made. This prohibition was set aside more and more in the patrilineal totemistic culture and that of the matrilineal agriculturalists, till finally we may say that nothing was left of it.

(d) This much is true, although Herbert Spencer did not adequately perceive it ; immediately after the primitive cultures, perhaps already in derivatives of them, the figure of the First Father, that is the first man, the ultimate ancestor of all men who came after him, is the first to obscure that of the Supreme Being. Sometimes the supersession is apparently amicable ; the father of the race appears as the intermediary between the Supreme Being and men, and so thrusts him aside, further and further into an exalted or otiose position, and thus himself becomes the Creator. Sometimes, however, their relations are more or less hostile, the primal man slandering the ethical strictness of the Supreme Being as cruelty, or his kindness as weakness, and painting his own different characteristics in favourable colours.

CHAPTER VII

ANIMISM

1. THE ANIMISTIC THEORY OF E. B. TYLOR

(a) CONDITIONS PRECEDENT TO THE THEORY

WE have already seen (p. 30 *sqq.*) that as early as the second half of the eighteenth century N. S. Bergier, in *Les dieux du paganisme* (Paris, 1767) had developed the idea that both fetishism and star-worship were the products of a childish mentality, which filled natural objects with genii or ghosts, and so made them alive and human. Bergier, however, did not make all religion a development from this origin. After him the continuity was broken, and no new development of his idea took place till a century later. It must, however, be granted that in the meantime a great improvement had taken place in the quality and quantity of the material for such an undertaking. During this time, certain series of savage peoples, lurking behind the races of the higher and middle cultures and the half-civilized, had become more and more widely and clearly known. These were the more or less matrilineal peoples of the horticultural and agricultural stages. Among them was found that very attitude of mind which Bergier had already proclaimed in his day, which sees under the material outside of things, their ' body ', a ' soul ' or *anima*, and explains remarkable characteristics of these things, especially movement, by reference to the powers of these things.

Now this new complex of data was acutely comprehended by Edward Burnett Tylor. He was not a philosopher nor a sociologist, entering the world of savagery to find therein facts to fit his theory ; this world was in itself his own chosen field of activity. Beyond a doubt he was one of the best-trained ethnologists of that day, and to natural acuteness and a wide-reaching knowledge of particular facts he united an extraordinary gift for systematization. He it was who for the first time collected the enormous mass of facts relating to animism, and, on inquiring into its origin, discovered it behind ancestor-worship, fetishism, and the adoration of nature, and thus identified it with the ultimate source of religion.

Thus he built up his animistic theory of the origin of religion. This, with its crushing weight of facts, its smooth and unbroken series of stages of development, and the concise, dispassionate style of its exposition left no room for opposition. As a matter of fact, for the next three decades it remained the ' classical theory ', as Andrew Lang called it, especially among ethnologists and students of the science of religion, almost without any loss of prestige. Even Spencer's ghost-theory, which immediately succeeded it, could not deprive it of pride of place, especially as Tylor had already included ancestor-worship in his own theory, but only as a later stage.

Tylor developed his view in a two-volumed work, *Primitive Culture : Researches into the Development of Mythology, Philosophy, Religion, Art and Custom* (London : ed. 1, 1872 ; ed. 4, 1903 ; ed. 5, 1913). The following quotations are from the first edition. He also gave a more condensed account of it in his book entitled *Anthropology : an Introduction to the study of Man and Civilization*, London, 1882, pp. 343-73.[1]

(b) ORIGIN AND DEVELOPMENT OF ANIMISM AND RELIGION ACCORDING TO TYLOR

We will now proceed to give, in brief outline, an account of the theory, keeping strictly to the order in which Tylor himself sets forth the several sections of it, regarded as successive phases of development. This review of his principal points will suffice to give a not too inadequate picture of both the form and the substance of his ideas.

(i) Primitive man forms his first idea of a something different from the body, *i.e.*, of a soul, from handling two groups of biological problems. The first of these is the phenomena of sleep, ecstasy, illness, and death ; the second, those of dreams and visions. In the former class of conditions, primitive man beheld the body more or less abandoned by the principle of life, and therefore isolated and by itself ; in the second, on the other hand, the figures in dreams and the appearances

---

[1] Both works were speedily translated into German, the former under the title *Die Anfänge der Kultur*, trans. J. W. Spengel and F. Poske, Leipzig, 1873 ; the latter, with the title *Einleitung in das Studium der Anthropologie und Zivilisation*, Brunswick, 1883.

in visions seemed to present this incorporeal principle, the soul,
in isolation. The conception of the soul thus developed
applied first and foremost to the soul of man. As corollaries,
there soon arose the belief in the continued existence of the
soul after death, and in transmigration. Hence arose tendance
of the dead. The idea of retribution in another life, on the
other hand, did not arise till later. (See *Primitive Culture*,
Vol. II, pp. I *sqq.*, 76 *sqq.*)

(ii) As, however, to primitive thought, man's own existence
was the measure of all other, and as he conceived of the
nature of other things by analogy with his own, whereof
alone he had immediate personal experience, he came to
think of all other things whatsoever, first of beasts and plants,
then of all the rest, as consisting of a body and a soul. Being
thus organized like man, it did not occur to him that there
was any difference of nature between man and other things,
and consequently man thought of the rest of the world as
related to himself.

(iii) Ancestor-worship was a cult of dead men who had no
longer an earthly body, and therefore were pure souls ; hence
primitive thought passed to the conception of pure spirits
(*ibid.*, p. 101 *sqq.*) These spirits could at pleasure take possession again, perhaps only for a time, of individual bodies not
their own ; this was the explanation of ' possession ' (*ibid.*,
p. 113 *sqq.*). Illness and death were considered as resulting
from nothing else than the entry and harmful effects of such
a spirit ; and the same explanation holds good for ' fetishism '
(*ibid.*, p. 131 *sqq.*) and the ' stock-and-stone worship ' (*ibid.*,
p. 147 *sqq.*), from which came idolatry proper ; ' a few chips
or scratches or daubs of paint suffice to convert the rude
post or stone into an idol ' (*ibid.*, p. 153).

(iv) The principle of separate or ' pure ' spirits having been
thus arrived at, it was now applied again to nature ; the
various parts of the natural world appeared to primitive man
as animated by such spirits, and their phenomena as due to
them. Hence arose the worship of nature, which was at the
same time a beginning of natural philosophy (*ibid.*, p. 169
sqq.), with its special forms, the worship of water, rivers and
the sea (*ibid.*, p. 191 *sqq.*) ; of trees and forests (*ibid.*, p. 196
sqq.), beasts (p. 208 *sqq.*), totems (p. 213 *sqq.*), and serpents
(p. 217 *sqq.*). All this development culminated in the ' species-
deity ', *i.e.*, the deification, not of a concrete individual, but
of a whole species (p. 220 *sqq.*)

(v) From this was developed the higher polytheism of the

civilized and half-civilized races (p. 224 *sqq.*), the sky-god
(p. 231 *sqq.*), the rain-god (p. 235 *sqq.*), the thunder-god
(p. 237 *sqq.*), the wind-god (p. 241 *sqq.*), the earth-gods
(p. 244 *sqq.*), the gods of water (p. 248 *sqq.*), fire (p. 251 *sqq.*)
and the sun (p. 259 *sqq.*) and moon (p. 271 *sqq.*). Another
line of development produced those gods who preside over
particular stages and functions of human life, the deities of
birth (p. 276), and of agriculture (p. 277), the god of war
(p. 278 *sqq.*) and of death (p. 280 *sqq.*), connected with whom
is the deified father of the race (p. 282 *sqq.*).

(vi) It must be admitted that traces of a dualistic system
are to be found even at the lower stages ; but ' good ' and
' bad ' here have no ethical significance, but mean simply
' beneficial ' and ' harmful ' (p. 287 *sqq.*). Generally helpful
or harmful natural forces helped in the production of this
idea, particularly light and darkness, as in the Zendavesta
(pp. 290 *sqq.*, 293 *sqq.*).

(vii) ' To mark off the doctrine of the lower races, closer definition
(of monotheism) is required, assigning the distinctive attributes of
deity to none save the Almighty Creator. It may be declared that,
in this strict sense, no savage tribe of monotheists has been ever
known. Nor are any fair representatives of the lower culture in
a strict sense pantheists. The doctrine which they do widely hold,
and which opens to them a course tending in one or other of these
directions, is polytheism culminating in the rule of one supreme
divinity ' (*ibid.*, p. 302).

(viii) Monotheism, according to Tylor, arises in various
ways : (*a*) ' by the simple process of raising to divine primacy
one of the gods of polytheism itself ', who may be either the
primeval ancestor or one of the nature-deities. (*b*) A sort
of pantheon may be formed ' arranged on the model of an
earthly political constitution, where the commonalty are
crowds of human souls and other tribes of world-pervading
spirits, the aristocracy are great polytheistic gods, and the
King is the Supreme Deity '. Or (*c*) a doctrine is arrived at
which conceives of ' the universe as animated by one greatest,
all-pervading divinity ', an *anima mundi*, in short. In this
last case a tendency arises either ' to fuse the attributes of
the great polytheistic powers into more or less of common
personality ' or else to ' remove the limit of theological speculation into the region of the indefinite and the inane ', which
results in ' an unshaped divine entity looming vast, shadowy,
and calm beyond and over the material world, too benevolent
or too exalted to need human worship, too huge, too remote,

too indifferent, too supine, too merely existent, to concern himself with the petty race of men ' (pp. 304–5).

(ix) ' Thus, then, it appears that the theology of the lower races already reaches its climax in conceptions of Supreme Deity, and that these conceptions in the savage and barbaric world are no copies stamped from one common type, but outlines widely varying among mankind. . . . Looked upon as products of natural religion, such doctrines of divine supremacy seem in no way to transcend the powers of the low-cultured mind to reason out, nor of the low-cultured imagination to deck with mythic fancy. . . . Among these races, Animism has its distinct and consistent outcome, and Polytheism its distinct and consistent completion, in the doctrine of a Supreme Deity.'

Such in brief is the comprehensive system of the animistic theory, which, erected by Tylor, soon set out on its triumphant career through the scientific world.

(c) THE SPREAD OF THE ANIMISTIC THEORY

(a) A notable proof of the extent to which Tylor's theory influenced the world is the fact that it was accepted by a number of prominent students of ethnology and religion almost without alteration.

Such unqualified acceptance is to be found in F. Gerland (Waitz-Gerland, *Anthropologie der Naturvölker*, Leipzig, ed. 2, 1873, pp. 324, 360, 454 ; Gerland, *Anthropologische Beiträge*, Halle, 1875, p. 274) ; O. Peschel (*Völkerkunde*, Leipzig, ed. 1, 1874, ed. 7, unaltered, 1887, p. 255 *sqq.*) ; G. A. Wilkens (*Het Animisme bij de Volken van den Indischen Archipel*, Leiden, 1885, p. 4) ; Preiss (*Religionsgeschichte*, Leipzig, 1888, p. 19) ; F. Ratzel (*Völkerkunde*, ed. 2, Leipzig and Vienna, 1894, Vol. I, p. 38 *sqq.*) ; A. H. Keane (*Ethnology*, Cambridge, 1896, p. 216 *sq.*) ; Ch. Letourneau (*L'Évolution religieuse*, Paris, 1896, p. 11) ; F. Tiele (*Einleitung in die Religionswissenschaft*, Gotha, 1899, p. 61) ; J. Deniker (*The Races of Man*, London, 1900, p. 215) ; F. Schultze (*Psychologie der Naturvölker*, 1900) ; H. Schurtz (*Urgeschichte der Kultur*, Leipzig and Vienna, 1900, p. 359 *sqq.*) ; F. Boas (*The Mind of Primitive Man*, Smithsonian report for 1901, p. 457) ; W. Bousset (*Das Wesen der Religion dargestellt an ihrer Geschichte*, Halle, 1903) ; E. Clodd (*Animism the Seed of Religion*, London, 1905). As regards the Leipzig school of Peschel, Ratzel and Schurtz, however, it must be added that they emphasize the desire to find a cause and the feeling of dependence as a deeper ground of religion.

(β) Against the nature-myth school, which was then still in full force in England under the leadership of Max Müller,

Andrew Lang, at that time Tylor's favourite pupil, led the animistic theory to a vigorous attack in *Custom and Myth* (London, 1884) and *Modern Mythology* (London, 1897), and that to such purpose that the nature-mythologists soon lost ground and Max Müller himself, as we have already seen (p. 40 *sqq.*), was forced to compromise.

A similar combination of the nature-myth theory with animism is to be found also in A. Réville, for many years editor of the *Revue de l'histoire des religions*, in a work entitled *Les religions des peuples non-civilisés*, Paris, 1883, Vol. I, p. 222 ; in H. Siebeck, *Lehrbuch der Religionsphilosophie*, Freiburg im Breisgau and Leipzig, 1893, pp. 52 *sqq.*, 62–3 ; and in Chantepie de la Saussaye, *Lehrbuch der Religionsgeschichte*, ed. 3, Freiburg im Breisgau and Leipzig, 1897, p. 13.

(γ) A further important conquest for the animistic theory was the field of Old Testament theology. Here the agent was J. Lippert, who in a book entitled *Der Seelenkult in seinen Beziehungen zur althebräischen Religion,** Berlin, 1881, declared the theory to hold good for the development of the Jewish people and its religion.

This application of the theory was at once accepted by two leading theologians of Liberal Protestantism, B. Stade (*Geschichte des Volkes Israel*, Berlin, 1884) and F. Schwally (*Das Leben nach dem Tode, nach den Vorstellungen des alten Judentums*, Giessen, 1892). They were joined by a long array of other authors, such as R. Smend, J. Benzinger, J. Wellhausen, A. Berthold and others, who sought support for their ideas, not only in the results of textual criticism, which they employed, but in these data provided by ethnological research, as transmitted to them by Tylor's theory. A good account of this tendency is to be found in A. Lods, *La croyance à la vie future et le culte des morts dans l'antiquité israélite*, Paris, 1906, Vol. I, pp. 1–42 and 265.

(δ) As the theory of Tylor continued to grow in volume like a mighty river, it received a remarkable tributary. A movement had taken place in Germany among the supporters of the nature-myth theory, in the province of Indo-Germanic studies. Helped by linguistic investigations in the area of these civilized peoples, it had arrived at results which might be brought into contact with the ethnological discoveries.

W. Schwartz, a colleague of Kuhn (see above, p. 38) had already upheld in his later works the view that it was not fully-developed mythology but the tales and fables of the common people which

* [' The Cult of Souls in its relations to Ancient Hebrew Religion.']

formed the beginnings of myth and religion, and that the latter had developed independently among the separate Indo-Germanic peoples. See his works, *Die poetischen Naturanschauungen der Griechen, Römer und Deutschen,* Berlin, 1864–79, and *Indogermanischer Volksglaube,* Berlin, 1885.

W. Mannhardt, whose earlier works, *Germanische Mythen* (Berlin, 1858) and *Die Götterwelt der deutschen und nordischen Völker* (Berlin, 1860), had followed the older school of nature-mythology, now applied this view with more thoroughness and wider range in *Roggenwolf und Roggenhund* (Danzig, 1865–6), *Die Korndämonen* (Berlin, 1868), *Wald- und Feldkulte* (Berlin, 1875–7) and *Mythologische Forschungen* (London and Strasbourg, 1884 ; a posthumous work, the author having died in 1880).* In these books he opposed to the ' high ' gods the figures of the ' lower mythology ', the fairies, genii, and spirits of the corn, woods and water. He maintained that they were not miserable relics of the ' higher mythology ' but survivals of the most ancient times and the first beginnings of the higher creations. These spirits and daimones found their proper place in Tylor's theory of animism, and with it their complement in the ethnological facts of the whole world, and their theoretical and psychological explanation.

In much the same spirit the results of ethnological investigation were applied, together with the theory of animism, to the classical civilizations by E. Rohde in *Psyche, Seelenkult und Unsterblichkeitsglaube der Griechen,* Tübingen, 1891–4, second ed. 1897, eighth ed. 1921 ; [tenth, with introduction by O. Weinreich, 1925] ; H. Usener, *Götternamen,* Bonn, 1896 ; A. Dieterich, *Mutter Erde,* Leipzig and Berlin, 1905 and 1913, 3rd ed. by E. Fehrle, Leipzig, 1925 ; H. Oldenberg, *Die Religion der Veda,* Berlin, 1894, second ed. 1917 ; H. Hirt, *Die Indogermanen, ihre Verbreitung, ihre Urheimat und ihre Kultur,* 2 Vols., Strasbourg, 1905–7, L. von Schroeder, *Mysterium und Mimus im Rigveda,* Leipzig, 1908 ; *Göttertanz und Weltentstehung,* Vienna, 1909, also *Die Wurzeln der Sage vom hl. Graal,* Vienna, 1910, *Herakles und Indra,* Vienna, 1914.

A notable step in the advance of this movement was the transference to its ranks of the periodical *Archiv für Religionswissenschaft.* This was founded and edited in 1898 by a Sanskrit scholar, E. Hardy, who, following the philological nature-myth school, made the following pronouncement, ' The religions of civilized peoples are there-

---

* [' Rye-wolf and Rye-dog '—' Corn-spirits '—' Cults of wood and field '—' Mythological Researches '. Besides the great merits of his work, the fruits of immense learning and admirable candour, Mannhardt is noteworthy for the influence he exercised upon Frazer, as the *Golden Bough* abundantly testifies.]

fore the very backbone of the science of religion ', Vol. I, p. 41.   In 1904 Dieterich became editor, and declared that now the question of the hour was 'not so much the investigation of particular historical religious developments, traceable to individuals, as that of the immemorial ethical background, eternal and still present, of all historical religion ' ; consequently, that in that field philologists and ethnologists could and should learn from one another.

This group of scholars has been not inappropriately called ' philological ethnologists ' or ' ethnological philologists '.[2]

[This school is supplemented and continued by a number of scholars outside Germany. Of these there may be mentioned, merely as examples, Dr. S. Eitrem of Oslo ; Dr. Martin P. Nilsson of Lund ; Dr. L. R. Farnell, late Rector of Exeter College, Oxford ; and, in her earlier work, the late Miss Jane Harrison of Cambridge. All these have in common the characteristic of using the Comparative Method, *i.e.*, of applying to the data of classical religion and mythology the relevant facts from other areas, and especially from savage and barbarous custom and belief.]

(ε) The last and most important continuation of Tylor's theory was that by W. Wundt, to be found in the section of his *Völkerpsychologie* which appeared under the separate title *Mythus und Religion* (three volumes, Leipzig, 1905, 1906, 1909, and second edition, 1915). He criticizes Tylor's views at many points as being onesided and all along one line ; but he accepts their basal principles and even extends them by introducing the concept of the ' body-soul ', that is, a soul connected with the body as a whole or some particular organ, essentially different from the independent soul or *psyche*, which appears as the breath- and shadow-soul. From the concept of soul and spirit develops, according to him, the daimon. This is a being of variable and vague personality, possessing superhuman power to help or harm. From an independent source, namely the mythologizing of natural processes, developed the gods, so Wundt holds, and these had originally only supramundane existence and power. A third source, the legends of heroes, brought about the idealization of the concrete individual man ; this introduced into the process a new factor, clearly defined personality ; and thus the gods produced from nature-myths were made into gods in the full and proper sense. Primitive peoples recognized no gods, only daimones ; the beginnings of the concept of gods are not found till we reach the higher types of savages ; and it is with the formation of the higher cultures and of

[2] Cf. H. Pinard de la Boullaye, *L'étude comparée des religions*, Vol. I, ed. 3, p. 377.

great nations that we meet fully-developed nature-gods and legends of heroes. Monotheism is the result of an advanced social culture, and absolute monotheism does not come into being at all save under the influence of philosophy. This theory of Wundt's, however, with its attempt to bring back animism into some sort of credit, appeared at a time when the latter view had already been much damaged from several sides, and did not succeed in overcoming the damage done.[3]

E. B. Tylor died at the advanced age of eighty-five. All these damaging attacks on his theory took place within his lifetime ; but he did not join in the lively discussions which raged all along the line from the beginning of the twentieth century. It is remarkable indeed that Tylor, after his three great works,[4] published nothing more on a large scale. There is a bibliography included in the memorial volume *Anthropological Essays presented to Edward Burnett Tylor* (Oxford, 1907) which was published on the occasion of his seventy-fifth birthday. It contains 262 items ; but apart from the three books they consist solely of articles and reviews in sundry periodicals and encyclopædias. Had he exhausted his great powers in the initial effort of producing his three important works ? It must not, however, be overlooked that he also did yeoman service as Curator for many years of the Pitt Rivers Museum in Oxford, and as the first Reader in Social Anthropology at that University.*

2. THE ACTUAL VALUE OF THE THEORY

(a) ITS PURELY EVOLUTIONARY CHARACTER

Tylor's theory, like Spencer's, was produced during the heyday of Evolutionism, and has all the marks of its origin, especially its *a priori* assumption of an upward development of mankind along a single line, and the absence of any proof that the single stages of the process have any historical connexion with one another. For indeed, no such proof is to be found for any step of Tylor's long evolutionary series. The order of the steps and their connexion one with another

---

[3] Cf. the more detailed account by the present author, *Ursprung der Gottesidee*, Vol. I.

[4] The two already mentioned were preceded by a work published in 1865, *Researches into the Early History of Mankind and the Development of Civilization.*

* [It should further be remembered that for some time before his death his health was far from good.]

is founded purely and simply on the psychological plausibility of this connexion; and the plausibility depends on the assumption that the simple always precedes the complex.

At the same time it is important to notice that Tylor did not go the whole length with the ethnological evolutionists of his day. His attitude towards the sociological evolutionism of Morgan and M'Lennan was always negative, and we may conclude that in this field he had at least an inkling of the inadequacy of the Evolutionist method especially. This is shown by his article *On a Method of Investigating the Development of Institutions, applied to Laws of Marriage and Descent*, in *Journ. (Roy.) Anth. Inst.*, XVIII (1889), p. 245 *sqq.* In this he tries to attain by a statistical method to the exactitude and objectivity which Evolutionism lacks.

'By a comparison of the greatest possible number of peoples he has come to the conclusion that certain phenomena belonging to particular categories of humanity appeared relatively often in combination with certain forms belonging to other categories. He concludes that there is a genetic connexion between phenomena which thus adhered one to another. By a comparison between the various phenomena of one category and their relations to the adhering phenomena, he believes that he has an unobjectionable method for determining the direction in which the phenomena of the categories in question had followed each other.' [5]

This is not the place to discuss in further detail this first serious attempt to break loose from Evolutionism. It contains a valuable element, although, as Graebner has shown,[6] by no means sufficient in itself. Unfortunately, however, Tylor did not think of applying this new method to his own theory of animism.

(b) PREANIMISM, A STATE PREVIOUS TO ANIMISM

Two theories succeeded in time in shattering the long undisputed predominance of animism. Both of them justly emphasized the fact that a whole series of the phenomena which Tylor derived from the fundamental concept of spirits really required no such concept; that rather, much if not all the evidence tended to show that the period of animism is by no means the oldest, but was preceded by an age of preanimism. In the latter, the concept of spirit was not yet so clearly developed and certainly not so extensively applied

[5] F. Graebner, *Methode der Ethnologie*, Heidelberg, 1911, p. 87.
[6] Graebner, *op. cit.*, pp. 88–91.

to the whole of nature as Tylor assumes. This preanimism is of two very different forms. One is the preanimism of magic, which we may call material preanimism; the other the preanimism of monotheism, which we may formally style personal preanimism. We shall later deal with each theory separately; for the present let it suffice to remark that as a matter of fact there are extensive regions which cannot be included or comprehended by the animistic theory, and are of earlier date than animism. Magical power, which is a supernatural force inherent in inanimate matter as such and preceding from it, really needs no indwelling spirit to explain its nature and effects. Likewise the living, undifferentiated personality, not analysed in any such definite way into body and soul, suffices fully to explain the characteristics and activities of which it is the centre. That remarkable personality, the Supreme Being of the primitive tribes, undergoes no such process as death, which in other cases brings about the separation of soul and body; naturally, there is therefore all the less occasion here to apply the concept of spirit.

These last considerations were urged especially by Andrew Lang, for many years Tylor's pupil, and the herald and champion of animism against Max Müller's nature-mythology, after his own researches in ethnology had made him better acquainted with the primitive high gods, whereof Tylor's theory had not taken sufficient account. He put forth his views especially in his epoch-making work *The Making of Religion* (London, 1898; second ed. 1900, third 1909).[7]

For further criticism of Tylor's theory, see F. Schleiter, *Religion and Culture*, New York 1919, pp. 74–100, and R. H. Lowie, *Primitive Religion*, New York 1922, pp. 99–135.

(c) Definition of the Nature of Animism : its True Scope

Meanwhile a series of special investigations of individual groups of peoples have brought about a more adequate comprehension of what animism really is.

Among these may be mentioned the following. For Melanesia, R. H. Codrington, *The Melanesians : Studies in their Anthropology and Folklore*, Oxford, 1891, pp. 117–73. For South America, T. Koch, *Zum Animismus der südamerikanischen Indianer*, Leiden, 1930, supplement to Vol. XIII of the *Internationales Archiv für Ethnographie*. For Indonesia, G. A. Wilken, *Het Animisme bij de volken van den indischen Archipel*, Amsterdam 1885 ; A. C. Kruijt, *Het Animisme in den indischen Archipel*, 's Gravenhage, 1906 ;

---

[7] See further, below, p. 172 *sqq.*

A. W. Nieuwenhuis, *Die Wurzeln des Animismus, eine Studie über die Anfänge der naïven Religion, nach den unter den primitiven Malaien beobachteten Erscheinungen*, Leiden, 1917, supplement to Vol. XXIV of the *Internationales Archiv für Ethnographie*. For Africa, B. Ankermann, *Totenkult und Seelenglaube bei afrikanischen Völkern*, in the *Zeitschrift für Ethnologie*, 1918, pp. 89–153. In general, A. Borchert, *Der Animismus oder Ursprung der Entwicklung der Religion aus dem Seelen- Ahnen- und Geisterkult*, Freiburg im Breisgau, 1900 ; A. Crawley, *The Idea of the Soul*, London 1909 ; G. Heinzelmann, *Animismus und Religion*, Gütersloh 1913.

From these and other researches it is clear (i) that animism is by no means equally well developed among all races. We can now recognize that it is especially prominent among the following groups of peoples : a part of the Melanesians and Indonesians ; the Africans of the West Coast ; the South Americans north-east and south-west of the Amazon ; the North American Indians of the north-west and the south-east. (ii) Even in these areas not everything is supposed to have a soul by any means. Among the Indonesians, inanimate objects have no soul at all ; it is simply that independent spirits live in objects of particularly noticeable shape or kind ; not even all plants have a soul. (iii) Human beings and certain beasts, domestic animals or soul-beasts, may have several souls, as many as seven apiece in Melanesia ; these are best thought of as faculties of the soul. Most commonly we find two souls, one belonging to the body and connected with the blood or the breath, the other the shadow or phantom, which probably owes its origin to memory-images of the departed and with which is usually connected a belief in a future life. (iv) Nor do all nature-spirits, as those of the earth, wind, fire and so forth, need to be derived from animism, for they may result directly from personification. (v) The concept ' spirit ' is not due solely to the phenomena of sleep, dreams and death, but may result directly from a logical search for a cause, as an appropriate basis for the rich world of phenomena belonging to the inquirer's own personality, for all his thinking, willing and feeling. Such a concept is moreover to be found almost everywhere, even among those peoples who are ethnologically the oldest.

Thus we see that animism, which Tylor had supposed nearly universal, is limited both in itself and in its geographical distribution. So much was made clear by subsequent investigations ; but recent ethnological studies of the history of culture have shown that there are likewise limits in time.

It has been found possible to establish that the matrilineal agricultural culture is especially the carrier of animism, which is aroused and cultivated there especially in the men's secret societies with their ghosts, skull-worship and masked dances, and later in connexion with head-hunting and bloody sacrifices, human and other.

From this it appears that animism does indeed find its ultimate origins partly in the primitive culture, which has already some idea of a soul; but that its full development does not take place till comparatively late. This alone shows that it cannot be the origin of religion, for it is these same primitive cultures which have developed religion in the form of a clear and decided ethical monotheism. What has taken place is rather that this monotheism, under the influence of animism with its offerings to the dead, its ghostly phantoms, its worship of ancestors and its cult of skulls, has often been overlaid, thrust into the background and stifled. Thus the figure of the Supreme Being is obscured and often quite disappears. All this process of degeneration is well described by Andrew Lang and A. W. Nieuwenhuis, see below, pp. 179 and 209.

(d) The Permanent Importance of Animism

The historical investigation of human culture is thus able to fix the *milieu* in which animism is, so to speak, at home, from the atmosphere of which it takes its rise, and whose outlook on the world it shapes. In so doing, it sets strict bounds in both time and space to the universality which Tylor claimed for animism in his theory; but on the other hand, it gives clearer comprehension of the essence and the origins of that belief, and so puts all the huge mass of material on which the animistic theory rests in the proper and appropriate light. The examination of the question is by no means over and done with yet, but is rather only beginning; but we can already perceive how much deeper and further reaching our understanding of animism can now be.

(i) In the matrilineal agrarian culture, which is to be sharply distinguished from the patrilineal and totemic, interest is concentrated not so much on life as on the painful and dark fact of death, the sundering of soul and body. The probable reasons for this are two. First, when women begin to occupy themselves with the cultivation of plants, the vegetable kingdom arouses a livelier interest; now in this, death occurs much oftener and at shorter intervals than among the animals which the totemistic culture hunts.   Secondly, women connect their own life and that of the growing plants closely with the moon, and this is not ever-living, like the sun, whose shape never changes, but passes away, dying over and over again at short intervals.   Now it cannot be doubted that the fact of death has had a very great deal to do with forming and developing the concept of an independent soul.   It is moreover obvious that the formation of this concept has been of far-reaching importance for the whole development of religion, philosophy and culture in general.   It was Tylor's great merit to have been the first to collect and draw attention to the importance of the data which form our material here ; and however much we may subtract from his estimate of its importance, however much allowance we may make for one-sidedness, omissions and exaggerations, his merit remains.

(ii) As regards the history of the human mind, the significance of animism is, beyond doubt, two-fold and its results of almost contradictory kinds.   It made possible the idea of pure spirit, divorced from matter ; but also of pure matter, divorced from spirit.   Hence the complete idea ' Man ' acquired two component parts ; and it depended on the importance given to each of these what sort of philosophy, materialistic or spiritual, would result.   Thus in India the materialistic Sankhyan philosophy most certainly arose from matrilineal animism.   Perhaps a closer investigation will show that on the other hand the matrilineal cultures of the Mediterranean region have played their part in establishing the spiritual philosophies of classical Greece.

(iii) The crux of the whole question is the Supreme Being of primitive peoples.   Undoubtedly the concept of pure spirit succeeds in disposing of many speculative difficulties connected especially with his attributes of eternity, omniscience and omnipresence.   So long, therefore, as this concept was not developed, the personality of the Supreme Being was not analysed, but generally imagined on the analogy of a concrete individual human being, which led but too easily to anthropomorphism.   (Compare the account given by Andrew Lang, *infra*, p. 181.)   But on the other hand we must not forget that even among these primitive peoples we meet with definite assurances of the Supreme Being's immateriality.   Thus, the Tierra del Fuegians say he is ' like air ', the Central Californians, ' like fire ', and so on.   How these ideas arose we cannot as yet explain (see below, pp. 266 *sqq.*, 284 *sqq.*)

(e) TYLOR'S ATTITUDE TOWARDS THE QUESTION OF PRIMITIVE
HIGH GODS

It is interesting to ask what attitude Tylor took up in
relation to the primitive high gods, who became known during
the concluding decades of his life. It has not been sufficiently
noted that for quite special reasons his need for taking some
stand must have been particularly pressing, and that he perceived this necessity at a comparatively early date. It is
well known that the discussions concerning savage high gods
were set going by the discoveries made in this connexion by
A. W. Howitt among the South-East Australian tribes, which
aroused much attention. In the course of his investigations
he was initiated into the secret puberty-rites of these peoples.
Before Andrew Lang could point out the value of these new
facts, Tylor felt himself compelled to express an opinion on
them. Howitt had published his first communications of
these discoveries in the *Journal of the Anthropological Institute*
for 1884 (Vol. XIII, pp. 185–99 and 432–59) under the titles
On Some Australian Beliefs and *On Some Australian Ceremonies of Initiation* ; the discoveries form the foundation of
his great work *The Native Tribes of South-East Australia*,
but this did not appear until 1904. The two papers were
read at a meeting of the Institute by Tylor himself, who was
then president ; he thus got the facts, so to speak, at first
hand, and could not ignore them.

It is to be noted that Howitt, in these first publications and
in that which followed in the next year (*The Jeraeil or
Initiation Ceremonies of the Kurnai Tribe, J.A.I.*, Vol. XIV,
1885, pp. 301–27), put forward the facts with far more of their
native freshness and purity, less influenced by his Evolutionist
friends and their theories, than in his later and more ambitious
work. Howitt himself of course could maintain his Evolutionist position by making out the South-East Australian
tribes to be ethnologically the most recent and culturally the
most highly developed ; for he took his sociology from the
Evolutionist theory of Morgan. But for Tylor, who owed no
such allegiance to Morgan (*v. sup.*, p. 82), this way of escape
was closed, and all the more so because of his better knowledge
of ethnology. On the other hand, neither he nor anyone else
could or did doubt that these beings whom Howitt had so
vividly represented and put in so clear a light were genuine
high gods. His only resource therefore was to amplify a
suggestion which he had tentatively made in the discussion

following Howitt's second article, and question the native origin of these gods, referring them to European, and specifically to missionary influence. Whether he realized how unsatisfactory this expedient was, or whether he needed this long time to mature his ideas, it was not till six years later that his article *Limits of Savage Religion* appeared (*J.A.I.*, Vol. XXI, 1891, pp. 283–301). In this he explicitly put forward the above explanation and sought to prove it.

But Howitt himself had already practically told him that no such resource was available, for he insisted on the genuinely native origin of these views, returning to the charge in his principal work, *Native Tribes*, and supporting his opinion with definite proofs. N. W. Thomas, in his article *Baiame and the Bell-Bird* (*Man*, 1905, pp. 44–52), exposed still more completely the untenable nature of Tylor's explanation so far as South-East Australia was concerned ; Andrew Lang had already done so for North America in *Magic and Religion* (1901, pp. 18–25) and *Myth, Ritual and Religion* (pp. xx–xxxix and 320–6). I have collected all these counter-proofs in my *Ursprung der Gottesidee* (Vol. I, ed. 2, pp. 248–56) and added a refutation of a like theory as regards the Tasmanians (pp. 256–73).

It therefore remains for us now only to maintain three facts : first, that Tylor recognizes the existence among the tribes of South-East Australia of genuine high gods ; second, that he recognizes these tribes as ethnologically too old to leave room for the previous stages which his Evolutionist theory postulates ; thirdly, that his attempt to explain these high gods away as due to the influence of Christian Europeans is shown to be untenable.

From this it follows that these South-East Australian facts alone suffice to expose the falsity of the conclusion and basic principle of Tylor's theory, as stated by him in the following words (*Primitive Culture*, Vol. II, p. 336).

' Among these (*sc.* primitive) races, Animism has its distinct and consistent outcome, and Polytheism its distinct and consistent completion, in the doctrine of a Supreme Being.'

But such high gods are to be found not only in South-East Australia but also among the Pygmies, the Bushmen, the oldest Arctic peoples, the natives of North Central California, the primitive Algonkin, the Tierra del Fuegians, in a word, all the primitive peoples with whom we have any close acquaintance. That they are found among these and these especially is the fact which finally and inescapably puts Tylor's theory out of court.

The following works deal specially with the criticism of Tylor's animistic hypothesis: A. Borchert, *Der Animismus oder Ursprung der Entwicklung der Religion aus dem Seelen- Ahnen- und Geisterkult*, Freiburg im Breisgau, 1900; G. Heinzelmann, *Animismus und Religion*, Gütersloh, 1913; J. Pascher, *Der Seelenbegriff im Animismus E. B. Tylors*, Würzburg, 1929; the last of these is by far the best, and is also just to Tylor on the positive side.

PART III

THE TWENTIETH CENTURY

CHAPTER VIII

STAR-MYTHS AND PANBABYLONIANISM

1. ASTRAL MYTHOLOGY

(a) CAUSES OF THE NEW TENDENCY

THE widening influence of the animistic school invaded the ranks of philologists and of theologians and suppressed the earlier nature-myth movement which had formerly existed there. But somewhat later, an invasion of the nature-myth school began to make itself felt in the domain of animism, and in time widened its conquests in that area. The causes of this were certainly in part the exaggerations and onesidedness of the animistic theory, which passed over important facts and discredited and rejected nature-myths more than they deserved. But another factor was at work, an outward and historical influence, comparable to that which the discovery of the unity of the Indo-Germanic languages had exercised in its day in calling the attention of workers in our field as in others to the nature-myths of the Indo-Germanic peoples ; see above, p. 37 *sqq.* In fact, it was once more a group of civilized peoples who, as a result of a succession of brilliant discoveries and decipherments during the preceding decades, came into the purview of science. These comprised the whole Babylonian and Assyrian world and their neighbours, predecessors and successors, the Sumerian, Elamitic, Semitic, Aryan, Chaldaean and other races. Now among these peoples a particular form of nature-myth, namely the star-myth, was very decidedly prominent in connexion with their religion ; and to this the new movement turned its attention with growing enthusiasm.

It is a doubtful question, hardly to be decided save by

more searching and almost personal inquiry, which of the two factors above mentioned had the earlier and the stronger influence, the negative one, due to animism itself, or the positive, coming from Babylon. This much is certain, that investigators came from both sides, that of mythology in general and that of Assyrian and Babylonian studies. But they soon perceived their essential relationship to each other and the community of their interests ; wherefore, in March 1906, they formed at Berlin a ' Society for the Promotion of Comparative Mythology ',* which proceeded to publish a ' Mythological Library ',† the first volume of which was E. Siecke's *Drachenkämpfe : Untersuchungen zur indogermanischen Sagenkunde*, Leipzig, 1907.

Although it is perfectly true that the interest in star-myths generally and the particular interest in Babylon affected each other mutually and combined one with the other, it is neces- sary for the sake of due clearness to treat of them separately.

(b) THE STAR-MYTH MOVEMENT

(a) The real founder and the most active supporter of this new mythological movement was E. Siecke. In face of pas- sionate opposition on the part of many of his fellow-experts, notably E. H. Meyer, he succeeded in attracting an increasing amount of attention to his ideas as set forth in a series of works, some of the most important of which are the following : *Liebesgeschichte des Himmels*, Strasbourg, 1892 ; *Mythologische Briefe*, Berlin, 1901 ; *Drachenkämpfe*, Leipzig, 1907-8 ; *Hermes der Mondgott*, 1908-9 ; *Götterattribute und sogenannte Symbole*, Jena, 1909 ; *Pûshan, Studien zur Idee des Hirtengottes*, Leipzig, 1914 ; *Der Vegetationsgott*, Leipzig, 1914.‡ He did not simply take over the ideas of the old school of nature-mythology, but gave them added precision in content, form and method. As regards content, he starts with the great heavenly bodies and particularly the moon with its 'wealth of forms' as being the oldest and most prolific source of the formation of myths. As to form and method, he emphasizes the principle that the subject of a nature-myth is always something really seen in the sky, and consequently the statements in myths are to be taken literally

* [In German, Gesellschaft für vergleichende Mythenforschung.]
† [Mythologische Bibliothek.]
‡ [Amatory History of the Sky—Letters on Mythology—Battles with Dragons, being Studies in the Legends of Indo-Europeans—Hermes a Lunar Deity—The Attributes and so-called Symbols of Gods—Pûshan, or Studies in the Idea of the Shepherd God—The God of Vegetation.]

and not allegorized away.   These ancient myths, he says, are
' childish judgements and questions, quite seriously meant,
concerning the marvels of the world around us ', and especially
the forms and movements of the great heavenly bodies.

(β) It was not, however, Siecke who drew up the actual
programme, the official manifesto so to speak, ' by agreement
with several members of the Society and particularly with
Dr. Hüsing '.   This was done by H. Lessmann in his *Aufgabe
und Ziele der vergleichenden Mythenforschung*.[1]   In this work
he treats of the definition, methods, the importance of the
' motifs and types ', the mythological material, and the characteristic feature of myths.   This, according to him, is ' a definite
series of motifs following each other in a definite order ' with
all the regularity of a natural law.   The Society for the Promotion of Comparative Mythology maintained the view that
probably all myths, certainly the great majority, dealt with
the history of the great luminaries, and that therefore a myth
had nothing to do with the other phenomena of the sky or
of nature generally, and most certainly nothing to do with
' belief in a soul, nor with dreams and nightmares '.   The
two most conspicuous figures of myth are the sun and moon ;
the Society tried to answer the question whether originally
it was the moon only, or had always been both, and was
inclined to assume the former solution.

(γ) Besides Lessmann, who is also the author of *Die Kyrossage
in Europa* (Berlin, 1905), the new movement was joined by E. Böklen, who applied its principles to the Old Testament and to folklore ;
moderation and method are notably lacking in his works, *Adam und
Qain im Lichte der vergleichenden Mythenforschung*, Leipzig, 1907 ;
Sneewitchenstudien, Leipzig, 1910 and 1914 ; *Die Unglückszahl
Dreizehn und ihre mythische Bedeutung*, Leipzig, 1913 ; *Die Entste-
hung der Sprache im Lichte des Mythos*, Berlin, 1922.   The Elamite
specialist G. Hüsing belongs partly to this, partly to a sub-
division of the Panbabylonian school ; he derives all myths from
Elam.   His writings comprise *Beiträge zur Kyrossage*, Berlin, 1906 ;
Krsaaxspa im Schlangenleibe, 1911 ; *Beiträge zur Rostahmsage*, 1913 ;
Der elamische Gott Memnon, 1917 ; *Purušalis und die achämenidi-
schen Lebenswehen*, 1918.   The importance of ' sacred ' numbers for
star-myths is brought out by W. Schultz in his works *Gesetze der
Zahlenverschiebung im Mythos und in mythenhaltiger Überlieferung*,
Mitteilungen der anthropologischen Gesellschaft [Reports of the
Anthropological Society], Vienna, Vol. XL, 1910, p. 101 *sqq* ; *Das*

---

[1] [' The Scope and Aims of Comparative Mythology.']   This was
Vol. I, part 4 of the above-mentioned Mythological Library, and was
published at Leipzig in 1908.

System der Acht im Licht des Mythos, in *Memnon*, Vol. IV, 1910, p. 110 *sqq.*; *Neue Beiträge zu den Gesetzen der Zahlverschiebung*, Mitteilungen der anthrop. Ges., Vienna, Vol. LIII, 1923, pp. 266–91 ; *Zeitrechnung und Weltanschauung in ihren übereinstimmenden Grundzügen bei den Indern, Iraniern, Hellenen, Italikern, Germanen, Kelten, Litauern* (Memnon-Bibliothek [' Memnon ' Library] No. 35). The last survivals of myth in pre-history are the subject of K. von Spiess' investigations in *Prähistorie und Mythe*, Wiener-Neustadt, 1910.

(δ) The new movement was freed from its narrow preoccupation with the myths of highly civilized peoples by P. Ehrenreich, who introduced it to the sphere of savage mythology. Consequently, he also modified the polemical attitude which the school had fallen into with regard to ethnology, and generally led it into a more universal importance, in the following works : *Die Mythen und Legenden der südamerikanischen Urvölker*, Berlin, 1905 ; *Götter und Heilbringer*, in *Zeitschrift für Ethnologie*, 1906, p. 536 *sqq.* ; and in his posthumous work, *Die Sonne im Mythos*, Leipzig, 1915.*

(c) Evaluation of Astral Mythology

It is beyond doubt that the animistic theory, in controversy with the older school of nature-myths, overshot the mark and failed to recognize and value aright the importance of such myths. It is a permanent merit of the new movement to have put this importance once more in a clearer light, and especially as regards what is certainly one of its chief branches, star-myths. It too, in the first zeal of discovery, and in polemic against animism, went too far and represented astral myths as being the only ones deserving of the name. But this we can understand and excuse as a natural human weakness ; the same may be said, to some extent, of the emphasis laid on the predominant importance of the moon. However, the ' panlunarism ' of Siecke, Böklen and Hüsing cannot be accepted.

(a) The new theory had the advantage of good criticism and far-reaching improvements at the hands of P. Ehrenreich, in his important work *Die allgemeine Mythologie und ihre ethnologischen Grundlagen*, Berlin, 1910.† This book is of the nature of a programme, and may be justly styled a text-book of mythology in general ; and Ehrenreich was especially

---

* [' Myths and Legends of the Primitive Peoples of South America ' —' Gods and Saviours '—' The Sun in Myth '.]

† [' General Mythology and its ethnological fundamentals.']

adapted to write one. By his very appeal to the general
fundamental principles of ethnology and his employment of
the myths of all peoples, he freed the new school from its
narrowness, and thus put 'panlunarism' in its proper place,
by giving the sun and the other heavenly bodies their due
rights among the various peoples. He agrees with Siecke in
rejecting the allegorical interpretation of myths, but supposes that certain metaphors are regularly connected with
them, although he holds that the inventors of the myths were
not conscious of these metaphors as such. A further service
was done by Ehrenreich in recognizing, like Andrew Lang,
the great antiquity, ethnologically speaking, of the Supreme
Being, and his freedom from astral myths. On this point,
however, he makes the mistake of supposing him to have had
no cult in the earliest times, and consequently refusing to
hear of 'primitive monotheism'.

(β) Numerous improvements, important in principle, of the
fundamental tenets of the nature-myth school were contributed
by F. Langer in his work *Intellektualmythologie : Betrachtungen
über des Wesen des Mythus und der mythologischen Methode*,
Leipzig and Berlin, 1917.* His immediate object of attack
is what he calls the objectivizing tendency of the older nature-
mythologists, a tendency from which the astral-myth school
had not freed itself sufficiently. Too exclusive attention had
been paid to natural objects, which after all could not in themselves adequately explain the myths. On the other hand,
however, he opposed the 'subjectivizing' tendency, to be
found to some extent in Wundt, which sought the explanation
of myths in the feelings and the 'twilight state, so big with
emotion, of the lower levels of thought'. We ought on the
contrary to lay the emphasis on 'the real mental kernel
of the content (of myths), and recognize that primeval man
was a being in possession of conceptual processes of thought
and of intelligence '. He admitted, however, that primitive
man was subject to the influence of subjective experiences
and especially prone to elevate the emotional forces to the
position of a 'subjective dominant'. It is a great pity that,
owing to his utterly inadequate knowledge of the material
(he knew only Christianity and Teutonic beliefs), Langer fails
altogether to work out his principles ; for he supposes that
mythopoeic thought began with theriomorphism, in other
words totemism, followed by 'mythical monism' or fetishism,

* ['Intellectualism and Mythology : being certain Considerations
of the Nature of Myth and the Methods of Mythologists.']

in which concept, word and object were all one and formed the basis of magic. After this, he supposes, came mythical dualism, or the separation of the world into a sacred and a profane, non-animate sphere. I have criticized his views in detail in *Anthropos*, xii–xiii (1917/19), pp. 1135–42, to which the reader is referred. Langer offers nothing but purely speculative deductions, which fall to pieces at the touch of historical facts.

(γ) Here as elsewhere it was the historical method which produced the most wide-reaching and decisive correction. On the one hand, it was able to work out the high importance of star-myths even for the ethnologically oldest stage of human development. On the other, it established in this connexion (i) that before and over all star-myths we find the figure of the Supreme Being. (ii) That the interest of primeval man lay, not primarily in the astral phenomena as such, but in important earthly happenings which deeply affected his own inner life. In particular, he projected into the celestial phenomena the thought of life and death, and used the former as symbols of the latter. (iii) We must recognize as one of the oldest forms of star-myth the dying moon taken as an image of the dying First Father; whereas the sun has not so much symbolical importance, but rather is treated as the source and giver of life.

Moreover, the historical method shows that we do not find all possible forms of astral myths in all cultures, after the fashion of Bastian's ' elementary concepts '. Rather is it true that each of the older cultures knows essentially but one astral theme, around which its mythology develops, and only with crossing of cultures do we get blending of these themes. In this connexion it has been possible to establish the facts that the matrilineal, agricultural peoples concern themselves principally with moon-myths, so that among them even the Supreme Being is often blended with the figure of the moon, a process which is already taking place in the boomerang-culture; while among the totemic, patrilineal cultures it is the sun which is the centre of interest, and the Supreme Being is often identified with it. The old sky-god of primitive times, of whom no myths were told, is best preserved in the pastoral nomadic culture, but he often vanishes into a far-off state of inactivity or else is identified with the material sky. The most varied combinations take place in course of time between all three of these forms. I have tried to set forth these matters, as regards the Austronesian peoples, in *Grundlinien einer*

Vergleichung der Religionen und Mythologien der austronesischen Völker,[2] and for South-East Australia in the section entitled *Die südostaustralischen Höchsten Wesen* [' Supreme Beings of South-East Australia '], in my *Ursprung der Gottesidee* (Münster, 1926), Vol. I, ed. 2, pp. 334–482.

2. PANBABYLONIANISM

(a) EXPOSITION OF PANBABYLONIANISM

(a) The three principal representatives of Panbabylonianism (they themselves accept this name) are H. Winckler, A. Jeremias and E. Stucken. All three are among the founders of the Society for the Promotion of Comparative Mythology, mentioned on p. 92. They thus are connected outwardly as well as in spirit with the star-myth school, of which indeed they are but a special branch, albeit a branch which puts forward maxims of its own, and takes all and every religion and mythology under its direction.

The foundations of the whole system were laid by H. Winckler, although still with some reserves, in his writings, namely : *Geschichte Israels*, Vol. II, Leipzig, 1900 ; *Die altbabylonische Weltanschauung*, in the May volume of *Preussische Jahrbücher* for 1901 ; *Himmels- und Weltenbild der Babylonier*, second edition, Leipzig, 1903.*

A. Jeremias was more emphatic, and was untiring in defence of the system in controversy. See his *Im Kampf um Bibel und Babel*, ed. 4, Berlin, 1903–5 ; *Monotheistische Strömungen innerhalb der babylonischen Religion*, Berlin, 1904 ; *Das Alte Testament im Lichte des alten Orients*, ed. 3, Berlin, 1912 [English translation, *The Old Testament in the Light of the Ancient East*, London, 1911] ; *Die Panbabylonisten*, ed. 2, Leipzig, 1907 ; *Das Alter der babylonischen Astronomie*, ed. 2, Leipzig, 1910 ; *Handbuch der altorientalischen Geisteskultur*, 1913.†

---

[2] [' Outlines of a Comparative Survey of the Religions and Mythologies of the Austronesian Peoples '], in the *Denkschriften der k. Akad. der Wiss. in Wien* [Transactions of the Imperial Academy of Sciences, Vienna], philologisch-historische Klasse, Vol. LIII, sect. 3 (1910). A brief survey of it will be found in my address to the Anthropological Society of Vienna, published in *Mitteilungen der anthropologischen Gesellschaft in Wien*, Vol. XXXIX (1909), pp. 242–59, under the title *Die Mythologie der austronesischen Völker*.

* [' The History of Israel '—' The Ancient Babylonian Conception of the Universe '—' Heaven and the Worlds as seen by the Babylonians '.]

† [' In the " Bible and Babylon " Controversy —" Monotheistic Movements in Babylonian Religion '—' The Panbabylonians '—' The Age of Babylonian Astronomy '—' A Manual of Ancient Oriental Thought ' (literally, ' culture of the *geist* ', a word which includes both ' spirit ' and ' intellect ').]

E. Stucken knew no restraint, and extended the system to all the peoples of the earth in his three-volume treatise *Astralmythen*, Leipzig, 1901–7.

(β) The whole Panbabylonian system may be summed up in the following axioms.

(i) All myths are concerned entirely, or nearly so, with the phenomena of the heavens; that is, they are star-myths. But in particular, they are concerned with the course of the sun, of the moon, and on occasion with that of the planet Venus, especially in relation to the twelve signs of the zodiac and the stars in them. Now the events in heaven and the relations between them are the model and guiding principle of the events on earth and their mutual relations; astronomy and astrology are one and the same. The two together form a general outlook on the universe.

(ii) This outlook on the universe is at the same time a religion, for the heavenly bodies and their movements are regarded as the principal revelation of the power and will of Deity. That Deity is something different from the stars is a secret known to the initiated, the priests (so Winckler). Their doctrine was set forth to the laity in myths, and its fixed tenets put before them in dramatic performances. In doctrine and myth alike, the numbers expressing the periodicity of the heavenly bodies' revolutions and their relations to each other played an important part, and were consequently 'sacred numbers'. They defined, not only the revolutions of the heavenly bodies, but also the dates of the festivals and in general the whole arrangement of holy days on earth.

(iii) The centre of this whole system is Babylon, in which place it was fully developed, according to this school, as early as 3000 B.C. Thence it extended, first over the whole East, particularly Egypt and Israel, and later to Greece and Rome, in consequence of which Christianity in the Middle Ages was also influenced by it. But the myths of every people on earth, even of the most distant and savage races, shows this influence, some part of which entered probably with the first human beings who came to people the continents.

(iv) Bastian's theory of 'elementary concepts', according to which these ideas developed in different parts of the earth as a result of the general sameness of human nature, is to be rejected. For firstly, the extensive astronomical knowledge involved in this system is quite out of keeping with the otherwise low culture of savage peoples, and secondly the agreement is too close, extending to the smallest details.

(v) This is especially noticeable in the great importance of the Pleiads among the most different peoples, who locate in them the occurrence of the spring equinox and the entrance of sun and moon into the same sign of the zodiac.   In the zodiac, the Pleiads form part of the constellation Taurus. Now it can be proved by calculation that the spring equinox entered the constellation Taurus about 3000 B.C.   The appearance of the era of this sign and the calendar reform which went with it, and signified a religious reform as well (the Era of Marduk) is historically proved by Babylonian cuneiform inscriptions of about the year 2000 B.C.   It is opposed to an older, Euphratean doctrine, which took as its starting-point the sign Gemini.*

Panbabylonianism is opposed to animism along two lines. Firstly, the latter is founded upon ' elementary ideas ', while the former is a historical method.   Secondly, animism is connected with progressive Evolutionism, begins with savages and ends with civilized peoples ; while Panbabylonianism on the other hand represents rather a theory of degeneration, begins with civilized races and goes back to savages.[3]

(b) VALUE OF PANBABYLONIANISM

In criticizing Panbabylonianism, we must be especially careful to differentiate the extent to which its various originators claim validity for it, distinguishing its inner and its outer geographical range.

(a) To begin with its validity over the inner range, it may be granted that the views put forth in (i) and (ii) above hold good to a large extent, not only for Babylon and the ancient East, but also for the non-European civilizations of India, China, Mexico, Central America and Peru, and indeed for the oldest savage races.   The abiding benefit conferred by this school consists in drawing more marked attention to the astounding uniformity which is often to be found in myths (in so far as they are astral), religion, cult, custom and law.

(β) But the attempt to trace the whole system back to Babylon, see (iii) above, is in a very different position.   This

---

* [These theories are in essence not original with the Panbabylonian school, but merely put forward with more learning and more insistence on the Babylonian origin of such ideas than elsewhere. A general similarity of outlook will be found for example in the works of the late Mr. Geo. St. Clair, to say nothing of sundry earlier treatises now forgotten.]

[3] On this point, however, anything but unanimity still rules. See W. Schmidt, *Ursprung der Gottesidee*, Vol. I, ed. 2, p. 65, note 3.

thesis is but vaguely expounded by Winckler and Jeremias, and they give no positive proof of it. Consequently Stucken,[4] in his *Astralmythen*, endeavours to provide this proof. But here we must begin by demurring at his fundamental principle. He holds that it was not entire mythical beings or types which were passed from people to people, but only single motifs, and that therefore only these can be used for purposes of comparison. Against this it was pointed out by Ehrenreich [5] that the motifs ought to be, not merely outwardly like, but identical, and as a confirmation of this, ought to appear in the same combination. In other words, we must here apply the double test of form and quantity; firstly, motifs must be produced which are beyond doubt alike in character, and therefore occur in fixed combinations; secondly, it is not enough to find one or a few motifs, but whole series of them. Besides this, Stucken does not know the Law of Continuity, that is, that where great gaps in time or space occur, we should bridge them with at least a few practicable intervening steps.

(γ) As regards the fourth axiom, namely, that Bastian's doctrine of elementary concepts does not suffice to explain the connexions of star-myths, I can but agree, and in this connexion I do not propose to maintain all that I said in my lecture on *Panbabylonianism and Ethnological Elementary Concepts*.[6] But there is absolutely no such agreement between the star-myths of savage peoples and those of Babylon as would suffice to demonstrate a historical connexion. For example, in Oceania and among most of the savages of South and North America, we look in vain for the division of the month into weeks and all the numerical complex connected therewith. Among the civilized peoples of Central America and Mexico, the ' week ' is twenty days long, a number which depends, not on anything stellar, but on the number of the fingers and toes. That the ' week ' of four or five days which is so common in Africa has a stellar origin is not to be assumed without proof. What we find among the savage peoples is, in comparison with the great self-contained Babylonian system, mere fragments; and the very point at issue is, whether these are remnants of a whole which once existed or incomplete beginnings of a system which might some day be evolved.

[4] Cf. Schmidt, *op. cit.*, p. 62, note 1.

[5] In *Die Mythen und Legenden der südamerikanischen Urvölker*, Berlin, 1905, p. 71.

[6] [In German, *Panbabylonianismus und ethnologischer Elementargedanke*] in *Mitteilungen der anthropologischen Gesellschaft in Wien*, XXXVIII (1908), p. 73 *sqq.*

But it can by no manner of means be said of these fragments which we know at present that they are above the level of the rest of the culture of the peoples concerned, if by that we understand not merely the stage to which their material civilization has advanced but their culture in general, with especial emphasis on the immaterial side thereof.

(δ) Again, the myths concerning the Pleiads, with which the fifth axiom deals, do not prove the Panbabylonian theory. Firstly, because here again the agreement in details is nothing like enough to oblige us to assume any such historical connexion ; secondly, because the savage races certainly could not have known the cycle of the passage of the sun through the zodiac and employed a new method of reckoning time after 2,200 years. The overwhelming majority, indeed, of savage peoples have never heard of a zodiac for the sun to pass through.

(ε) All this shows that one of the props of the Panbabylonian hypothesis, that erected in the savage area, will not hold. We must note finally that the other, that reared in Babylon itself, is demonstrably very cracked and insecure. For the postulate that the Babylonians, as early as 3000 B.C., knew that the sun moved through the zodiac in a fixed period of time (the precession of the equinoxes), and were capable of reforming their calendar in accordance therewith, is declared to be quite untenable by Father F. Kugler, S.J., a scholar equally eminent in Assyriology and in astronomy. He proves his point in several works, viz. *Kulturhistorische Bedeutung der babylonischen Astronomie*, Cologne, 1907, pp. 38–50 ; *Auf den Trümmern des Panbabylonianismus*, in *Anthropos*, Vol. IV, 1909, pp. 477–99 ; *Sternkunde und Sterndienst in Babel*, Book II, pt. 1, Münster, 1909, with supplements, Münster, 1913–14 ; *Im Bannkreis Babels*, Münster, 1910.* He points out that the age of Babylonian astronomy is far from extending so high, and that it was not until the turn of the eighth and seventh centuries B.C. that a change took place in this matter ; even in the middle of the second millennium B.C. the precession of the equinoxes was unknown. Kugler's views are supported also by C. Bezold in *Astronomie, Himmelschau und Astrallehre bei den Babylonier*† (in *Sitzungs-*

* [' The Importance of Babylonian Astronomy for the History of Civilization '—' On the Ruins of Panbabylonianism '—' Astronomy and Astrolatry in Babylon '—' In Babylon's Bounds '.]

† [' Astronomy, Observation of the Heavens, and Astral Doctrine among the Babylonians.']

berichte der Heidelberger Akademie der Wissenschaften, Philologisch-historische Klasse, 1911, Heidelberg, 1913).

(ζ) And finally, the opposition of Panbabylonianism to
Animism is of little account. Winckler, for example, admits
that the civilization of Babylon itself must have been preceded by a long period of lower culture, and he, Jeremias and
Stucken all avoid the central question, the origin of religion.[7]
Another adherent of this school, B. Baentsch, wishes, it is
true, not to derive the Mosaic religion directly from an ' age
of barbarism or semi-barbarism which worshipped trees, stones
and springs in animistic fashion, and had the cult of ancestors,
fetishism, totemism, magic and other such-like pretty things ',
but not because it never passed through such a state, but
only because ' by that date the Semites with whom we are
concerned had long ago left the most primitive stages of
religion behind them ' [8]. This author supposes therefore that
those Semites also had (like all other peoples, of course) passed
through these ' pretty things ' which he names as ' the most
primitive forms of religion'. So the hope that was for a
while aroused by many Panbabylonians, that their school
would free the historical study of religion, or at least that
part of it which deals with the Old Testament, from the bonds
of the various Evolutionist systems, was not fulfilled.

[7] See Winckler, *Religionsgeschichtliches und geschichtlicher Orient*,
pp. 27, 33 ; Jeremias, *Die Panbabylonisten*, p. 33 *sq.* ; Stucken, *Astralmythen*, p. 431 *sq.*
[8] Baentsch, *Altorientalischer und israelistischer Monotheismus*,
Tübingen, 1906, p. 107.

CHAPTER IX

TOTEMISM

1. ITS INTRODUCTION BY J. F. M'LENNAN AND (SIR) J. G. FRAZER

(a) TOTEMISM, that enigmatic phenomenon, the belief of certain peoples that their families and clans stand in a definite blood relationship to particular species of animals, has exercised great influence, not only on religion, but also on human schemes of relationship. It was first made known to more extended scientific circles by J. F. M'Lennan, the discoverer of exogamy [1]; and at the same time, it was brought by him into connexion with religion, in his essay *On the Worship of Animals and Plants*.[2] From that time on, totemism appeared as a later integral part of all succeeding Evolutionary theories, as those of Lubbock, Tylor, Spencer and others. These authors, if only because of the utterly insufficient material which was then accessible to them, could not possibly reach a correct understanding of so complicated a phenomenon as totemism, which we find hard enough to understand even to-day. Still less were they able at that date to appreciate correctly its relation to religion.

However, knowledge of totemistic races and peoples meanwhile gained ground little by little. Faded survivals of it, indeed hardly any longer recognizable, were to be found even in the religions of barbarian and civilized peoples, the objects of study for the schools of nature-myths and star-myths. Such traces were more clearly to be made out among the more advanced savages, with whom fetishism and ancestor-worship were the most prominent features, and they obtruded themselves among the primary cultures of the matrilineal agricultural peoples, those from which the animistic theory

---

[1] See his *Primitive Marriage*, London, 1866; second issue, with additions, under the title *Studies in Ancient History*, London, 1876.
[2] *Fortnightly Review*, Oct.–Nov. 1869, Feb. 1870.

got its principal evidence ; indeed, totemistic features were often an inseparable part of such cultures. But the main body of totemism was not reached until research had got behind the animistic horticultural peoples. At first this main body seemed very scattered and fragmentary, its representatives being separated one from another by broad intervening spaces ; yet the progress of research brought to light more and more new totemic areas, which often filled the gaps in the most unexpected fashion, and thus the phenomenon of totemism was revealed as something increasingly impressive and important.

(b) The most noteworthy service in collecting these data was performed by (Sir) J. G. Frazer. His little book *Totemism* (Edinburgh, 1887) was the first general collection of the facts ever made ; he followed it up with an article in the *Fortnightly Review* for April-May 1899, entitled *The Origin of Totemism.* The extraordinary facts brought to light by Spencer and Gillen in their researches among the natives of Central Australia moved him to write another essay, *The Beginnings of Religion and Totemism among the Australian Aborigines* (*Fortnightly*, July-September, 1905). By that time he was already busy with a larger work, to include a collection of the facts of totemism for the whole world ; that the number of new discoveries in this connexion had greatly increased was largely due to his zealous encouragement. This *magnum opus* appeared in 1910 under the title *Totemism and Exogamy* (Macmillan, London, 4 vols.) ; its first volume contained reprints of Frazer's earlier works, already mentioned. It will be for all time to come the foundation of all collections of material. The last volume contained also a critical sketch of the various theories of the origin of totemism, among which three hypotheses of Frazer's own appeared, for he had three times changed his opinion on the subject.

He likewise made great changes in his views of the relations between totemism and religion. In his earliest publication he still thinks that totemism is a half-religious, half-social phenomenon, and speaks of its religious and its social aspect.[3] But in his second work, he already lays down the axiom ' The aspect of the totemic system, which we have hitherto been accustomed to call religious, deserves rather to be called magical'.[4] In his third work he goes further in this direction, and begins with the following declaration :

[3] *Totemism and Exogamy*, Vol. I, p. 4 *sqq.*
[4] *Ibid.*, p. 115.

' The theory that in the history of mankind religion has been preceded by magic is confirmed inductively by the observation that among the aborigines of Australia, the rudest savages as to whom we possess accurate information, magic is universally practised, whereas religion in the sense of a propitiation or conciliation of the higher powers seems to be nearly unknown.' [5]

Frazer thus ranks himself among the supporters of the Theory of Magic, in connexion with which we shall have to treat of him later. As regards totemism, however, his principal work rejects the idea of its religious character more strongly than ever:

' Pure totemism is not in itself a religion at all ; for the totems as such are not worshipped, they are in no sense deities, they are not propitiated with prayer and sacrifice. To speak therefore of a worship of totems pure and simple, as some writers do, is to betray a serious misapprehension of the facts.' [6]

We shall probably not be far wrong if we assume that this increasingly emphatic denial that totemism is a religion which we find in Frazer, backed by the authority which his knowledge of the facts gives him, has been one of the most important reasons why there never has really been a definite school which made totemism the foundation of all religions, but only isolated appearances of such views.

2. W. ROBERTSON SMITH AND HIS THEORY OF SACRIFICE

(a) EXPOSITION OF THE THEORY

(a) Before ever Frazer had published his first collection of the data concerning totemism, W. Robertson Smith,[7] a pupil of M'Lennan, had given the world his *Kinship and Marriage in Early Arabia* (Cambridge, 1885 ; second ed., London, 1903), preceded by an article, *Animal Worship and Animal Tribes among the Arabs and in the Old Testament*, in the *Journal of Philology*, IX (1880), p. 75 *sqq.*, and followed by his work *Lectures on the Religion of the Semites*. First Series, London, 1889 (second ed., London, 1894 [reprinted, 1907 ; new ed., edited by S. A. Cook, 1927]).

In these writings, following an idea of his teacher, he makes totemism the starting-point of all religions, and believes that he can demonstrate it at the root of Semitic and in particular

---

[5] *Ibid.*, p. 141.   [6] *Op. cit.*, Vol. IV, p. 27.
[7] It was he who induced Frazer to write his article *Totemism*, originally intended for the *Encyclopædia Britannica*.

Hebrew religion, ' and thus ' to use Frazer's words, ' of the faith which is now embraced by the most civilized nations of the earth '.[8] By way of proof he adduces the names of the tribes, which were at the same time names of beasts; the nature-worship of stars, stones, springs, trees, and beasts; the distinction between clean and unclean beasts and the tabus on foods connected therewith ; the figures of beasts on the Israelitish standards ; the Jinn or demons, which he supposes to have been originally beasts; and finally the existence of matriarchy.

(β) The purple patch of his whole theory is his view of sacrifice among the Semites. He holds that the victim was the totem animal, of the same blood and the same stock as the god to whom the sacrifice was made and as the man who made it. Generally, this animal might not be killed or eaten. But on the occasion of certain festivals the tribe gathered together, and then the totem animal, which was identical with the god, was killed, a communal meal made of its flesh and blood, the intimate connexion with the totemic god renewed and his vital powers newly absorbed by this common feast, or communion. Of positive proof for this hypothesis Smith under the circumstances could give none, save for one incident related in the life of St. Nilus the hermit concerning that saint, and therefore post-Christian.[9] According to this, the Bedawin of the Desert of Sinai, who usually lived by brigandage, hunting, and on the milk of their herds, in case of need would also kill some of their most precious possessions, their camels, and eat them. Only one was slaughtered for each horde, and its flesh, only slightly roasted, was then eaten with dog-like greed. This, according to Robertson Smith, was a classical instance of totemic sacrifice.[10]

(γ) This theory was more or less warmly welcomed by a number of Protestant Biblical critics of Liberal views, for instance B. Stade,[11] who used it as evidence of the existence of animism, fetishism and worship of ancestral spirits in the Old Testament ; J. Benzinger,[12] who found evidence of the former existence of totemism among the

[8] Frazer, *Totemism and Exogamy*, Vol. I, p. 92.
[9] *Nili Opera*, in Migne, *Patrologia Graeca*, Vol. LXXIX, p. 612.
[10] See *Religion of the Semites*, Lecture VIII, p. 281 *sqq.* of the 1907 ed. [It should be added that S. Nilus goes on to describe a sacrifice of a camel to the Morning Star, in which the entire victim is consumed by those present: Nilus, *op. cit.*, p. 613.]
[11] *Geschichte des Volkes Israel*, Berlin, 2 vols., 1884–7, second impression, 1889.
[12] *Hebräische Archäologie*, Freiburg im Breisgau, 1894.

Israelites in certain of their names, derived from those of beasts ;
G. Kerber,[13] who assumed that in the most ancient times totems
received divine honours among the people of Israel ; and also, at
that time, it was supported by Andrew Lang in *Custom and Myth*,
London 1884 [new impression, London 1901 ; p. 115].

(δ) Especial enthusiasm, indeed fiery zeal, for the hypothesis was
shown by a French archæologist, Salamon Reinach.   Being on the
lookout for totemism among the classical peoples, he was delighted
to find it also among the Semites and especially the Hebrews.   He
added but little of his own to support and extend Smith's thesis ;
he had not the means, and especially he had not the ethnological
knowledge to do so.   But he proved himself an energetic popularizer
in his three volumes of collected essays, *Cultes, Mythes et Religions*,
Paris 1905–6, and still more in his little work *Orpheus, Histoire
générale des Religions*, Paris 1909, of which he himself says that it is
constructed after the fashion of card-castles (*châteaux des cartes*).

(ε) Decidedly the most serious, profound and wide-reaching
extension of Robertson Smith's views to be found among his
followers is that of an Anglican theologian, F. B. Jevons, who
was his pupil.   It was Jevons also who, consciously taking up
the idea which his teacher had but obscurely expressed, that
totemism is the origin of all religions, put it on a wider
foundation and worked it out fully.

This was done in his treatise *Introduction to the History of Religion*,
London, 1896 (third ed. in 1904).   He tries to derive Tylor's animism
from a yet earlier stage of universal personification, which however
had no religious character as yet, but acquired one only from
observation of unusual occurrences.   The religious development thus
brought about passed at once into totemism, for the mixed product
of this personification has projected upon a totemic spirit, which was
always incorporated in an animal.   Thus Jevons reaches Smith's
sacrificial communion.   A sort of primitive monotheism is established by the fact that each tribe had only its own totemic deity ;
polytheism was not produced until several races had combined.
In the second and shorter part of his book, the boldness of this
theory of 'totemic monotheism', for bold it certainly is, seems to
trouble the author's theological conscience.   It is obvious that
Jevons is here trying to reconcile the Protestant doctrine of an
inborn idea of God, testified to by the individual consciousness, with
the complicated facts of totemism.   It is no easy task to reduce
them to harmonious agreement.

His later work, *The Idea of God in early Religions*, Cambridge
1910, is mostly a speculative discussion of the facts of ethnology

[13] *Die religionsgeschichtliche Bedeutung der hebräischen Eigennamen*,
Freiburg im Breisgau, 1897.

and of the history of religion.   In it he says that only among ' some peoples ' do we find that the (sacrificial) feast is ' not an occasion of " eating with the god " but what has been crudely called " eating the god " ' (p. 77).   This is tantamount to abandoning the attempt to derive all sacrifices from the supposed totemic communion sacrifice.

In his last work, *Comparative Religion* (Cambridge, 1913), the last chapter, *Monotheism*, pp. 117–44, gives him occasion to discuss Andrew Lang's investigations into the high gods of savages.   Here he departs so far from his earlier views that he not only admits the existence of such gods even among the most primitive peoples, but even ventures on the conjecture (p. 120) that they are survivals of an age of belief in one God.

(b) REFUTATION OF ROBERTSON SMITH'S THEORY OF SACRIFICE

(a) With our present knowledge of totemism, which of course is far better than was then at hand, it is often very hard to realize what sort of evidence was then accepted as an indication, or even proof positive, of its existence.   But even the knowledge then available through Frazer ought to have sufficed to deter Robertson Smith and his followers, particularly Reinach, from indulging in such extravagant theories as theirs.   G. Foucart opposed this whole movement from the point of view of the historical method in two works full of penetration and irony, *La méthode comparative dans l'histoire des religions*, Paris, 1909, and *Histoire des religions et méthode comparative*, Paris, 1912.   In the latter (p. lxvi) he writes very delightfully, ' And as regards St. Nilus' camel, I am still of the opinion that it does not deserve to have so heavy a weight as the genesis of a part of the history of religion laid on its hump '.

(β) A thoughtful and substantial refutation of the application of the totemic theory to the Old Testament is to be found in the thorough investigation by V. Zapletal, *Der Totemismus und die Religion Israels*,* Freiburg, Switzerland, 1901.   In this he examines the proofs brought forward by Robertson Smith in minute detail, and gives an excellent demonstration of their untenability or insufficiency.   To-day of course such a proof could be made much more stringent. J. Nöldeke also agrees in essentials with Zapletal, who was his pupil, in his *Beiträgen zur semitischen Sprachwissenschaft*,† 1904, p. 74.

* [' Totemism and the Religion of Israel.']
† [' Contributions to Semitic Philology.']

(γ) As to Smith's theory that all sacrifice is derived from the totemic communion-sacrifice, Frazer never shared it:

' It is true,' he says, ' that in my *Totemism*, and again in the present work, I noted a few cases (four in all) of solemnly killing a sacred animal which, following Robertson Smith, I regarded as probably a totem. But none even of these four cases included the eating of the sacred animal by the worshippers, which was an essential part of my friend's theory. . . . Hence . . . I became more and more doubtful of the existence of such a practice at all.' [14]

Even after the discovery of the ' totem sacrament ' among the Arunta in Central Australia, Frazer persists that this discovery is not what Robertson Smith was looking for. He had in mind a sacrament, meaning thereby a religious rite, in which the beast sacrificed was divine and put to death only for this mystical meal. But in reality the Australian ceremony was not a sacrament, in that sense, but a magical ceremony, in which the totem was in no way reverenced or regarded as a god, but treated with magical rites for the prosaic purpose of increasing the food-supply, and in that connexion, simply eaten.[15]

The hopeless situation in which Robertson Smith's theory of sacrifice found itself at that time, on Frazer's testimony, is no better to-day ; on the contrary, it has grown worse and is now absolutely untenable, thanks especially to researches along historical lines. We shall have later to go further into this matter.

3. SIGMUND FREUD AND THE OEDIPUS COMPLEX

The prospects for totemism being found to be the origin of religion, or indeed a religious phenomenon at all, were thus anything but bright by the end of the first decade of this century, as we have seen. It is therefore all the more remarkable that two works appeared, one shortly after the other and for all practical purposes simultaneously, which strengthened this claim of totemism to be the initial stage of all religions by making it the source of all culture, morals, and social organization in general. The coincidence is all the more extraordinary because these claims were put forward from two utterly different points of view, and, moreover, by

[14] *Golden Bough*, preface to ed. 2 ; reprinted in ed. 3, Vol. I, p. xxiii.
[15] See Frazer in *Proceedings of the Australasian Association for the Advancement of Science*, Melbourne, 1901, p. 316 *sqq.* ; *Totemism and Exogamy*, Vol. IV, p. 231.

the leaders of two important schools of thought, whose intention was to do their followers the highest and best service in their power, to say, if I may so express myself, their last word on the subject.

One of these works is a collection of four articles, *The Horror of Incest*; *Tabu and the Ambivalence of Stimuli*; *Animism, Magic and the Omnipotence of Thought*; and *The Reappearance of Totemism in Infancy*,* contributed by Sigmund Freud in the course of the year 1912 to the periodical *Imago*. As a separate publication they bear the title *Totem und Tabu: einige Übereinstimmungen im Seelenleben der Wilden und Neurotiker* (Leipzig, Vienna and Zurich, 1913).† Despite all the progress made in the meantime by ethnology, a third, unaltered edition made its appearance in 1922. The other publication is Emil Durkheim's *Les formes élémentaires de la vie religieuse*, Paris, 1912.‡ We shall deal with Freud's work first.

(a) EXPOSITION OF THE OEDIPUS COMPLEX

Freud forms and expounds his theory principally in the fourth essay contained in the above-mentioned book. I give it here in a synopsis, as formulated by Krœber in a criticism of Freud,[16] supplementing it in places by citations from Freud himself.

' He (Freud) commences with the inference of Darwin, developed further by Atkinson,[17] that at a very early period man lived in small communities consisting of an adult male and a number of females and immature individuals, the males among the latter being driven off by the head of the group as they became old enough to evoke his jealousy. To this Freud adds the Robertson Smith theory that sacrifice at the altar is the essential element in every ancient cult, and that such sacrifice goes back to a killing and eating by the clan of its totem animal, which was regarded as of kin with

* [In the original, *Die Inzestscheu; Das Tabu und die Ambivalenz der Gefühlsregungen; Animismus, Magie und Allmacht der Gedanken; Die infantile Wiederkehr des Totemismus.*]
† [' Totem and Tabu: Points of Agreement between the Mental Life of Savages and of Neurotics.' There is an English translation, by A. A. Brill, New York, 1918.]
‡ [English translation, ' The Elementary Forms of the Religious Life ', London, 1915.]
[16] *American Anthropologist*, Vol. XXII (1920), pp. 48–55.
[17] In an appendix to Andrew Lang's *Social Origins*, London, 1903. Lang was Atkinson's cousin, and, being so much better known, gave publicity to this short article, which otherwise would probably have remained unnoticed, owing to its own insignificance.

the clan and its gods, and whose killing at ordinary times was therefore strictly forbidden.' [18]

These then are the two ethnological theories which Freud adopts ; they surely ranked already as the weakest of their day. Now he adds his own contribution from psycho-analysis. This is the application of his own creation, the so-called Oedipus complex, the substance of which is that the male child, one may almost say as a normal thing, entertains quite early sexual desires directed towards his own mother, and consequently regards his father as a rival. He therefore has, on the one hand, a hatred, even a murderous hatred, for his father, but on the other, for his feelings are ' ambivalent ', he also loves his father for the latter's care for him. Owing to certain ' phobias ' which children feel towards animals, the son's hatred for his father is often transferred to some beast, with which consequently the child feels himself to be related ; and this is the key to the new explanation of totemism.

' The Oedipus complex ', Kroeber continues, ' directed upon these two hypotheses welds them into a mechanism with which it is possible to explain most of the essentials of human civilization, as follows. The expelled sons of the primal horde finally banded together and slew their father, ate him, and appropriated the females.' I now cite Freud himself. ' That they should also eat their victim is a matter of course among cannibal savages. Their powerful father had certainly been the envied and dreaded exemplar of every one of the brothers. Now, by the act of devouring him, they attained to identity with him, each making a portion of his strength his own. The totemic banquet, perhaps the first feast mankind ever celebrated, was the repetition, the festival of remembrance, of this noteworthy criminal deed, with which so much began—the organization of society, moral restrictions, and religion.' [19]
' For ', again to cite Kroeber, ' at this point the ambivalence of emotions proved decisive. The tender feelings which had always persisted by the side of the brothers' hate for their father, gained the upper hand as soon as this hate was satisfied, and took the form of remorse and sense of guilt. What the father's presence had formerly prevented they themselves now prohibited in the psychic situation of " subsequent obedience ", which we know so well from psycho-analysis. They undid their deed by declaring that the killing of the father substitute, the totem, was not allowed, and renounced the fruits of their deed by denying themselves the liberated women. Thus they created the two fundamental taboos of totemism ' (*i.e.*, not to kill the totem and not to marry within the

[18] *V. sup.*, p. 69.   [19] Freud, *Totem und Tabu*, p. 110.

totemic clan) ' which *ipso facto* necessarily coincided with the two suppressed desires of the Oedipus complex ' (viz. to kill the father and marry the mother).[20]

Totemism as a religion is thus inseparably connected with the killing of the animal totem. The totemic sacrifice and the eating of the totem which follows are the means by which the consciousness of guilt is relieved, and also by which the rebellious feelings of the sons are satisfied by a continually renewed killing of the father. It was this latter tendency which conquered.

But Freud goes further still. He holds that God is nothing more or less than the sublimated physical father of human beings ; hence in the totemic sacrifice it is God Himself who is killed and sacrificed. This slaying of the father-god is mankind's ancient original sin. This blood-guilt is atoned for by the bloody death of Christ.

' Hence in Christian doctrine mankind confesses in the most open manner the primeval guilt, because it has now found the most perfect satisfaction for it in the sacrificial death of the only Son . . . But the Christian communion is fundamentally a renewed removal of the father, a repetition of the deed that needs atonement.' [21]

(b) CRITICISM OF FREUD'S THEORY

Professor Kroeber, at the end of his synopsis, adds :

' This mere extrication and presentation of the framework of the Freudian hypothesis on the origin of socio-religious civilization is probably sufficient to prevent its acceptance.' (*Ibid.*, p. 49.)

However, he proceeds to give us a series of criticisms which can be read with profit. I may be allowed to indulge in a short criticism here, from a somewhat different point of view. It would not be necessary because of any importance of the theory itself, for of all that have been put forward in the historical investigation of religion, this is perhaps the most hopelessly untenable, on account of the wide gulf between the facts and the claims made by its author ; but it may be of some use in view of the wide popularity which that theory has won. For it is Freud's theory of the formation of the Oedipus complex that has proved—to use the rather inæsthetic but highly modern metaphor of one of his supporters—' the

[20] Kroeber, *op. cit.*, supplemented from Freud, *op. cit.*, p. 112.
[21] Freud, *op. cit.*, p. 206 *sq.*

locomotive which has drawn Freud's triumphal car all around the globe '.[22]   It is supposed to be the crowning work of the whole psycho-analytical school, whereof Freud, as every one knows, is the founder and head.[23]   I will sum up my criticism in five propositions, referring the reader, if he wishes to supplement them, to the more detailed account in my lecture *Der Ödipus-Komplex der Freudschen Psychoanalyse und die Ehegestaltung des Bolschewismus.*[24]

(i) Totemism, with which Freud begins the development of mankind, is not at the beginning of human culture. We know a whole series of peoples, ethnologically the oldest, who have neither totemism nor mother-right ; the Pygmoids,* the Pygmies of Asia and Africa, the South-East Australians, the Ainu, the primitive Eskimos, the Koryaks, the Samoyeds in the extreme north of the globe, the North Central Californians, the primitive Algonkins of North America, the Gez-Tapuya tribes of South America, and the Tierra del Fuegians of the extreme south.[25]   Even if Freud's theory were right in itself, it would have nothing to do with the origin of religion, morals or society ; for the origins of all these lie much further back, in pretotemic days, and are utterly different from Freud's phantasies.

(ii) Totemism is now seen to be a later stage of development ; but even as such, it is not universal, nor have all peoples passed through it.   In the first place, as Graebner has shown, mother-right does not belong to totemism.   In the second, Frazer has proved, and since Frazer wrote it has been even more clearly demonstrated, that the three great ruling races in particular, the Indo-Europeans, the Hamito-Semites and the Ural-Altaics, had originally no totemism, but merely acquired it here and there on their many travels, mostly in

[22] Quoted by Clemen in *Die Anwendung der Psychoanalyse auf Mythologie und Religionsgeschichte (Archiv für gesamte Psychologie,* Vol. LXI, 1928, p. 124).

[23] See, for ethnological criticism of the theory, W. H. Rivers, *Instinct and the Unconscious,* Cambridge, 1920 ; *The Symbolism of Rebirth,* in *Folk-Lore,* Vol. XXXIII, 1922, pp. 14–23 : F. Boas, *The Methods of Ethnology,* in *American Anthropologist,* N.S. XXII, 1920, p. 311 *sqq.* ; Kroeber, *Totem and Taboo : an Ethnological Psycho-analysis, ibid.,* pp. 48–55 ; Malinowski, *Sex Repression and Savage Society,* London, 1927 ; Clemen, *loc. cit.*

[24] *Nationalwirtschaft,* Vol. II, 1929, pp. 401–32 ; also published separately by this Review, Berlin, W. 57, 20III Bülowstrasse.

* [I.e. those peoples who resemble the Pygmies but are not actually Pygmies themselves.]

[25] See W. Schmidt in *Anthropos,* Vol. X–XI, 1915–16, p. 597 *sq.*

decidedly weakened forms.[26] Thus the attempt to make the psycho-analytical explanation of the Oedipus complex of universal and inevitable validity has the ground cut from under it, even as regards the later phases of culture.

(iii) Freud takes over from Robertson Smith the assumption that the totemic sacrifice and totemic communion, that is the ceremonial killing and eating of the totem animal (he would say ' totem-god ') is an invariable feature of totemism. But this is ethnologically impossible. Of the many hundred totemic races of the whole earth there are just four who know any rite even approximating to this one, and they all belong, ethnologically speaking, to the most modern totemic peoples.

But even if Freud's theory of totemism would hold water, these totemistic sacrifices and communions would not be of general significance, for as we have seen, totemism is not a stage through which even all the later peoples have passed. Still less would such rites have anything to do with the origin of sacrifice, since totemism, as also we have seen, does not occur at all in the oldest cultures. In a part of these very ancient pre-totemic tribes, no sacrifice has hitherto been discovered ; but among the most of those which seems to be ethnologically the most ancient, as the Pygmies, the Arctic peoples, and some of the Algonkins, a form of sacrifice, that of the first-fruits, is already in existence. The first-fruits are those of their hunting and plant-collecting, and they are offered to the Supreme Being as the Creator and Lord of Life and of that which sustains it. The little morsel of meat or food-plant which is thus offered has no sacral significance ; it is invariably ' profane ' food. Nor is any sacramental banquet connected with it, but only a ' profane ' meal. Everything that Freud has written, therefore, concerning the close relation of his totemic primeval sacrifice to the Christian sacrifice of the Cross and the Christian Eucharist, is shown, on this side as on all others, to be mere castles in the air.

(iv) The pre-totemic peoples know nothing of cannibalism, and patricide among them would be a sheer impossibility, psychologically, sociologically and ethically. As to patricide, the authority of the father is firmly rooted, among the oldest peoples, in their social organization, their morals and their affections ; and the murder of anyone, especially within their own clan, is something so rare that the thought of murdering a father could simply never enter these people's heads at all.

[26] Schmidt, *ibid.*, 597–601, 607 *sq.*

(v) The form of the pre-totemic family, and therefore of
the earliest human family we can hope to know anything
about through ethnology, is neither general promiscuity nor
group-marriage, neither of which, according to the verdict
of the leading modern ethnologists, ever existed at all.[27]
Nor is it, as Atkinson imagined, a horde, in which an old
male possesses all the females himself and drives the young
males out. On the contrary, it is a clear, fully developed
marriage in the proper sense, which is monogamous among
a large number of these peoples, moderately polygamous
among some few.

All this certainly does not provide an atmosphere in which
the Oedipus complex could spring up and flourish. We must
moreover remember that among these most ancient peoples
in general, sexual matters are far from playing the dominant
part which Atkinson and Freud attribute to them.

The picture which we thus get of the earliest men is certainly
very different from that which Freud constructs in his theory.
To bring such men into connexion with modern sex-ridden
neurotics, as he would have us do, and from this connexion
to deduce the alleged fact that all thought and feeling, especially subliminal, is founded on and saturated with sex, must
remain lost labour. Thus Freud's hypothesis loses its last
shadow of hope ever to corroborate or establish any single
part of itself, for every part collapses in ruin.

4. THE PANTOTEMISM OF E. DURKHEIM

Since a great part of the criticism directed against Freud's
theory can justly be applied also to E. Durkheim's work,
Les formes élémentaires de la vie religieuse, we may spend
less time on the latter, although in content and in method
it is far superior to Freud's book. Indeed, of all recent works
dealing with ethnology and the history of religion, there is
none which has reaped such a harvest of praise for its details,
combined with such general rejection of its main thesis. The
reason for this latter occurrence was that, owing to the long
time the work took to mature, the development of the whole
sciences of ethnology and comparative religion had in the
meantime left it a great way behind.

The question was asked how it was possible not merely to
defend the religious character of totemism, as this book does,
but actually to exalt it to the position of the source of all

[27] Cf. W. Schmidt, *Ursprung der Gottesidee*, Vol. I, ed. 2, pp. 215–36,
for a list of the authors in question and their attitudes.

religion, at a time when all other researchers were more and more definitely denying any connexion between totemism and religion whatsoever. Again it was asked why Durkheim so onesidedly and so arbitrarily confined himself to Central Australian totemism, with no more than an occasional reference to that of North America, when the world-wide distribution of the various kinds of totemism and their manifold variety were already well known. And finally it was asked how Durkheim, who revelled in the forms of the most orthodox Evolutionism, could so stubbornly maintain that the Central Australians were the oldest stratum of their race, at a time when research into the history of culture had revealed another and a totally different stratification. For according to this, the Central Australians in general, and the Arunta in particular, are the latest, the most modern, of the six strata or so into which the native culture of that continent is divided. The only explanation psychologically possible is the following ; all the researches of that school had for a long while been devoted with remarkable persistency and conscious direction to these theories ; that fossilization had already set in ; and that in consequence the only way left for them to deal with the disturbers of their peace who had arisen in the meantime was to brush them aside with Archimedes' cry of *Noli turbare circulos meos.*

At the same time, it is very much to Durkheim's credit that, faced with the high gods who are particularly common in South-East Australia, he refused to apply Tylor's desperate remedy and attribute them simply to missionary influence. Rejecting this, he expresses himself decidedly in favour of the original and native character of this ' concept of a god who, if not the only one, is at least supreme, and to whom there is attributed a pre-eminent station relatively to the other religious entities'. [28] He indulges indeed in polemic against Andrew Lang and me, but he is ready to allow these gods actually elevated characteristics, if only ' in a relative sense, in harmony with Australian mentality '.[29] At last, however, he comes to the conclusion that they are nothing but ' the logical result and the highest form ' of totemism.[30] They are, according to him, the product of the totemistic ancestors of the Central Australians, and passing through the intervening stage of culture-heroes, they have become the Supreme Beings of the natives in the south-east.

As this whole theory supposes the Central Australians to

[28] *Formes élémentaires*, p. 409.
[29] *Ibid.*, pp. 414–15, note 4.   [30] *Ibid.*, p. 415.

be very old and the South-East Australians modern, the ground is cut from under Durkheim's feet by the demonstration which I undertook in the same year (1912) in the first edition of my *Ursprung der Gottesidee* and completed in my *Gliederung der australischen Sprachen,** p. 218 *sqq.* and especially 264 *sqq.* This is, that it is these same South-East Australians who form the oldest stratum of the native population, while on the other hand it is the Central Australians and especially the Arunta who are the most modern. Now these oldest tribes have either no totemism at all to show, or only fragments of it, acquired at a later date ; what we do find among them is the figure of the Supreme Being, clear, definite, and quite independent of totemism. I was therefore justified in writing, in the preface, to the latter of the works just mentioned, ' On the other hand, I hope that one beneficial result will follow from the present work, namely that the appearance of treatises so purely speculative and *a priori* as E. Durkheim's *Formes élémentaires de la vie religieuse* will be rendered a scientific impossibility in the future.'

Durkheim's theory is criticized from points of view not wholly the same as mine, but still emphatically rejected in every way, by A. A. Goldenweiser in his *Early Civilization*, New York, 1922, p. 360 *sqq.*, and by R. H. Lowie, in *Primitive Religion*, New York, 1924, p. 153 *sqq.*

But totemism is very closely connected, not indeed with religion but with magic. This point has been grasped, almost instinctively, by sundry authors who to begin with accepted the totemic theory of religion ; in consequence, they have gone over to the ' magical ' theory, with which we shall soon have to deal. Frazer was one of the first ; and the entire sociological school founded and led by Durkheim has been occupied almost more with magic than totemism.

* [' The Grouping of the Languages of Australia.']

CHAPTER X

MAGISM AND DYNAMISM

1. INTRODUCTION: THE FIRST PIONEER

(a) THE PREANIMISTIC TENDENCY AND ITS RELATION TO ITS TIMES

(a) IT has already been made clear in the preceding chapter that various derivatives of the totemic theory made a place for themselves; these postulated magic as the initial stage of religion or as leading up to it, and in any case, claimed that magic was prior in time to animism. And as a matter of fact, these attempts did largely correspond to real, objective conditions. It is a perfectly solid fact that magic is particularly flourishing in those very races which belong to the older totemic culture, while animism is either poorly developed among them or not developed at all. We shall see later that there exists between these two facts an inner connexion, depending on the form taken by these peoples' view of the universe. Now both the patrilineal totemic culture and that characterized by agriculture and mother-right belong to the primary cultures which follow upon the primitive stage; to this extent, then, they run parallel to each other; but nevertheless, in many parts of the world the totemic culture actually appears before the agricultural and matrilineal, and therefore is in those places older than it; the same therefore is of course true of the relation in time of magic to animism.

But a movement set in from another direction which attempted to get beyond and behind animism. It was clear enough that animism involved the division of a unity into two parts, for it separates the whole man into body and soul; and if, as supposed by Tylor's theory, spirits were projected into lifeless things and natural objects and processes also, on the analogy of human beings, then a dualism was set up there again, in place of an earlier unity. Logically

118

and psychologically therefore, it seemed inevitable to treat the idea of the unity as older than this duality which had arisen from dividing it ; in other words, to regard magic as earlier than animism.

Before going further, we would emphasize the following point. The very consideration which makes plausible the greater antiquity of magic tells even more strongly in favour of the greater antiquity of the concept of a still undivided personality contrasted with the division which man feels in himself. In other words, the currents of preanimism which began to flow during the opening decades of this century divided into two diametrically opposite streams. The first of these is the theory of magic, whose starting-point is the priority of material substance, as yet not regarded as animate, not credited with an *anima*. The second is the theistic theory, which begins from a personality, single because not affected by a separation into body and soul. Both streams began to flow about the same time. After a short time, during which both were of equal strength, the former left the latter behind in the race for the general attention and forced it for some time into the background. For this there are not only reasons inherent in the theories themselves, but others depending on the background of contemporary history ; these we must consider later.

For the immediate present, this temporary victory of the former current gives the theory of magic the right to be considered first. We will therefore deal with it in more detail in the following sections.

(β) It will facilitate our understanding of both streams if we also take into consideration their relationship to the parallel events of their time, which are in part not merely parallels, but also forces which prepared the way for them and set them in motion.

The concluding years of the last century had seen the fading of the crasser kind of materialism. This doctrine had on the one hand falsified the hopes it had raised of explaining the universe and satisfying mankind. On the other, recent investigations on modern lines made clearer than ever the independent nature of man's immaterial part. Those who remained faithful to materialism tried to save it by converting it into a monism of philosophical colouring ; in the natural sciences the watchword was no longer Karl Bücher's formula ' force and matter ', but matter also was resolving itself into force, as for instance in Oswald's monistic philosophy of science. In biology, Häckel produced a sort of monism, artificially saturated with the 'psychism' of the ultimate elements. Both these monistic doctrines were curiously like the Theory of Magic, for that too soon sought refuge in a general magical force, that is, in dynamism.

However, it became obvious that all this re-shaping was no more than a disguising, an ineffectual attempt at revivification of systems which were past their prime. As research progressed it became more and more evident that spirit was something peculiar and independent, and this was expressed in Wundt's 'psycho-physical parallelism', which found approval. Consequently, in the sphere of our science also, theories arose which no longer made material magic the first stage, but declared a more or less decided blend of magic and religion to have been the point from which the evolution of religion started. As we shall concern ourselves in the following sections with these different variants of the theories of magic, we need not yet dwell in any detail upon the fact that in the history of our times research has progressed even beyond Wundt's 'parallelism' and that now the independent nature of spirit is widely recognized. The corresponding effects of this recognition upon the science of religion is a subject into which we must go more fully later on.

(b) The Pioneer, J. H. King : His Failure to Obtain a Following

(a) It is not easy to give a sketch of the Theory of Magic which shall be at once brief and adequate. Its supporters are many ; their peculiarities are so marked, and their relations to each other so vague, that a description of them is very apt to degenerate into a long catalogue of individual savants. Here we find no noteworthy leader, to set forth the entire theory at one stroke in a great work, train a great number of pupils and attract a multitude of followers. Rather do we find, and it is a curious fact, that the formal beginning of this long series was made by an author so many years earlier than the remaining members of the succession that no actual connexion exists between them and him. This pioneer, this best representative of the school, produced no effect at all and passed away without finding a follower.

His name is J. H. King, and his book is entitled *The Supernatural, its Origin, Nature and Evolution*.[1] This is the first

[1] London, Williams and Norgate, and New York, G. P. Putnam's Sons, 1892, 2 vols.

work to put magic, instead of animism, at the beginning
of the development of religion. Moreover, it remains so far
the best and most complete work of the whole movement.
Nowhere is the proof of the theory he puts forward undertaken on a wider basis or with more methodical stringency.
If we may call Tylor the father and the classical exponent of
animism, it cannot be doubted that King has earned the title
of classical exponent of the preanimistic, or magical theory,
but not of its father, since he begot no sons. At first, his
book remained completely unnoticed on its appearance.
Possibly the reason for this was, that in those days animism
was still too potent a force, and King was much ahead of his
times. But even eight years later, when at the beginning
of the twentieth century other authors came forward with
this hypothesis, though they were far less thorough than
King and covered a much less wide field, his book remained
in total obscurity. Even after I ' discovered ' it in the library
of the Vienna Anthropological Society and drew attention to
it in the first edition of my *Ursprung der Gottesidee* (this was
in 1912, twenty years after its appearance), there was no
change. The literature dealing with the Theory of Magic is
extensive enough ; yet I do not remember to have found
in it a single first-hand quotation of King.

(β) King recognizes two kinds of ' powers ' in the world ; the
mental, in man and beast, and the impersonal (physical, chemi-
cal, etc.). From the former man derives the theory of spirits ;
from the latter, that of magic, *i.e.*, of good and ill luck and so
forth. Both often coalesce ; but magic is the older. Magical
beliefs and practices form at first when the usual order of
things in nature or in the individual's consciousness is broken
by something unusual. This unexpected event is then classi-
fied as good or bad, as bringing good or ill luck, and corresponding desire or fear is produced. The latter feeling is
much commoner and in this connexion stronger as well ;
for man feels himself faced with an indefinite material something which he has at first no means of influencing, and so
his fear develops into terror.

This universal feeling of good and ill luck is the first germ
of all religion. It is a phase in which the reasoning faculties
are at a low level, the power of forming ideas not yet awakened,
and immediate sense-perceptions can arouse only crude
associational series in the mind. Man at that time, discovering what he supposed to be the causes of these feelings
of good or ill luck, used these supposed causes as means of

attracting good luck and avoiding ill luck ; and this was the beginning of magic. In the earliest stage, every man was his own sorcerer ; in the second, outstanding individuals developed greater magical powers, and the professional sorcerer, the shaman or what not, began to come into being. King repeatedly insists that in all magical media there is no trace to be found of spirit or spiritual power ; the power inheres directly in the material object, without the intervention of a spirit ; consequently material magic is prior to animism.

(γ) Thus King had already clearly perceived both the intellectual and the emotional origins of magic. The social origins, however, he paid less attention to, or overlooked them altogether. The priority in time of human magic over an animistic belief in spirits he has not indeed everywhere proved, but has made it very likely. His defects are, first, that he does not perceive sufficiently how the 'mental' powers give rise to personification, which arose at least as early as ideas of material magic ; secondly, that religious thought does not have to wait to be aroused by the appearance of extraordinary events interrupting the normal processes of consciousness, but springs also, indeed earlier, from reflection upon the ordinary and regular happenings, which are the veritable source of the idea of causation ; while this idea, applied to the universe as a whole, produces the assumption of a Creator as the personal vehicle of power.

(δ) Eight years had now to pass before the first tentative and timid movements were made to overthrow the animistic theory and to raise up that of magic. Exactly at the end of the nineteenth and the beginning of the twentieth century, on November 15, 1899,* an address was delivered before the Folklore Society by R. R. Marett, which appeared in the next year's volume of *Folk-Lore* (XI, 1900, pp. 162–82) under the title *Preanimistic Religion*. After this there came out, almost every year of the first decade of the present century, articles and books which in the most varied ways drew attention to the idea of magic and its priority to animism. At last, in 1912, appeared Durkheim's work, *Les formes élémentaires de la vie religieuse*, which was meant by its author to

* [Father Schmidt adopts the reckoning approved by the Vatican, by which the twentieth century begins on January 1, 1900, in accordance with the astronomical custom of beginning our era with the year 0, not 1 ; for which custom, see Fotheringham in *Nautical Almanac* for 1931, p. 745.]

form the very zenith and crown of the movement, but in reality marked the beginning of its decline.   The new tendency developed but one special branch during the second decade of the century ; it entered upon a close partnership with the psychology of religion which had in the meanwhile developed.

If, in trying to explain the various theories of magic, we wish to escape the danger alluded to above, of giving a scattered list with no unity, we have no choice but to try to group them in some fashion.   And this grouping can be carried out with no violence to our material ; we have but to note what element the several authors treat as the initial and fundamental one from which to derive magic itself. Now we find that they turn their attention to the three fundamental powers of the mind, one after another, namely, intellect, will and emotion.   Correspondingly, we can distinguish between (i) intellectualist, (ii) volitionalist, and (iii) emotionalist theories ; whereof those of the second class all have as a matter of fact a sociological character.

2.   THE INTELLECTUALIST THEORIES OF MAGIC

J. H. King, J. G. Frazer, K. Th. Preuss, A. Vierkandt, E. W. Hopkins

(a) The first and best representative of this theory, J. H. King, whose acquaintance we have already made, belongs undoubtedly to the intellectualist movement.   His primary object indeed is to establish the manner in which the component parts of magic come about, and the direction which the natural desire to find a cause must take in accordance with them, in order to recognize and master the origins of impressions of good and ill luck.   True, he also grasped very well the importance, for the development of magic, of the emotion of fear which arises out of the uncertainty of magical judgements.   The sociological element he scarcely recognizes at all.

(b) It is equally certain that (Sir) J. G. Frazer belongs to the intellectualist category ; a superficial handling of the subject might call him the first to put forward such a theory.   His opinion concerning magic is set forth in his great masterpiece, *The Golden Bough*, which indeed has the sub-title *A Study in Magic and Religion*.   But here, as in other fields, his opinion has in course of time and in the progress of the work through various editions, undergone changes.   In the first edition (1890) Frazer supposed that for primitive man the world was governed by personal beings, characterized, like himself, by perception and will, and also by impersonal forces, the forerunners of the natural laws one day to be discovered by science. In the latter region, he held (see *Golden Bough*, ed. 2, Vol. I, pp. 9 *sqq.*, 30), sympathetic, or homœopathic, magic grew up. In the second edition (1900) he laid more stress on the difference between these two views of the world ; the former he declared to be that belonging to religion, while the latter was that of magic. He now assumed that ' in the mental evolution of humanity' magic, the lower intel-lectual stratum, had probably everywhere preceded religion. Only with the passage of time had man, despairing of his power to control the impersonal forces by the help of magic, bowed before the personal and moral forces and endeavoured to secure their favour by prayer and sacrifice. But, on the other hand, the false science, magic, had gradually progressed into true science, alchemy becoming chemistry, astrology astronomy and so forth (*op. cit.*, Vol. I, pp. 62–75). Essen-tially the same opinion, only more decidedly expressed and more fully worked out, is entertained by Frazer in the third and greatly enlarged edition of his work, in the first volume of what is now the first part and bears the separate title *The Magic Art and the Evolution of Kings* (1911).

The proof which Frazer offers of his theory is very short and almost entirely of a psychological and Evolutionist nature. To conceive of what goes on in nature as personal is a more complicated and therefore a later idea than to think of it as impersonal ; magic also is everywhere more uniform than religion, which is many-sided ; it therefore is older than religion. The only historical evidence he produces is the predominance of magic among the Australians, ' the rudest savages as to whom we possess accurate information' (*Golden Bough*, ed. 3, I, p. 234). This is wrong to begin with, for the Pygmies, who practise magic but little, are ethnologically older ; and Frazer bases his contention exclusively on the latest of the five or six strata of Australians, the Arunta of Central Australia. This is also the judgement of Lowie in his *Primitive Religion* (New York, 1924, p. 147), who says :

' In short, Frazer's argument breaks down at every point, and even if we adopt his definitions there is no reason to ascribe greater antiquity to magic than to religion.'

(c) K. T. Preuss is uncompromisingly intellectualist, without the least trace of emotionalism, in his article *Der Ursprung*

der Religion und Kunst.[2] It is described by Preuss himself
as an 'interim report', intended only 'to put forward a
tolerably coherent chain (of evidence), to be completed later '.
But this completion seems never to have followed.   However,
it was this article which did for Germany what Marett's did
for England in bringing the idea of magic to the front.

Preuss wishes to push back preanimism to the earliest
possible date, the first emergence of man from the bestial
state which the author presupposes.

' As soon as this factor appeared, as soon as instinct ceased to be
the only guide of the living creature that was becoming human, he
must of necessity pass through an endless series of blunders which
failed to annihilate him in the struggle for existence only because
the essential thing, instinct and the tendency to imitate what already
existed, still remained.   This " primeval stupidity " [*Urdummheit*,
a favourite and widely quoted term of Preuss] of mankind . . . is
the ultimate origin of religion and of art.   For both of these are
produced immediately from magic, which in its turn is the direct
result of the endeavour for self-preservation, which survives instinct. . . . Magic and purposeful action with real effects, as we
understand it, blend with one another for primeval man.'

It was not till later that practically useful actions and magical
acts separated.[3]

This position is of course quite untenable.   With the
negative talent for ' primeval stupidity ' and a consequent
' endless series of blunders ', humanity would never have
reached any higher development at all, but, instinct or none,
would have perished miserably.   In order to rise, it needed
a positive force, and this was the power of forming general
concepts and connecting cause and effect.   This must inevit-
ably have been stronger than the ideas of magic, which in any
case are nothing but rational judgements gone wrong.   Preuss
therefore does not adequately grasp the concept of causality,
nor does he understand personification aright.   For in this
there is always a central ego, which remains self-identical and
unchanged amid all metamorphoses ; so that in this connexion
magical acts, involving a change of the whole, are unthinkable.[4]

The proofs Preuss brings forward, work-songs, working
dances, masked dances, are all examples from his own especial

[2] In *Globus*, Vol. LXXXVI, 1904, pp. 321–7, 355–63, 375–9, 388–92 ;
Vol. LXXXVII, 1905, pp. 333–7, 347–50, 380–4, 394–400, 413–19.
[The title may be rendered ' The Origin of Religion and of Art '.]
[3] *Globus*, Vol. LXXXVII, 1905, p. 419.
[4] Cf. Schmidt, *Ursprung der Gottesidee*, I, ed. 2, pp. 527–33.

area, the mythology and religion of Mexico. They therefore do not belong to the earliest ages of mankind, nor anywhere near them, and so can tell us nothing about the ' origin of religion and art '.⁵ Besides this, numerous ethnological objections might be raised. As to the high gods of the ethnologically oldest peoples, those figures which are so intimately connected with the rational ideal of creation, of the cause of the world, Preuss has never a word to say about them in this treatise.

Ten years later, Preuss himself modified and laid aside the exaggerations and the one-sidedness of his theory. Thus, in his bibliographical article on *Savage Religions*,⁶ he writes of his own work *Die geistige Kultur der Naturvölker*,⁷

' it represents in some measure a complement to my first essay, *Ursprung der Religion und Kunst*, in that it drops certain opinions incapable of sufficient proof and is principally interested in expounding the whole subject, including the concept of a Supreme Being among savages, in its various aspects, in accordance with the present position of our knowledge '.

We shall have later (p. 198) to discuss further the alteration which the trend of his opinions had by this time undergone.

(*d*) The work of A. Vierkandt is likewise intellectualist throughout. His essay *Die Anfänge der Religion und Zauberei* ⁸ is so decidedly of this character that even in the passages where he touches upon the position of the emotions, he himself does not realize how very important they are for the question, among others, of the origin and development of sorcery. Vierkandt tries to go on from where Preuss left off, but is distinguished from him by his greater lucidity, sober moderation, and subtle psychological insight. One of his especial merits is the sharp distinction which he draws between magic operating close at hand and that effective at a distance ; he considers the former to be the older. Between the two he interposes what he calls ' initial magic ' as a transitional form. He distinguishes also between magic of aversion and magic of attraction,* but it must be admitted

---

⁵ Cf. Schmidt, *Ursprung der Gottesidee*, I, ed. 2, pp. 525 *sqq.*, 533 *sqq.*
⁶ In *Archiv für Religionswissenschaft*, Vol. XVIII, 1914, pp. 544–6.
⁷ [' The Mental Culture of Savages.'] Teubner, Leipzig and Berlin, 1914. It is No. 542 of the series entitled *Aus Natur und Geisteswelt*.
⁸ [' The origins of Religion and Magic '], in *Globus*, Vol. XCII, 1907, pp. 21–5, 40–5, 61–5.
* [These five forms are termed, in the original, *Nahzauber, Fernzauber, Anfangszauber, Abwehrzauber* and *Strebezauber* respectively.]

that he is less successful here in trying to prove the former to be the earlier. He has also correctly perceived the great importance of expressive gestures in the development of magic, and explains excellently that in their earliest stage these are spontaneous reflex actions resulting from emotion, and nothing more ; they have at that level no intention of being magically effective, for this comes only at the last stage. With commendable insight, moreover, he realizes that analogical magic is in itself not primary at all, but simply the illegitimate extension of a procedure which, to use his own words,

' is perfectly rational in its own sphere, that is, well adapted to its ends and perhaps even accompanied with a consciousness of those ends '.

He suffers, however, from the following weakness : his attitude towards the subject is not yet free from Evolutionism, for he says that ' an important negative predisposing condition for the rise of magic ' was ' the lack, in the mind of primitive man, of any clear idea of causality ' and his ' obscure and muddled processes of thought ' (p. 44).

In setting out to describe the relations between magic and religion, he begins with cult, many parts of which, he admits, have originated independently. Nevertheless, he is of opinion that the origin of the overwhelming majority of cult-practices from magic is demonstrated, especially in the cases of the sacraments and mysteries of the Christian church, such as the Eucharist, Baptism, and the blessing of water. He therefore fails to see, firstly, that there is in the rites a simple and perfectly natural symbolism ; secondly, that they owe their efficacy, not to any idea of impersonal magic, but to the operation of the will of God's omnipotent personality ; and finally, that they demand in addition a certain moral attitude on the part of the recipient. His description of prayer, moreover, is absolutely self-contradictory, for while he begins by deriving certain simple forms of it, which he regards as original, from a natural extension of the communi-cations between man and man, and other forms from the magic of words and names, he then goes on to make all prayer result from magic.

It is curious that Vierkandt, although desirous of writing on ' the origins of religion and magic ', and although he has so much to say about the magic of the Australians, has not a word on the subject of the Supreme Being among the

South-East Australians and other peoples who are ethnologically the most ancient. For these beings have nothing whatsoever to do with magic, but are connected with the second 'stage' which he allows, with the rational idea of causality.[9]

(e) *The Origin and Evolution of Religion*,[10] by E. Washburn Hopkins, is a book showing remarkable acuteness, and contains good criticism of Tylor's and Spencer's animism and ghost-worship, which the author calls 'the English theory', Max Müller's nature-worship (the 'German theory'), Frazer's doctrine of magic and Durkheim's collectivism (the 'French theory'), all of which he rejects. Hopkins' own theory is as follows. For primitive man, the distinction between spirit and matter did not exist as yet, and everything was gifted with magical 'power'. But this was not a general force like *mana* and its equivalents; each thing had its own special power. Turning now to the origin of religion, he rejects those hypotheses which begin with the irrational and emotional element simply; he holds that intellectual activity was also present even at that time. He perceives, moreover, that the conception of a personality as a whole and undivided is prior to the distinction of soul from body which is brought about by animism; that this conception found expression in personification, which even in later times long continued to develop. But notwithstanding he arrives at the position that in the beginning no distinction was made between religious and non-religious, natural and supernatural; that the starting-point was an undifferentiated something. With the help of a doctrine of unlimited evolutionary progress he succeeds in producing from this plurality of objects and persons endowed with power a single great power, either by way of 'inclusion', which leads to pantheism, or of 'subordination', which brings us to monotheism. The latter was a long journey and made step by step.

All this is unfortunately nothing but a piece of Evolutionist construction without a trace of historical investigation, and the series of stages given is of the most orthodox Evolutionary type: stones, hills, plants, beasts, the elements, the heavenly bodies, the sun, human beings, ancestors. Each and all of the high gods, so characteristic of the peoples who are ethnologically the most ancient, and so awkward for this theory,

[9] See further Schmidt, *Ursprung der Gottesidee*, Vol. I, ed. 2, pp. 544-53.
[10] New Haven, New York, London and Oxford, 1924.

are dismissed with exactly six words, ' Primitive monotheism is a modern dream '.

(*f*) By way of giving a short summary of the characteristics of the Theory of Magic in its intellectualist form, let me point out that all these theories more or less assume a prerational stage in the history of mankind, which, in accordance with the Evolutionist theory of the descent of man, they naturally put near the beginning of man's development from the beasts. In particular, Preuss considers that this prerational stage should be described as the first in the process of ' humanizing '. King allows even in beasts a certain apprehension of things as ' canny ' or ' uncanny ', but nothing like the practice of magic.

The interest of these writers is directed principally to the first comprehension of a real causal nexus, which they generally suppose to be late, or derive from a previous indefinite and nebulous condition of thought. Here they generally neglect the capability of even the most ancient human beings to form general ideas, which is revealed by all their languages, and implies the ability to arrange things in order, and therefore to master them. This primeval occurrence of causal thought is revealed by the existence of tools adapted to certain ends. It had already emerged from man's perception of the essential connexion between his own thought and will and the movements of his immediate instruments, the parts of his own body, especially the hands and feet, whereof those tools which are not parts of the body are merely prolongations.

Another point which is missed or imperfectly understood is the importance of personification for the oldest stages especially. Frequently the concepts of person and spirit are not distinguished. Personification makes it easier to form even an outward connexion between the person and the desire to find a cause, and this occurs at the very birth of the idea of causality. Thus the concept of personal Supreme Beings is easier, logically and psychologically, than that of impersonal ones.

Thus we see the true importance for religion of normal and ordinary events, and can correct the over-emphasis laid by this movement, as a rule, on extraordinary happenings.

3. THE VOLITIONALIST AND SOCIOLOGICAL THEORIES OF MAGIC

H. HUBERT, M. MAUSS, E. DURKHEIM, L. LÉVY-BRUHL

It is a surprising fact that Frazer, the most energetic collector of the facts regarding totemism, has never put forward a volitionalist and sociological theory of magic, but remains true to his intellectualist hypothesis. For no one can have learned so soon or so well as he how closely totemism and magic are connected. Spencer and Gillen's discovery of the Central Australians with their wealth of magic rites, so inseparable from their remarkable form of totemism, almost compelled him, one would think, to adopt a volitionalist theory ; but, as he had long lacked any predisposition that way, he did not essentially modify his intellectualist attitude.

These same Australian data had a quite different effect on a series of French researchers, fellow-countrymen of Auguste Comte. There sociology was in the air they breathed, so to speak. In 1896, E. Durkheim founded *L'Année sociologique* as the principal mouthpiece of the new sociological school, which owed its existence to him. Early in its career appeared his article *De la définition des phénomènes religieuses* [11], in which we already find the characteristic features of this school, its over-emphasis on the community and its undervaluing of the individual, which often amounts to completely ignoring him.

(*a*) This characteristic likewise appears in the first important work in which this school dealt with magic and its relation to religion. This was the *Exquisse d'une théorie générale de la Magie* of H. Hubert and M. Mauss [12], two leading disciples of Durkheim. These two authors trace the labyrinthine and often unintelligible laws of causality as magic understands it to

' a social agreement, which translates a social need . . . the need, being felt by all, suggests the goal to all ; between these two extremes an infinite number of terms may be intercalated . . . a choice must be made between these, and it is made, either by the force of tradition, the authority of some famous magician, or the sudden unanimous pressure of the entire group ' (p. 126).

This universally felt want keeps up confidence in magic, owing to the feelings of excitement, expectation, hope and

[11] *Année Sociologique*, Vol. II (1897–8), p. 1 *sqq.*
[12] *Ibid.*, VII (1902–3), pp. 1–140.

fear which are connected with it and are capable of rising at times to hallucination or illusion. These conditions are collective, the result of a blending of the individual's feelings with those of the whole community. From this common source, the social organism, arise both magic and religion, according to these authors (see p. 138) ; religion, according to them, is ' essentially and in all its parts a collective phenomenon ' (p. 86).

Belief in magic and the confidence felt therein can indeed be to a large extent traced to the pressure of strongly felt collective needs and collective emotions. However, it must not be forgotten, in the first place, that the original belief is formed in the individual mind and must be explained with reference to it ; here King's explanation, drawing attention to the effects of unusual experiences, is good, though partial. Then later on, the choice of magical materials, which are as various as humanity itself, is strongly characterized by the presence of individuality, especially that of the magician.[13] As regards religion, on the other hand, its source is as a rule the far wider sphere of the workings of a natural desire to classify and find reasons for normal, ordinary things and events. It moves smoothly and without arousing excitement ; the judgements as to classification and causation are in a still greater majority of cases individual products ; and they must of necessity be first developed in the individual. It is not till later, when religion is an affair of doctrine and cult, with more rigid ceremonial forms, that the influence of the community makes itself felt ; but even so, it is expressed for the most part in the quiet and uniform power of tradition, rather than in states of excitement, to say nothing of hallucinations. These last are everywhere a religious phenomenon of late date.

(b) One of these two authors, M. Mauss, published in the same year (1904), in Paris, a monograph under the title of *L'Origine des pouvoirs magiques dans les sociétés australiennes*. It was in fact *en partie destiné a montrer sur quelle substructure de documents critiques repose notre théorie* [14], those, namely, on which the authors had founded their joint work [15]. How

---

[13] See also J. Meier, *Die Zauberei bei den Küstenbewohnern der Gazelle-Halbinsel, Neupommern*, in *Anthropos*, Vol. VII, 1913, pp. 5–11.

[14] Mauss, *op. cit.*, p. 3, note 2.

[15] It gave no references to authorities, *pour ne pas dépasser la place dont nous pouvions disposer dans l'Année Sociologique*. This, for a scientific periodical, is surely rather naïve !

weak a foundation for so wide-reaching a theory is laid by this exclusive attention to Australia, and in particular Central Australia, we shall see further on.

(c) Although they look for support preferably, I might say almost exclusively, to Australian and Central Australian data, they nevertheless do not succeed in discovering the intimate connexion of the Central Australian facts in particular with the local totemism. This does not apply to the leader of the school, E. Durkheim himself. He had occupied himself early with an exact study of totemism,[16] and in his principal work, *Les formes élémentaires de la vie religieuse*, of which we have already spoken, see p. 115 *sqq.*, he had recognized that totemism and magical power are very close akin. Hence his theory of the origin of religion, while it is totemistic and sociological, must also be classed as belonging to the volitionalist form of the Theory of Magic ; in his opinion, totemism is nothing but the appearance in concrete form of this same magical power.

As a matter of fact he devotes a separate chapter, the sixth (p. 268 *sqq.*) of his work, to the *notion de principe du mana totémique et l'idée de force*. In this he expounds the origin of the ' holiness ' of totemic animals or plants, etc., persons, tabus, emblems, and rites from one general principle.

' In other words ', he says, ' totemism is the religion, not of this or that animal, man, or image, but of a kind of nameless, impersonal force, to be found in each of these, but not to be confused with any of them. . . . Using the word in a very wide sense, we may say that it is the god which every totemic cult adores. Only, it is an impersonal god, with no name, and with no history, immanent in the world and diffused throughout a countless multitude of objects ' (p. 269).

This power he recognizes in the Sioux *wakan*, the Iroquois *orenda*, the Algonkin *manitu*, the Melanesian *mana* and the Australian *arungquiltha*.

There is a great deal of truth in all this, and Durkheim has done very good service in grasping the close connexion of magical force with totemism. His examples, however, Algonkin *manitu*, Iroquois *orenda* and Melanesian *mana*, are ill chosen, for some of them do not belong to totemic races at all, and also they are faulty for another reason, as we shall see. Another serious defect is his exclusive attention to Central Australian totemism, as already pointed out, p. 116 *sqq.*

[16] See his article *Sur le Totémisme*, in *L'Année Sociologique*, Vol. V (1900–1).

(*d*) It would at first sight appear impossible to include under the volitionalist form of the magical theory the three works of L. Lévy-Bruhl, *Les fonctions mentales dans les sociétés inférieures* (Paris, 1910), *La mentalité primitive* (Paris, 1922) and *L'âme primitive* (Paris, 1927). His preoccupation with the origin of concepts, one would think, places him in the intellectualist wing of this theory. However, a somewhat closer examination of these books suffices to show how volitionalist they really are. Their object in fact is to expose the error of the intellectualist treatment of man's mental development hitherto in use. The author sets out to prove that primitive man, the forerunner of the higher civilizations, does not start from logical and causal thought, but is essentially 'prelogical' and 'prenotional' in his mental processes ; that is, that he has not as yet any such things as concepts, or reasoning from premises to conclusions, while the idea of a cause has never occurred to him. That which essentially influences his mental life is rather the general atmosphere, of totemism especially, and the emotions aroused thereby. He feels himself one with the (totemic) group in which he lives, so completely indeed that he has neither any feeling for his own identity nor any inkling that such principles as those of identity and contradiction exist.

A long list of serious objections must be raised against this doctrine. Here are some of them. In the first place, Lévy-Bruhl nowhere gives a scientifically accurate definition, or any other for that matter, of what he means by 'primitive'. In his first book he uses that term to include all non-Europeans, including the civilized races. In the second, possibly as a result of my criticism [17], he has less to say of the latter. Secondly, we look in vain in his works for the slightest indication of any arrangement of the various groups of peoples which he mentions in their historical sequence ; in this respect he indulges in a wild confusion, to be equalled only in the writings of the oldest Evolutionists ; all uncivilized races are flung without distinction into one huge melting-pot. Thirdly, and in consequence of this, he fails to make the least attempt at a historical arrangement of the several stages of prelogical thought, or any investigation of the question whether there is more prelogicality in the earlier or the later stages, or whether it is more marked in the one or the other. Consequently, it is impossible that there should be any determination of how it arose. Fourthly, he com-

[17] See *Anthropos*, Vol. VII, 1912, p. 268.

pletely neglects the fact that there are plenty of prelogical states to be found even in the civilization of Europe and America (witness our fashions, our ' movements ', our superstitions, our prejudices, yes, and the theories and ideas of certain expositors of ' exact ' sciences) ; and on the other hand wide fields of activity, theoretical and practical, in which the savage is guided by the light of rational, causal thinking. And fifthly, it is astonishing how much sheer ignorance he is capable of displaying in such pronouncements as the following : that primitive man comprehends *nothing* as we do ; that he refers *everything* to a mystical [i.e., non-natural] origin ; that he *never* regards sickness or death as due to natural causes ; that no such thing as an accident exists for him ; that he does *nothing* without magical means ; that he derives *everything* from a universal magical force ; and that he knows *no* difference between man and beast.[18]

In this last respect and in the absence of any restraint on his Evolutionism, Lévy-Bruhl makes the collapse of the sociological and volitionalist school perfectly clear. Even his merit of having drawn attention to features of savage thought which had not hitherto received enough attention is much lessened by the exaggerations which cloud the truth ; also by the innumerable confusions between different mental states, belonging to wholly different cultures or coming from totally different sources, which prevent us getting a clear picture.

For good refutations of Lévy-Bruhl's ' prelogism ', see O. Leroy, *La raison primitive*, Paris, 1927 ; R. Allier, *Le non-civilisé et nous*, Paris, 1927 ; A. Goldenweiser, *Early Civilization*, New York, 1922, pp. 380–9. Meanwhile, at a recent meeting of the Société française de Philosophie, a thorough discussion took place (June 1, 1929), following on a lecture by Lévy-Bruhl. P. Aupiais, Franz Boas, L. Brunschwieg, R. Lenoir, X. Léon, M. Mauss, P. Rivet, M. Blondel and E. Meyerson took part, thus representing ethnology, sociology, psychology and philosophy. Scarcely one of them defended the lecturer's fundamental principles, while on the other hand he was subjected to wholesome criticism, some of it positive. He himself denied that his ' prelogical ' mentality was intended to be entirely different from the logical thought of civilized peoples, and also declined the suggestion of Mauss that he should rely for the explanation of his theory wholly on the sociological school of Durkheim. See *Bulletin de la soc. fran. de philos.*, Vol. XXIX, 1929, pp. 105–39.

[18] For an appalling list of such unintelligibilities, see O. Leroy, *La raison primitive*, pp. 47–51.

4. THE EMOTIONALIST THEORIES OF MAGIC

(a) THE EARLIER DEVELOPMENTS : R. R. MARETT, E. S. HARTLAND

(a) If the belief which prevailed for a while were true, that R. R. Marett was the founder or at all events the pioneer of the theory of magic, the latter would have appeared first in the emotionalist form. But I have shown that eight years earlier, J. H. King had led the way with a full-blown magical theory which was rather intellectualist than emotionalist. It is true that the latter scholar found no followers ; so it may after all be held that it was Marett who gave the first impulse to the opening of the period of what we may style Magism, in his article *Preanimistic Religion*.[19]

This article, in quantity and in quality, presents a sharp contrast to King's good development of all sides of his theory in the two volumes of his work. The author hopes he will be ' acquitted of any design to dogmatize prematurely about Religious Origins ' ; his proofs are ' culled hastily from the few books nearest to hand ' [and are not spoken of as proofs, but simply as illustrations] ; they are put together ' on the chance of their proving useful to this or that researcher who may be in need of an odd piece of twine wherewith to tie his *scopae dissolutae* into a handy, if temporary, besom '. Moreover, by his own admission, the examples which he produces from the worship of stones, plants, corpses, diseases and blood (pp. 175–80 = 14–29) mostly belong, not to a preanimistic stage, but to that of animism ; they therefore can hardly prove anything for the greater antiquity of magic and for an origin of religion going further back into the past.[20]

Marett, therefore, founds his theory of the origin of magic and religion on an insecure basis. There is no mistaking the emotionalist character of this hypothesis. It traces the origin of religion to the ' emotions of Awe, Wonder and the like ', which are wellnigh universal ; to the ' vague but dreadful attributes of Powers ' which man saw in the things around him, and ascribed to a ' mysterious or " supernatural " something felt ' and not comprehended (pp. 174, 168 = 19, 11).

But primeval man was far from being the sluggish dreamer

[19] Originally delivered as an address to the Folklore Society on November 15, 1899, and then published in *Folk-Lore*, Vol. XI (1900), pp. 162–82 [republished in *The Threshold of Religion*, London, 1909, pp. 1–32].

[20] See also *Threshold of Religion*, p. viii *sq.*

that Marett seems to picture him as having been, standing
in stupid astonishment and fright at the world that was so
new to him. The prehistoric tools and weapons and those
of the ethnologically oldest peoples of to-day are alone enough
to show that he was a vigorous and daring man of action.
To begin with, his mental powers made their way through
nature and analysed her phenomena ; his synthetic activities
mastered her by forming generalizing and classificatory
ideas ; he grasped the conception of cause and effect, and
then adapted that to the relationship of means to end. His
means, to effect the ends he desired, were his tools, which
he invented and used. Now all this sufficed to lead him to
a real religion, to the recognition of a personal Supreme Being ;
for he was able to apply these same mental powers to the
contemplation of the universe as a whole.

Marett indeed already makes an advance towards this
consideration when he writes, speaking of early times,

' There arises in the region of human thought a powerful impulse
to objectify and even personify the mysterious or " supernatural "
something felt ' (p. 168 = 11).

It is a pity that he did not extend and deepen this valuable
recognition of the great antiquity of personification.[21]

(β) Some years later another British writer, E. Sidney
Hartland, put forth an emotionalist theory of magic which
was more thoroughly developed, in his presidential address
to Section H (Anthropology) of the British Association at
its meeting in York, 1906. A shorter form of this was delivered
as a presidential address to the Third International Congress
for the History of Religions, in the section dealing with savage
religions,[22] and it was expanded in the essay on *The Relations of Religion and Magic*, which is the first chapter of his
collected work *Ritual and Belief: Studies in the History of
Religion*. London, 1914. I base my remarks on the second
of these publications.

Hartland starts from the same point as Marett, with the
feeling of awe and wonder, of a power behind the phenomena,
with which primitive man was oppressed. But he increases
the emphasis already laid by Marett on personification, and
makes primitive man interpret these phenomena as manifestations of a personality possessed of needs and potential-

[21] See in general Schmidt, *Ursprung*, Vol. I, ed. 2, pp. 507–10.
[22] *Trans. of the Third Intern. Conf. for the Hist. of Religions*, Oxford,
1908, pp. 21–32.

ities akin to his own. Such personalities he would then endeavour to conciliate or to control by means of his own potentiality, that power which is called *orenda* by the Iroquois, *wakan* by the Sioux, *manitowi* by the Algonkins, and *mana* by the Melanesians (p. 28). The characteristic thing about this potentiality is its vagueness, even though it is found only in persons. In order to conciliate or to control this non-human, ' supernatural ' personality, man would employ the same means as he used in dealing with other human personalities about him, namely his own words and actions. These words and deeds of man were either magical or religious rites ; religious, if directed towards personalities which he must approach with fear and reverence ; magical, if towards those which he thought he could coerce. But the difference between the two is not constant.

' Man's *orenda*, or at least the *orenda* of some men, reaches often even to the coercion of the transcendent beings of his imagination. Hence magical procedure is found interwoven with the most solemn religious rites.' The beginning of the next paragraph sums the matter up. ' Thus according to this theory, magic and religion spring from the same root. Nay, I should hardly be wrong if I changed the metaphor and said : Magic and religion are the two faces of one medal.'

Here, in the first place, all that was urged in criticism of Marett can be repeated with regard to Hartland. He, like Marett, fails to recognize the rational and causal nature of primitive thought and action ; now these have nothing to do with magical powers and consequently cannot be subsumed under the idea of *orenda*, or whatever it is to be called. Moreover, Hartland does not see that even in the earliest period there is discovered by means of these rational and causal powers a personality superior to all others, which at that time and among these oldest peoples no one, not even ' some men ', imagined he could coerce by means of *orenda*, but in relation to whom only prayers, submission and obedience were employed. Hence among these oldest peoples, magical procedure is by no means ' interwoven with the most solemn religious rites ', but, if it exists at all, exists alongside them and quite separate from them. Nor is this all. While genuinely religious actions and expressions are clearly and definitely to be found, and govern the main lines of their life, it would seem that magical expressions are there only as unconnected and occasional phenomena, growing chiefly on the edges and in the dusty corners of their existence, like any other weed. It is unthinkable that these two forces, so different in quality and in size, should have sprung from the same root.[23]

(b) The Later Emotionalist Developments: K. Beth, Archbishop Söderblom, R. Otto, J. W. Hauer, G. Wobbermin

It is extraordinary that for nearly a decade no scholar was found to develop the emotionalist form of the Theory of Magic any further, and that in England it quite died out.* Its further development had to wait for the middle of the second decade of this century, and then it took place in Germany. The circumstance that it is chiefly Protestant theologians who have developed it justifies us in conjecturing that other causes have been at work besides mere adherence to the views of the two British pioneers of what we may call emotionalist magism. I find these causes in the developments of the psychology of religion which took place under the guidance of the late William James and his pupils, E. Starbuck, M. J. B. Pratt and others. These psychologists took their material chiefly † from the emotional experiences of members of the Protestant Churches of North America and also of England; whence it came about that through the agency of Wobbermin and Stählin their results became known to Protestant theologians in Germany also. The seed fell on fruitful soil, particularly because these circles, under the pressure of scientific and still more of philosophical and historical attacks, were coming more and more to doubt whether religion was tenable at all from the rationalistic and intellectualist point of view. They therefore welcomed the religious psychology of this American school, which, being pragmatist, took as its standard of importance and value not intellectual verity but the active power to produce results [asking, in its own language, not so much ' Is it true ? ' as ' Will it work ? ']. It is easy to see that this whole movement had much in common with the Theory of Magic, and with the idea of an imper-

---

[23] See in general Schmidt, *op. cit.*, pp. 354–63.

* [So far from dying out, it continued and still continues in full vigour. Father Schmidt has been misled by the absence of formal treatises dealing with it at length. The ten years in question for practical purposes reduce to six, as they include the whole period of the Great War.]

† [Somewhat of an exaggeration, see James, *Varieties of Religious Experience*, Lectures XI–XVII.]

sonal power which that theory placed at the beginning of the whole development.

(a) Probably the first expression of such a line of thought as this is to be found in K. Beth's *Religion und Magie bei den Naturvölkern*[24]. He criticizes adversely the theories of magic hitherto put forth by Frazer, Preuss, Marett and Vierkandt, and insists on the profound distinction between magic and religion, which cannot be derived one from the other. Before either he postulates an indifferent stage, in which neither magic nor religion yet existed, lasting for an unknown length of time. In this stage, man received only general impressions from life ; he reacted to these in two ways. He might have self-centred consciousness of his own powers ; this produced magic. He might, again, humbly recognize a power higher than himself ; and hence came religion. The two may therefore be of equal antiquity (p. 226).

But religion too had its first beginnings in something impersonal ; it started from the recognition of an unknown power, beyond experience and above nature (p. 236). From this idea arose ' not among all peoples ' but only ' here and there, as the result of a continued process of personification ', the idea of a supreme God (p. 228). The fundamental belief in power was ' as yet not a belief in a god in the narrower sense of the word, but capable of being the root of a lofty theism ' (p. 238).

Here we must note that Beth's supposed ' premagical and prereligious period ' of unknown duration is pure assumption. It is a case of filling a gap in the argument by speculation, and neither has nor can have any ethnological facts to support it. Moreover, we miss in this theory precise historical determination of the ethnological age of the peoples which Beth adduces to show the great antiquity of the belief in an impersonal power. He mentions the Melanesians, Polynesians, Sioux-Dacota, Algonkins, Iroquois, Sea Dyaks, Bantu, Malagasy and Central Australians ; but not one of these goes back to pure primitive culture, most of them belong to the primary cultures, either patrilineal and totemic or matrilineal and agricultural, and others, as the Malagasy and Bantu, are actually as late as the secondary cultures.

Now it is just in the primitive culture that we find no trace

---

[24] [' Religion and Magic among Savages '], Berlin, 1914 [ed. 2, under title *Religion und Magie*, Leipzig and Berlin, 1927.] See also his smaller work, *Die Urreligion* [' Primeval Religion '], Berlin-Lichterfelde, 1917.

of a universal belief in impersonal powers, but the quite concrete and decidedly personal Supreme Being. But if we
examine the various peoples among which Beth tries to find
this impersonal power, the result is that the great majority
of them are agricultural races, but with an admixture of
totemism. Now if the magical ideas peculiar to totemism
combine with the belief in spirits belonging to matrilineal,
agricultural peoples, we have the very conditions necessary
to turn magic, which in itself is material and objective, into
an affair of spirits and spells. The phantasmal spirits of
their belief receive an access of more robust potency, and
the idea of such potency takes on the peculiar, unstable form,
fluctuating back and forth between personal and impersonal,
material and spiritual, of those powers of which Beth speaks.
These powers are of very great significance for the further
development of religion, that is, for its disintegration ; but
they throw no light on its origin, for they did not then exist
as yet.[25]

(β) Archbishop Nathan Söderblom, of Upsala, admits
into his work *Das Werden des Gottesglaubens* [26] a good deal
which might rank him as a member of the intellectualist
school ; but on the crucial points he shows himself an emotionalist.

He shows diagreement with Beth in the following proposition :

' In the beginning, so far as we can discover it, magic and religion
are unrecognizably blended with each other ' and in allowing no
more than the beginnings of a distinction ; ' Even in primitive man,
however, we can trace the germ of a differentiation between the
two ' (p. 223).

This differentiation appears in the recognition of those
personal high gods whom Söderblom calls ' originators '
(*Urheber*), as regards whom he shows himself more just to
modern historical investigation than Beth.

However, this admission loses much of its value from the
circumstance that Söderblom will acknowledge this Supreme
Being only as an ' originator ', that is, as satisfying human

[25] Cf. Schmidt, *op. cit.*, pp. 592–5.
[26] [' Development of the Belief in God '], Leipzig, 1916 ; second
and shorter ed., 1926. The following criticisms are founded on the
first ed. Cf. also, by the same author, *Einführung in die Religionsgeschichte* [' Introduction to the History of Religion '], Leipzig, 1920,
and his revision (Berlin, 1920) of Tiele's *Kompendium der Religionsgeschichte* [' Outline History of Religion '].

curiosity concerning the origin of things, in other words the tendency to find a cause. He will not admit that such beings are real deities, much less the only deities, because he contends that they have no cult and no sacrifices, and that therefore man's relation to them is not a religion. But he arrives at this view only by means of an almost complete neglect of the really primitive peoples, and an unjustifiable emphasis on the latest Australian stratum, the Arunta of Central Australia. To these alone he devotes sixteen pages (116–33), which is more than he allows to all the other peoples and races put together (pp. 133–46). He also takes the average of these other peoples, which of course results in an unjustifiable prominence being given to the faded, unworshipped high gods of the later stages.

Where Söderblom, however, agrees with Beth and shows himself a good emotionalist in his version of the Theory of Magic is, that he allows little importance to the element of personality in religion, and definitely places its essential being in the impersonal, provided only that the impersonal be conceived fervently and whole-heartedly as ' something holy '. This he considers a more important criterion of essential religion than the belief in or the worship of a god (pp. 143 and 211). Here again he does not see that, in primitive times especially, the universal originating activity of the Supreme Being, who is decidedly personal, together with the great importance even in secular life of the individual personality, leaves no room for the religious acknowledgement of impersonal, neuter powers.

(γ) The strongest emphasis is laid on the emotional side, indeed on irrationality, by R. Otto, throughout his work *Das Heilige : über das Irrationale in der Idee des Göttlichen und sein Verhältnis zum Rationalen.*[27] He begins with sharply adverse criticism of the intellectualist attitude of earlier researchers in the science of religion ; according to him, they have quite missed the real essence of religion, which is irrational. The particular form this irrationality takes is ' the Holy ', from which he even excludes ethical elements, as not belonging to religion. He further describes it as ' numinous ', and declares that it cannot be intellectually comprehended, but only felt by intuition.

[27] Breslau, ed. 1, 1917 ; ed. 9, 1922. [Literally, ' The Holy. On the Irrational in the Idea of Deity and its relation to the Rational '. English translation, ' The Idea of the Holy ', by J. W. Harvey, Oxford University Press, 1926 (fourth impression).]

The historical sequence of the development of religion is in his opinion as follows (p. 146) :

' At the beginning of the development of religion there stand certain remarkable things which form as it were its vestibule . . . such things as the ideas of purity and impurity, beliefs concerning the dead and their tendance, concerning the soul and the cult of souls; magic, folk-tales, myths, the worship of natural objects . . . the curious ideas concerning " power " . . . fetishism and totemism, cult of beasts and plants, daimonism and polydaimonism ; in all of which there is no more than a certain haunting element of the numinous. Before all these vestibules came a yet earlier " stage," in which these all existed only as the purely natural products of primitive imagination, belonging to the times of primeval simplicity, in which they had not yet even that much flavour of the numinous.'

Only after passing these ' vestibules ' do men conceive the figure of the ' daimon ', which is still only half personal (p. 152), and only after passing through various stages does fright at demons rise to the level of fear of gods, or of God. Hence an endless amount of time must have elapsed and a vast process of development have been gone through before the first element of rational belief in a personal deity emerged.

In maintaining the existence of a supposed profane stage, previous to and free from all religious feeling, Otto follows Beth, but with this difference, that he makes not the faintest attempt at proving any of his propositions whatsoever. If we must say even of Beth's prereligious and premagical stage that it is the product of pure speculation, the same is true of Otto's ' previous stage '; but not even that much can be said of his ' vestibules ', which are in plain fact the kaleidoscopic result of purely arbitrary dealing, and nothing else.

It is alleged that Otto's book is of value and importance less as a contribution to the history of religion than to the psychology of the subject. But F. K. Feigel in his treatise *Das Heilige* : *kritische Abhandlungen über R. Ottos gleichnamiges Buch* [28] has proved sufficiently that Otto makes serious mistakes also in the psychology and the philosophy of religion. I have gone fully into its historical blunders in my work *Menschheitswege zum Gotterkennen.* [29]

[28] Haarlem, 1929. [' The Holy : critical studies of R. Otto's work with the same title.']
[29] [' Humanity's ways to the knowledge of God '], Munich and Kempten, 1923.

(δ) The emotional side of religion is considered by J. W.
Hauer in his work *Die Religion, ihr Werden, ihr Sinn, ihre
Wahrheit. Erstes Buch : das religiöse Erlebnis auf den unter-
sten Stufen.*[30]   He brings to his task not only a good knowledge of the methods and literature of psychology but also
remarkable ability for the subject.   By his handling of it,
he provides valuable complements and corrections to the
one-sided views of sundry intellectualist researchers into
the science of religion.   His mistake, however, lies in confining
his attention wholly to the emotional aspect, he being of the
opinion that religion in what he calls its lower stages consists
of religious ' experiences ' (pp. 33, 38).   He goes further
and declares that ' primitive religion is to a very large extent
ecstatic ' (pp. 68, 85 *sqq.*), meaning that it is the result of
the intensest form of religious experience, ecstasy.   This
primitive religious experience, he holds, is irrational.

Hauer can be guilty of such over-emphasis on the ' affective '
side of religion only because he has almost wholly omitted
to examine the historical evidence for the ethnological age
of the primitive strata.   He is consequently unstable in his
views, and does not venture to put forth his own chronology
as such but only as an ' auxiliary construction '.   It is contained in a note on p. 310 and runs as follows :   ' Belief in
mana, and magic, in other words primitive panpsychism ;
animism and resultant polydaimonism ;   tellurian monotheism
(worship of Mother Earth) ;   formation of a tellurian polytheism ;   celestial monotheism (worship of Father Sky) ;
celestial and astral deities ;   . . . ethical and spiritual monotheism.'

He really has refuted himself by his admission, as early
as p. 6 of his book, that the belief in a celestial high god is
to be found nearly, if not quite, everywhere among primitive
peoples.   He does indeed state that he is not competent to
decide whether this belief represents the poor remainder of
a once fuller form or is something inchoate and as yet incomplete, and is of opinion that ' the one attitude of mind appropriate to the subject is extreme reserve and caution '.   If
only Hauer, and others as well, had exercised this same
' extreme reserve and caution ' in dealing with beliefs in magic
and *mana* !   If Hauer had also equipped himself with a better
knowledge of ethnology and its appropriate methods, he

[30] [' Religion, its genesis, meaning and truth.   Book One :   the
religious experience at the lowest levels ').   Berlin, Stuttgart and
Leipzig, 1923.   The second volume has not yet appeared.

would have realized that the ethical and spiritual monotheism which in his system forms the last stage is to be found just in the oldest strata ; that belief in *mana* and magic does not reach its full development till we reach totemism, in the primary culture ; that tellurian monotheism, or the cult of Mother Earth, belongs to no earlier stratum than the secondary agricultural and matrilineal ; that celestial monotheism has its roots partly in primitive culture and partly in the primary nomadic culture ; and consequently, that we have to do, not with one line of development, but with several parallel ones, each following its own path in the primary cultures and not blending until a later period, in the secondary and tertiary stages.[31]

It remains therefore for Hauer to supplement his remarkable gifts for and training in psychology with an equivalent training in historical research ; thus only will he be able to understand the data of religion as a whole and to see them in their true succession.[32]

(ε) Hitherto we have been obliged to review a whole succession of Protestant scientific theologians, who recognize the existence of religion even where they find only an irrational idea of something impersonal, or even consider this as having been originally the only form. The real meaning of this is an attempt to retain the actuality and importance of religion, at any cost of concession to the attacks hitherto made by Evolutionism in the fields of history and philosophy. The whole process is sketched by J. H. Leuba, a Protestant and a psychologist, from his own point of view, in a work entitled *A Psychological Study of Religion*.[33] After explaining that in earlier epochs of religion the personal Deity occupied the foreground, he goes on as follows :

' In a second phase, this formless but personal God was gradually shorn of all the qualities which make for individuality. He became the passionless Absolute in which all things move and have their being. Thus the personifying work of centuries is undone, and humanity, after having, as it were, lived throughout its infancy and youth under the controlling eye and the active guidance of personal divinities, finds itself, on reaching maturity, bereft of these sources of life. The present religious crisis marks the difficulty in the way of an adaptation to the new situation. As belief in a personal God seems no longer possible, man seeks an impersonal, efficient

[31] For these stages, see Chapter XIV, sect. 3, p. 237 *sqq.*
[32] Cf. Schmidt, *op. cit.*, pp. 605-9.   [33] New York, 1912.

substitute, belief in which will not mean disloyalty to science (p. 125).

Protestantism, especially Liberal Protestantism, is for quite definite reasons particularly exposed to and particularly unable to cope with the effects and the assaults of this 'science'; consequently it has gone further in yielding ground to it than other faiths.* It must be admitted, however, that one of the best and most thorough refutations of these assaults and these concessions is furnished by a Protestant scholar, K. Girgensohn, in his work *Der seelische Aufbau des religiösen Lebens*.[34] In opposition to the exaggerations of Emotionalism and Irrationalism, he re-emphasizes the fundamental importance of the intellectual element in all religious occurrences. And we shall make the acquaintance in a moment of another Protestant scholar, whose keen wits have done battle with the errors and dangers of Irrationalism, Emotionalism, and impersonality in religious matters, although he himself has not been able to keep entirely free of them.

(ζ) I mean G. Wobbermin, who was, it is true, one of the first to introduce into Germany the North American movement in religious psychology of James and his school, but whose great caution and circumspection would not allow him to draw all its conclusions with regard to the problems of religion. He has in consequence escaped many errors, and also given much positive and valuable help towards solving the problem. However, he has not quite avoided such mistakes. He expresses his own views in his principal work, *Das Wesen der Religion*,[35] which was preceded by an article, *Die Frage nach den Anfängen der Religion in religionspsychologischer Bedautung*.[36] I base my criticisms on the larger work, referring only here and there to the other.

Wobbermin deals at length with the question of primitive high gods and recognizes their existence (pp. 334–50). He

---

* [To anyone who knows Protestant thought the above remarks need no criticism ; indeed, the rest of this paragraph and the following one largely refute them.]

[34] ['The Building of the Religious Life in the Soul'] ; Leipzig, 1922. See also his inaugural lecture, *Religionspsychologie Religionswissenschaft und Theologie*, delivered at Leipzig and published there in 1922.

[35] ['The Nature of Religion'], Book I, Leipzig, 1921 ; Book II (with continuous pagination), Leipzig, 1922.

[36] ['The Question of the Origin of Religion and its importance for Religious Psychology']. In *Zeitschrift für angewandte Psychologie*, Vol. IX, 1915, pp. 333–90.

refuses to accept Tylor's explanation of them as the products of Christian missionary influence, holding that the examples of them are too numerous and too closely connected with the secret tribal initiations. He further refuses to admit that these deities are inactive, as has been alleged, or if they are, supposes this inactivity to be a thing of later growth ; in his opinion, the common occurrence of the relation of son and father among these high gods is a particularly clear proof that they have an actively religious character (p. 83 *sqq.*).

As to the question whether the first object of religious activity was a person or a thing, he is indeed of opinion that the former alternative cannot be postulated without demur by psychologists of religion, but adds,

'The tendency to personalize the object of religious interest is really one of the fundamental factors in all phenomena which have religious experience behind them ' (p. 169).

Accordingly he holds that a belief in *mana* could have started religion going only ' occasionally ', and further, that examples of such a belief in primitive religion are to be considered only as rather rare peripheral or border-line phenomena (p. 174 *sqq.*).

Unfortunately Wobbermin does not succeed in sufficiently distinguishing the lower elements of the most ancient and primitive religion from the higher ones according to the methods of ethnology and the history of culture. This is especially true as regards the belief in high gods. So he begins to make psychological conjectures at a point where historical research has still something to say. This is true especially of his treatment of my sketch of South-East Australian religion. He does indeed say in this connexion that the services which my studies in this field have rendered ' must be unreservedly recognized, all criticism notwithstanding, and deserve the heartiest thanks '. He also passes the following judgement on the research into culture-horizons (p. 385) :

'This principle of examining horizons or strata of culture undoubtedly means that science is provided with a new and very valuable tool, and its worth has already been shown in many ways.'

While as for the defects which he finds in my results from the point of view of the psychology of religion, I have elsewhere shown [37] that his criticisms spring either from imperfect acquaintance with the ethnological facts or from too great a trust in the competence of psychology.

But all these are but defects of detail. Where Wobbermin goes wrong on a large scale and fundamentally—for this, notwithstanding all his previous merits, he eventually does —is in his account of the relation between religion and magic. It must be admitted that even here he emphasizes their essential difference and also, for good reasons, rejects the theories of Durkheim, Frazer, and Leuba, that magic came first (pp. 355 *sqq.*, 371 *sqq.*). But at last he expresses his own opinion, which is that the two have always been closely related one to another, always 'contained in each other' [*ineinander*], as he puts it (pp. 174 *sqq.*, 265 *sqq.*, 350). Indeed, he arrives at this proposition :

' The great mass of the phenomena which come into question show religion and magic side by side in one way or another. Magic without religion cannot be historically proved ever to have existed, while religion without magic is to be found only in Christianity ; and indeed even there not always and everywhere as an accomplished fact, but at least set up as an ideal ' (p. 362). A little earlier (p. 350) he had summed up his position thus : ' Religion, magic and mythology seem to have been originally contained in each other. . . . For that very reason we may find here and there a belief in a god, of decidedly monotheistic colouring, springing direct from the original substratum. For the magical and mythical elements do not belong to the essence of religion itself, although in the course of its historical development they have played a very great part, from the original substratum that belongs to them all alike onwards.'

This is a last surviving fragment of old-fashioned Evolutionism, from which Wobbermin at this point cannot quite free himself. As the belief in a Supreme Being is found in its strongest and clearest form among the oldest peoples in particular, and among all of them without exception ; and as the oldest religion we can reconstruct from a comparison of the later ones is on the same lines ; three things are clear :

(i) That the belief in a god emerges from the ' substratum ' and ' with a strongly monotheistic colouring ', not only ' here and there ', but to the widest possible extent ; being indeed the characteristic of the oldest strata which the history of culture reveals to us.

---

[37] Schmidt, *op. cit.*, p. 479 *sqq.* ; and cf. p. 628 *sqq.*, where I discuss his definition of the relation between the psychology and the history of religion.

(ii) Since it can be historically proved that the belief in one God appears so vigorous and widespread, it is impossible that psychological research can then proceed to show that this kind of theistic belief is, so to speak, on an equal footing as to strength and value with mythology and magic, or blended with them both in an undifferentiated something, to say nothing of all three being ' contained in one another '.

(iii) The above psychological conclusion is in turn historically confirmed when we are able to show that mythology and magic did not attain to their full vigorous development until later periods of culture, and that the earlier they appear the weaker they are.

(c) REVIEW OF THE TWO EMOTIONALIST DEVELOPMENTS

In concluding with a short review of the whole emotionalist and magist movement, it seems to me that there are in it two principal points which we must recognize as representing valuable progress, and two or three weak points to criticize.

(a) I find both the former well set forth in A. Vierkandt's article, *Das Heilige in den primitiven Religionen*.[38] They are, firstly, a partial abandonment of old-fashioned Evolutionism and a recognition of the true nature of religion, which is something *a priori*, something that has always existed, from the very beginning, and did not ' develop ' in course of time out of a previous state in which there was no religion.[39] This advance, however, is more than half lost again if, with Otto, we again admit this ' development ', and allow that believers in it are more or less right in their sketch of the external history of religion. Such an admission is made easier by the mistaken assumption that the original object of religion was an impersonal ' something '.

The second advance is the observation and understanding of the emotional side of religion, which must always be there whenever a really vital religion exists. This is an advance on one-sided intellectualism and no less one-sided ritualism and institutionalism ; since the former of these views can see nothing but religious ideas, the latter nothing but usages and ordinances.[40] Vierkandt rightly accuses the animistic theory of this inadequate intellectualism ; a charge of being purely institutional could by equal justice be brought against the magical and sociological hypotheses of the movement

[38] [' The Holy in primitive religions '] ; in the journal *Die Dioskuren*, Munich, Vol. I, 1922, pp. 285-324.
[39] Vierkandt, *op. cit.*, p. 286 *sqq.*   [40] *Ibid.*, p. 296 *sqq.*

represented by Durkheim and his followers. It is past all doubt that this deeper understanding of the emotional side of religion has led also to a far better grasp of its living warmth and value. For many elements in it which, considered purely intellectually, seem low and uncouth, reveal themselves as much more intimately human if treated from the side of the affections. The individual religious life, also, can probably be more sympathetically grasped if approached from this angle.

(β) But this advantage is nullified or at least diminished by a one-sided neglect, wholly or in large measure, of the intellectual factor in man's spiritual life, and especially by the exclusion from the first beginnings of religion of the search for a cause. This is the first weak and retrograde point in this movement. It cannot be doubted that the mistake is largely due to two tendencies of the present day ; on the one hand, distrust of the objective reality of all thought and consequent prevalence of the idea of Relativity ; on the other, an exaggerated fideism.[41] Also, it cannot be denied that we have here another sequel of old-fashioned Evolutionism, the still existing unwillingness to allow anything but the lower and more imperfect at the beginning. Now that thought, if it can be called thought, which goes purely by feeling and the law of association is the more imperfect ; consequently, on this theory, it must be held to be prior in time to true rational thinking.

From the same muddy spring, in my opinion, comes the second defect of the magistic or psychological movement, which is, that it prefers to postulate at the earliest stage of religion, not the conception of a personality, but of a thing, or at best of an undifferentiated something. For this also would appear to represent a more imperfect or lower stage, which consequently, *secundum legem euolutionis*, must have been the earlier. Such a postulate has the further advantage that it does not involve making morality start at the same time as religion ; for a mere thing cannot be the author of moral commands.

But I believe that yet another cause has contributed to the defect in question. This is the psychological character of this movement, for psychology is mainly concerned with the

[41] Cf. H. Pinard de la Boullaye, *La théorie de l'expérience religieuse*, in *Revue d'histoire ecclésiastique*, Vol. XVII, 1927. [Fideism is the denial of a rational basis for faith. It was condemned, along with Rationalism, *i.e.*, the exclusion of faith altogether, by the Vatican in 1870. See Pinard de la Boullaye, Vol. I, ed. 3, p. 274.]

emotions. In dealing with them it is far easier and far oftener possible to abstract them from their object than in considering conceptual thought ; or rather, in the case of the emotions the subjective aspect, the condition which they bring about in the feeling subject, is so prominent that the cause of emotion, the so-called object, may quite disappear ; but in an intellectual process on the other hand, the object comprehended is in the foreground. Hence it is that this school is able to represent a certain state, a particular attitude of the soul, as the characteristic of religion. Or when it does turn to an object, that object is represented as being a vague ' something ', lacking the clear outlines of a personality. At the highest and best, we have here no more than the darkling and uncanny features of a goblin or a demon.

The mistake is all the more easily made because as a matter of fact these strong emotions did exist at the very beginning. But they were not the result of some ' intuition ' of an undefined ' something ' labelled ' holy ' ; they arose from the profoundest depths of a conviction of the person of the Supreme Being as the Universal Cause. Upon this Being, the ' Father ' who was the author of all good and of nothing but good, were concentrated in the most intense fashion the sunlit emotions of love and gratitude ; to him, as the Creator from nothing of the boundless universe, were directed the amazed admiration of his creature, conscious of its own helplessness ; before him, as the absolute Lord over life and death, his adorers trembled in fear of losing life's highest good ; and before him, as the unescapable Judge and Avenger, they hid themselves in terror and shuddering. Indeed, the emotions aroused by this great and mighty personality were far greater, far more overwhelming, than any caused by a dumb, vague, neuter ' something ' could ever have been.

But it is no *a priori* reasoning of Evolutionary type which enables us to place this sublime personality at the beginning of religious history, instead of a deaf and dumb ' something '. We have but to take in earnest the principle that the lot of mankind, like the life of the individual, is history and must therefore be ascertained by historical research, directly applied if possible, but if this is not practicable, then indirectly. The neglect of this historical method is the third defect which this school suffers from, doubly as we may say ; for both its magical and its psychological aspects are affected.[42]

[42] This, in certain circles, is apparently declared in so many words to be the right, or perhaps I should say the privilege, of this move-

5. POSITIVE AND CRITICAL EVALUATION OF THE VARIOUS THEORIES OF MAGIC

In the preceding sections I have been obliged to deal critically with those scholars who maintain that magic preceded religion. It has been my endeavour throughout not merely to indicate and refute the errors which I discovered, as such, but also to draw attention to the services which these researchers have done to science. These are perfectly real and often by no means slight, and I have tried to increase them by my own efforts. In the conspectus of the whole theory which I now proceed to give, I shall still keep this double object in view.

(a) ORIGIN OF THE IDEA OF MAGIC

I hold that King's account of the real origin of the idea of magic is still the best, while the contributions of Frazer, Hubert and Mauss and Vierkandt do not go so deep, although they form a useful continuation to the work begun by King.

(a) I therefore agree with King that magic begins from the encounter with the new or extraordinary, with that which cannot be brought into any sort of relation to anything else previously and clearly known, and is at the same time too significant to be merely neglected.[43] All such encounters bring about a condition of excitement, and this in turn results in forming associations, which bring the object into connexion with other things after their own fashion, treating it now as cause, now as effect, often as both at once.

(β) At first sight it would seem an original idea, a new and rather volitionalist explanation, as opposed to King's, which may in its turn appear too intellectualist, when Durkheim, Hubert and Mauss put forward the lively social need felt by all as the origin of magic.[44] But we should very quickly go astray if we failed to apply King's principle here also.

ment. W. Brahm, in his article *Über die Wechselwirkung des Rationalen und Irrationalen in der religionsgeschichtlichen Arbeit* [' On the mutual influences of rational and irrational in work on the history of religion '], *Zeitschrift für Theologie und Kirche*, N.F., Vol. I, 1920, p. 102, grants that what he calls historical typology ' employs a method which is chiefly rational ', while ' psychological typology ' according to him has one which is ' chiefly irrational '.

[43] See above, p. 121.   [44] See p. 130 *sqq.*

Not all acutely felt needs become the starting-point of magical practices, but only such as leave helpless before them such knowledge and power as man may hitherto have possessed. So here again, quite in harmony with King's postulates, we find the extraordinary, in face of which it is hopeless to connect the new phenomenon with what is already known and mastered, and so to make it ordinary.   The theory of Hubert and Mauss is thus of value because it emphasizes a particularly active cause of the origin of magic.   For if not only the intellect but also the will is left unsatisfied, the emotional effect is of course all the stronger, and thus the possibility of forming associations of ideas is increased ;   and it is upon such associations that magic depends.

   (γ) Another source, and a far from unproductive one, is tapped by Marett and Vierkandt, whose merit it is to have drawn attention to it by the stress which they lay on the expressive gestures caused by lively emotion.[45]   These gestures in themselves, in their first origin and in their continuance, have nothing magical about them, of course.   They are simple, involuntary, spontaneous discharges of lively emotion, carried out without the intellect or intelligence having part or lot in creating them.   But as soon as the emotion is so far calmed as to allow reflexion to become active, the itch to find a cause for everything will extend to these same gestures. It fails to discover any ' profane ' purpose for them ;   still less, in the then condition of man's mind, is he capable of recognizing them for the purely psychological discharges that they are.   Now the person or the object comes in sight which was the psychological cause of this lively emotion and, with it, of the gestures which expressed the emotion.   The inquirer, who assumes that the gestures had some end in view, can find no other reason for them than this person or object, which he therefore brings into association with them.   The incommensurability still existing here between subject and predicate is bridged again by associations, which are all the more easily produced because the emotion was lively.   In sum, one may describe the process as a kind of popular etymology of expressive gestures.

   (δ) Analogy, which Preuss makes almost the only form in which magic arises, while Vierkandt allows it to be one of the forms, is, if we examine it carefully, not the latter and still less of course the former.   It is rather one of the lines along which the associations move, perhaps the commonest

[45] See p. 127.

of them ; it being these associations which in their turn give rise to magical ideas.[46]

(b) MAGIC AND RELIGION

We may thus hold that King's explanation of the origin of magic is adequate, and also the extensions which Hubert, Mauss and Vierkandt have made therein. But we must begin to dissent as soon as these scholars set about determining the relationship of magic to religion. All have a common fundamental error, their erroneous evaluation and treatment of what King styles ' normal ', Hubert, Mauss and Vierkandt ' profane ', causation. Not one of those I have named realizes its decisive importance for the origin of religion. In addition, their attitudes towards it vary. King simply ignores it ; Preuss, Frazer and above all Lévy-Bruhl boldly put magical causation before normal ; Durkheim, Hubert and Mauss, still more Vierkandt, Hartland, Hopkins and Söderblom try to construct an undifferentiated whole in which the two methods of causation were combined, and suppose that this lay at the beginning of the whole course of development. Beth, who distinguishes sharply between magic and religion, supposes that there existed before either of them a wholly ' profane ' period, from which magic developed in one direction, religion in another. Wobbermin, while admitting that magic and religion are essentially different, declares that from the beginning they have been ' contained one in the other '.[47]

(a) Against all these theories I consider that I have proved in each instance that the facts, psychological, ethnological and prehistoric alike, justify but one assumption, namely the absolute priority of ' normal ' or ' profane ' causation, magical causation being later. I will not repeat what I have said in this connexion, because I intend, in the last volume of my *Ursprung der Gottesidee*, to take up once more the whole demonstration and to go deeper into it. I content myself for the present with emphasizing the fact once again, that we must begin with power, not impotence ; with the positive, not the negative ; with effort and efficiency in the search for a cause, and not with ' primeval stupidity '.

Naturally, this efficiency had its limits, and certainly

---

[46] For Preuss and Vierkandt's views see above, pp. 125, 127. On the whole question see also J. Leuba, *The Varieties, Classification and Origin of Magic*, in *Amer. Anthropologist*, N.S., Vol. XIV, 1912, pp. 350–67.

[47] See p. 147.

narrower limits then than now. But it is quite wrong to
imagine that these limits were then wholly obliterated, that
in consequence man was not even clear as to how far his own
powers would reach, and that this and nothing else is the root
of magic practices, which therefore go back to the very
beginnings of human history. As Vierkandt, speaking of
magical causation, makes magic acting close at hand precede
that which is effective at a distance, so for normal causation
among primitive men we must exclude all *actio in distans*.
Only when primitive man is actually in touch with a thing,
especially when he can reach it with his own hands, does he
feel that ' consciousness of his own power to bring about an
event ' in which Berkeley and Wundt [48] find the psychological
origin of the idea of causality. This feeling of certainty is
also present when the object can be touched immediately
with an implement which all the while remains in the hand
and under the self-controlled influence of the user, like a
craftsman's tool or a weapon for close fighting. It begins to
waver if the implement must be let go, and when some time
must elapse before it reaches the object at which it is directed ;
for during this time human power has ceased to control it,
and foreign, incalculable influences can reach it. This is the
case, for instance, with missiles sent from the hand or a bow.
This region of wavering between knowing and not knowing,
between power and impotence, is the most favourable soil
for those associations to grow up in to which is due the development of magical conceptions. But it is at once apparent
that this region is of later origin and comparatively small
extent.

In relation to everything else, however, and particularly in
relation to all the events in nature and all natural conditions,
primitive man had absolutely no doubts and no hesitation
as to whether he could affect them causally or not. At this
stage, which excluded *actio in distans*, he was perfectly certain
in regard to them that he could not. Moreover, he had not
as yet made many observations on nature which could have
provided him with material for false analogies, such as did
no doubt lead him in later times to imagine the possibility
of influencing natural processes and especially the weather.

Primitive man then felt himself utterly and absolutely
helpless in face of the immensity of nature, except in so far
as he could directly accomplish a result by the work of his

[48] See W. Wundt, *Völkerpsychologie*, Vol. II (*Mythus und Religion*),
pt. 2, p. 183.

own hands ; and that was at first but a small exception.   If, in that whole period, he could not take refuge in magical causation, what refuge did he seek in his sore need of help for his impotence ?

(β) Now appears a second force, which all the authors I have dealt with misestimate or undervalue ; Personification comes into play.   King put the formation of this faculty far too late ; Preuss swamps it with his wrong notion of meta-morphosis ; Vierkandt again does not make it appear early enough ; Hubert and Mauss never mention it ; Marett and Hartland put it fairly early, but cannot draw the right con-clusions from their excellent discovery.   As I will explain in the further course of this work, it is this very tendency to personify, combined with the desire to find a cause, which leads to the recognition of a Supreme Being, who as Creator and Lord of nature has also power over all its activities.   In this period of personification, it is to the Supreme Being that man turns, as one person to another, with words and prayers ; for the prayers are not couched in words only, but the whole body takes part in them, that is to say, they are dramatically expressed.   All this is but the natural result of the personal conception of the universal cause, which is the prevailing one among mankind at this stage.

Magic, on the other hand, is of a conspicuously and entirely impersonal character.   That is to say, it avoids or denies the supreme personal Cause and turns to material objects them-selves, striving, by means of the secret powers latent in them, to reach its ends.   These new methods were capable of finding supporters even in preanimistic days, wherever men, for one reason or another, wished to cast off their reverence for and obedience to the Supreme Being and thrust him into the background.   But it must have been decidedly strengthened when animism began to appear ; for this both drove the Supreme Being still further out of sight and also, by producing the idea of spirit, enabled magic to act at a distance, thus conquering new and wide fields for it and increasing its superiority as against the old personal conception.   Once grasped, magical force would necessarily be more agreeable to man's self-confidence than prayer to another personality than his own.   In the course of time it often developed into a pseudo-science, as astrology by the side of astronomy, alchemy along with chemistry, and so on.   Thus it gained a further advantage, for it could claim to be more impersonally objective ; while the ancient concept of a personality, the belief in a Supreme Being, was more and more discredited as mere anthropomorphism.

(c) Existing Theories of Magic : Their Speculative and Deductive Character

The most perilous defect which attaches itself to all theories of magic so far, and has especially influenced the question of priority as between magic and religion, lies in their almost complete lack of historical research. The phases of development, and in particular their chronological relation to one another, are determined entirely on psychological grounds. Now these, in any given case, can but show us possibilities, ways in which development might take place ; hence all theories of magic hitherto are but cloud-castles, for they lack positive, exact and concrete support.

(a) Their authors should have had their attention drawn to this defect by a fact of which no observer reasonably well trained in ethnology could be ignorant. Neither the extent nor the intensity of the belief in magic is at all uniform for all peoples ; some show more of it, others less. Now which of these two classes of peoples is ethnologically the older and more ' primitive ' ? To try and answer this question on the basis of the development of magic is merely to reason in a circle.

Naturally, it is equally inadmissible to lay down, as is commonly done, the principle that, since the body of man developed out of a bestial state, his mental development must also of necessity have passed at first through such imperfect conditions as that represented by a belief in magic. Even granted the bodily descent of man from the lower animals, it is possible to conceive another origin for the mind, viz., that it came into being suddenly, all at once, at a stroke, so to say.[50] No one of course can doubt for a moment that the Evolutionist conception of the origin of man's body has, consciously or unconsciously, influenced most if not all upholders of the magist theory hitherto.

(β) A further prejudice, namely that among ' savage ' peoples no historical development can be traced, and consequently that no precise determination of the chronological succession

---

[50] For a more detailed discussion, see Schmidt, *Die Stellung der Pygmäenvölker in der Entwicklungsgeschichte des Menschen*, Stuttgart, 1910, p. 301 *sqq.*

of events is possible, is now disposed of by the historical method.[51] This teaches us that the ethnological age of individual peoples can be determined objectively, and there-fore, of course, that of particular elements of their culture, and consequently, in the case we are considering, that of their religious and magical beliefs. It may be impossible to deter-mine the absolute dates ; but at least the relative chronology can be settled. This method therefore has something very important to say as regards the question of which came first, magic or religion.

It has not indeed as yet had time to carry out all the investi-gations necessary to decide the question from all sides. But at least it has already determined one pertinent fact of importance. Every one of the Pygmy peoples, which with-out doubt belong to the oldest strata of humanity, is seen to have magical beliefs and practices only to a relatively small extent, certainly to a less extent than we find them among the greater part of the ethnologically later peoples, whose material culture is on a far higher level.[52] Much the same is true of nearly all peoples of the lowest stratum. In the arctic culture-area, the Caribou Eskimo of the Barren Grounds and the Koryaks display decidedly less magic, and less malign sorcery, than their neighbours ; among the Samoyeds and the Ainu, the comparatively recent origin of magic, which is rather more prevalent here, from foreign sources, can be proved ; among the inhabitants of North Central California and the Old Algonkins only the simpler and less harmful forms of magic are used for the most part, or we may find that they have no genuinely professional sorcerers. In the region of the southern primitive culture, both among the South-East Australians and in Tierra del Fuego, the older, ethnologically speaking, the race is, the weaker is the develop-ment of magic, both as to quantity and quality. Thus, in South-East Australia it is the Kurnai, in Tierra del Fuego the Halakwulup, among whom we find the feeblest and most infrequent magical practices ; while as for the remaining races, it can be shown that their more vigorous sorceries result from foreign influence. Even among the Bushmen, although magic is more prominent there, it has not nearly the high development nor the vigour which it displays among their neighbours, the Hottentots and Bantu, with their much

[51] See Schmidt, *Ursprung*, Vol. I, ed. 2, chap. XI.
[52] See Schmidt, *Die Stellung der Pygmäenvölker*, Stuttgart, 1910, pp. 218 *sqq.*, 224 *sqq.*, 231, 234.

higher material civilization, their cattle-breeding and their agriculture.[53]

Now on the other hand, among all these peoples of the lowest stratum, and among them especially, we find clearly and definitely the recognition and worship of a personal and moral Supreme Being. Thus by the methods of historical research we find a certain proof that this religion of a high god is not later than magic nor developed out of it, but in all probability has preceded it.

(*d*) THE ETHNOLOGICAL DATE OF MAGIC, AS DETERMINED BY THE HISTORY OF CULTURE

These two facts, that on the one hand belief in a high god is already to be found, past all dispute and in full vigour, in the oldest strata of culture, and on the other hand, that magic does not attain its highest development or its greatest triumphs in these particular stages, are naturally of the greatest value in themselves towards determining the origin of religion and of magic. But the way the problem has been handled hitherto, by Evolutionists quite innocent of historical research, involved yet another weighty defect, which historical inquiry is able to get rid of.

(*a*) If we cannot determine the ethnological age of an element of culture, such as an implement, a social custom, or a religious attitude, we cannot know the quite definite, perhaps unique circumstances under which its origin came about ; we cannot name a time and place and say that it can have happened then and there only. In the case of religious attitudes and cult-forms, such inability would be due especially to lack of knowledge concerning the quite peculiar condition of mind which must have existed in order to produce them. Investigation of the history of culture, however, has succeeded already, by purely objective means, in proving that magic, which did not attain its full and characteristic development in the primitive cultures, did at length find it in later stages of civilization, those of patrilineal totemism and of matrilineal agriculture, both primary ; while it reached still higher developments at yet later levels, the secondary and tertiary cultures. Starting from the

---

[53] For detailed proofs of all these propositions, see the author's *Ursprung der Gottesidee*, Vol. II (Munster, Westphalia, 1929), for the primitive peoples of America ; Vol. III for those of Asia and Australia, and Vol. IV for those of Africa.

knowledge that its first efflorescence took place in the two primary cultures just named, we may now ask the definite question : What new forces came into play at this point, after the primitive culture, in order to bring the idea of magic to so vigorous a growth ?

(β) And now we find that, firstly, two important new factors came in with the totemic culture which favoured the development of magic, and of active magic, or magic properly so called, in particular. The first of these was a series of discoveries which men (not women) made in the course of perfecting their tools and implements and in learning to coerce and make their profit of the beasts they hunted. They invented weapons of the dagger and spear type, also defensive armour and the throwing-stick ; they introduced and elaborated traps for game. All this must have increased their self-confidence very decidedly and produced a strong conviction that, even if extraordinary objects and events came their way, they need not remain enslaved to the resultant horror and fright, but could contrive ingenious and powerful ways and means, speedily and by force if need were, to coerce both the forces of nature and their fellow-men. To this end they called to their aid, for example, also their most virile faculty, the active power of reproduction. The second new and important factor which had now to be reckoned with is the increased significance of the tribe as a whole, as opposed to the individual and the family. From this there now began to arise the confusing and hampering effect of general opinion on a man's judgements, feeling and action. The volitionalist and sociological school of Durkheim gets its best materials from these same totemic tribes, although it quite fails to see that since totemism is relatively late the origin of magic is so likewise.

(γ) But there is another kind of magic, which I would style passive, and this does not appear to have arisen and attained its first decided development in the totemic and patrilineal culture, but in that of the matrilineal agriculturalists. This is the magic of omens, especially evil omens, of signs which foretell, at first, merely what must not be done, and consequently must be left undone ; whereas the magic proper to totemism gives means for the active accomplishment of something, the positive attainment of an end. This ' passive ' magic is equally easy to explain, from the more passive and timid character of women. For they now began, for the first time, to take a predominant place, owing to the discovery of agriculture ; but plants, the objects of their agricultural activities, are utterly out of the control of mankind and exposed beyond all else to the influence of the weather ; consequently, much helpless anxiety and fear must be felt on their behalf. I have already (p. 140) noted that the blending of totemic and agrarian culture brought magic to a still more advanced stage of elaboration.

The further development of magic is due chiefly to continually increasing specialization in magical materials and practices ; to the forming of a hierarchy among those persons who engage in them, in accordance with their degree of activity and the size of their clientèle ; and to the establishment by inheritance of an equipment of magical knowledge and implements.

6. THE ALLEGED UNIVERSAL MAGIC FORCE AMONG VARIOUS PEOPLES

(a) GENERAL CONSIDERATIONS

The first exponent of a theory of magic, J. H. King, already produced in proof of his hypothesis the alleged universal magic forces among certain peoples, *e.g.*, the Melanesian *mana*, the Sioux *wakan*, and the Australian *boylya* (see *The Supernatural*, Vol. I, pp. 132–64). Recourse is had to these also by nearly all later theoreticians of this group, and the range is extended more and more, in accordance with apparent new discoveries of such forces as more peoples became known.

Thus, Marett adduced the Masai *ngai* and the Malagasy *andria-manitra*, while Vierkandt adds the Iroquois *orenda* and the Central Australian *arungquiltha*. Sidney Hartland further appeals to the Algonkin *manitowi*. Frazer and Beth especially expend their whole ethnological learning in long lists of such peoples and their forces ; the latter, besides citing *mana*, *wakanda*, *manitu*, *orenda*, *andria-manitra* and *arungquiltha*, adds further the Sea Dyak *ngarong* and *petara*, the Bantu *mulungu* and the Central Australian *churinga*.

All these alleged forces need examination one by one, and a methodical comparison with each other. Lack of these precautions has brought things to such a pass with not a few writers that they actually speak of this universal magical force as a mysterious central reservoir of all mystical powers, a sort of ubiquitous, invisible fluid upon which the worker of magic draws on every occasion for such of them as he wished or needed for the time being.

This view had already been upheld by J. N. B. Hewitt in his article 'Orenda and a Definition of Religion'[54] as regards the Iroquois *orenda* ; later he also explained the Algonkin *manitowi* and the Sioux *wakan* as analogous forces. Somewhat later, Miss Alice C. Fletcher accepted it as regards the Sioux *wakanda*[55], and W. Jones similarly for the Algonkin *manito*[56], Franz Boas correlates all these views and declares that magical power is the fundamental concept of individual religious life among the Indians[57].

But we may now say in general that no such a universal magical force exists among any people. Further, no general examination of these alleged forces has ever been made, to discover what common features those which have been adduced may possess. Such investigations have been carried out only for two of them, which however belong to the most important, best known and oftenest mentioned. I give their results here. The forces in question are Melanesian *mana* and the *orenda, manitowi* or *wakanda* of the Amerindians.

(b) Melanesian *Mana*

There have been published of late two useful monographs on *mana*, namely F. R. Lehmann, *Mana: eine begriffsgeschichtliche Untersuchung auf ethnologischer Grundlage,* and J. Röhr, *Das Wesen des Mana*[58]. Having to review the former of these for the *Literarisches Centralblatt*,[59] I took the opportunity to go into the linguistic context of the word *mana,* while investigating the material collected by Lehmann. I was then able to show that *mana* is derived from the word *manang* or *menang,* which occurs in Indonesian languages and means fundamentally nothing but 'superior or victorious force', whether of a religious or secular kind, and whether attaching to persons or things.

[54] *American Anthropologist*, N.S., Vol. IV, 1892, pp. 33–46, also the art. 'Orenda' in the *Handbook of American Indians* (Bureau of American Ethnology, Bulletin 30, part 2, Washington, 1910).
[55] In 'The Omaha Tribe', in 27th Annual Report of the Bur. Amer. Ethn., Washington, 1911, p. 597 *sqq.*
[56] See 'The Algonkin Manitou', in *Journal of American Folk-Lore*, Vol. XVIII, 1905, pp. 183–90 ; see also his article in *Hand. Amer. Ind.,* part I.
[57] In his art. 'Religion', in *Handbook Amer. Ind.,* part 2.
[58] The former at Leipzig, 1915, second ed. in 1922 ; the latter, an article in *Anthropos,* Vol. XIV–XV, 1919–20, pp. 97–124. [The titles may be translated *Mana : an examination of the history of a concept on an ethnological basis* and *The nature of mana.*]
[59] October, 1916, No. 2, pp. 1091–3.

This fact was obscured in the first edition of Lehmann's work by the inclusion of a series of other stems which have nothing to do with *mana* or *manang*. While Lehmann, as a result of my criticism, left these out in his second edition, Röhr keeps them in his essay and even increases their number. This damages his work, which in other respects is clearer and more concise than Lehmann's, since the latter, who makes a great number of critical observations and establishes a number of propositions dealing with particular points, gives no concise summary of his results, except as it were casually, in remarks dropped in the course of his criticisms.

At all events, the critical studies of both authors agree in establishing the fact that *mana* is by no means a word of exclusively or specifically religious meaning. Still less does it signify a universal magical power with which everything is filled ; nor is it right to suppose that each thing has its own *mana*, as it were a psychic power. On the contrary ; *mana* means superior power, unusually great and efficient, which may be ' supernatural ' and mystical, but can equally well be ' natural ' or profane. It is therefore of no use to ask, as Röhr does, when and how a thing is regarded as *mana*-ful, or whether *mana* is to be treated as a sort of fluid or as something psychic. Röhr comes to an affirmative answer to the latter question, but only because he has included in his list of derivatives words such as *manawa*, which have no connexion with *manang*.

Lehmann has done good service by giving a critical account of the use made of the word *mana* in the various pre-animistic theories. The results above mentioned should logically lead to a considerable restriction of its employment.

For the sake of completeness and lucidity, I would add this much. The description of *mana* which has hitherto ranked as ' classical ', that of Codrington in *The Melanesians* (Oxford, 1891, pp. 119, 191) [60] declares that *mana* is possessed only by spirits (of nature), ghosts (of ancestors) generally *, and if by men, only through the medium of ghosts or spirits, never by things as such. This needs a certain amount of correction, since *mana* may signify conspicuous non-magical power ; but, and this is very significant for our purposes,

[60] See further Schmidt, *Grundlinien einer Vergleichung der Religionen und Mythologien der austronesischen Völker*, in *Denkschriften der k. Akademie der Wissenschaften in Wien*, philologischhistorische Klasse, Vol. LIII, third article, p. 114 *sqq*.

* [The original has *nur wenigen Ahnengeistern*, ' only a few ancestral spirits ' ; but Codrington, p. 119, says definitely ' ghosts generally ' (have *mana*).]

Codrington's statement holds good for *mana* in the sense of conspicuous supernatural power, mysterious force; this belongs properly to spirits only, and to these, as we shall see presently, not as spirits in the sense of Tylor's animism, but rather as personifications, as embodiments of a certain undivided personal factor of power.

(c) Amerindian *Orenda, Wakanda* or *Manitowi*

It is interesting to note that Hewitt's article in which he conceives the Iroquois *orenda* as a universal magical power appeared in 1892 [61], almost simultaneously with Codrington's book (1891). Hewitt, however, since he brought in Sioux *wakanda* and Algonkin *manitowi* as well, put the matter on a broader basis; and this basis was much noticed and used by later exponents of the theory of magic, the more so as the author had declared this power to be a universal, unattached source of energy.

(*a*) The whole idea expressed by these authors is emphatically opposed by P. Radin in his article *Religion of the North American Indians* [62], in which he declares it to be ' quite untenable '. Examining critically the descriptions of the writers in question he shows, to begin with, that their ideas concerning the force of which they speak are not so uniform, and consequently the forces themselves not so identical, as they themselves would have us believe. Radin holds, and quite rightly, that the fundamental principle of *orenda* as set forth by Hewitt is to be found in Hewitt's own statement, ' The possession of *orenda* is the distinctive characteristic of the gods.' But in this connexion Hewitt, he holds, has blundered by dividing the gods into higher entities and their magical powers, no such division being really possible, since entity and power form an indivisible whole. The same mistake disfigures the account of *manito* in the work of W. Jones. The linguistic arguments, moreover, which Hewitt and Jones produce are saturated in and interpreted beforehand by the theory already formed.

After this criticism, which, while chiefly negative, is in itself enough to prove his case, Radin proceeds to support his own position by positive considerations, the fruits of his

[61] This was also the year in which the first statement of the theory of magic, that of J. H. King, appeared ; see above, p. 120.
[62] In *Journal of American Folk-Lore*, Vol. XXVII, 1914, pp. 335–73, especially 344 *sqq.*

own investigations, on the one hand, of *wakanda* among a Sioux tribe, the Winnebago, and on the other, of *manito* among an Algonkin people, the Ojibwa.

' In both tribes ', he says (p. 349), ' the term always referred to definite spirits, not necessarily definite in shape. If at a vapor-bath the steam is regarded as *wakanda* or *manito*, it is because it is a spirit transformed into steam for the time being ; if an arrow is possessed of specific virtues, it is because a spirit has either transformed himself into the arrow or because he is temporarily dwelling in it ; and finally, if tobacco is offered to a peculiarly-shaped object, it is because either this object belongs to a spirit, or a spirit is residing in it. The terms " *wakanda* " and " *manito* " are often used in the sense of " sacred ". If a Winnebago tells you that a certain thing is *waka* (*i.e.*, sacred), further inquiry will elicit from him the information that it is so because it belongs to a spirit, was given by a spirit, or was in some way connected with a spirit.[63] It is possible that Dr. Jones, Miss Fletcher, and Mr. Hewitt interpreted a certain vagueness in the answer, or a certain inability (or unwillingness) to discuss objects that were regarded as *manito* or *wakanda*, as pertaining to the nature of sacred. In addition to the connotation of " sacred ", *wakanda* and *manito* also have the meaning " strange ", " remarkable ", " wonderful ", " unusual ", and " powerful ", without, however, having the slightest suggestion of " inherent power ", but having the ordinary sense of these adjectives '.

(β) When, however, Radin then proceeds to say (p. 351), ' Animism, then, in the old Tylorian sense of the term, is the belief of the Indians ', I am compelled to differ from him. I do not deny that in quite a number of cases the ' spirits ' included under or signified by the terms *manito* and *wakanda* are spirits in the sense of Tylorian animism ; that is, that they are opposed to and separate from body. But I deny that this is always or even generally the case. Rather are there numerous instances in which no such distinction is made, consciously or unconsciously, but the agent is conceived as undivided, as a person.[64] I perceive moreover that Radin himself holds at least a very similar view, as may be seen especially from the following remarks (p. 352) :

[63] That *manito* means a spirit or something connected with a spirit is emphasized also by E. W. Hopkins in his article ' Manitu ' in Hastings' *Encyclopædia of Religion and Ethics*, Vol. VII, Edinburgh, 1915, col. 403 *sqq.* ; a contribution, in some respects, not above criticism. H. B. Alexander also, in his article ' Orenda ' in the same work, Vol. IX, 1917, col. 553 *sqq.*, agrees with this and says the same of *wakanda*.
[64] See my remarks on this point in *Ursprung der Gottesidee*, Vol. I, ed. 2, pp. 499 *sqq.*, 509, 529, 541 *sq.*, 572.

' It is, I believe, a fact that future investigations will thoroughly confirm, that the Indian does not make the separation into personal as contrasted with impersonal, corporeal with impersonal, in our sense at all. What he seems to be interested in is the question of existence, of reality ; and everything that is perceived by the sense, thought of, felt and dreamt of, exists. It follows, consequently, that most of the problems connected with the nature of spirit as personal or impersonal do not exist.'

If investigations as thorough as those we have described in connexion with Melanesian *mana* and Amerindian *orenda*, *manitowi* and *wakanda* were carried out for the other peoples who, as we are assured by numerous upholders of the Theory of Magic, believe in a similar magical force, we may be sure that similar qualifications, even eliminations, would result. We should then see the employment of this diffuse nebula from the chaos of magic in the service of such theoreticians decidedly lessened, or even excluded altogether.

PART IV

THE SUPREME SKY-GOD IN THE NINETEENTH AND TWENTIETH CENTURIES

CHAPTER XI

THE SKY-GOD IN THEORIES OF THE NINETEENTH CENTURY

1. THE SUPREME SKY-GOD IN THE PASTORAL NOMADIC CULTURE

IN our review of the many theories which in recent decades have sought to discover the origin of religion, we have made our way further and further into the remotest past of religions, till, leaving behind us the faiths of the tertiary and secondary cultures, we have arrived at the primary. (See below, p. 238.) Here also we have now completed our examination of most of the religions of this area. We found the data relative to animism in the matrilineal agrarian culture; this was the foundation of Tylor's theory that animism was the origin of all religions. In the patrilineal totemic culture we discovered the very nest of magic, close by totemism itself, and its strongest development. This magic a whole series of theoreticians had introduced into their explanations of the origin of religion, either supposing it to be a stage earlier than religion itself, or postulating an undifferentiated mixture of both as the primal state.

(a) NEGLECT OF THE SKY-GOD

(i) Consequently there remains only one of the primary cultures, that of the pastoral nomads, the great cattle-breeding peoples. These are still to be found in their natural state, their representatives being Altaic, or Ural-Altaic, and Hamitic

167

races ; but all the Indo-European and nearly all the Semitic
peoples, who once belonged also to this culture, have long
ago become, as a result of various crossings in the course of
millennia, civilized or semi-civilized peoples of the secondary
or tertiary cultures. In their natural state, however, the
great cattle-breeding peoples display a quite characteristic
form of religion, not to be found in this peculiar shape in any
other cultures. They steadfastly believe in and worship a
supreme sky-god. Now it is a really remarkable fact in the
history of our science that whereas, as we have seen, the
religions of every other culture have been made the starting-
point of theories concerning the origin of religion, no one
has ever made the religion of these pastoral peoples the basis
of his hypothesis, or troubled to inquire if perhaps the
starting-point of religious evolution was to be sought here.
No existing work even gives a comparative study of the
religions of these pastoral races ; no one has so treated either
the African or the Asiatic representatives of this culture,[1]
and still less has there been a comprehensive comparison made
of both, or even a comparison between their beliefs and those
of the ancient Indo-Europeans and Semites.

(ii) Connected with this is a still more wide-reaching fact,
to which I would draw attention. Till quite recently there
was no comprehensive work whatsoever dealing with the
figure of the sky-god, which yet is so important for the history
of religion. Not till the year 1922 did the first volume appear
of a work by Pettazzoni, *Dio : formazione e sviluppo del
monoteismo nella storia delle religioni.* It bore the separate
title, *L'Essere Celeste nelle credenze dei popoli primitivi.* This
book, to which we will recur later, is an attempt to fill the
gap. Under these circumstances it is rather surprising and
certainly commendable that the late Dr. J. Hastings included
an article ' Sky and Sky-Gods ' in his *Encyclopædia of Religion
and Ethics*, Vol. XI, 1920, pp. 580–5. Its author, G. Foucart,
remarks (p. 585) that ' there is no monograph on the subject '.
His own handling of the matter, to which we will return later
(see p. 214 *sqq.*), is not faultless but, in several important directions, does not lack merit.

(b) The Sky-God in Indo-Germanic Philology

In order to appreciate the present situation adequately, we
must grasp the fact that it was more favourable at a quite

[1] Miss M. A. Czaplicka gives a short account of the latter in *Aboriginal
Siberia*, Oxford, 1914, pp. 277–90, but it is of course insufficient for this
purpose.

early date than it has been for the last few decades. When the comparative philology of the Indo-Germanic languages discovered that a supreme sky-god existed among the various peoples of that group, whose great antiquity was guaranteed by the common root DIV, to shine, from which his name was derived, the attention of researchers in the field of religion was drawn to him for a considerable time.[2] A. Kuhn, who made the meteorological phenomena of rain, storm, thunder and lightning the beginnings of religion and mythology, was already making investigations along this line. C. Ploix, in his work *La nature des dieux : études de mythologie gréco-latine* (Paris, 1888), laid down the principle that the sky was the chief object of myths and of religion. The most energetic and best working out of the great importance of the supreme sky-god among the Indo-Europeans is that by L. v. Schroeder in the first volume of his standard treatise, *Arische Religion*, Leipzig, 1914 (see above, p. 43 *sqq.*). Unfortunately we have not either for the Semito-Hamites nor for the Ural-Altaic peoples any exposition of the place taken by their supreme sky-god in a work which, for importance, can be compared at all to von Schroeder's.

2. THE THEORY OF THE SKY-GOD : ITS BIRTH AND DEATH

(a) ITS BIRTH

It was at this earlier date also that attempts were made at a theory of the origins of religion, founded upon this sky-god. It was then believed, under the influence of Schelling's *Philosophie der Mythologie*, that a vague and uncertain monotheism might be assumed as the earliest state ; that this monotheism, however, was not definitely realized as such, and so could easily pass into polytheism. We find a theory of this kind in O. Pfleiderer's first work, *Die Geschichte der Religion*, Leipzig, 1869, Vol. II, p. 47 *sq.*, in which he writes as follows :

'The preeminent position taken from the beginning by the sky-god furnished a natural starting-point for monotheism . . . we must not, however, as is often done, try to find true monotheism in this position of the sky-god in and for itself.'

Other researchers of that day, who were Protestant theologians, took up a similar position ; for example, E. G. Steude in *Ein Problem der allgemeinen Religionswissenschaft und ein*

[2] See above, pp. 38 and 39.

Versuch einer Lösung ['A Problem of the general Science of Religion and an attempted Solution'], Leipzig, 1881, and C. von Orelli, *Allgemeine Religionsgeschichte* [' General History of Religion '], Bonn, 1899. Max Müller also, in the early days of his activity, belongs to this group, and his ' kathenotheism ' is probably an outgrowth of it (see above, p. 40). Quite recently G. Wobbermin (see above, p. 147) shows signs of wishing to return to this theory.

However, all this was but a tentative approach to a theory which was never fully worked out, and, moreover, it was a little later given up by its own creators, if one may so call them. A typical example of this change of front is that of Pfleiderer himself in his later works, *Religionsphilosophie auf geschichtlicher Grundlage* [' The Philosophy of Religion on a Historical Basis '], Berlin, 1878, and *Religion und Religionen* [' Religion and Religions '], Munich, 1906. His series of starting-points for religion is nature-myths, animism, totemism (à la Robertson Smith), and analogical magic [*Analogiezauber*, Frazer's ' homœopathic ' magic], so that his account of the evolution of religion reads almost like an outline of the modern developments of our science.[3] In the work of Max Müller, again, we discovered much the same series of adaptations to the different theories concerning the origin of religion, beginning after the breakdown of the school of nature-myths. Here also it is obvious that the fundamental change which set in about this time both in ethnology and in the general attitude of European educated thought had a not inconsiderable share in preventing this theory of the supreme sky-god in primitive times from reaching its full development, and causing its own originators to abandon it almost entirely.

(b) Its Death

The change, which began, for ethnology, as early as Lubbock, and was completed by Spencer and Tylor, was the new interest in savage races. Such a change would not in itself have sufficed to kill the theory of the sky-god so completely ; for among savages also such a supreme deity is widely distributed. But the doctrine of progressive Evolution, which was then being put forward from the most various quarters and soon mastered the mind of all Europe, necessarily brought about such a result if it was understood and developed in a materialistic spirit, as was then the case. Under this twofold influence, all framers of theories concerning fetishes, ghosts, animism,

[3] See Schmidt, *Ursprung der Gottesidee*, Vol. I, ed. 2, pp. 86–8.

totemism and magic, if they agreed in nothing else, were at one in this, that the figure of the sky-god must be got rid of from the earliest stages of religion, as being too high and incomprehensible.   For, as they held, these stages must have been extremely low, not far removed from that of the beasts ; therefore the sky-god must be referred to quite late stages of development, unless it was preferred to deduce him from Christian influence.   The strength of this universal current of thought was so great, and the resulting discredit into which it brought the notion of the great age of the sky-god so complete, that hardly anyone found courage to oppose it and to draw attention to the quite frequent examples of this exalted sky-god appearing among decidedly primitive peoples, where not the least trace of Christian influence was to be found.

CHAPTER XII

THE PRIMITIVE HIGH GOD

1. GENERAL HISTORICAL SURVEY

(a) THE APPEARANCE OF ANDREW LANG

DESPITE all this, about the same time that the theory of magic began to spread, there arose another opponent of animism, whose attack on that theory was made from the side of the high gods of low races. It is dramatically effective that this assailant was one of Tylor's leading pupils, the most successful assailant of the nature-myth school in Britain and of its most important representative, Max Müller.

The author of the new theory was a Scot, Andrew Lang. Enjoying a high reputation as poet, historian, especially of literature, and essayist—perhaps the first modern essayist in Great Britain—Lang had also been busied for decades with sociological, mythological and religious studies. In this sphere as in others, his literary art stood him in good stead. It was he who, fighting steadily in the foremost ranks of the new anthropological school against the authority of Max Müller, then paramount, especially in England, was at length successful in defeating the nature-myth theory and establishing that of animism in general approval.[1] Such a battle and such a victory shed great lustre on Lang's name in every country of Europe and America, just at the time when the new animistic explanation of mythology was making its triumphant way through them, one after another.

Lang belonged at first entirely to the school of Tylor, and had not the least hesitation in accepting that one of its axioms which declared that monotheism had everywhere developed out of a lower animistic form of worship. The first time that he found, in reading a mission report, certain facts which did not exactly fit that theory, his impression was that the

[1] See Schmidt, *Ursprung der Gottesidee*, Vol. I, ed. 2, p. 25.

missionary in question had somehow made a mistake. But the further his studies took him, the more examples of this kind he met with, and at last he came to the conclusion that this fundamental Tylorian tenet would not hold water.

To this conviction he gave public expression in 1898, in his book *The Making of Religion*.[2] It was so successful that a second enlarged edition appeared in 1900 and a third in 1909. He widened and deepened his new views in revisions, in part very extensive, of his earlier works, *Magic and Religion* and *Myth, Ritual and Religion*,[3] and to some extent *Custom and Myth*.[4] The two new works, moreover, which he published after 1898 on sociological topics, *Social Origins* and *The Secret of the Totem*,[5] bear the marks of these ideas so far as they deal with the science of religion. Apart from this, Lang was unweariedly busy and on the watch for new particulars to discover and publish, mistakes and misunderstandings to clear up, attacks to repel ; he wrote alike in the technical ethnological publications, *Journal of the Anthropological Institute of Great Britain and Ireland*, *Man*, *and Folk-Lore*, and also (for such questions interest a wider circle in Great Britain than in most countries), in non-technical journals, such as the *Edinburgh*, *Contemporary*, and *Fortnightly Reviews*.

(b) THE OPPOSITION TO LANG

Seeing then that this discussion found lively expression in the leading British periodicals, which of course are known everywhere abroad also, and that they represented the new views of a scholar of such wide repute ; considering also that they constituted a complete break with a theory which was then almost universally accepted ; it is hard to understand why the majority of specialists and of specialist publications outside Great Britain received Lang's utterances with the deepest silence.* Year after year, the *Revue de l'histoire des religions* in France, the *Journal of American Folk-Lore* and the *American Anthropologist* in the United States, the *Archiv für Religionswissenschaft* and the *Zeitschrift für Ethnologie* in Germany, either said nothing at all or gave Lang only short and unimportant notices. The general opinion

[2] London, Longmans, Green & Co. ; hereinafter quoted as M.R.
[3] Same publishers, the latter 1901, the former 1899 ; cited respectively as Mc.R. and M.R.R.
[4] Same publishers, 1904 ; cited as C.M.
[5] Same publishers, 1903 and 1905 respectively.
* [It is not unworthy of remark that the translator, at Lang's own university, had considerable difficulty in obtaining some of Lang's works. His deservedly high literary repute seems actually to have militated against recognition of his services to science.]

regarding Lang at the time is expressed by E. Lehmann in the following sentence : ' This unexpected theory of Lang's has been received with due mistrust.' [6]   He does not, however, explain to whom or what exactly the ' mistrust ' is ' due '.

This whole attitude of silent rejection was all the more remarkable because the theory of magic, which appeared simultaneously, was everywhere accorded ready discussion and, in a short time, wide acceptance ; yet according to the testimony of its first three supporters themselves, Marett, Hubert (and Mauss) and Preuss, it rested on insecure and merely provisional foundations.

Lang himself had no illusions on the reception which his theory might expect in the then prevailing current of opinion. He wrote as early as 1901 (Mc R., p. 14) :

' Like other martyrs of science, I must expect to be thought importunate, tedious, a fellow of one idea, and that idea wrong.   To resent this would show great want of humour, and a plentiful lack of knowledge of human nature.'

He had dedicated his work *The Making of Religion* to his own old University, St. Andrews, which, as he says in the preface :

' fostered in the past the leaders of forlorn hopes that were destined to triumph, and the friends of lost causes who fought bravely against Fate '.

And to the very end of his life he never ceased fighting valiantly and imperturbably for his ' anachronistic ' views. He died in the year 1912, the same year in which the first edition of the present author's *Ursprung der Gottesidee* was published.[7]

2.   LANG'S CRITICISM OF THE ANIMISTIC THEORY

(a) Its Fundamentals

Lang, in his doubts of and attacks upon the animistic theory, relied especially on the startling discoveries of A. W. Howitt concerning the Supreme Being of the South-East Australian tribes, published by their author in the years 1882 to 1889 in the *Journal of the*

[6] In his article *Die Anfänge der Religion und die Religion der primitiven Völker*, in Hinneberg's *Die Kultur der Gegenwart*, pt. 1, sect. 3, pp. 1–27.

[7] For laudatory notices of his death, see *Folk-Lore*, Vol. XXIII, 1912, pp. 336–75 (obituaries by R. R. Marett, A. van Gennep, W. H. Rivers, and W. Schmidt).

Anthropological Institute,[8] and upon the information given by Mrs. Langloh Parker concerning the Euahlayi and related tribes in *Australian Legendary Tales,* Melbourne, 1887, and *More Australian Legendary Tales,* London, 1898,[9] together with E. H. Man's investigations of the high god Puluga among the Andamanese pygmies; see his work *On the Aboriginal Inhabitants of the Andaman Islands,* London, 1883.[10] He also made use, but in rather incidental fashion, of facts from the Bushmen, Hottentots, Zulu, Yao, the West African peoples and the Tierra del Fuegians, and somewhat more extensively from the North American Indians.[11]

Neither his material nor his handling of it is everywhere of the same value, and not all his examples will hold good in the present more advanced state of our knowledge. On the other hand, a whole series of peoples who later provided apposite data were at that time quite insufficiently known. Moreover, at that date the historical method was not yet developed; if it had been, it might have furnished Lang with really deadly weapons with which to combat animism. He himself remained a moderate Evolutionist.

Yet with all these defects which we can to-day easily recognize as such, the ceaseless attacks which Lang conducted with such spirit and skill had plenty of effectiveness left, and the foundations of his criticism were wide and solid enough to cut the ground from under the feet of the animistic theory.

(b) ITS HEADS

(a) He begins at the beginning by shaking the pillars on which the whole system of animism rests. That theory teaches that the idea of God as a spirit could not be attained to until the conception of spirit had itself been reached; and that this developed from the phenomena of sleep, dreams and death. Lang simply asks whether these primitive peoples regard the Supreme Being as a spirit at all. To us, whose ideas have been influenced by Christian conceptions from our youth up, it may seem that they must do so; but have

[8] Afterwards published as a separate work under the title *The Native Tribes of South-East Australia,* London, 1904.
[9] She published later *The Euahlayi Tribe,* London, 1905.
[10] Puluga's existence denied by A. R. Brown in *The Religion of the Andaman Islanders,* in *Folk-Lore,* Vol. XX, 1909, pp. 257–71, and *The Andaman Islanders,* Cambridge, 1922. But see my account of the matter in *Ursprung der Gottesidee,* Vol. I, ed. 2, p. 162, and the detailed exposition, *op. cit.,* Vol. III, pp. 50–145.
[11] For a synopsis of these data, see *Ursprung der Gottesidee,* Vol. I, ed. 2, pp. 142–79.

these peoples any such ideas ? Not at all ; in many cases they have nothing of the sort. They do not deny the spiritual nature of the Supreme Being, but neither do they affirm it ; such ' metaphysical ' questions have not as yet entered their heads. For them God is simply a Being, and a Being who really exists. That the idea of a spirit, derived from the phenomena of death, is applicable here, is impossible ; for it is nearly always directly asserted that this Being has existed from all eternity, or at least since before death was, and that he never dies.[12] (See M.R., chaps. IX and X ; M.R.R., Vol. I, p. 309 *sqq.*)

Thus the fundamental idea of the animistic theory, the origin of the idea of God from the idea of spirit, misses its mark. The former concept need not have been developed out of the notion of a soul at all.

(β) But more than this, the animistic theory in its further development is contradicted by the facts. From the idea of the soul, according to it, is developed on the one hand the concept and the worship of nature-spirits, and on the other the cult of ancestral ghosts. Then came polytheism, and from some form of this monotheism was at last developed. But it is just the most primitive peoples, whose acquaintance we have made here, the Australians, the Andamanese, who do not possess any tendance of the dead, at least no religious tendance, no ancestor-worship. But where no ancestor-worship exists, no monotheism can develop out of it. The case is much the same for the adoration of nature-spirits, religious animism. For these same most primitive peoples worship no spirits whatsoever. So this stage precedent to monotheism, as supposed by the animistic theory, is likewise lacking. Lang adds also that among the primitive peoples mentioned the state of their social development is such that no chiefs, in any proper sense of the word, exist ; we must therefore say that the social model for the supremacy of the One God over many others is not to be found.[13] Hence the further development of the animistic theory is likewise completely unsuccessful. (See M.R., ed. 3, p. 162.)

(γ) Animism is just as obviously bankrupt as regards the connexion between ethics and religion. The position that

---

[12] ' Between them (high gods) and apotheosized mortal ancestors there is a great gulf fixed—the river of death,' M.R., p. 206.

[13] As I have explained in *Ursprung*, Vol. I, ed. 2, p. 213, Lang seems to me to go too far in this last point ; but it is not essential to his proof.

no such connexion existed in the earlier stages of religious development was intelligible only on the basis of this theory. It certainly is obvious that ancestral ghosts, whose cult rests largely on fear of them, and nature-spirits, whose helpful or harmful influence alone moves men to worship them, have nothing to do with morality. But if neither animism nor ghost-worship is the beginning of monotheism, as we have found it among the most primitive peoples, the theoretical basis for denying the ethical character of this religion collapses. The solid objective facts point the same way, for among these primitive races we not only find moral precepts, but these are the expression of the will of the Supreme Being, who watches over their observance with all his omniscience, and by his justice rewards their keeping and punishes their neglect, on this side, and frequently also on the other side the grave. A closer connexion between religion and morality can be found even in the higher religions only to this extent, that in them God Himself is recognized as essentially good and holy. Even the content of these ethical laws is essentially the same as with us. Here Lang does not forget to emphasize that precepts in favour of altruism and unselfishness are everywhere to be found in this connexion. (See M.M.R., Vol. I, pp. 316, 332, 336 *sqq.*)

3. LANG'S OWN THEORY CONCERNING THE AGE AND ORIGIN OF HIGH GODS

(a) THEIR ORIGIN

Andrew Lang did not content himself with criticizing the theory of animism, but passed on to a positive exposition of his own view concerning the development of the idea of God and the part played by animistic and manistic beliefs in the further evolution of religion. He does not indeed attempt to give a definite and final solution of the problem of the origin of religion, for, he held, we have no data and no means of getting back to the really oldest human beings.

(i) A further difficulty, he declares, confronts us. When we leave the region of hypotheses and take our stand upon the firm ground of facts, we find it is true no peoples which possess only the lower, mythical elements, but also none which has only the higher, or religious ones. We invariably find both together. It can be shown that the higher elements need not have developed out of the lower, that both, therefore, may have originated independently. But whether one of them was earlier than the other cannot be proved by the ethnological facts. We can only produce examples of later date, which show how religious ideas are gradually overgrown with popular mythic imagery, as was the case with medieval Christianity (see also M.R., ed. 3, p. xv *sqq.*), with its popular tales of the Saviour, the Virgin Mary, the apostles, and so forth. Hence there is only a certain probability at the very beginning of religion the higher conceptions were again the earlier. As to the origin of these conceptions, nothing more than conjectures is possible. Hence Lang attempts no more than to put forward a theory which has a high degree of possibility, nay a decided probability in its favour.

(ii) 'As soon', he says (M.R., ed. 3, p. xii), 'as man had the idea of " making " things, he might conjecture as to a Maker of things which he himself had not made, and could not make. He would regard this unknown Maker as a " magnified non-natural man ". . . . This conception of a magnified non-natural man, who is a Maker, being given ; his Power would be recognized, and fancy would clothe one who had made such useful things with certain other moral attributes, as of Fatherhood, goodness, and regard for the ethics of his children ; these ethics having been developed naturally in the evolution of social life. In all this there is nothing " mystical ", nor anything, as far as I can see, beyond the limited mental powers of any beings that deserve to be called human.' (Cf. Mc R., p. 225.) [14]

Thus religion grew in a natural way out of the nature of man and satisfies his speculative curiosity, his moral sense and his feelings. It is

'the speculative belief in a power superior to man' and 'the emotional belief that he loves his children' (Mc R., p. 69).

(iii) Lang describes the relation of the higher, religious element to the lower or mythical as follows :

'Among the lowest known tribes we usually find, just as in ancient Greece, the belief in a deathless " Father ", " Master ", " Maker ", and also the crowd of humorous, obscene, fanciful myths which are in flagrant contradiction with the religious character of that belief. That belief is what we call rational, and even elevated. The myths, on the other hand, are what we call irrational and debasing.' . . .
'For the present, we can only say that the. religious conception uprises from the human intellect, in one mood, that of earnest contemplation and submission : while the mythical ideas uprise

[14] He gives a rather more detailed account in controversy with E. Sidney Hartland, *Folk-Lore*, Vol. X, 1899, pp. 9–13.

from another mood, that of playful and erratic fancy. These two moods are conspicuous even in Christianity. The former, that of earnest and submissive contemplation, declares itself in prayers, hymns, and " the dim religious light " of cathedrals. The second mood, that of playful and erratic fancy, is conspicuous in the buffoonery of Miracle Plays, in *Märchen*, these burlesque popular tales about our Lord and Apostles, and in the hideous and grotesque sculptures on sacred edifices. The two moods are present, and in conflict, through the whole religious history of the human race. They stand as near each other, and as far apart, as Love and Lust.' (M.R.R., I, pp. 4–5.)

But it is just at the most primitive levels that we find the religious element still in greater purity and comparatively uncorrupted, both elements being still clearly distinguishable. But then, according to Lang's theory, the mythical element begins to develop more and more strongly, intrudes more and more upon the religious, overgrows it, and finally covers it so as nearly to strangle it altogether.

(b) Origin of the Lower or Mythical Elements

(i) Having sought for the origin of the higher element, we must now examine the reasons for the appearance of the lower, and furthermore, the reasons why it was able to develop so much more strongly than the higher. At this point Lang rejoins the modern animistic school and accepts its theories of the origin of this element. Like that school, he assumes that those remarkable fables, folk tales and myths arose at a definite period in the history of human thought through which all peoples have passed, and in which the savage races to some extent still are. At such a stage of mental development, these things which we often find so childish and so tasteless were created in simple sincerity and accepted in all seriousness as true. As intellectual progress went on, they were maintained in the first place by the power of tradition, and were especially defended by the priests. At this stage poets invented new tales on the lines of the old, or collected scattered legends into a system. With yet further development of the intelligence, when these things appeared more and more quaint and absurd, priests and in later times philosophers tried to allegorize them away. (See M.R.R., Vol. I, pp. 1–122.) Clearly this is simply the explanation of mythology supported by the new ' anthropological ' school, as opposed to the older ' philological ' one.

Lang disassociates himself here from the animistic theory

on two important points. (*a*) He does not suppose that this stage of development was the first in human history, for he does not say that all peoples began with it, but only that all have passed through it ; see M.R.R., Vol. I, p. 138 ; Vol. II, pp. 345–51. (*β*) He denies that even at this stage the irrational element was the only one active (*op. cit.*, Vol. I, p. 41).

(ii) How, then, did fetishism, ancestor-worship and the cult of deified natural phenomena develop out of this transitional stage in the history of the human mind ? How did these forms, belonging to a new ' religion ', gradually overlay the original and higher one, till they smothered it and caused its disappearance ? I give the answer in his own words.

' " How ", it has been asked, " could all mankind forget a pure religion ? " That is what I now try to explain. That degeneration I would account for by the attractions which animism, when once developed, possessed for the naughty natural man, " the old Adam ". A moral creator in need of no gifts, and opposed to lust and mischief, will not help a man with love-spells, or with malevolent " sendings " of disease by witchcraft ; will not favour one man above his neighbour, or one tribe above its rivals, as a reward for sacrifice which he does not accept, or as constrained by charms which do not touch his omnipotence. Ghosts and ghost-gods, on the other hand, in need of food and blood, afraid of spells and binding charms, are a corrupt, but, to man, a useful constituency. Man being what he is, man was certain to " go a whoring " after practically useful ghosts, ghost-gods, and fetishes which he could keep in his wallet or " medicine bag". For these he was sure, in the long run, first to neglect his idea of his Creator ; next, perhaps, to reckon Him as only one, if the highest, of the venal rabble of spirits or deities, and to sacrifice to Him, as to them. And this is exactly what happened ! If we are not to call it " degeneration ", what are we to call it ? It may be an old theory, but facts " winna ding ", and are on the side of an old theory. Meanwhile, on the material plane, culture kept advancing, the crafts and arts arose ; departments arose, each needing a god. . . . But, at this stage of culture, the luck of the state, and the interests of a rich and powerful clergy, were involved in the maintenance of the old, animistic, relatively non-moral system, as in Cuzco, Greece, and Rome. That popular and political regard for the luck of the state, that priestly self-interest (quite natural), could only be swept away by the moral monotheism of Christianity or Islam. Nothing else could do it. In the case of Christianity, the central and most potent of many combined influences, apart from the Life and Death of Our Lord, was the moral monotheism of the Hebrew Religion of Jehovah ' (M.R., ed. 3, pp. 257–8 ; the question at the beginning is from Menzies, *History of Religion*, p. 23).

(c) IMPORTANCE OF ANIMISM FOR THE HISTORY OF RELIGION

On realizing what a corrupting effect has been exercised upon religion by the whole growth of which animism is the root, many have not hesitated to declare animism itself to be quite worthless. But is this really so ? Is animistic belief only degenerative in its effect, a ruining and destroying force ? To this question Lang answers with a decided No.

(i) Primitive man's conception of God, he explains, was high as regards its content, but unreflecting, naïve and undeveloped in its form. In particular, the formal question, whether God is a spirit, a body or both, had never been asked. But this question must arise, in one shape or another, as soon as man, with his progress in mental development, began to think seriously of further questions, for example, of the divine properties of omnipresence and eternity. Where was man to get the conception of pure spirit, which he does not meet with as such in nature ? This is the merit of animistic belief, that it gradually evolved this conception from primeval conjectures concerning sleep, dreams and death, which of course did not at once attain to the whole truth, yet put men on the track of true understanding, little by little ; and this track in turn led them in the end, when philosophy had developed, to valuable final results. The idea of spirit thus attained could then be applied to God.

(ii) Moreover, the morality of primitive men was also lofty in content, being sanctioned by rewards and punishments, not only in this life but in the next. But here again it was unreflecting and undeveloped. And now the question must arise, whether it was man as a whole, as he is in his present life, that was rewarded or punished after death. In that case, how did his body get there, seeing that it remained here, decaying in its grave ? Or again, how was it that in the afterlife there was no death, and how was anyone to feel either pleasure or pain there ? These and other questions could have no satisfactory answer save by the assumption that there was an immortal soul, essentially different from the body, which went alone into eternity, while the body remained here. This belief in a soul whose interests related to eternity and were quite different from those of the body, indeed often opposed to them, demanding the sacrifice of the latter to the former, could thus produce the idea of spiritual health and preservation. Then and not till then could the cry *salua animam tuam* be raised and be effective. The ultimate formation of this idea of an *anima*, albeit at the cost of many errors by the way, is again to be set down to the credit of animism (M.R., p. 264 *sqq.*).

(iii) Lang points out that the Israelites, in the earlier stages especially of their history, displayed a thorough indifference and vagueness with regard to its ideas concerning the fate of the individual soul in the other world.[15] Their destined path was rather to be absorbed in an unperturbed development of the theistic conception, belief in one eternal and righteous God. On the other hand, Egyptian and Roman paganism, and numerous other pagan peoples, showed the most lively interest in the destiny of the individual soul after death—fear of the punishments awaiting it there and an energetic desire to avoid them by any possible means.

' " In the religion of our Lord and the Apostles ", says Lang in conclusion, " the two currents of faith in one righteous God and care for the individual soul were purified and combined. ' God is a Spirit, and they who worship Him must worship Him in spirit and in truth ' ". And a little earlier : " Christianity, last, combined what was good in Animism, the care for the individual soul as an immortal spirit under eternal responsibilities, with the One righteous Eternal of prophetic Israel, and so ended the long, intricate, and mysterious theological education of humanity " ' (M.R., ed. 3, pp. 299, 303).

4. THE SUBSEQUENT FATE OF ANDREW LANG'S THEORY

(i) Anyone who reviews the whole of Lang's system and keeps in view the all-powerful influence of the animistic hypothesis, which had made its way even into theological circles, will have some idea of the astonishment which it must have awakened on all sides, contrary as it was to everything that modern scientific circles held in honour.

In Great Britain, at all events, criticism began to make itself heard. Considering the revolutionary opposition between modern theories and this, the most modern of all, and likewise the high esteem which its author enjoyed, one would have expected that discussion and, it might be, opposition would be universal and extremely lively. Lang, however, in answering the first criticisms, as he did immediately, admitted some mistakes he had formerly made, and conceded some quite

[15] But it must be noted that the Assyrian *Araltu* is little less comfortless than the Israelitish *Sheol* ; see Father Lagrange, *Études*, p. 336 *sqq.* Yet the level of Assyrian culture was higher.

unimportant points. This produced the impression that he had at least half abandoned his position, and in its new form, so it was felt, the theory was not so outrageous and might be better endured.

If we except the decided, but generous, opposition of E. Sidney Hartland, the fact remains that the other principal opponents of Lang, Tylor and Frazer, could not be induced to speak, despite Lang's direct challenges to them. The example of these two savants was for the most part followed abroad, as I have explained in *Ursprung der Gottesidee*, Vol. I, ed. 2, p. 133 *sqq.*, and thus an admirable proof was given of the international nature of scientific ' activity '. Only Hartland and A. W. Howitt carried on a thorough criticism of Lang in Great Britain, and to them we may perhaps add, for France, A. van Gennep ; and for Germany, F. Graebner. The whole of this polemic is confined, almost without exception, to the Australian facts which Lang had produced to support his theory. In my above-mentioned work I have reproduced these criticisms in full detail (pp. 211–483), and added my own counter-criticism. In this condensed synopsis we cannot go into all minor points at length, and for the most part we need not, for much of the controversy has been left behind and made pointless by historical investigation, aided by the production of better data.

(ii) It therefore will suffice to set down the general outcome of the criticisms and of Lang's replies to them, as detailed in my former work. To begin with, one principal point has been placed beyond all doubt. The information concerning the Supreme Beings was in all essentials correct in itself, and represented native belief. Wide-reaching doubt of their native origin and assumption of missionary influences were really confined to a single authority, E. B. Tylor. But that was some thirty years ago. His objections have since been refuted by several researchers, notably Lang himself and N. W. Thomas, and as for the remainder, especially as regards the Tasmanians, I flatter myself that I have disposed of them.[16]

If then the facts which have already been given concerning the worship of a good Supreme Being are native and authentic, their far-reaching importance for any theory which may be put forward concerning the genesis and development of religion can no longer be doubted. Ethnology and the science of religion have thus the decided duty of paying more attention to these matters than has hitherto been the case.

[16] *Op. cit.*, pp. 256–73.

(iii) Two important points, it must be emphasized, have so far been quite missed by the critics.   One is Lang's attempt to explain how the idea of the Supreme Being arose and to make out that such an idea was easy, simple, and in accordance with the whole nature of primitive peoples.   Hartland, it is true, had something to say of the ' antecedent improbability' that these savages could evolve ideas of so high a kind. But he did not deal with Lang's attempted explanation at all, nor notice that it is their very simplicity which enables these children of nature to reach such a height.   We shall have more to build on this fundamental principle, which is the one and only basis for a theory of development in the true sense of the word.   This basis, as laid down by Lang in his attempted explanation, is capable of a decided psychological deepening and a still more extensive historical substantiation ; the result of which is that the entire superstructure gains proportionally in stability and steadfastness.   The other point has been left almost as completely unnoticed.   It is the universal distribution of the worship of a Supreme Being over the whole earth.   The critics, one and all, have so far busied themselves with the Australian data, save for an excursus on North America by Tylor and a brief discussion of South African facts by Hartland.   It is quite inadmissible to say that the facts outside Australia are of no significance ; rather do they include some which are every whit as important as any in that continent.   But this very fact, the equal value for the proof of the materials from all over the world, increases immensely the cogency of that proof as a whole, by excluding *ab initio* all purely external attempts at explanation, especially the theory of borrowing, and shows convincingly that we are dealing with ideas which go back to the earliest days of humanity.

CHAPTER XIII

THE PROGRESSIVE RECOGNITION OF THE PRIMITIVE HIGH GOD, DURING THE TWENTIETH CENTURY

1. THE INITIAL SITUATION

WHEN Andrew Lang departed this life in 1912, the first volume of the present author's *Ursprung der Gottesidee* was coming out. It was the enlarged and revised German edition of certain studies which had already appeared in French, in the periodical *Anthropos*, under the general title *L'origine de l'idée de Dieu* (Vols. III, IV and V, 1908, 1909 and 1910). These same studies, since *Anthropos* has an international circulation, had made Andrew Lang's appearance with his new theory familiar to such wide circles that his hypothesis could no longer be simply ignored. Criticism, in many ways useful, and consequent broadening of Lang's theory made a further contribution to the same result. But how poor a welcome and what small chances of success awaited the German edition of *Der Ursprung der Gottesidee* in 1912 may be judged from the outline of the situation given by an unprejudiced observer, Dr. E. W. Mayer, the Protestant Professor of Theology at Strasbourg, in an article entitled *Zur Frage vom Ursprung der Religion*.[1] He says :

'The theories of the two British savants (Spencer and Tylor) are fiercely attacked on two sides ; on the one, by a small, almost microscopic group which has inscribed upon its banner the motto " Primitive Monotheism " ; on the other, by a strongly massed battalion, which rallies to the cry of " A Preanimistic Period ". . . . Any distinct reverberation produced by the thesis of the Oxford savant (Lang) is more than the most delicate ear of the most audacious optimist can hope to catch. It has simply not been heard. But now, at the last moment, it has been caught up by an ethno-

[1] In the *Theologische Rundschau*, edited by W. Bousset and W. Heitmüller, Vol. XVI, 1913, pp. 33–48.

logist of repute, Father W. Schmidt, of Vienna, who has done good service as editor of *Anthropos*. He has just published a work on the Origin of the Idea of God. . . .

'Whether Father Schmidt will make more impression, especially on ethnologists, than his predecessor Lang, I do not pretend to decide. That must be left to the seer who knows the past and can prophecy after the event ; but it is not likely. Clearly, the discussion has long been tending to stray, and the sins of an earlier time still have power to confuse us. It has too often happened before now that the doctrine of a primitive monotheism has been put forward purely in the interests of dogma, and supported by facts, more or less, but rather less than more. Even Schmidt's theory might produce the impression here and there—I say it with all critical reserve—that it reads into the earliest belief in a god more prefection than can unconditionally be allowed it, even if we admit the cogency of his line of argument. On the other hand, among the opponents of dogmatism, the fear of dogma has led gradually to a sort of negative dogmatism. It is often passionately denied, *a priori*, that the history of religion could by any possibility have begun with so naïve and undeveloped a belief in a single deity. There are researchers whom the mere hint of such a theory will put into a rage which certainly is not adequately justified by the fundamental idea of Evolution, that the differentiated and complicated has developed out of the simple. In that mood, even the facts are sometimes treated with rather scant courtesy. I know no recent work which denies such views as those of Lang and Schmidt and at the same time takes the trouble to sift, quite quietly, the evidence, which grows more abundant every day, of the existence of a faded and ineffective belief in a Supreme Being among numerous savage peoples, and to do so with the requisite thoroughness. Only when this is done shall we have a really satisfactory explanation of what is in any case a remarkable phenomenon. This must be said once and for all, even at the risk, which is by no means slight, of being misunderstood.'

The serious reproof which Professor Mayer makes in this passage was and remained for a long time only too just. But the ' seer who knows the past and can prophesy after the event ', that he then wished to be, has proved a false prophet in declaring that my work would probably make no more impression than Lang's. Slowly, very slowly I must admit, the views expressed therein made their way, and the facts put forward compelled attention. We will now briefly review their progress.

2. RECOGNITION OF THE HIGH GOD IN PARTICULAR AREAS

That the great antiquity of high gods, although slow in winning recognition, did at last force its way to acceptance all the more powerfully, is due partly to the investigations of a series of researchers in special fields, who were in some cases quite independent of Andrew Lang, but came each in his own area, and as a result of his special studies, to affirm the existence of a genuine Supreme Being in that area. I now give a list of these particular areas in the order in which the investigators in question have examined them in this direction.

(a) THE INDO-EUROPEANS

In this area that prominent Indologist and student of the history of religion, Professor Leopold von Schroeder of the University of Vienna, although he had formerly been an adherent of Tylor, soon recognized the importance of Lang's work and set about a corresponding investigation in his own special subject. He gave a brief report of his findings in a paper entitled *Über den Glauben an ein höchstes gutes Wesen bei den Ariern* [' The Aryan Belief in a good Supreme Being '], read before the Second International Congress for the general History of Religion, at Bâle, in 1904 [2] and in *Wesen und Ursprung der Religion, ihre Wurzeln und deren Entfaltung* [' The Nature and Origin of Religion : its Roots and their Growth '].[3] Since then, his great work *Arische Religion* has appeared, Vol. I at Leipzig in 1914, and Vol. II in 1916 ; he had planned a third, but his untimely death prevented its appearance. In the first volume of this, he dealt with the fundamental principles of religion in general, and also threw a flood of light on the facts concerning the Aryan Supreme Being. Postulating as the three ' roots ' of religion the worship of nature, the cult of the dead and the recognition of a good and supreme creative Being, he does not decide whether one of these three is older than the rest, and if so, which. In one passage he states that the question can hardly be answered ; in another, that it calls for further investigation. I have already dealt with this in a detailed criticism of the first volume in *Anthropos*, Vols. X and XI, 1915–16, pp. 285–92. As stated earlier, the whole account of the religion of the Indo-Germanic peoples given above (p. 42 *sqq.*) is drawn from von Schroeder's work.

---

[2] Afterwards published in *Wiener Zeitschrift für die Kunde des Morgenlandes*, Vol. XIX, pp. 1–23.
[3] Part 2 of *Beiträge zur Weiterentwicklung der christlichen Religion*, Munich, 1906.

(b) THE AMERINDIANS

(i) As early as 1906, one of the foremost Americanists of Germany, Paul Ehrenreich, declared his agreement with Lang's hypothesis, in an article entitled *Götter und Heilbringer* ['Gods and Saviours '].[4] He appealed especially to the American material, of which he had such extensive knowledge. He dealt chiefly with the relation between the ' saviour ', culture-hero or First Father and the Supreme Being, and not only established the mutual independence of both figures, but declared the Supreme Being to be an older conception than the ' saviours ', who indeed are usually the first beings made by the supreme Creator, while the rest of mankind derive from them, at his behest. This position is further developed, from a different point of view, by P. Radin (see below, p. 202 *sqq.*).

(ii) At about the same time, another veteran Americanist, Dr. A. L. Kroeber, Professor at the University of California (Berkeley, Cal., U.S.A.), published a long series of special studies, and finally summed up his results in an essay, *Types of Indian Culture in California.*[5] He demonstrated that the tribes living in the central part of that state belong to the oldest and most primitive in all North America.[6] Then, in two monographs, *Indian Myths of South Central California* and *The Religion of the Indians of California*,[7] he showed that, contrary to the animistic and preanimistic theories of the late development of a high god, these very tribes had a clearly developed Supreme Being and an idea of a real creation much more decidedly than any other Amerindian peoples, despite the relatively great advances of the latter in other aspects of culture. All these studies are now summed up and supplemented in his monumental work, *Handbook of Californian Indians.*[8]

Kroeber describes the Central Californian region in general as follows :

[4] *Zeitschrift für Ethnologie*, 1906, pp. 536–610.
[5] University of California Publications of American Archaeology and Ethnology, Vol. II, 1904, pp. 82–103.
[6] The same result was reached by F. Krause also, in his very penetrating study *Die Kultur der kalifornischen Indianer in ihrer Bedeutung für die Ethnologie und die nordamerikanische Völkerkunde*, Leipzig, 1921, which I reviewed thoroughly in *Anthropos*, Vols. XVI–XVII, 1921–2, pp. 502–10. For his position regarding the religion of these tribes, see *Ursprung der Gottesidee*, Vol. I, ed. 2, p. 657.
[7] Univ. of Calif. Pubs., Vol. IV, pp. 167–250 and 319–56 respectively.
[8] Bulletin 78 of the Bureau of American Ethnology, Washington, 1925.

' In Central California there is always a true creation of the world, of mankind, and of its institutions. The conception of the creator is often quite lofty, and tricky exploits or defeats are usually not connected with him. Often there is an antithesis between this beneficent and truly divine creator and a second character, usually the Coyote, who in part co-operates with the creator but in part thwarts him, being responsible for the death of mankind and other imperfections in the world-scheme. In the northern half of the Central region the creator is generally anthropomorphic ; if not, he is merged into one personage with the more or less tricky Coyote ' (Univ. Calif. Pub. Am. Arch. Eth., Vol. IV, p. 343).

Elsewhere, in Vol. II of the same series, he gives a still more adequate account of the Central region, whose theology he describes (p. 97) as follows :

' Instead of a human divinity there is almost everywhere a true creator, a god who makes. . . . Often he makes the world from the primitive water. Generally he also makes mountains and rivers. Usually he creates food. Almost always he creates men, and frequently he divides them by languages and localities. He gives men their arts and occupations. . . . However much their power may be kindred or alike, the character and the functions of the Coyote and the Creator invariably differ fundamentally in the myths of the Indians of this culture area. The Creator's names are indicative of his nature. With the Yuki he is Going-alone, with the Wintun Existing-in-the-above, with the Maidu Earth-initiate or Earth-maker ; where he appears in animal form it is often as the Eagle.'

(iii) R. B. Dixon,[9] speaking of one of the Central Californian tribes, the Maidu, had described the figure of their Creator in the following terms :

' The importance given in the Maidu mythology to the creation is another feature characteristic of the stock. The problems of the origin and beginning of things seem to have appealed strongly to the Maidu imagination ; and they have not been content to assume a world already created, and ready for occupancy when the ancestors of mankind should reach it after an earlier sojourn elsewhere, as did to a great extent the tribes of the South-west, for example. Nor is the creation here merely an episode—a re-creation after a deluge brought on by one cause or another—as it is in some mythologies. Here the creation is a real beginning : beyond it, behind it, there is nothing. In the beginning was only the great sea, calm and un-limited, to which, down from the clear sky, the Creator came, or on which he and Coyote were floating in a canoe. Of the origin

[9] In *The Northern Maidu*, Bulletin of American Museum of Natural History, Vol. XVII, 1905, pp. 119–346. The following quotations are from p. 335 *sq.*

or previous place of abode of either Creator or Coyote, the Maidu know nothing. . . .

' One of the most striking features of the myths is the sharp and consistent contrast of the characters of the Creator and Coyote. Throughout the whole series the Creator is uniformly dignified, benevolent, never stooping to trickery, and always striving to make life easy for man, and to render that life deathless and happy. On the other hand, Coyote is at all times opposed to him, striving to render life hard, and insisting that man must die and suffer. Not only does Coyote thus constantly at all times oppose the benevolent desires of the Creator, but he is mischievousness personified, a prince of tricksters, playing tricks on others, and as frequently being tricked himself, and led into innumerable scrapes by his greediness and sensuality.'

Dixon (*op. cit.*, pp. 336–7) quite rightly rejects the Evolutionist theory then held by Boas, that the combination of a grave and a playful element in one person was the older stage, and that it was only with the advance of culture that the two were separated. That theory is very simply disposed of by the fact that it is on the contrary the ethnologically oldest tribes among whom the separation of the two elements is most marked, those tribes whose outward and material civilization is the lowest.[10] Besides, Boas himself would now hardly maintain this purely Evolutionist hypothesis, for since that time he has worked his way more and more completely around to the historical method and paved the way for its triumph in North America.[11]

The reason why the Creator apparently yields to Coyote's onsets is really that mankind lets itself be misled by Coyote into following him and deserting the Creator. Therefore the latter lets them have their way, and at the same time prepares the most condign punishment thereby. On this point, compare the present writer's remarks in *Ursprung der Gottesidee*, Vol. II, p. 140 *sqq.*, and that volume generally, which treats of the religions of the oldest races in North and South America.

(c) THE PYGMY PEOPLES

(i) Attention has already been drawn to the races of dwarfish people inhabiting Central Africa, the Andaman Islands, the peninsula

[10] Cf. also the views of P. Radin, cited in *Ursprung der Gottesidee*, Vol. II, p. 406 *sq.*

[11] Cf. his article, *The Methods of Ethnology*, in *American Anthropologist*, N.S., Vol. XXII, 1920, pp. 311–12 ; and also the present author's remarks in *Anthropos*, Vols. XIV–XV, 1919–20, on the same subject, under the title *Die kulturhistorische Methode und die nordamerikanische Ethnologie.*

of Malacca and the more retired parts of the Philippines, by
J. L. A. de Quatrefages in his treatise *Les Pygmées*, Paris, 1887,
and by A. Le Roy in a work with the same title, published at Tours
(no date). Both mentioned their religion especially. Following on
them, the present author undertook a comprehensive investigation
of the anthropological, ergological, sociological, psychological,
ethnological and religious conditions of these tribes in a work
published at Stuttgart in 1910 and entitled *Die Stellung der Pygmäenvölker in der Entwicklungsgeschichte des Menschen* [' The Position of
the Pygmy Peoples in the History of Human Development ']
The conclusion arrived at was ' that the Pygmies, generally considered, represent the oldest stage at which we can arrive of the
ethnological development of humanity ', exceeding in primitiveness
even the tribes of South-East Australia. (See *op. cit.*, p. 280.) In
replying to A. Padtberg, *Zwerge als Stammväter des Menschengeschlechtes* [' Dwarfs as the progenitors of humanity '], in *Stimmen der
Zeit*, Vol. CVII, 1924, I recently put the theory on a yet firmer basis
in an article entitled *Die Pygmäenvölker als älteste derzeit uns
erreichbare Menschengeschicht*, in *Hochland*, Vol. XXXIII, 1925–6,
pp. 574–92.[12]

Under these circumstances, it is of course of especial interest
to know what is the religion of these peoples. After establishing that neither personification of natural forces, animism
nor ancestor-worship is to be found among them, and that
their belief in magic is decidedly less than among their
neighbours of greater stature and more advanced material
culture, the following summary is given in the above-mentioned
work :

(ii) ' If now we pass to points of positive comparison, we are
struck by one very remarkable fact above all others. That is, the
clear acknowledgement and worship of a Supreme Being. He is
everywhere the creator and sovran lord of the whole world, thus
refuting the theories of those who suppose that such primitive
peoples are quite incapable of envisaging the bewildering variety of
the universe as a single whole, much less of referring it to a single
cause. On the contrary, as we see, the supremacy of this Being
is so energetically and comprehensively expressed that all other
supernormal beings are far inferior and invariably subject to him.'

But it is not merely that every Pygmy Supreme Being
has the prerogative of unity and of lordship over all other
beings. His remaining attributes, which make his character

[12] [' The Pygmy peoples as the oldest stratum of humanity at present
known to us '.] An important detail of the problem is treated by me
in *Das ethnologische Alter von Pfeil und Bogen* [' The ethnological age
of the bow and arrow '], in *Zeitschrift für Ethnologie*, 1925, pp. 68–78.

as a veritable Supreme Being yet more universally manifest, are the subject of very far-reaching agreement among them.

(iii) Other forms of their worship of the Supreme Being are short informal prayers (here and there, however, longer ceremonies exist), offerings of first-fruits, *i.e.*, from the game they catch, or of plants which they have gathered, and in one tribe, the Semang of Malacca, a sin-offering of their own blood, which they mix with water and throw up towards the sky during a thunder-storm.

All the information which has come in since the book was written concerning these peoples, and in some cases it has been decidedly increased, has been able to modify the above sketch only in small details, while confirming and strengthening it in all the important features. This will be seen from the thorough and comprehensive account of the religion of the Pygmy peoples to be published in *Ursprung der Gottesidee*, Vol. III.

(d) THE SEMITES

(i) One of the most prominent Semitists of our day, Professor D. C. Brockelmann, of the University of Halle, handles a peculiarly important area, lying between savagery and important civilizations, in his monograph *Allah und die Götzen, der Ursprung des vorislamischen Monotheismus*.[13] He deals with the question of monotheism before the days of Muhammed, rejecting the view that it is derived from Christian or Jewish sources, and also the suggestion that Allah is developed out of the more ancient god Hubal, whose image is said to have stood in the Kaaba.

He then examines Wellhausen's view that Allah owes his existence to the peculiarities of the Arabic language, in which each tribe fell into the way of calling its own deity simply ' God ', with the result that the particular gods gradually disappeared. This view also Brockelmann rejects.

' It is impossible ' he says ' to understand how this general name could have raised itself so decidedly over the specific ideas that it could triumphantly survive their annihilation ' (p. 104) ; and he rightly conjectures ' that Wellhausen, when he put forward this theory, was more or less consciously under the influence of the hypotheses put forward by the British school of anthropology under E. B. Tylor, of whose supporters in the field of Semitic studies Robertson Smith and besides him Wellhausen have exercised the

[13] [' Allah and the Idols : the Origin of Preislamic Monotheism '] ; in *Archiv für Religionswissenschaft*, Vol. XXI, 1922, pp. 99–121.

strongest directing influence on studies of the history of religion '. (Cf. above, p. 78.) ' It is well known that the most important tenet of this school is the origin of the idea of God from animism. . . . Thus, as Wellhausen, after the fashion of this school, supposed animism to be the only source of the religious life, logical consistency impelled him to derive the Arabian Allah, who could not be evolved directly from animism, out of animistic deities by the way of a process of abstraction ' (p. 104 sq.).

(ii) Brockelmann then asks the question whether this theory is still consistent with the history of religion, as the progress of research in the last few decades reveals it. To answer the question, he begins by examining the conceptions which the old, preislamic Arabs associated with the name of Allah. Then follows a very valuable collection of these ideas, exact references to his authorities being given.

Allah is above all the creator of the world, of the earth and of mankind. Therefore he is also lord of the whole world. In particular, he sends the refreshing rain which is the source of all life. He is moreover the absolute master of men, and determines their fates. He knows their thoughts, words and deeds, and is the guardian of oaths, the supreme judge of conduct, and, as such, the author of rewards and punishments. He is eternal and immutable, almighty and all-good. The expression ar Rahmân, ' the Merciful', is older than Islam. Therefore men may trust in his mercy, and honour and praise him. The very phrase al hamdu l'illah, ' praise be to Allah ', is of preislamic date.

(iii) The question whether this belief in Allah is to be considered the common property of all Arabs or a sort of esoteric doctrine must in Brockelmann's opinion be answered in favour of the second alternative. The reasons he gives are not particularly cogent ; they are equally consistent with a state of things in which the belief in Allah was held and practised in different degrees by different individuals. He continues as follows :

' If then, after defining the position of Allah in ancient Arabian belief, and establishing the fact that it cannot be explained either by borrowing from one of the revealed religions nor by animism, we look for analogies to such a divine figure, the " Originators ", as Söderblom calls them in Das Wesen des Gottesglaubens, immediately suggest themselves ' (p. 118 sq.).

As Brockelmann immediately afterwards refers to my views (' as Father W. Schmidt has shown in his work on the Origin of the Idea of God '), one may conclude that he does not use the word ' originator ' precisely in Söderblom's sense, since he speaks as if I there maintained this theory also. It is clear enough from my criticism of Söderblom's ideas that I definitely reject it, as inconsistent with ethnological facts (see above, p. 140). Moreover, the attributes and functions with which Brockelmann credits Allah make him far too great for the narrow bounds within which Söderblom's ' originators ' are confined. In particular, a high god who intervenes to such purpose in the physical world and the ethical life of man and is the object of such lively hopes and fears, such fervent prayer and praise from men, is very different from an otiose deity who receives no worship.[14]

Even supposing the monotheism of the preislamic belief in Allah fully established, this is as yet no ethnological proof of primitive monotheism. Neither I nor anyone else needs to spend time on discussing this point, seeing that the Semites are a comparatively long way from the real origin of humanity. It merely establishes a certain presumption in favour of it, because of the general fact that the pastoral nomads have remained truest to the conditions of the primitive religion as compared with the rest of the later and more advanced peoples.[15]

(iv) I have therefore no hesitation in agreeing with Brockelmann when he goes on to say :

' There can really be no more question of Renan's hypothesis concerning the original tendency of the Semites to monotheism. Our tradition gives no indication of an older conception of Allah, lying behind the idea of him as an " originator " ; we must therefore leave it an open question whether or not he, as perhaps other such figures did, may have arisen out of a culture-hero or other mythical personage. No such assumption, indeed, is necessary ; for it cannot be denied that the belief in an " originator " could arise out of primitive man's need of an explanation of the world ' (p. 120).

Professor Brockelmann may convince himself, from the whole of this present work, how completely right he is in that last sentence.

In conclusion, Brockelmann raises the question whether other Semitic races knew of such divine figures. He holds that no deity comparable to Allah can be shown to have

[14] For further discussion of Brockelmann's views, see *Ursprung*, Vol. I, ed. 2, pp. 679 *sq.*, 693.
[15] See my remarks on this subject in *Anthropos*, Vol. IX, 1914, p. 675 *sqq.*

existed by the inscriptions of the Northern and Western
Semites, nor by those of South Arabia. He agrees with
J. Hehn (*Die biblische und babylonische Gottesidee* [' The Idea
of God in the Bible and at Babylon '], Leipzig, 1913, p. 150
sqq.) in rejecting the suggestion of Lagrange, that among the
primitive Semites, El was the personal name of God, and
that the several national deities were produced only by the
splitting up of this single personality (p. 121). I have taken
the liberty, in my review of Hehn's work, to make a number
of criticisms of and reflections on this view and others connected with it [16]; perhaps Brockelmann will find in them
reasons for a more optimistic attitude towards this question.
Now that his meritorious initiative has disburdened the study
of Semitic religion of the load of animism which lay upon it,
I cannot but think that this will prove a pioneer work, in the
sense that it leaves the way clear for further investigations
on the same lines. Compare also H. Grimme, *Die altsinai-
tischen Buchstabeninschriften*, Berlin, 1929, p. 96 *sqq.*, for a
collection of preislamic epigraphic material bearing on
Semitic theism.

3. THE RECOGNITION OF THE HIGH GODS BY PSYCHOLOGISTS AND HISTORIANS OF RELIGION

(a) PSYCHOLOGISTS (J. H. J. LEUBA, K. ÖSTERREICH)

It is noteworthy that the facts and the high antiquity of
primitive high gods were early recognized and frankly acknowledged by two prominent religious psychologists, James H.
Leuba in America and K. Österreich in Germany.

(a) In his book *A Psychological Study of Religion, its Origin,
Function and Future*, New York, 1912, Leuba writes as follows :

' It is an old opinion that even the lowest savage entertains a belief
in a Supreme Being, however dimly conceived and little reverenced.
. . . Although this opinion suffered temporary discredit . . .
recent anthropological researches furnish sufficient evidence to
warrant a return to this view ' (p. 100). He concludes his synopsis
of this evidence with the words ' the general existence of the belief
in High Gods is now accepted by most anthropologists ' although, he
adds, ' there is no unanimity of opinion in regard to the origin of
this belief ' (p. 103). In this respect he shows his own apprehension
of the matter to be remarkably just. ' The truth of the matter as
I see it is that the High Gods *proceeded from an independent and
specific source* ; they are, or were originally, the Makers. The

[16] *Ibid.*, pp. 344–8.

essential elements of my theory are that man comes to the idea of superhuman beings along several routes, that the characteristics of these beings depend upon their origin, and that one—or one class —of these beings, the one arising from curiosity about the making of things, is necessarily a relatively lofty conception, awe-inspiring, and suggestive of power and benevolence. . . . And, whenever that conception appeared, the god would have possessed the comparatively high and noble endowment naturally belonging in the mind of even the lowest savage to the Creator of man and things ' (p. 103). He also finds fault with scientists for neglecting this origin of the idea of God, namely ' the problem of creation '. ' This very early and potent source of the idea of great unseen beings has been very insufficiently taken into account. The idea of a mighty Maker of things may safely be attributed to men as low in intelligence as are the lowest tribes now extant, for it appears very early in the child ' (p. 96). Speaking of the relation between magic and religion, he lays down, among others, the following propositions (p. 176) : ' 1. Magic and religion have had independent origins. Neither of them need be regarded as a development from the other. 2. Magic contributed very little directly to the making of religion. 3. The simpler forms of magic probably antedated religion '. Here he forgets that he himself, a little earlier, in speaking of the idea of a maker, which he supposes to be the origin of a high god, had said (p. 104), ' The idea of a Maker I suppose to have originally presented itself to the race very much as it does to a five- or six-year-old child who is suddenly struck with the idea that some one must have made the world '.*

(β) Three years later, one of the most prominent German authorities on the psychology of religion, Dr. K. Österreich, Professor at the University of Tübingen, likewise acknowledged the fact that a Supreme Being is worshipped, particularly in the oldest phase of religious development.

In his *Introduction to the Psychology of Religion* [' Einführung in die Religionspsychologie '],[17] he writes as follows with regard to the Pygmy peoples :

' In view of the quite rudimentary condition of these peoples' culture, it came as a great surprise to all investigators who took any especial interest in them, that in regard to ethics and also to religion they stand far higher than the peoples of normal stature who live around them ' (p. 104). And, a little further on, ' It is however surprising that they appear to have an almost monotheistic outlook. Certainly, much has still to be explained in the field of religion especially ; but in general, one cannot escape the impression that the

* [Why Leuba is supposed to have forgotten this when he wrote his remarks on magic, I cannot imagine.]

[17] See also, by the same author, *Weltbild der Gegenwart* [' The World as it seems to-day '], Berlin, 1920, p. 93 *sqq.*

truth is to be sought along the lines laid down by Father W. Schmidt in his meritorious monograph *Die Stellung der Pygmäenvölker in der Entwicklungsgeschichte des Menschen*' (p. 106).

Österreich emphatically defends the facts concerning the existence of the Supreme Being against the supposition, favoured by some, that they can be traced to Christian influences, as Martin and Wundt would have it. He writes (p. 107) :

' The demonstration that a religious stage relatively so high exists among populations culturally so backward was a great surprise for every investigator brought up in the usual doctrines of Evolutionism. . . . But these objections (*i.e.*, the hypothesis of influence from without) lose force if, as we know is the case, monotheistic ideas exist also among numerous other peoples who certainly have not been influenced by Christianity. Such objections are the fruit of dogmatical Evolutionist prejudice.'

He fully recognizes also (p. 124 *sqq.*) that a Supreme Being of moral character is widely distributed among the remaining peoples.

As regards the relation between religion and magic, he is decidedly opposed to deriving the former from the latter.

' No cogent proof ', he writes (pp. 115, 126), ' that we must see in magic a stage preliminary to religion, as many investigators, including Frazer, Marett, Preuss and Vierkandt, now hold, has hitherto been produced. Certainly magic is in principle lower than religion ; but it remains to be shown that there ever was a preanimistic stage in which magic alone existed. . . . Everywhere, we find magic and primitive religion side by side. For magic to represent a genuinely preanimistic grade of religion, it would be necessary to show that in an original form it lacked all belief in a soul, also that it can exist isolated and without religion.'

(*b*) ETHNOLOGISTS AND HISTORIANS OF RELIGION : K. T. PREUSS, J. R. SWANTON, P. RADIN, R. H. LOWIE, F. HEILER, A. W. NIEUWENHUIS

The numbers of ethnologists and historians of religion who joined the recognizers of ancient high gods has increased steadily. The Americanists are the largest section ; but the reason for this is simply, that Evolutionism, the great bar to the acceptance of these high gods, was shaken off earlier and more emphatically in America than elsewhere.[18]

[18] See my two articles, *Die kulturhistorische Methode und die nordamerikanische Ethnologie* (*Anthropos*, Vols. XIV–XV, 1919–20, pp. 546–63) and *Die Abwendung vom Evolutionismus und die Hinwendung zum Historismus in der Amerikanistik* (*ibid.*, Vols. XVI–XVII, 1921–2, pp. 487–519).

(*a*) The first recruit was most unexpected, no other than one of the pioneers of the theory of magic, Dr. K. Th. Preuss, Professor at the University of Berlin and Director of the National Museum (*Staatsmuseum*) there. He made a beginning as early as 1914 in a bibliographical review of works on savage religions.[19] Immediately afterwards there appeared his treatise on *The Spiritual Culture of Savage Peoples* [' Die geistige Kultur der Naturvölker '],[20] in which we read the following :

' That animism and ancestor-worship are the foundations of religion is a theory which goes back to the earliest days of ethnology. Fifteen years ago, however, Andrew Lang introduced the view that an earlier monotheism existed among savages, independent of animism ; and this has of late been zealously maintained by Father W. Schmidt.   This surprising state of affairs, which cannot be got rid of by blank denial, although " monotheism " is hardly the right word for it, we must try to understand on the basis of the general outlines of religious forces already given ' (p. 59).

Preuss makes it decidedly harder for himself to understand it by paying too little attention to just these most ancient peoples and persistently speaking of the Supreme Being as having no cult.

Preuss speaks yet more decidedly and to a great extent more definitely and correctly in a later work, *Die höchste Gottheit bei den kulturarmen Völkern*,[21] as follows :

' The discovery of these beings (*sc.*, " saviours " and high gods) cut so decidedly across the ideas previously entertained by anthropologists concerning a steady development from lower to higher, that for some decades there was considerable reluctance to deal with the matter, and it has been clearly envisaged only in very recent times.   Now that the suggestion of Christian influence on the formation of the high gods has been given up, we can understand that their attributes have impelled many investigators to idealize them, or to find in them a sort of primitive monotheism or primeval revelation.[22]   Those on the other hand who try to reconcile such beings with the results of earlier research have had their ideas

[19] In *Archiv für Religionswissenschaft*, Vol. XVII, 1914, p. 544 *sqq.*
[20] No. 542 of the series *Aus. Natur. und Geisteswelt*, Leipzig and Berlin, 1914.
[21] [Practically ' high gods of low races ', to borrow Lang's formula] ; published in the journal *Psychologische Forschungen, Berlin*, Vol. II, 1922, pp. 161–208.   Preuss developed much the same ideas in a paper read on January 15, 1921, before the Berlin Society for Anthropology, Ethnology and Prehistory, afterwards published in the *Zeitschrift für Ethnologie* under the title *Die oberste Gottheit bei den Naturvölkern*, Vol. LIV, 1922, pp. 123–9.
[22] Cf. Schmidt, *Ursprung der Gottesidee*, Vol. I, ed. 2, p. 637.

revolutionized to a certain extent ; for it is now clear that even at a low level there are to be found, along with a more or less un-intelligible magical cult, lofty ideas, worthy of a religion in our sense of the word ' (p. 161 *sq.*).

Turning to the evaluation of the figure of the high god, Preuss recognizes that ' all students of the subject who have deliberately concerned themselves with these supreme deities now agree that they are not the last stage of a development, the headstone of the corner in the temple reared by human thought to its gods, but may be an early religious testimony. In fact there are cases in which the only information we possess is that such a single god exists ' (p. 164).

At the end of his article (p. 207), Preuss puts forward the fruitful idea that one cause of closer consciousness on the part of mankind of the supreme Deity may have been the blending of such a deity with lower nature-gods who were more nearly human.

From this it would appear that nature-gods and nature-spirits arrived at a higher form and a nobler cult, not in accordance with the formula of a so-called ' inner ' evolution, steadily advancing from lower to higher, but by a contact, the result of historical events, with the Supreme Being, who was quite independent of them and arose from a totally different source. Hence Preuss develops, and quite rightly, a methodological principle which is opposed to the facile schemata of Evolutionists.

' In any case ', he says (p. 207), ' the two poles [of religious thought] take shape and meet each other in a remarkable variety of ways ; and we must do justice to both sides alike, in their historical sequence and in our psychological analysis of them, never forgetting that historical development is one thing, and progress from what is supposed to be lower to higher is quite another.'

Preuss gives utterance to another fruitful suggestion in his recent work, *Glauben und Mystik im Schatten des Höchsten Wesens* [' Belief and Mysticism in the Shadow of the Supreme Being '], Leipzig, 1926. He there points out that the religion of savages does not consist in a disconnected assembly of single ideas, but that these single ideas are but the parts of a great scheme of the universe, and can be evaluated only in connexion with it. The upholder, or, as Preuss elsewhere less happily calls him, the personification of this great scheme of the universe is often the Supreme Being, the sky-god (p. 25 *sq.*, cf. 41 *sq.*). Even a great number of things which seem

unintelligible to us and have a look of magic about them are
to be explained in this way. He says (p. 38) :

> ' The necessary complement thereof lies in the simultaneous belief
> in a Supreme Being who, as the savages hold, bestowed upon them
> the ceremonial of their worship at the beginning of the world. The
> first men were already provided therewith by the supreme deity,
> in order that they might continue to operate for the benefit of the
> world at large and control the supernatural powers. This worship
> is consequently not directed to the Supreme Being, who, being a kind
> of order of the universe, sits enthroned above all events, but only
> to the powers to which such functions in the world were entrusted
> at the beginning.'

Preuss is perfectly right in treating the Supreme Being not
merely as satisfying the intellectual desire to find a cause, but
also as helping man in the needs of life ; a help which primitive
man, being sorely in need of succour, feels he cannot do without. But it is startling to find that here again Preuss, who
makes no pretence at historical research, and consequently
does not consider the profound difference between the more
and less ancient forms, makes remoteness from the world and
absence of worship the characteristics of the Supreme Being
as such (p. 40). These fit only the later form of that Being,
when pushed on one side and thrust into the background.

(β) On laying down the office of President of the Anthropological Society of Washington, one of the veterans of North
American ethnology, John R. Swanton, delivered a retiring
address on *Some Anthropological Misconceptions*.[23] In this
he made a sharp attack on Evolutionism in the fields of sociology and of the science of religion alike. He sketched, sometimes with subtle irony, the various Evolutionist theories,
Spencer's manism, Tylor's animism, and Frazer's magism,
rejecting them all as too one-sided and ' particularist ', not
taking account of the multiplex nature of the truth. He also
assailed the unilinear schema of this kind of Evolutionism
and declared for the real existence of several parallel and
independent lines of development. He writes :

> ' Even in the case of our regnant monotheism it is a fair question
> whether it does not tie on to a belief in a sky-god extending back
> to the earliest days of religion among men, the only change which
> it has undergone being the relatively greater importance and deeper
> spiritualization of the concept in later times.'

[23] *American Anthropologist*, Vol. XIX, N.S., 1917, pp. 459–70 ;
the citation is from p. 466.

Swanton explains his point of view even more completely
and more positively in an important article, *Three Factors in
Primitive Religion*,[24] wherein, first, he once more shows himself
an outspoken opponent of the theories of Tylor, Marett, Read
and Lévy-Bruhl. Religion, he holds, has indeed in the course
of time come into connexion with the phenomenon of death,
with dreams, with magic and so forth ; but it is not the product of these things, but rather is obviously one of the primary
components of human nature, not to be connected with any
such specific origin as death or dreaming (p. 360). He believes
that religion was to begin with a complex whole, composed of
many particulars as yet undefined, which were differentiated
only in the course of time (p. 363 *sq.*).

Regarding the genesis and growth of primitive monotheism,
he first explains that even in many forms of Christianity, both
in official theory and in popular belief, in Islam, in Chinese
deism and in the religion of Zoroaster, an undeniable monotheism has absorbed other elements also in increasing proportions. He then continues as follows :

' When we consider the limitations and dilutions of monotheism
above indicated, the difference between the monotheistic religions
of more developed peoples and those primitive cults which include
the idea of a superior or supreme deity is not so great. Such a
conception, usually associated with the sky or the sun, is, indeed,
surprisingly common. . . . Its occurrence among certain races
regarded as most primitive from other points of view is still more
surprising, peoples such as the natives of south-eastern Australia, the
Negrillo, and even the Bushmen and Andaman Islanders. Therefore even the assumed advanced monotheism, or something very
close to it, may have originated in various parts of the world at an
early date through specialization out of the third element of the
complex above given [referring to a list of known beliefs on the
preceding page, the third of which is " a germinal monotheism "].'

These words certainly bear clear enough testimony to the
reality and genuinely native origin, the wide distribution and
the great antiquity which Swanton ascribes to the primitive
high gods, and also to his refusal to derive them from manism,
animism or magism.[25]

(γ) A third prominent Americanist, P. Radin, delivered on
April 27, 1924, an address before the Jewish Historical Society
in London. It has since been published under the title *Mono-*

[24] *Ibid.*, Vol. XXVI, N.S., 1924, pp. 358–65. The quotation is
from p. 363.
[25] Cf. Schmidt, *Ursprung*, Vol. I, ed. 2, pp. 648–52.

theism among Primitive Peoples, and republished, with slight modifications, as Chapter xviii (*Monotheistic Tendencies*) of the same author's work, *Primitive Man as Philosopher* (New York and London, 1927). In the setting which it there receives its effectiveness is further increased; for Radin's thesis is that the mental equipment of primitive man was exactly the same as our own, and that he had his poets and thinkers whose genius far excelled the capacity of the vulgar; a thesis which he supports on all sides in this work with abundance of examples. Beginning with a short sketch of the old Evolutionist theories concerning the genesis of monotheism from animism or some other source, he describes the entry of Andrew Lang upon the scene in the most sympathetic manner. The smallness of the following which Lang's new views won among ethnologists he accounts for by the weaknesses in his proofs; but at the same time, he holds that the real reason for it was the then prevalence of Evolutionism.

' To have admitted ', he says, ' among primitive peoples the existence of monotheism in any form would have been equivalent to abandoning the whole doctrine of evolutionary stages. And this they were not prepared to do nor did the facts at that time definitely warrant it.' However, ' twenty-five years have elapsed since Lang wrote his book and his intuitive insight has been abundantly corroborated. The ethnologists were quite wrong. Accurate data obtained by trained specialists have replaced his rather vague examples. That many primitive peoples have a belief in a supreme creator no one to-day seriously denies ' (*Primitive Man as Philosopher*, p. 345 *sq.*).

However, Lang's view that this monotheistic belief represented a degeneracy from a higher and purer faith has not received the smallest corroboration, according to Radin. Anything low, worthless, or immoral that may be found attaching to the figure of a Supreme Being is not the product of degeneration, but of a combination with a figure of the kind known as ' the Transformer, Culture-hero, Trickster '. There were to begin with two concepts :

' the supreme deity, creator of all things, beneficent and ethical, unapproachable directly and taking but little interest in the world after he has created it ; and the Transformer, the establisher of the present order of things, utterly nonethical, only incidentally and inconsistently beneficent, approachable, and directly intervening in a very human way in the affairs of the world. These two figures represent two contrasting and antithetic modes of thought, two completely opposed temperaments continually in conflict. All that

has been called contamination and degeneration is but the projection
of the image of the Transformer upon that of a supreme creator
and vice versa ' (*Ibid.*, p. 347 ; Radin then proceeds to give specific
proofs of this double thesis from his wide range of knowledge,
particularly of American facts).

All that Radin here adduces is very meritorious. But it is
hard to see how it is to disprove degeneration. It touches
only that form of the theory, to which indeed Andrew Lang
apparently inclined, which teaches that degeneracy did not
come about until animism arose. Radin's statements make
it clear that degeneracy arose from older origins than that,
namely the combination of the Supreme Being with a lower,
less worthy, more human figure, that of the ' Transformer '
or tribal father. But this is simply the theory of degeneration
in a special form. Compare what has already been said (above,
p. 190) concerning the development of the First Father.

By way of a basis for his own explanation of the manner in
which the idea of a Supreme Being originated, Radin lays
down the general axiom that among primitive men the gen-
erality are equipped exactly as we are with regard to thought
and feelings ; but also that the proportion of outstanding
abilities, persons of genius, exceeding the general average, is
the same as it is among ourselves.[26] At all times and among
all peoples, he maintains, ' the idealist and the materialist,
the dreamer and the realist, the introspective and the non-
introspective man ' have existed, and likewise ' the devoutly
religious, the intermittently, the indifferently religious man '.
Monotheism is the creation of the devoutly religious who were
also aesthetic. These were always few in number, for the
vast majority of mankind is indifferently religious, materialistic
and realistic.

' Monotheism would then have to be taken as fundamentally an
intellectual-religious expression of a very special type of tempera-
ment and emotion. Hence the absence of cults, for instance, the
unapproachability of the supreme being, his vagueness of outline,
and his essential lack of function. Whatever dynamic force he
possesses for the community is that with which the realists endowed
him ' (*Ibid.*, p. 367).

Radin's basal facts are in themselves true beyond all doubt,
and he has deserved very well in bringing them to notice.
They have had moreover a very considerable influence on the

[26] The present writer had already expressed these ideas. See W.
Schmidt and W. Koppers, *Völker und Kulturen*, Vol. I, Regensburg,
1924, p. 59 *sq.*

fixing and shaping of the idea of the Supreme Being. But I do not believe that they alone can provide a full explanation of its genesis. Against this, among other things, is the fact that, whatever Radin, like Ehrenreich and Preuss, may say, the oldest form, and especially the oldest form, of the Supreme Being is neither without function, without cult, nor unapproachable. Far from it ; he stands in full, vigorous and effectual relations to mankind. Hence what Radin supposes to have arisen only at a later date in consequence of the combined activities of two differently gifted types of men appears in reality as the first and most ancient form of the Supreme Being. Hence it follows that this idea is not the product of one type of mentality only, but owes its origin to the general average endowments of the human mind. Of course this is not to deny that men of outstanding religious gifts at once grasped this conception more deeply and with more vigour than the rest, and worked with greater energy to shape and to propagate it.

As regards explicit monotheism, Radin says that it

' is rare among primitive peoples, but possibly not quite so uncommon as the literal reading of the facts might seem to indicate. . . . From my own experience I am inclined to assume that a limited number of explicit monotheists are to be found in every primitive tribe that has at all developed the concept of a supreme creator ' (*Ibid.*, p. 371 *sq.*).

In conclusion, I would draw attention to the decisive way in which Radin rejects Evolutionism. After expressing [in the original lecture] a fear that his thesis might seem exaggerated and clean contrary to the ideas which we generally associate with primitive peoples, he continues (*Ibid.*, p. 373) :

' Most of us have been brought up in or influenced by the tenets of orthodox ethnology and this was largely an enthusiastic and quite uncritical attempt to apply the Darwinian theory of evolution to the facts of social experience. Many ethnologists, sociologists, and psychologists still persist in this endeavor. No progress will ever be achieved, however, until scholars rid themselves, once and for all, of the curious notion that everything possesses an evolutionary history ; until they realize that certain ideas and certain concepts are as ultimate for man as a social being as specific physiological reactions are for him as a biological entity.' [27]

[27] I have already shown (above, p. 197) that the reaction against Evolutionism has gone pretty far. I have expressed views very similar to Radin's in controversy with Wundt, see *Ursprung der Gottesidee*, Vol. I, ed. 2, pp. 52 *sqq.*, 504 *sqq.*

(δ) R. H. Lowie, who devotes a part of his book, *Primitive Religion*,[28] to the question of the Supreme Beings, is yet a fourth leading Americanist. He begins with a thorough criticism of the animistic theory of Tylor, the magism of Frazer, and incidentally of Durkheim, and the collectivist hypothesis of Durkheim, all of which he rejects.

In criticizing Tylor's animism, he begins by countering the criticisms directed by Durkheim against that savant, which he finds very unsatisfactory, since Durkheim's arguments suffer from a

' combination of arbitrary assertions and rationalistic psychologizing and, above all, from a misunderstanding of the question at issue ' (p. 110).

Durkheim's assumption that totemism is older than animism he attacks at its foundations ; for Durkheim supposes that the totemic Australians are the most primitive of peoples, whereas Lowie opposes this emphatically, referring to really primitive races such as the Semang, the Andamanese and the Paviotso, who know nothing of totemism. He is still more emphatic and briefer in his rejection of G. Elliot Smith and W. J. Perry's pan-Egyptian theory, which derives all animism from Egypt and supposes that it reached the other peoples of the earth from there only ;

' The historical evidence ', he says (p. 114), ' adduced to support this inference seems to me to be precisely nil '.

Against Tylor he objects especially that, following the lines laid down in his day by Darwin and Huxley, he connected with the idea of spirit far too many things which might equally well have some other origin. This Andrew Lang, who had a more independent mind, rightly perceived in so far as the Supreme Being of primitive peoples is concerned ; for he saw that such a Being need not and in many cases cannot have been developed out of animism. Further, Lowie agrees with my development of Lang's position, which I reached by investigation of ' culture-circles.' He makes no difficulty about admitting that the existence of a Supreme Being among so many primitive peoples, so far separated geographically and often sharply differentiated as to race, can be explained neither by casual borrowing in

[28] New York, 1924. Cf., by the same author, *Primitive Society*, New York, 1920, a pioneer work directed against Morgan and other Evolutionists ; reviewed by the present author in *Anthropos*, Vols. XVI–XVII, 1921–2, pp. 487–93, *q.v.*

later times nor from independent development of fundamental ideas.

'Any religious traits held by these Negroid groups (the Negritos, Bushmen and Tasmanians) prior to their specialization', he says (p. 126), 'must be of hoary age ; and if these features are common to them and the rudest American aborigines, we are indeed carried back to as early a period of human belief as we can reasonably expect to attain by means of an historical reconstruction. In short, on the score of logic I have no objection to Father Schmidt's premises.'

He feels bound, however, to object to my views on the ground that the facts adduced in support of them are not convincing nor certain enough. This he tries to show by a brief criticism of the data regarding the Tasmanians, the Pygmies of Central Africa, the Semang, the Andamanese and the Bushmen. I have to note that there are inadequacies in this criticism which I cannot understand, and a considerable number of deficiencies in the use of the data which were even then available ; the facts have been much augmented in number and their quality improved since that date.

It is therefore unnecessary to go into Lowie's criticism in detail, for it may be confidently expected that he will soon take up a quite different position and judge otherwise than now, both of the theoretical side of the question and of the facts which go to prove that the Supreme Beings have been independently existent and real from time immemorial.

(ε) F. Heiler, in his admirable work *Das Gebet*,[29] treats the subject from a very important angle, namely prayer. He takes up a definite attitude towards the question of primitive monotheism, not only expressing complete acceptance of it, but recognizing also that it is the starting-point of prayer, and that without it prayer could not have reached full development.

After dealing with Andrew Lang's and my views, he continues as follows :

'It has been suggested, and not without some reason,[30] that both these writers have idealized the savages and the primitive Being of their belief alike, Lang owing to his prejudice in favour of the romantic, Schmidt from a theological predisposition to the theory of primitive monotheism. Be that as it may, the facts prove quite

[29] Munich, 1918, ed. 1 ; 1922, ed. 4 ; the following quotations are from the fourth edition. [The title means simply ' Prayer '].

[30] He does not specify with how much reason ; therefore I do not feel called upon to go into this criticism at present. Cf. *Ursprung der Gottesidee*, Vol. I, ed. 2, p. 81 *sq.*

plainly that these " high gods " occupy a place of their own in the religious conceptions of savages, and owe their genesis neither to belief in spirits nor to ancestor-worship ' (p. 118 *sq*.).

He then, in agreement with Söderblom, emphasizes the character of these high gods as creators, first causes of all that is, and as institutors and legislators, whose deeds often belong to a distant past, but continues as follows :

' But in the overwhelming majority of savage peoples, the Supreme Being is more than a first cause, creator, institutor and legislator of long ago ; he is also the maintainer of his work, a god of destiny and the guardian of his own commands.   Söderblom has not sufficiently emphasized this side of the picture of the First Father ' (p. 119).   This statement Heiler proceeds to support with a long series of good examples.

Although, among many peoples, no sacrifices are made to the Supreme Being, there are others, notably the oldest races, the Pygmy peoples, among which the offering of first-fruits, and that alone, is made to him.   It is therefore certain that this sacrifice is not derived from a food-offering to the dead. Heiler, although his views concerning sacrifice are not always quite just,[31] recognizes this (p. 96).

' These offerings of first-fruits ', he says, ' which are distributed over the whole world and are stated to be the only form of sacrifice known among these extremely backward Pygmy peoples, are considered by Aristotle * and by many modern investigators (as Brinton and Father W. Schmidt) to be the primitive form of offering. It is certain that they arise from other motives and ideas than the ordinary gift-sacrifices, intended to feed or at any rate to please a superior being.   The offerings of first-fruits are nothing else than expressions of veneration, acknowledgement and thanksgiving. . . . The pious worshipper testifies, by offering the first-fruits, that he owes his meat and drink to the bounty of the deity ; he recognizes his entire dependence upon superior powers, and their complete suzerainty over that which he possesses.'

He concludes his account of the matter as follows :

' Thus we get a view of . . . a vista, historical and philosophical, utterly different from the traditional theories of the genesis of the idea of God.   Primitive man, when he prayed, did not turn to a plurality of spiritual beings, but to the One God, the First Father, the Lord of Heaven and earth ' (p. 130 *sq*.).

[31] See my criticism of Heiler on this point in a review of his book in *Anthropos*, Vols. XII–XIII, 1917–19, p. 723 *sq*.
* [*Eth. Nicom*., IX, 1160 a 25 ; but Aristotle is speaking of agricultural communities and their harvest-thanksgiving.]

(ζ) That prominent Dutch explorer, Dr. A. W. Nieuwenhuis, now Professor at the University of Leiden, delivered, in his capacity as Rector Magnificus of that University, a speech in commemoration of its 345th anniversary on February 9, 1920. This he afterwards published under the title *Der Mensch in de Werkelijkheid, zijne Kenleer in den heidenschen Godsdienst* [' Man as he is ; his doctrine in pagan worship '].[32] At the conclusion of this address he deals with the question of the Supreme Being among primitive peoples and his origin. He writes (p. 25) :

' The genesis of this belief in a universal spirit is still unexplained, and this has grown more important in the last few years, owing to the theses maintained by such savants as Andrew Lang and W. Schmidt, to the effect that the belief in question is not the end or culmination of a long development of belief in spirits, but should be placed at the beginning of it.'

He then marshals facts proving a belief in such a Supreme Being, chosen from his own especial area, the peoples of Indonesia. He holds, however, that the origin of the Supreme Being cannot be explained from this area, since there he has already been subjected to wide-spread contamination with mythological, magic and ghost-worshipping beliefs and practices belonging to later and more civilized peoples. He therefore (p. 29 *sqq.*) turns to older peoples, among whom no such mixture has yet occurred. He bases his argument on the present writer's two works, *Stellung der Pygmäenvölker* and *Ursprung der Gottesidee*, using and agreeing with their conclusions.

He then proceeds to give his own explanation of the origin of the Supreme Being, and finds it in the logical quest for a cause ; the same quest which, according to his own investigations, results in personification, and hence in the idea of nature-spirits.[33]

' My researches ', he says (p. 30 *sq.*), ' have . . . shown that the idea of spirit owes its origin to the activities of the mind in the logical search for a cause, in response to a stimulus from without. Consequently, we must consider the Universal Spirit as the first stage in the development of an idea of God, produced by the impression which the universe made as a whole on reflecting men, as soon as they set about trying to understand the world around them. This origin of the concept of the Universal Spirit accords with the fact

[32] Brill, Leiden, 1920. He calls the Supreme Being by the less suitable name of ' Universal spirit ' (in Dutch, *Allgeest*).
[33] See the review of the relevant works of Nieuwenhuis by the present author in *Anthropos*, Vols. XIV–XV, 1919–20, pp. 1151–9.

that later on came the personification of the lords of day and night, sun, moon and some of the principal stars, which were made into gods without an attendant host of spirits ; this we find even among the lowest savages. The idea of spirits came later, and resulted from the very strong impression which the subdivisions of nature made upon the thinking minds among primitive men. Such a state of things exists among the Malays, who to this day, unless moved thereto by something which particularly affects them, show no tendency to form any concept of spirits. This being the way events have moved, we can explain the remarkable fact that the idea of the Universal Spirit and the worship given to him fall into the background in proportion as the ideas of spirits become more numerous and include more of the special parts of nature, having greater importance for the people in their daily life.'

Professor Nieuwenhuis has here put a fundamentally important fact in its true setting, namely, that the idea of a Supreme Being resulted from the impression made by the universe as a whole upon primitive man. All other and lesser deities, on the other hand, arose out of the impressions made by the various parts of nature upon men's minds. I had expressed similar ideas earlier, in my work on the Pygmies (p. 249) in 1910, and again in the first edition of my *Ursprung der Gottesidee* (p. 406–p. 669 of the second ed.), in 1912.

4. MONOTHEISM AND BELIEF IN A SKY-GOD

(a) R. Pettazzoni's new Theory of the Sky-God

A yet stronger proof of the increasingly rapid and universal recognition of the Supreme Being of primitive peoples as the starting-point of religious evolution is the fact that a work has already appeared which sets out to collect all the relevant material and estimate the importance of this supreme sky-god in every direction and for the whole of religious development. Its author is R. Pettazzoni, Professor of the History of Religion formerly at the University of Bologna, now at Rome. The general title is *Dio : formazione e sviluppo del monoteismo nella storia delle religioni :* and so far the first volume has appeared, dealing with *L'Essere celeste nelle credenze dei popoli primitivi*, to be followed by a second volume, *Il Dio supremo nelle religioni politeistiche*, and a third, *Il Dio unico nelle religioni monoteistiche*.[34]

[34] Rome, Società editrice Athenæum, 1922. [General title, *God : the formation and development of Monotheism in the History of Religion.* Vol. I, *The Celestial Being (sky-god) in the beliefs of primitive peoples.* Vol. II, *The supreme God in Polytheistic Religions.* Vol. III, *The One God of Monotheistic Religions.*]

In the long introduction * to his work, Pettazzoni begins
by setting forth the inability of Tylor's theory of animism to
explain the rise of a genuine monotheism. When Andrew
Lang and I appeared as opponents of this theory, and placed
monotheism at the beginning, not the end of religious development, he asked himself the question how the same set of facts
could give rise to two hypotheses so directly contrary. He
then perceived that mere polemic would not be so useful as a
collection of the largest possible number of facts ; for if Lang's
theory was right, then these facts would support it. But the
more facts he gathered, the more they appeared in a quite
different light.

' Thus ', he says (p. xvi), ' on the one hand, the supposed primor-
dial monotheism, which should have been the sole representative
of the first and original impulse of man's religious consciousness,
reduced itself, in my eyes, to the more modest proportions of belief
in a celestial being, envisaged in the form of the personified sky,
according to the fashion of that mythopœic thought which governs
all forms of primitive religious mentality.'

Traces of this idea he claims to have found, not only among
savage peoples in all parts of the world, but also in the polytheistic religions of the past and present. Furthermore, it
had, according to him, a leading part in shaping the true and
genuine monotheism of the Israelites.

The further statement of his theory does not come till Chapter II, which is oddly entitled *Intermezzo* ; for Chapter I deals
at once with the Australian evidence. The first half of Chapter
II is no more than a review of the controversies which have
taken place in recent years concerning Australian religion ; it
leaves much to be desired in completeness and consequently
in correctness. Upon this follows the statement of Pettazzoni's own theory (pp. 67–83). The Australian Supreme
Beings (he assumes their number to be very much greater
than anyone has yet found them to be) are in his opinion all
sky-gods, meaning by sky-god or sky-being [*essere celeste*] ' a
being who lives in the sky and whose life is the life of the sky
itself ' (p. 67).

This *essere celeste* he takes to be the result of a personification,
which, however, does not belong, as I would have it, to the
faculties of reason and imagination together, but only to the
latter, to that intuitive activity which is myth [*quella forma
dell' intuizione ch'è il mito*, p. 71]. The resulting Supreme

* [It is twenty pages long, not a disproportionate size.]

Being is the personification of an element perceptible by the senses, namely the sky (pp. 71–72). Pettazzoni sees what difficulties lie in the way of personifying the sky, owing to its lack of individual distinctness, which, he adds, is why so experienced a mythologist as P. Ehrenreich, in his article *Götter und Heilbringer* (*Zeitschrift für Ethnologie*, Vol. XXXVIII, p. 587 *sqq.*) refused to assume any real personification of it for the earlier stages of human history, although these very stages have already a clear idea of a Supreme Being. But he tries to get out of the difficulty by the suggestion that in these circumstances that form of personification takes place which alone is possible at that stage ; namely, that a being is assumed to exist beyond the celestial phenomena and yet united with them,

' a less definite figure, with less distinct outlines, in comparison with others which represent objects of a more individualized nature, such as the moon and the sun ; but having on the other hand the advantage of those characters of loftiness, supreme power and uniqueness which the sky could bestow upon him' (p. 72).

(*b*) CRITICISM OF PETTAZZONI'S THEORY

Pettazzoni himself feels that this is the fatally weak point of his theory. As a matter of fact, the theory is here weak in itself ; for such ' lesser' personification is really not personification at all, because the essential element of intuition, simplicity, is lacking in it. A being who lives in the sky, who stands behind the celestial phenomena, who must ' centralize ' in himself the various manifestations, is not a personification of the sky at all. The theory, moreover, is feeble here again in its relation to the facts ; for it is quite untrue that the figures of Supreme Beings among the most ancient peoples are ' less definite ' and have ' less distinct outlines ' than other figures, ' such as the moon and the sun '. Rather are they more individualized than the latter ; compare, for example, the Andamanese Puluga, the Semang Kari, the Central Californian or Tierra del Fuegian Supreme Beings with the Sun and the Moon in the corresponding mythologies. The outlines of the Supreme Being become dim only among later peoples. For that reason alone, that for psychological reasons the material sky cannot be personified as a single individual form, Pettazzoni fails hopelessly also when he attempts to explain the unity of the Supreme Being from the unity of the vault of heaven. For if personification here means imagining a single person in the sky, it is hard to see why there could not equally well be several persons, one, for instance, to produce thunder, another to send rain, and so on.

But, as Pettazzoni lays down the axiom (p. 75),

'As if there could be a thought in which the two cognitional faculties, the intuitive and the logical, did not co-exist',

why does he exclude the simultaneity of the two forms of cognition, the logical and the mythical, at the very beginning of the formation of the concept of God ?   Why does he suppose only the mythical to have been active ?   It was only later, he tells us, that a logical element was combined with the purely mythical, and it came as a secondary development (p. 75).

And, however dogmatically they may be expressed, all these statements are nothing more than mere opinions.   For what proofs of these astonishing propositions are there ?   Since he lays so much weight on earlier and later, where does he set about establishing by scientific methods which is which ?

And here the reader is sorely disillusioned.   For what Pettazzoni offers him is nothing at all but a bare collection of material, roughly arranged in large geographical sections ;   his so-called proofs are no more than a bibliography, with a very summary account of the contents of the works mentioned.   There is not the faintest attempt to prove by objective means any historical connexion between the individual beings mentioned and to put the particular connexions thus established together into larger culture-groups.   And least of all do we hear anything of the question concerning the earlier and the later.   The particular sky-gods are not investigated in order of their ethnological age ;   the question is not asked whether their attributes, especially the celestial ones, are all of the same date ;   still less does he inquire whether their celestial attributes are all from the earliest period.   Thus all high gods are lumped together, provided only they have anything about them which suggests the sky.   The entire work of analysis that is bestowed upon them consists, as a matter of fact, of printing in spaced lettering * references to any features that are in any way celestial, such as ' he lives in the sky ' or ' he sends the rain '. Positively no theory can be proved by such a mere heaping up of material ;   certainly not so daring and wide-reaching a hypothesis as Pettazzoni's.   For his purpose he ought necessarily to have used the method of culture-history, which he

---

* [This, and not italics, is the ordinary continental method of emphasizing words.]

himself had previously declared to be correct and most promising,[35] but now entirely neglects.

When therefore we finally reach the end of the nine chapters, extending to 348 pages, which I have described, the meagre *sintesi* of twenty-four pages is not a synthesis at all, but a mere external summary and grouping. Even here—and it would indeed be too late to begin it here—there is not the faintest attempt to group the facts according to their real historical connexion ; still less is there any endeavour to determine by objective means the question of earlier and later, *i.e.* the actual sequence of the various figures. Consequently, after making not the least effort to ascertain the relative ethnological ages of the various ' celestial beings ', Pettazzoni finds himself in the enviable position of being able to lump forty-three of them together as being quite, and thirty-two more as being largely, without cult (p. 365), whereat he triumphantly remarks :

' The fact is that in the majority of cases the celestial being is not an object of worship.'

Pettazzoni gives a shorter summary of his work in a paper read before the Congress of the History of Religion in Paris and published [in *Actes du congrès international d'histoire des religions tenu à Paris en octobre* 1923, Champion, Paris, 1925, Vol. I, pp. 70–82, and], with some additions, in *Revue d'histoire des religions*, Vol. LXXXVII, 1923, pp. 193–229. In this he defends himself against the present writer's criticisms expressed in *Ursprung der Gottesidee*, Vol. I, ed. 2, pp. 674–84.*

He expressly admits in this article that despite his great appreciations of the method of the history of culture, he is not in a position to apply it himself. As a critical student of religion, he must wait until ethnologists have brought it to a definite conclusion (*Rev. Hist. Rel.*, p. 221). He further states that he has collected his material almost without touching it (pp. 220, 229), *i.e.*, without handling and sifting it by ethnological methods. It is hardly tolerable that a scientific student of religion, engaged in discussing the religions of savages, should thus leave all real research of the kind to ethnologists.

In any case, if he is not in a position to settle the ethnological age of the individual sky-gods for himself, he thereby puts out of court what he calls his *methode combinatoire intégrale* [*Actes*, p. 81 ; *Rev. Hist. Rel.*, p. 219], a method of his own invention, on which he

---

[35] In his article *La science des religions et sa méthode*, in *Scientia*, Vol. XIII, 1913, p. 135 *sq.*

*[See also, by the same author, the article 'Monotheismus und Polytheismus' in *Die Religion in Geschichte und Gegenwart*, Mohr, Tübingen, Vol. IV.]

lays great stress, despite the fact that it explains the older by the more recent. For he has absolutely no exact and scientific knowledge of which are the older and which the more recent forms. He ends his article on a note of resignation with the following words :

' In view of the importance which this theory may have, especially for the history of religions in general, I hope I am justified in putting it forward without awaiting the final conclusions of ethnology. Its present form is partial and provisional, and I am ready to modify it or even to abandon it as soon as it appears untenable in view of the further progress of science, ethnological or other.'

This is certainly a praiseworthy and most correct attitude ; it is a pity that he has not always kept to it.

(c) G. FOUCART ON THE ORIGIN OF THE SKY-GOD

Having now set forth Pettazzoni's theory, it will be both interesting and useful to listen to another authority on the science of religion, G. Foucart, well known for his pointed criticisms of totemistic extremists in France. Some two years before Pettazzoni, Foucart had given his views on the subject to the world in a meritorious article, SKY AND SKY-GOD, in Hastings' *Encyclopædia of Religion and Ethics*, Vol. XI, pp. 580–5.

(i) He begins by emphasizing the world-wide distribution of the sky-god among all peoples, savage and civilized, and concludes that :

' We may safely assume that the concept of sky-god belongs to the most ancient period in the history of religious feeling, and that it is at least as ancient as primitive naturism and animistic fetishism. Whether it is even pre-animistic in its fundamental aspect is a question which must be reserved in the meantime.'

Since he will not allow ' any historical or proto-historical motive ' as a sufficient explanation of this world-wide phenomenon, he appears at first sight to approach Pettazzoni's standpoint, for he declares (p. 581) that the only explanation is the ubiquitous presence of the material sky and the characteristics of its various manifestations.

(ii) He now, however, proceeds to ask :

' Is the conception of sky-god itself explained by an exclusive application of the processes of pure and simple animism or by the usual mechanism of naturism ? ' (*Ibid.*).

This question he answers in the negative. He too is obliged to resort to personification as being the force here at work ; but he defines it in a way which can no longer be accepted, as follows :

'Personification . . . starts from the idea that under the appearance and within or behind the material exterior there exists a being, or, rather, a personal force . . . closely bound to the substance of which it is the energy and the life, unable to exist without this substance, but distinct from it *and, if necessary, separable from it —at least momentarily* ' (*Ibid.*).

These last few words, which I have italicized, contain something not strictly germane to the concept of personification ; they involve an extension which cannot be arrived at save by way of the animistic concept of spirits. Foucart himself feels that he is on unsafe ground, for he adds ' at least momentarily '. But he needed that addition, for he perceives and immediately after states the truth of the matter : ' The sky-god is therefore radically different from the substance which forms the material sky '. On the other hand, however, he once more insists that this substance is ' indispensable to its [the god's] existence, for without it it would return to the vortex of the impersonal forces of nature '.

(iii) So far Pettazzoni would probably follow Foucart's line of thought only with mixed feelings. But he surely must halt and involuntarily break off at the question which Foucart now asks, as he ruthlessly pursues his inquiry :

' Does this imply that primitive man imagines a time when, as the sky was not yet in existence, the sky-god could not exist ? ' But Foucart also falters here ; he sees that this is the crucial question, but he adds hesitatingly, ' This vital question cannot be definitely answered in the present state of ethnological information.' He admits that ' numerous myths ' represent the sky-god as creating the sky itself ; but he adds the sceptical question, ' But are these myths primitive ? '

(d) Criticism of Foucart's Theory

Foucart does not try to solve this problem by the application of the historical method, which would surely be appropriate here when the subject is the age of these myths ; he does but reply with a new question, so *a priori* as to betray its descent from psychological Evolutionism very clearly, namely, ' Can primitive reasoning reach the problem of the origin of the sky ? '

(i) This is that same Foucart who, when faced by the Evolutionist arbitrarinesses of S. Reinach and his kind, could

so eloquently eulogize the superiority of historical investigation, as he well knew how to conduct it in his own field of
Egyptology, not without pitying glances at ethnology and
its lack of any really historical method! Twice over, in
1910 and again in 1913, I reviewed in *Anthropos* (Vol. V,
p. 576 *sqq.*, and Vol. VIII, p. 906 *sqq.*) his *Histoire des religions
et méthode comparative* (Paris, 1909 and 1913), and took occasion
to refer with some emphasis to the true historical method,
which ethnology had created for itself some years earlier.
After that, one might really have expected something better
from Foucart. A little later in the same article, on p. 582,
note 2, he writes: ' Creation *ex nihilo* is unknown to the intellect of primitive and semi-civilized man.' Yet this was in
1920, when Kroeber's and Dixon's data (see p. 189 *sqq.*) were
already known, and they tell a very different story, and
could have given him the answer to the question asked previously, whether primitive man was able to conceive of the
origin of the sky.

(ii) Under these circumstances there is not much to interest
us in the provisional solution which Foucart proposes with
all reserve (p. 582) :

' In the formless mass of impersonal forces there spontaneously
appeared forces endowed with personal consciousness ; the most
efficient of these released the liquid mass from the universal chaos
and formed the material sky, which has ever since been its vital
substance and its special property.'

An answer so wanting in lucidity can hardly clear up anything, and in particular the ' spontaneous ' appearance of
these personal forces does but illumine the darkness by means
of another and a deeper darkness.

However, it remains to Foucart's credit that he has pursued
the whole subject without halt or check to its last problem
and has not stopped short, content with some new ' theory '
of his own invention. But it would have been more in accordance with reality and likelier to lead to some result if he had
declared that he personally could not at present solve the
problem.

The rest of Foucart's article, dealing with the rôle and
functions, the specific aspect and representations, and the
characteristics of the sky-god, contains much useful information. At the end, however, when he should have written
a history of the sky-god, he contents himself with describing
his ' evolution '. Here again many particular ideas are of

value, but there is too much hypothetical construction to
serve instead of historical investigation, which alone is able
to bring us nearer a solution of the important problem of the
sky-god, and thus to cast a flood of light on many other
important questions in the history of religion.

5. THE PRESENT SITUATION

No one who has read the long list of eminent researchers
given in the preceding sections can fail to realize that the
question of 'high gods of low races' has passed beyond
the first stage, in which it fought for existence or was
tacitly neglected, and has at last reached a certain degree
of quiet security. Its strong support in known fact, the
authenticity and genuinely native origin of the beings in
question, is no longer disputed by any investigator of repute.
The great antiquity, ethnologically speaking, of such beings
is also openly acknowledged by most, and at least not seriously
attacked by any. Furthermore, the number of those who
attribute to them an independent origin, unconnected with
animism, magic or totemism, continues to grow. A respect-
able body of opinion now puts their origin, if not actually
earlier than that of these elements, at least contemporaneous
with them. At the same time the leading investigators at
all events have cast off the yoke of Evolutionism, and the
principles of historical research have won recognition ; whence
there opens a prospect of a quieter, more circumspect and
therefore more solid treatment of the whole problem, as a
result of influences both within and without our science.

But the first necessity, now as formerly, is very decidedly
the production of fresh material, less superficial and less
narrow in scope, especially as regards the peoples ethnologically the most ancient.

A second desideratum is the thorough study of particular
regions in accordance with the historical method. Of such
studies we have hitherto but a very few examples. But
without them we cannot arrive at a tenable establishment
of the boundaries of real 'culture-circles,' the fixing in
space of organic culture-complexes. Still less can we
hope to restate them as phases of culture, i.e., to establish
their sequence in time. Only by such studies will the conditions be fulfilled under which we can settle the real and
proper evolutionary development of cultures, and distinguish
this from the accidental phenomena produced by mixture
and contact. Not till then will it be possible to state

the question with due regard to the inner motor forces and the outward influences which have had their part in bringing about any given cultural element. Of this more will be said further on, p. 235 *sqq*.

Applying all this to the problem of the Supreme Being, we find that firstly, the facts regarding his attachment to certain small culture-areas, then to larger complexes and horizons of culture, must be tested. Next, when these culture-horizons are restated as cultural phases, we have at last an objective basis on which to determine the ethnological age of the various Supreme Beings, within long periods of time. Following up the subject through the individual phases of development it then becomes possible to get an insight both into their inner development and also into the influences from without which have affected them, and to look for the causes of the one and the other.

But this undertaking is so important, so crucial in fact, that to describe it thoroughly demands a special chapter.

PART FIVE

METHODOLOGICAL BASIS. CONTENT OF THE PRIMITIVE BELIEF IN HIGH GODS

CHAPTER XIV

THE HISTORICAL METHOD AND ITS RESULTS FOR ETHNOLOGY

IN the preceding chapter we began by making the acquaintance of the sky-gods belonging to the third culture of the primary stage, that of the pastoral nomads. Continuing the subject, we met with investigators and trends of research which also recognized and drew attention to those Supreme Beings, almost all of them likewise sky-gods, who are to be found in other primary cultures, and especially in those cultures of an earlier date still, belonging to a more remote past, which we style primitive.[1] So we arrived at the last cultures, which bring us, in our search for the real origin of religion, to the point where our present data and means begin to fail us.

Great as are the merits of those researchers who have drawn scientific attention to the figures of these high gods, so long unrecognized and thrust into the background ; wholesome though the criticism is to which they have thereby subjected the earlier theories which left them out of sight ; yet there is scarcely one of them who was in a position to determine, by means of an unvarying and competent method, the first question, namely the ethnological age of these high gods, who as a matter of fact differ much in kind from each other. Consequently they were of course prevented from finding their way to the veritable nature of these beings, for that is very closely connected indeed with the dates at which they make their first appearance. It was equally impossible for

[1] See below, p. 238.

them to write a real history of the development of these high gods and of their connexion with other religious factors and elements.

This last and most crucial task could not be accomplished until science had recovered from the confusion and darkness of the Evolutionist period and discovered, or rediscovered, the broken road leading to a true historical method. Further, it was not till then in a position to produce a final proof that these high gods in their oldest form, that in which we meet them in the primitive cultures, come before all other elements, whether nature-myths, fetishism, ghost-worship, animism, star-myths, totemism or magic, from one or another of which the earlier theories of preceding decades had derived the origin of religion. It is the object of the following pages to sketch this method briefly in its essential traits.

1. THE HISTORICAL MOVEMENT IN ETHNOLOGY AND THE HISTORY OF RELIGION

The Evolutionist method, which we have sufficiently characterized earlier in this work (above, pp. 5, 13), dominated almost the entire nineteenth century. The whole earlier period of ethnology, sociology and the science of religion worked along its lines ; in this connexion we may mention, among others, Sir John Lubbock (Lord Avebury), Herbert Spencer, E. B. Tylor (with certain exceptions), Andrew Lang, Sir J. G. Frazer, F. B. Jevons, E. S. Hartland, J. Lippert, F. Gerland, L. H. Morgan, J. F. M'Lennan, H. Post, J. Kohler, A. Bastian, O. Peschel (with some reserves), H. Schurtz, F. Müller, C. Letourneau, A. Réville, J. Deniker, Goblet d'Alviella, Salamon Reinach, E. Durkheim, H. Hubert, M. Mauss, L. Lévy-Bruhl. True, Th. Waitz, F. Heger, P. Ehrenreich, W. Wundt and, in his earlier work, A. Vierkandt would exempt the historical peoples, in the narrower sense of the word 'historical', from the dominion of natural laws, and allow in their case the appearance of outstanding individuals, the creators of an historical existence in the proper sense. But this is of no consequence for our questions regarding origins, since these must plunge into the deepest depths of savagery, and in any case it is a departure from the older point of view in degree only, not in principle.

(a) THE HISTORICAL MOVEMENT IN GERMANY

(i) The first to oppose this whole doctrine was F. Ratzel. He declared that all peoples without exception were 'historical', and drew attention to the necessity for research into their history, especially as shown in the migrations of peoples. When he found agreement between forms, such as did not arise automatically from the nature and purpose of the object in question, or the kind of material used for it, he postulated an historical and genetic connexion, even though the forms in question were distributed over a wide and discontinuous area. Hence he proposed what is called the criterion of form, and was the author of a theory of migration, which he employed first in an investigation of the history of the bow in Africa.[2]

(ii) Leo Frobenius, a pupil of Ratzel, enlarged the above theory into the doctrine of ' culture-circles ' [or ' spheres ', *Kulturkreise*, a word usually rendered in this translation by ' culture-horizons' or simply ' cultures ']. While investigating the cultures of West Africa and comparing them with those of Melanesia, he discovered, in 1898 and the following year, that a genetic connexion such as Ratzel had drawn attention to existed, not only between single elements, but between these cultures as a whole, including their material, sociological and mythological sides, in fact the entire ' circle ', and that it was not only single parts but, even more, entire cultures which were capable of such migrations. He therefore turned his attention to a criterion which he was the first to examine extensively, that of quantity, as it is called. Later, Frobenius abandoned his theory, altering it so as to postulate the working of ordinary natural laws ; but in the last few years he seems to have been championing it once more.

(iii) Two assistants at the Berlin Ethnological Museum (Museum für Völkerkunde), F. Gräbner and B. Ankermann, took up the subject, drawing upon the rich stores of their museum and working with method and system. They published their first researches in two lectures, one by Gräbner, *Kulturkreise und Kulturschichten in Ozeanien* [' Spheres and strata of culture in Oceania '], the other by Ankermann, *Kulturkreise und Kulturschichten in Africa* [' Spheres and strata of culture in Africa '].[3] In these they worked out a number of such ' spheres ' in both the areas mentioned, and settled their relative chronology as culture-strata. Gräbner's activity, which concerned itself especially with material and social culture, led to a wider extension and confirmation of the views then in vogue in several individual areas. In 1911 he produced an important work, *Methode der Ethnologie* [' The Method of Ethnology '], founded upon all his previous works ; to this we shall have to refer again later.

[2] A bibliography including this and succeeding publications is given by Ankermann in the *Zeitschrift für Ethnologie* for 1905, p. 54, note 2.
[3] Published in *Zeitschrift für Ethnologie*, XXXVII, 1905, pp. 28 *sqq.*, 57 *sqq.*

The new movement was joined by W. Foy, who had already been working along similar lines, and by the present author, who, having come to much the same results from work on the languages and mythology of South-East Asia, Oceania and Australia, later included South America in the territory covered by the new theory in *Kulturkreise und Kulturschichten in Südamerika*.[4]

While the old ethnologico-psychological school lost ground in Germany, the historical tendency exercised a growing attraction for the younger men, although they did not always agree entirely with the doctrine of 'culture-circles'. They included, F. Krause in his treatise *Die Kultur der kalifornischen Indianer in ihrer Bedeutung für die Ethnologie und die nordamerikanische Völkerkunde*[5]; W. Krickeberg, author of the section *Amerika* in Buschan's *Illustrierte Völkerkunde*[6]; W. Lehmann, in his *Central-America*[7]; W. Koppers, in *Die ethnologische Wirtschaftsordnung*[8], also in *Völker und Kulturen*[9]; and H. Ulrich, in *Logische Studien zur Methode der Ethnologie*.[10]

[4] [' Spheres and Strata of Culture in South America ']; *Zeitschrift für Ethnologie*, 1913, pp. 1014–1124.

[5] Leipzig, 1912; an account of it by the present author in *Anthropos*, Vols. XVI–XVII, 1921–2, pp. 502–10. Cf. also his later work, *Das Wirtschaftsleben der Völker*, Breslau, 1924, especially p. 113 *sqq.*, and cf. W. Koppers in *Anthropos*, Vol. XVII, 1923–4, p. 1124 *sqq.*

[6] Ed. 2, Stuttgart, 1922, cf. *Anthropos, ibid.*, pp. 516–18.

[7] Berlin, 1920, cf. *Anthropos*, Vols. XIV–XV, 1920–1, pp. 1175–8.

[8] Vienna, 1917, see *Anthropos*, Vols. X–XI, 1915–6, pp. 611–51 and 971–1079.   [9] Vol. I, pt. 2, Regensburg, 1924.

[10] *Anthropos*, Vols. XVIII–XIX, pp. 447–64 and 700–32. The following works show the same or a similar tendency. D. Kreichgauer, *Die Klapptore am Rande der Erde*, in *Anthropos*, Vols. XII–XIII, 1917–18, pp. 272–312. Same, *Die Religion der Griechen in ihrer Abhängigkeit von den mutterrechtlichen Kulturkreisen*, in the St. Gabriel *Jahrbuch*, Vol. II, 1925, pp. 106–52. Same, *Neue Beziehungen zwischen Amerika und der alten Welt*, in *Festschrift für W. Schmidt*, Vienna, 1928, pp. 366–77. P. Schebesta and G. Höltker, *Der afrikanische Schild*, in *Anthropos*, Vols. XVIII–XIX, 1923–4, pp. 1012–62 and Vol. XX, 1925, pp. 817–59. P. Schebesta, *Die religiösen Anschauungen Südafrikas*, *ibid.*, XVIII–XIX, 1923–4, pp. 114–24. Same, *Die Zimbabwe-Kultur in Afrika, ibid.*, Vol. XXI, 1926, pp. 484–545 and 621–64. M. Gusinde, *Die geheimen Männerfeiern bei den Feuerländern und deren kulturhistorische Wertung*, in *Zeitschrift für Ethnologie*, 1926, pp. 261–312. Same, *Kulturheroen in der Mythologie Südamerikas*, in XXIII International Congress of Americanists, New York, 1928. M. Schulien, *Kleidung und Schmuck bei den Atchwabo in Portugiesisch-Ostafrika*, *Anthropos*, XXI, 1926, pp. 870–919. E. Vatter, *Der australische Totemismus*, Hamburg, 1925, see *Anthropos*, Vol. XXI, 1926, pp. 566–79. P. Leser, *Geschichte und Verbreitung des Pfluges*, Vienna, 1930. Same, *Westöstliche Landwirtschaft*, in *Festschrift für W. Schmidt*, pp. 416–18. L. Lips, *Einleitung in die Völkerkunde*, Leipzig,

(b) THE HISTORICAL SCHOOLS OUTSIDE GERMANY

(a) In America also, F. Boas stood forth quite early (1885–
98) and more definitely in his lecture *Ethnological Problems
in Canada*, 1910,[11] as an advocate of the necessity for historical analysis, as opposed to the older psychological methods.
Despite his criticisms of the German school of culture-history,
he advocated such methods yet more strongly in his article
The Methods of Ethnology, in 1920.[12]

Similar views have been expressed by R. B. Dixon, G. C. Wheeler,
C. Wissler, A. L. Kroeber, H. R. Swanton, H. H. Lowie,
1928. Same, *Fallensysteme der Naturvölker*, Leipzig, 1926. Same, *Die
Anfänge des Rechts an Grund und Boden bei den Naturvölkern und
der Begriff der Erntevölker*, in *Festschrift für W. Schmidt*, pp. 485–
94. A. Gahs, *Blutige und unblutige Opfer bei den altaiischen
Hirtenvölkern*, in *Internationale Woche für Religionsethnologie*, Vol.
IV, 1925, Paris, 1926, pp. 217–32. Same, *Kopf-, Schädel- und
Langknochenopfer bei Rentiervölkern*, in *Festschrift W. Schmidt*, pp.
231–68. R. v. Heine-Geldern, *Die Megalithen Südostasiens, Anthropos*,
Vol. XXIII, 1928, pp. 276–315. Same, *Ein Beitrag zur Chronologie
des Neolithikums in Südostasien*, in *Festschrift W. Schmidt*, pp.
809–43. F. Röck, *Kalenderkreise und Kalenderschichten im alten
Mexiko und Mittelamerika, ibid.*, pp. 610–28. Same, *Die Kultur-
historische Bedeutung von Ortungsreihen und Ortungsbildern, Anthropos*,
Vol. XXV, 1930. F. Kern, *Stammbaum und Artbild der Deutschen*,
Munich, 1927. Same, *Die Welt, worein die Griechen traten, Anthropos*,
Vol. XXIV, 1929, pp. 167–220. H. König, *Das Recht der Polar-
völker, ibid.*, pp. 87–114. G. Höltker, *Zeit und Zahl in Nordwesta-
frika, Festschrift W. Schmidt*, pp. 282–302. E. M. v. Hornbostel,
Die Massnorm als kulturgeschichtliches Forschungsmittel, ibid., pp. 303–
23. L. Walk, *Die ersten Lebensjahre des Kindes in Südafrika, Anthropos*,
Vol. XXIII, 1928, pp. 38–109. Same, *Initiationszeremonien und
Pubertätsriten der südafrikanischen Stämme, ibid.*, pp. 861–966. J.
Wölfel, *Die Trepanation, ibid.*, Vol. XX, 1925, pp. 1–50. W. Hirsch-
berg, *Die viertägige Marktwoche in Afrika, ibid.*, XXIV, 1929, pp.
613–20. F. Flor, *Das Pferd und seine kulturgeschichtliche Bedeutung*,
in *Wiener kulturhistorische Studien*, Vol. I, 1930. H. Baumann,
Vaterrecht und Mutterrecht in Afrika, Zeitschrift für Ethnologie, 1926,
pp. 62–161. H. Trimborn, *Methode der historischen Rechtsforschung*,
in *Zeitschrift für vergleichende Rechtswissenschaft*, Vol. XLIII, 1929,
416–64. Same, *Die Organization der öffentlichen Gewalt im Inka-
Reich, Festschrift W. Schmidt*, pp. 740–59. W. C. MacLeod, *On the
Diffusion of Central American Culture to Coastal British Columbia and
Alaska, Anthropos*, Vol. XXIV, 1929, pp. 417–40. T. L. Seifert, *Von
Bogomil über Hus zu Lenin*, in *Zeitschrift für Völkerpsychologie und
Soziologie*, Vol. III, pp. 128–58.

[11] *Journ. Roy. Anth. Inst.*, Vol. XL, 1910, p. 529 sqq. For his earlier
attitude, see further *Anthropos*, Vol. VII, 1912, p. 253.

[12] In *Amer. Anthropologist*, N.S., Vol. XXII, 1920, pp. 311–21.
For my reply to his criticisms see *Anthropos*, Vols. XIV–XV, 1919–20,
pp. 546–53. Cf. also Boas, *Evolution or Diffusion*, in *Amer. Anthrop.*,
N.S., Vol. XXVI, 1924, pp. 140–4.

A. A. Goldenweiser, and E. Sapir.[13] In consequence, it must be admitted that in North America the historical movement has already triumphed completely over the older methods. The resemblance to the German historical school is becoming increasingly close, the only serious difference being the reluctance of the Americans to assume historical connexions when the distribution of the culture in question is broken by very considerable intervals in space ; see above, p. 221, and below, pp. 227, 231.

(β) In Great Britain the older school has held the field longest and most strongly. Here, N. W. Thomas had adopted similar methods of historical study for Australia and Africa,[14] but did not follow them to their logical conclusion. Later on, the eminent psychologist and sociologist, the late Dr. W. H. D. Rivers, broke loose from the old school in his presidential address, *The Ethnological Analysis of Culture*, 1911.[15] In his *History of Melanesian Culture*, the first volume still follows the lines of the old Evolutionist method ; but in the second he broke completely away from it, and tried to work entirely on historical lines, an attempt, however, which did not entirely succeed. Unhappily, a too early death robbed science of him.

There is an approximation to the historical method in the work of Dr. G. Elliot Smith, the physical anthropologist, who makes Egypt the starting-point of the ' archaic culture ', and of W. J. Perry, his pupil ; but their lack of any real method is so complete that it can bring only discredit upon the new movement. [See especially W. J. Perry, *The Children of the Sun*, London, Methuen, 1923.]

(γ) In France, A. de Quatrefages had at an earlier date made some attempts at historical research ; but these efforts of him and others had not reached full development nor appreciation, for the physical anthropology and pre-history of those days worked on materialistic principles, with the result that for a time ethnology was of little importance.[16]

[13] I have listed and commented on their works in *Anthropos, ibid.*, pp. 546–63 (*Die kulturhistorische Methode und die nordamerikanische Ethnologie*) and Vols. XVI–XVII, 1921–2 (*Die Abwendung vom Evolutionismus und die Hinwendung zum Historismus*). For Kroeber, Swanton, Goldenweiser and Lowie, see further *Ursprung der Gottesidee*, Vol. I, ed. 2, pp. 643 *sqq.*, 656 *sqq.*, 782 *sqq.*

[14] See *Anthropos*, Vol. VI, 1911, p. 1019.

[15] [To Section H of the British Association. See their Report for 1911, pp. 490–9 ; *Science*, Vol. XXXIV, pp. 385–97 ; *Nature*, Vol. LXXXVII, p. 356 ; and] *Anthropos, ibid.*, pp. 1016 and 1019. [For a full list of Rivers' publications, see *Man*, Vol. XXII, 1922, No. 61.]

[16] See Pinard de la Boullaye, *L'étude comparée*, ed. 3, Vol. I, p. 426 ; Schmidt, *Die moderne Ethnologie*, in *Anthropos*, Vol. I, 1906, p. 335 *sq.*

Later, A. van Gennep, in the introduction to his work *Mythes et légendes d'Australie*, Paris, 1905, took a similar line ; but his *Rites de passage*, Paris, 1909, is a regression to the old ways. In his own special province, Africa, M. Delafosse has always worked along strictly exact and historical lines in his detailed researches. This is true also of P. Rivet for South America. Of late he has recognized the important results of historical investigation regarding the connexion between American cultures of the older and oldest strata and those of Oceania and Australia ; these results he is trying to supplement by linguistic investigations of his own.[17] Father Pinard de la Boullaye, in his important work *L'étude comparée des religions* [see above, p. 18], takes his stand on the side of the historical method, which he describes, together with the psychological, most excellently, and thus leads it on to further development and popularity.

(δ) In Sweden, the works of so eminent an investigator as E. von Nordenskiöld (*Eine geographische und ethnographische Analyse der materiellen Kultur zweier Indianerstämme in El Gran Chaco; The Changes in the material culture of two Indian Tribes under the influence of New Surroundings; The Ethnography of South America seen from Mojos in Bolivia*,[18] etc.), are wholly on the lines of geographical and historical methods, although he does not go all the way with the German school.

(ε) In Denmark the historical method has been developed chiefly by the study of the Eskimo region, which is of large extent and presents great variety. How far-reaching its results are, particularly for religion, is clear from the thorough study of W. Thalbitzer, *Die kultischen Gottheiten der Eskimos*,[19] in which he proves that so distant a source as the ideas of the inhabitants of Central Asia has influenced the Eskimo religion. Knud Rasmussen's journeys in Thule were made on a magnificent plan, and inspired wholly by the spirit of geographical and historical investigation ; the volumes which

[17] See *Anthropos*, Vol. VI, 1911, p. 1017, for criticism of van Gennep by the present author ; Vol. XX, 1925, pp. 51–4 for Rivet.

[18] Göteborg, 1918, 1920 and 1924 respectively ; I have reviewed them in *Anthropos*, 1921–2, pp. 497–502. His pupils follow the same lines, for instance S. Linné, *Darien in the Past*, Göteborg, 1929, and G. Montell, *Dress and Ornaments in Ancient Peru*, London, 1929, and other works. Another follower of Nordenskiöld's school is A. Métraux, now Director of the Museum of Tucuman, Argentina, see his two excellent treatises *La civilisation matérielle des tribus Tupi-Gurani*, Paris, 1928, and *La religion des Tupinamba*, Paris, 1928.

[19] In *Archiv für Religionswissenschaft*, Vol. XXVI, 1928, pp. 364–430.

he and his collaborators, K. Birket-Smith, Mathiassen and others, are bringing out on the basis of the materials thus collected are first-rate examples of that method well applied.

(ζ) Finnland has reached a very high level in historical investigation. This resulted from the labours of Finnish scholars seeking for the origin of their national epic, the *Kalevala*. The earlier investigators, such as Lonrött, Castrén, J. Krohn and others belonged to the school of nature-mythologists ; Comparetti explained everything by magical practices and shamanism ; but investigators were already beginning under J. Krohn to make their way, through a process of mapping and studying the geography of their data, to a fully historical method, and this movement has grown stronger under K. Krohn. The result is that the origin of the *Kalevala* can be placed in the historical period, between paganism and Christianity ; as is very instructively set forth by J. Krohn in his most interesting lecture *Kalevala und die finnischen Heldenlieder*.[20] This method has specialized on folklore, and a whole host of distinguished investigators have been working in Finnland by means of it ; it is explained with exemplary thoroughness by K. Krohn in his treatise *Die Folkloristische Arbeitsmethode* ['The Folklorist's method of work'], Oslo, Leipzig, Paris and London, 1926.

(c) Helpers in the Formation of a Regular Method

The defect, as compared with the German method, of the above historical tendencies which have appeared in various countries, is that they have not yet produced any complete statement of their principles.

(a) The nearest, comparatively, to forming such a statement are the North American ethnologists. Besides a whole series of studies on single points, mostly dealing with the idea of convergence, that continent possesses the work of E. Sapir, *Time Perspective in Aboriginal American Culture, A Study in Method*,[21] which might well be called a handbook of methodology. Sapir goes straight to the central problem, 'how inject a chronology into this confusing mass of purely descriptive fact ? ' [p. 2]. Among uncivilized peoples we have, side by side, certain ethnological data, which seem, historically speaking, to go but a little way back. How shall

[20] ['The Kalevala and the Finnish heroic ballads'] ; in *Germanisch-romanische Monatschrift*, Vol. XVI, 1928, pp. 337–57.
[21] Ottawa, Govt. Printing Bureau, 1916 ; fully reviewed by the present author in *Anthropos*, 1921–2, pp. 510–16.

these be made deeper and richer by giving them their true succession in time? Towards the solution of this problem he offers a series of sound criteria, founded upon the inner connexion and outward extension of the various phenomena. He even takes the decisive step of including discontinuous extension, which he perceives must take us further back still in time. He does not, however, succeed in realizing that whole complexes or 'circles' of culture can as such travel a great distance; and, not realizing this, he loses a powerful instrument for detecting deeper stratifications. Finally he remains the victim after all of a kind of agoraphobia, or ethnological Monroe doctrine, for he says (p. 50) that

'the culture stratum must not be freely handled as a universal counter, but needs to be restricted to the bounds set by at most a continent or parts of two adjacent continents'.

the last words alluding to the American expedition, financed by Jessup, to the north-western corner of America and the north-eastern extremity of Asia.

(β) R. H. Lowie comes still nearer the method of culture-history in the third part (*Historical and Psychological Aspects*) of his treatise, *Primitive Religion*. It is indeed an interesting blend of the historical and psychological methods of research which is here represented, and much may be learned from it ; for instance, from the first two chapters, *Historical Schemes and Regional Characterization* and *History and Psychology*. He upholds the necessity of historical investigation, but does not venture to extend it over such a large area as the German school does ; he confines himself mostly to the narrow limits of American ethnology, but passes on to postulate connexions between North-Western and even North-Eastern America and East, even West Siberia. This contention he bases on a number of details, clearly characterized ; some of these even refer to the farthest parts of South America. Hence his declaration that in applying the historical method he has no fear of either space or time is justified. The one real difference between him and the German school is that he prefers (p. 183)

'to establish sequences where the distribution is *spatially continuous* or rendered plausible by documentary evidence or at least by known ethnographic principles'. (The italics are mine.)

It is not clear whether he includes under 'known ethno-graphic principles, the fundamental axioms laid down by

Graebner in his *Methode der Ethnologie* with regard to ' distant interpretation of the second degree' [*Ferninterpretation zweiten Grades*] ; see my *Ursprung*, Vol. I, ed. 2, p. 749. If so, then there exists between him and the German school at most a difference of degree, not of kind.

(γ) Sapir and to a less extent Lowie laboured under the disadvantage that the detailed investigations upon which they based their methodological positions were all within the boundaries of North American ethnology, which after all has its limits. Here F. Graebner was better off. Even the region with which he began, Australia and Oceania, provided decidedly more varied relations than America, and since then he has been able to make good progress in other regions also, though it must be admitted that, very unlike Sapir and Lowie, he is weakest in knowledge of North America. In the South Seas, he started from material culture, but at the same time included the social relationships in his investigations.

Graebner had the further advantage that he was a historian to begin with and had been trained in historical method. His *Methode der Ethnologie* (Heidelberg, 1911) is based on E. Bernheim's well-known work *Lehrbuch der historischen Methode und der Geschichtsphilosophie* [' Manual of Historical Method and the Philosophy of History ' ; ed. 1, 1899 ; eds. 5 and 6, 1908], which is much to its advantage as regards construction and handling of the subject. It is, however, to be regretted that he has not added thereto the manageable outward form of Bernheim's treatment.

He makes a decided and undoubted step forward even in the opening chapter, by treating seriously the term ' history of culture' and completing the introduction of ethnology into history. This gives Graebner the advantage, which greatly lightens his task, that he can fall back upon history in working out his method. But he repays the debt thus contracted by reminding historians how much they in turn can learn from ethnology, if they will not confine themselves, as they have done hitherto, to written sources, but will also learn to use the unwritten documents from the past. How this may be done safely and by a new method he proceeds to show ; we shall have more to say of his method later, see p. 230.

(δ) We meet with a fourth noteworthy methodologist in the person of Father H. Pinard de la Boullaye, whose meritorious book, *L'étude comparée des religions*, Paris, Vol. I, 1922, Vol. II, 1925 (third ed. of both vols., 1929), devotes its second volume wholly to ethnological method and to that of the science of religion. The historical method is considered (pp. 88–152) along with others, and approved in all essential points. The author is, however, no mere copyist. Almost at the same time as Graebner, but independently of him and from a different point of view, he had set about studying methodological problems; see his two articles, *Quelques précisions sur la méthode comparative* and *Essai sur la convergence des probabilités*,[22] both now included in his larger work, pp. 1–81 and 509–54, with additions and slight alterations. Clearly his interests are, on the formal side, those of a logician; as regards content he is principally concerned with the science of religion. To the former source are due his accuracy, clearness and system, conspicuous from beginning to end of his discussion, and the profound philosophical basis which characterizes it. Both advantages are seen to good effect even when he enters Graebner's own field; the same questions are past all doubt handled by Pinard with far greater lucidity and in a more comprehensible way. But of course the pioneer task of cutting a road through such a thorny jungle of problems and difficulties was the harder, and it was Graebner who accomplished that.

Graebner gives no rule of any sort for the very difficult case of two cultures which we have to compare when they have no sort of contact or crossing with each other. Father Pinard also does not treat this case specifically; but we can easily deduce a rule from that which he gives for the case where, to use his own words,

' we have to study a territory uniformly coloured [*i.e.*, on a polychrome map], in other words a single cultural type, filling by itself a single continuous area ' (Vol. II, ed. 3, p. 271).

Graebner, on the other hand, gives us some useful hints for deciding the age of a culture for the whole world.[23] I am not sure if Father Pinard does not intend to raise the same point on p. 283 *sqq.* of his work. But in any case, the answers which he gives there are not sufficient for the basal problem which is in question.

Father Pinard is superior to Dr. Graebner, in my opinion, as regards the lucidity and handiness of his exposition; but

[22] Respectively in *Anthropos*, Vol. V, 1910, pp. 534–58 and *Revue néo-scolastique*, Vols. XX, 1914–19, pp. 394–418, and XXII, 1920, pp. 5–36.

[23] *Methode der Ethnologie*, p. 160 *sq.*

Graebner is superior in that his long activity as an ethnologist provides him with more concrete examples, drawn from that source, to illustrate his views ; although the number of these ought to be still greater.[24]   On the other hand, the bibliography furnished by Father Pinard is incomparably the richer and more varied, and therefore is in more lively contact with the present-day controversies.

2. EXPOSITION OF THE HISTORICAL METHOD

(a) INTERPRETATION AND COMBINATION OF DATA

The following sketch of the historical method in ethnology and the history of religion is founded in substance upon Graebner's, and, in particular, the arrangement of the various parts is that given in his *Methode der Ethnologie*.[25]   Short references to Pinard de la Boullaye's account are also given in the notes.[26]

Graebner's work can be naturally divided into three sections. The first of these deals with the criticism of sources, and provides the means of establishing the facts with exactitude and fidelity.   The second treats of interpretation, and leads to discovering the true meaning of each fact.   The third, which is the most important for ethnology and the history of religion, as well as the longest, gives an account of combination.   In other words, it teaches us, when the facts are accurately known and rightly interpreted, so to combine them that they show us the veritable course of a development, whether of the whole or some part.   Concerning the first two parts I say nothing here, for they offer nothing really new.   I wish only to touch briefly on the two kinds of interpretation.   That of the first degree, or direct interpretation, is easier to accomplish, for it deals with objects which belong to the same cultural unit.   But as regards indirect interpretation, that is, that which compares objects from cultural units separated in space, Graebner rightly lays down the principle that it must be of the second degree.[27]   That is to say, it can be accomplished only by a process of combination, often anything but simple, which

[24] See *Anthropos*, Vol. VI, 1911, p. 1027.
[25] A similar sketch will be found also in the present author's article, *Die kulturhistorische Methode in der Ethnologie*, in *Anthropos, ibid.*, pp. 1010–36, where a selection of criticisms on Graebner's work and my own are dealt with.
[26] Cf. Pinard, Vol. II, p. 243 *sqq.*
[27] The border-line between two cultures forms a partial exception to this rule.   In this case we may get mixed forms ; see *Anthropos*, Vol. VI, 1911, p. 1031 *sqq.*

proves that the two objects to be compared belong to the same cultural unit. He then continues :

'Hitherto, direct interpretation has been almost alone in vogue. I feel perfectly certain that, if tested by this requisite, a large part of the ethnological work which has been done, particularly in the field of the history of religion, loses much of its value, if it does not become entirely negligible ' (p. 67).

The important third section, that dealing with combination, begins with a historical and critical account of the theories of development which have so far governed the great bulk of all ethnological research, and which claim that the combination of data will result most especially in establishing series of development.

The damage done by Evolutionism may have been lessened, but has not been made good, by the conception of convergence, as introduced by Thilenius and developed by Ehrenreich. Still less is it done away with by Wundt's division of mankind into peoples who have a history and (savage) peoples who have none (see above, p. 220).

The main part of his book has four sub-divisions. He first treats of the criteria by the help of which particular culture-contacts may be put together into whole circles and strata of culture, and how these in their turn connect with one another by juxtaposition and mixing. He then gives directions for establishing the chronology of the development of the partic-ular circles and strata of culture. Finally, he examines the process by which the causal succession of the particular cultures and the reasons for their rise may be arrived at.

(b) THE ESTABLISHMENT OF SPATIAL AND TEMPORAL RELATIONS BETWEEN CULTURES [28]

(i) The two main criteria on the basis of which the historical connexion between cultural elements and complexes can be assumed are those of Form and of Quantity (see above, p. 221). The second of these completes and strengthens the former, and does so the more in proportion as it is itself stronger. There is no reason, on principle, why we should not conclude to such connexions even when the distribution is discontinuous, although the separation may be very wide, extending over entire continents or seas ; but if we do so, the two Criteria of Form and Quantity must be proportionately stronger. Furthermore, in such cases the possibility of continuous

[28] Cf. Pinard, Vol. II, p. 250 sqq.

connexion at an earlier date must be made out; in other words, the Criterion of Continuity must be appealed to. For the original distribution of course did not take place *per saltum*; we cannot assume here that anything acts where it is not.

This possibility of former connexion is strengthened if we can still discover in the intervening areas islands of peoples with the same or similar cultural elements. These can be nothing but survivals and vestigial remains of the connexion which once existed. The cogency of our argument will be still more increased by using the Criterion of Degree of Relationship; that is, if we find that the resemblances in question increase in strength and in number in proportion as we approach the two chief areas, which are now separated from each other. This would amount to a proof that the resemblances did not arise *en route* independently, but owe their origin and existence solely to a historical connexion with the two principal areas.

By the help of these criteria and others of the same tendency, we are able to determine the spatial connexion of cultural areas, and to do so by an objective process, free from subjective judgements of value and developmental series constructed *a priori*; and with scientific certainty, without any excessive heaping up of merely possible hypotheses, whether or not the areas in question are separated by areas of different culture.

(ii) But the historical method also makes it possible to determine the temporal connexion; this is naturally of especial value among savage peoples who have no written chronological documents. If two cultural areas of different character touch one another, then either they will overlap at the borders, and so produce crossings, or else will merely touch at the edges and so produce the phenomena of contact. It is obvious that forms arising either out of a crossing or a contact must be more recent than the parent forms. This is the first objective ethnological criterion of time, and it may lead to still further chronological results; for those forms due to mixture or contact in which the two components are still clearly to be recognized as such are thereby shown to be less ancient than those in which the component elements have blended into a unity; since this process must needs demand a longer time.

(c) THE SPATIAL RELATIONS OF CULTURES [29]

(i) If now we take a large region, say a continent, and establish by the above methods the existence of individual culture-areas, their crosses and their contacts; if we have

[29] See Pinard, Vol. II, p. 250 *sqq.*

everywhere differentiated the latter from the former ; then it becomes clear that a certain number of the areas characterized by crossings and contacts stand in one of the two following relations to each other.

The relationship of the individual elements of culture to one another in each subordinate area may be organically close, and therefore its resemblance to other subordinate areas clearly visible,—in this case there is generally agreement in language also,—as we find it in the Polynesian culture of the Southern Pacific. In such a case we have cultures of a more recent order.

Or it may be that a certain number of cultural elements which seem to have no organic connexion with one another are yet as a matter of fact found more or less together in sundry areas. We then have cultures of older date. The apparent lack of connexion now between the individual elements in individual areas indicates a long-continued crossing with other cultures ; but that we do find them together, again and again, shows that there was once a historical relation between them.

(ii) That these individual regions belong to a cultural horizon which once existed as a historical fact is proved by the large number of the individual and characteristic agreements ; in other words the Criterion of Quantity is applicable. But a legitimate application may also be made of the Criterion of Form. The agreement of the individual forms affects all parts of the life of the culture in question, material, economic, social, ethical and religious. Hence, wherever a region spatially separate of the culture-horizon in question is found, these elements of the separate parts of that culture likewise appear, in more or less constant association.

But this constantly recurring association of the separate elements is not of internal character; one element cannot be necessarily deduced from the very nature of another. For instance: what possible organic connexion is there between the use of weapons of the club type, which we find in cultures having mother-right, and the matrilineal organization ? Or how are the pointed weapons of the patrilineal, totemistic culture connected with their sun-myths ? The connexion is a purely outward fact, a matter of history.

(d) CULTURE-STRATA IN THEIR CHRONOLOGICAL RELATIONS [30]

(i) As individual cultural areas come into contact with others of a different kind and produce forms due to crossing and juxtaposition, so also of course do entire circles of culture. In the case of the individual groups we were able to establish differences in time, by noting that the forms arising from

[30] Cf. Pinard, Vol. II, pp. 270–87.

crossing and contact must always be later than the forms in the two cultures from whose combination they arose. This is naturally true likewise of the similar forms which arise from the contact of two entire circles of culture ; the areas where such forms occur and the forms themselves must be later than the cultures themselves and the simple forms belonging to them. Thus our power to establish a chronology extends its scope very considerably. Also, in this connexion we acquire two other useful measures of time.

(ii) One culture may not only touch another at a particular point, but may cut the other culture in two, thus splitting it into halves which from then on have no connexion with each other. It is obvious that the victorious culture must be the later at the spot where it has broken through the other. Or, one culture may so overlay another that only scattered and rudimentary survivals of the second are left in the area in question. Such survivals are thus seen to be older than the victorious culture, at least on the spot where the overlay has taken place. For certainly there must once have been a time when the rudimentary survivals which we now find stood in a living and organic connexion with each other.

(iii) Assuming that the human race originated in Asia—a proposition contradicted by no reliable results of any other science, such as physical anthropology or prehistory, but on the contrary receiving continual accessions of support from them—and that it gradually migrated thence to the other portions of the globe, we get a second objective measure of time. Precisely those portions of the world which contain the savage races of to-day, namely Africa, Oceania and America, are not connected with Asia by any broad land-bridge, across which migrations might have entered them on an indefinitely wide front. Their connexions with that continent consist of isthmuses or strings of islands, so narrow that the bulk of the migrations must have followed this one way, especially in the earliest times, when the art of navigation was but little developed. Thus we come to the result, as concerns these three portions of the earth's surface, that in all cases the oldest movement of population made its way to the farthest district, or at least was thrust there by the following waves of migration ; while on the other hand, the most recent strata of peoples in those parts of the world are those who are nearest the entry. Apart from this, however, remnants of older populations can maintain themselves more easily in out-of-the-way districts, such as mountainous tracts difficult of approach, primeval forests, deserts, and other inhospitable regions ; also on distant islands.

With the help of these criteria we can succeed in determining, in each of the several parts of the world, what is the sequence, in other words the age, of the various cultures there. It must be the ultimate goal of our comparisons to establish, first of all, the distribution of the several cultures over the whole earth ; and then, by comparing them reciprocally, to find which is the oldest in the whole history of cultural development, and also the absolute sequence in which the others follow it. Perhaps then we shall also be able to establish, for each several culture, in what region it arose. I need hardly say that at present we are far from an answer to this great problem.

(iv) Nevertheless, we can even now lay down two useful rules which may help to solve it. Firstly, a culture which appears as the oldest in every part of the world in which it occurs, must be regarded as absolutely the oldest. Secondly, a culture-area which divides another in two, or overlays it, can in no case have arisen on the spot where the dividing or overlaying occurs.

(e) THE ORIGIN AND DEVELOPMENT OF CULTURAL ELEMENTS [31]

(i) Having learned now to judge of cultures, their boundaries, overlays, crossings, and relative and absolute chronology, we are at last in a position to attempt, with due caution, to solve that difficult problem, how the several cultural elements developed. How are we to answer the questions regarding the development of the family, the state, religion, industry and tool-making ? What were their beginnings, and how did their later development proceed ?

To answer these questions, we need no previously adopted theory of development, whether that of progress upwards or that of degeneration downwards. We simply let the facts speak for themselves, having first established them on the basis of purely objective criteria.

To begin with, it is obvious that even the determinations of time which we have attained to with the help of the criteria hitherto mentioned are of very great importance for the question of development ; for they reveal to us, at least in its main outlines, the general course of development and the sequence of the several phases thereof. But the historical method has yet more service to do for us. Firstly, it teaches us what things the investigator must leave on one side when trying to

[31] Cf. Pinard, Vol. II, p. 288 *sqq.*

determine the inner development of an object, an institution, or an area, because they are due to an external cause, namely crossing.

But it is not only forms which owe their existence to outward (and secondary) crossing which must be excluded from comparison, if we wish to arrive at an undistorted picture of the inner development. No element belonging to one culture can have any inner connexion with the analogous element in another culture, so far as its development is concerned. For the many-sided peculiarity of a culture is the result of its separate and independent existence throughout a considerable extent of time, apart from all other cultures. Consequently, the development of its several elements has been wholly independent likewise, and not in any way affected by the analogous elements of another culture, or in any way affecting them in their development.

Hence, as soon as we are confronted with question concerning the inner development of a cultural element, we can compare only those forms of it which lie within the range of the same culture ; any others are wholly outside the comparison, and are disparate. It is easy to see what a world of cloud-castles in the form of comparisons and developmental series are annihilated by this principle. Forms belonging to a foreign culture can be taken into consideration only if the two cultures in question are themselves inwardly connected with one another, either because one has developed out of the other or because both are the offspring of some older culture still.

Let us now consider the way in which the several forms of one and the same cultural element are to be arranged as regards their age, and therefore how the individual points in the series of development are to be fixed. Only objective criteria will guide us here, and these we have already made the acquaintance of ; there are still some few extensions and specifications to make, but these must be omitted here, because to consider them would take too long.

(ii) On the other hand, we must, in conclusion, say a few words about the last and decisive question, that of the origin of the individual cultural forms.

It is especially in regard to this question that the historical school is fundamentally dissociated from the Evolutionist, or psychological. The latter raises questions of origin at every turn, and is continually engaged in explaining the genesis of a cultural form, a tool, a usage or a social institution on the basis of the relations in which it is now found, and of the factors now in existence. The historical school, on the contrary, leaves these questions to the very last, which is methodologically the only permissible thing to do. All the operations which we have hitherto undertaken with the help of the various criteria must first be accomplished before we can lawfully set out to answer the question how a cultural element originated.

For firstly, we must establish to what particular culture this element belongs ; next, we must follow up the individual phases of the development of this element through the whole of that culture, for only thus can we make sure which is the oldest form of the element concerned. This oldest form of the tool, institution, belief or custom in question is the only one immediately proceeded by the origin, and therefore it must be put in the foreground when we ask what the origin was. The later forms, it is easy to see, can help us but little to learn the origin, and the further they are from the origin itself, the less help they can give.

And now we can lay down an important and general rule, consisting of two parts :

(a) Every cultural element can be explained, as regards its origin, only from the ideas and associations belonging to that culture to which itself belongs, and not from any general guesses as to what may have been ; still less of course from the ideas and associations of a foreign culture.

(β) Within a given culture, it is the oldest forms of any element which are especially significant for the explanation of its origin, for they come nearest to reflecting the influences, physical and mental, to which the first appearance of that element was due.

In another place [32] I have made a few remarks by way of supplement and criticism of Graebner's method, as above described. My points were three in number. First, different individual elements of culture have different capabilities of dissemination. Second, especially close and accurate observation is needed in areas where crossing and contact take place ; for here tendencies of an arbitrary and non-organic kind are formed, for instance, in mythology. Third, there is need for particularly accurate grasping of the combined factors of comparison, and care to recognize aright what element is really the nucleus of the phenomenon studied.

3. THE NOMENCLATURE AND GROUPING OF THE CULTURES

The earliest nomenclature of the culture-horizons which had so far been discovered was made by Graebner for Oceania and Anker-

---

[32] See the author's article *Die kulturhistorische Methode in der Ethnologie*, in *Anthropos*, Vol. VI, 1911, pp. 1010 *sqq.*, 1027 *sqq.*

mann for Africa, in their above-mentioned lectures (see p. 221). The terms they use are founded on the special circumstances prevailing in those regions. Later, W. Foy introduced a set of names which could be applied to both the above areas indifferently. The present author worked out a still more extensive and complete unification, starting from the social structure and especially from the form of exogamy in use in each culture-horizon.

Complete agreement has not yet been reached as to the number and kind of cultures established as existing. While Foy and Ankermann practically agree with the author in holding the Pygmy culture to be the oldest, Graebner wishes to look further ; he also does not as yet feel certain of the existence of the culture of nomads who are pastoral on a large scale, which is likewise postulated by me. On the other hand, I no longer recognize the boomerang culture, postulated by Graebner, as an original and independent culture-horizon but only as an early cross between matrilineal elements and those of the primitive culture. I accept, however, the Arctic culture-horizon which Graebner, in his *Ethnologie*,[33] gives as forming a division of primitive culture.

We must thus distinguish three stages, primitive, primary and secondary. To the first of these belong all those races whose members still belong to the so-called food-gatherers ; that is, in which man does not as yet assist nature to increase her productivity, but contents himself with gathering from her what she offers of her own accord. At this stage the men get flesh-food by hunting, the women vegetable food by collecting plants. To the second stage belong those cultures in which the exploitation of nature has begun. Women pass from gathering plants to cultivating them, that is, to the primitive horticultural stage. This occurs in the exogamous, matrilineal culture. In the culture characterized by the undivided family and patrilineal organization, the men's hunting develops into cattle-breeding ; while in another, the exogamous patrilineal, it produces totemism, which is a kind of animal worship. Finally, in the secondary stage new culture-horizons appear ; these are the result of crossings of the primary cultures with one another or with primitive cultures. Particularly conspicuous here are the free matrilineal culture, resulting from a cross between patrilineal, with the undivided family, and the exogamous matrilineal ; also the free patrilineal culture, which springs from a cross between the two primary patrilineal types, the exogamous and that having the undivided family.

[33] In Hinneberg's *Kultur der Gegenwart*, Leipzig and Berlin, 1923 ; cf. *Ursprung der Gottesidee*, Vol. I, ed. 2, note on p. 709.

In the primitive stage we begin by differentiating three cultures. The first, or Central, is exogamous and monogamous ; it includes the African Pygmies and those of Southern Asia, perhaps those of New Guinea and the New Hebrides also. The second, or Southern, is exogamous and has sex-totems; to it belong the tribes of South-East Australia (and the extinct Tasmanians); the Tierra del Fuegians of the southernmost parts of South America are connected with it, as also the Bushmen of South Africa. The third, or Arctic, is exogamous with equal rights for both parties ; it includes North and North-Eastern Asiatic peoples, also the primitive Eskimo. Related to it are the Central Californians and primitive Algonkin, in North America. A fourth, the Boome-rang culture, includes, in Australia, the tribes bordering on those of the second culture, and in Africa, certain races of the upper Nile and of South Africa. (See above, p. 238). In South America, it would seem that all three primitive cultures have combined into one. In all these original cultures of the primitive stage, a kind of father-right exists.

Passing now to the primary stage, we again find three cultures. Of these, the first is that of the pastoral nomads, characterized by the undivided family and father-right. These peoples become later conquerors and rulers ; they include the Ural-Altaics, the Indo-Europeans and the Hamito-Semites. The next, the exogamous patrilineal culture of the higher hunters who practise totemism, is the founder of art, crafts-manship, and trade ; it is therefore the originator of town-culture. Its distribution cannot be defined within such narrow limits ; it is scattered over South and Central Australia, New Guinea, Hither India, and wide areas in Africa and North and South America. In like manner the exogamous, matrilineal culture of the horticultural peoples, the founders of village-culture, is not confined within a fixed area. It is to be found in East and West Australia, in central Melanesia, parts of Indonesia, India, both Farther and Hither, West Africa and the central part of East Africa, and portions of North and South America.

It is still less possible to define briefly here the distribution of the secondary cultures. It must be emphasized that both the free matrilineal and the free patrilineal cultures are found here and there as late as the earliest historical times in Western Asia and in Europe.

It is very important to remember that the three primary cultures did not arise essentially one after another, so that

every people, or even the majority of peoples, must needs
have passed through them all. On the contrary ; a part of
the tribes having primitive culture developed into the higher,
totemistic hunting stage, another part became cattle-breeders,
the third horticulturalists. It was not till later, by means of
crossings, which of course took place in different degrees of
strength of the various components, that elements of one or
both the other cultures could be taken up by a third ; the
internal development of each culture always went on independently. The same is true, *mutatis mutandis*, for the secondary cultures as well. In the primitive cultures a similar
independence of each of the three cultures of that stage existed.
However, in Oceania, Asia and Africa it is probable that the
third appeared later than the other two, and of these two, the
first is older than the second. All three alike presumably go
back to an earlier culture still, the primitive culture properly
so called ; but hitherto no concrete examples of this can be
established anywhere, nor is it likely that we shall ever be
able to do so directly.

In an article contributed to *Festschrift für W. Schmidt*, Vienna,
1928, p. 490 *sqq.*, and entitled *Der Begriff der Erntevölker* ['The Idea
of Harvest-Peoples '], J. Lips supposes the existence of a group of
Erntevölker, [literally ' harvest-peoples '], who gather the fruits and
so forth of wild plants and store them for use in the colder season of
the year. These he takes to be identical with the totemic peoples,
and credits them with originating both agriculture and cattle-
breeding. The discovery of such peoples within the primitive
culture is very important ; but their position as a separate culture-
horizon and the consequences deduced therefrom by Lips are highly
problematical. Further inquiries must be awaited here.

We may thus represent the number, names and grouping
of the cultures diagrammatically as follows :—

I. PRIMITIVE
CULTURES
(*Food-
gatherers*)

1. Central Primitive Culture ; exogamous, with monogamy.
2. Southern Primitive Culture ; exogamous, with sex-totems.
3. Arctic Primitive Culture ; exogamous, equal rights.
And, by crossing of one of the above with a very old matrilineal culture,
4. Boomerang Culture.
General characteristics of all these : occupa-
tion of men, supply of flesh-food by hunting ; of women, supply of vegetable food
by plant-gathering.

II. PRIMARY
    CULTURES
    (*Food-
    producers*)

   1. Exogamous, patrilineal. Totemic, higher stage of hunting; 'city culture.
   2. Exogamous, matrilineal. Horticulturalists; 'village' culture.
   3. Patrilineal, with undivided family; to this culture belong the pastoral nomads, who become ruling races.

III. SECONDARY
     CULTURES

   1. Free patrilineal cultures (Polynesia, the Sudan, Hither India, Western Asia, Southern Europe, etc.).
   2. Free matrilineal cultures (Southern China, Farther India, Melanesia, the North-East of South America, etc.).

IV. TERTIARY
    CULTURES

Oldest civilizations of Asia, Europe and America.

4. HISTORIANS OF CULTURE AND THEIR ATTITUDE TOWARDS THE HIGH GODS

Even in their enumeration of the several cultures, we have seen differences in the attitude of individual inquirers using the modern historical method. Such differences in details are yet more in evidence with regard to the religions of the different cultures, and particularly to the question how old, ethnologically speaking, the high gods are. However, it is to be noted that the amount of attention devoted by individual investigators to this problem varies greatly. W. Foy and B. Ankermann could pay but little heed to it ; F. Graebner studied it more closely ; the most intensive study of this matter is my own. But we must also keep the fact in view that the time during which the new method could be employed has been comparatively short, and that unfortunately, the number of those pioneers who have used it has already been lessened by the death of Foy, while Graebner and Ankermann have been prevented from going on with their work by ill-health.

(*a*) W. FOY

This savant gave only a rather short account of his views on the history of religion, in his Guide to the Rautenstrauch-Joest Museum in Cologne, of which he was the director for a long time (Cologne ; ed. 2, 1908 ; ed. 3, from which the following quotations are taken, 1910). It is, however, sufficient to show what his attitude was. In describing what he calls the ' first and oldest cultural heritage of mankind as it spread over the world', he says, speaking of non-material culture :

'Promiscuity did not prevail among them, but rather individual marriage ([*Einzelehe*]; meaning perhaps monogamy); cannibalism was unknown. The religion of primitive man was rooted in belief in magical force and the efficacy of magical practices, also in a belief in the ghosts of the dead, who were feared. To what extent these beliefs were already connected with faith in a Supreme Being living in the sky can no longer be determined ; in any case, such a faith belongs to the oldest strata of culture, where a more or less feeble glimpse of it can always be caught' (pp. 25–6). He adds a little later (p. 26), 'There are nevertheless still other backward peoples, as the dwarfish races of Africa, the South-East Australians and the Tierra del Fuegians in South America, whose poverty of culture makes an impression of antiquity, despite many borrowings from foreign sources, and who agree with the Tasmanians in many cultural matters.'

As his picture of the oldest condition of mankind is derived only from the scanty Tasmanian material, it needs correction, or explanation, on two points. For the Pygmy peoples especially, it is clear that belief in magic is not nearly so developed among them as in later cultures, while on the other hand the figure of the Supreme Being is far more definite and distinct ; but neither of these is due to a 'borrowing from foreign sources', for conditions among their neighbours are entirely different.

Speaking of the Australians, Foy says :

'The population of Australia is dark-skinned, and both the physical and their cultural characteristics have preserved remarkably primitive features, dating from the first development of mankind. No such features are found to so large an extent anywhere else on earth.'

He agrees that among the Australian tribes those of the south-east are the oldest. Concerning their religion he writes:

'It is at first sight surprising to find, especially in South-East Australia, a belief in one god, known as "father" or "grandfather", who is supposed to have created man and the principal phenomena of nature, to have taught men how to make weapons and tools, and to watch over the preservation of the tribal laws, especially the correct performance of the complicated ceremonial connected with the initiation of the young men. This belief is probably the result of an attempt on the part of primitive man to understand the phenomena of meteorology, and we can well understand that he would suppose these caused by a human, but gigantic and enormously powerful being, whose breath for example was the wind, his voice the thunder, and so on. Now vegetation is very closely connected with these meteorological processes, such as rain, thunder-storms and the like ; hence this Supreme Being acquired at an early date the traits of a vegetation-god. He likewise blended with leading figures of solar and lunar myths, for these, like the moon and sun themselves, have in their turn especially close relations with plant-life. So we find this god in Australia ; often his son stands, as an independent mythological creation, at his side, acting as mediator between him and man, and especially as guide of the dead. Other beliefs concerning gods and spirits grow up around these figures ; we also notice a dualism, the result of an antithesis between sun and moon, or between the bright and the dark moon ' (pp. 58–9).

In so short an account as this, it was obviously hard to avoid a certain confusion between the various South-East Australian high gods, despite their characteristic differences, which I have expounded in detail in *Ursprung*, Vol. I, ed. 2, pp. 334–477 and Vol. III, Division III. But Foy, more clearly here than anywhere else, emphasizes the independent origin of the Supreme Being, before all star-myths and apart from them. It is only ' later ', in his opinion, that he is ' blended ' with solar or lunar figures, and beliefs in other gods and spirits ' grow up around ' him. As the Supreme Being is also the Creator, the explanation of his origin from ' the attempt of primitive man to understand the phenomena of meteorology ' is certainly too narrow. But Foy is perfectly right when he lays down that the Supreme Being is closely connected from the very beginning with the observance of tribal law, *i.e.*, that he has an ethical character.

(b) B. ANKERMANN

Of all the pioneers of the historical movement, Ankermann is the least uncompromising and the most loath to abandon the older views. This is visible also to some extent in his attitude towards the question of how religion originated. He has stated his views in his article *Die Religion der Naturvölker*.[34] After attacking the earlier unilinear theories of Evolution, he continues (p. 133) :

' It would seem rather that we have to do with several lines of thought, running parallel to each other, which originated independently, but soon blended in all manner of relations. Instead

[34] In the fourth edition (edited by A. Bertholet and E. Lehmann, Tübingen, 1924) of Chantepie de la Saussaye, *Lehrbuch der Religionsgeschichte*, Vol. I, pp. 131–92.

244 THE ORIGIN AND GROWTH OF RELIGION

of a simple process of development, everywhere following the same course, we must assume a number of different developments, from whose crossing and mutual influence the manifold forms of religion which we may observe to-day have sprung up as history progressed.'

But unfortunately he departs from this great multiplicity of religious forms, because they cannot be expounded in the brief space available, and attends exclusively to the ' equally great uniformity in certain fundamental traits ', which, as he asserts, is no less unmistakable. He thus proceeds to set forth in order the ' elements ' from which religions have arisen, arranging them in accordance with his scheme in six sections : worship of the dead and belief in ghosts, including ancestor-worship and animism ; ideas of power and magic ; totemism ; gods ; cults and priesthood ; mythology.

No attempt is made anywhere to connect one or another of these elements with particular cultures. Only at the very end (p. 192) do we find this general statement :

' The division of mankind into races and separate families was certainly accompanied by a differentiation of the original and primitive culture. Religion also must have been differentiated. The migrations of peoples, which resulted in their being subjected to new conditions of life, no doubt also brought about a divergent development of the elements of religion, and thus each culture must have created a religion of its own.'

Considering that the author of this sketch is so important an historian of culture as Ankermann, one would have liked at least some example of this religion which is peculiar to a particular culture.

As regards his attitude towards the high gods, Ankermann agrees that such beings, living in heaven and sending thence rain, lightning and thunder as transitory expressions of the workings of their will, are especially to be found among the races who, ethnologically speaking, are the most ancient. He not only recognizes, with Andrew Lang, their existence ' among quite primitive populations ', but also rejects the theory that they arise late, as the head of a hierarchy of gods, and like-wise their derivation from animism (see p. 179 sq.). But he does not succeed in forming a completely just idea of these high gods, because his apprehension of their attributes is incorrect or incomplete. Following Söderblom's example, he treats them as ' originators ', who have created the world once for all, but have since retired and have no cult. He is obliged, however, to modify his statement by admitting that they punish transgressions of their ethical laws.   It is also to be remembered, as I have already (above, p. 140 *sqq.*) mentioned in criticism of Söderblom, that among the ethnologically oldest peoples in particular, the Supreme Beings show vigorous vitality and frequently intervene in the progress of events.[35]

(c) F. GRAEBNER

Graebner's views on the origin of the idea of God are expressed in several passages of his *Ethnologie*,[36] but still more is said in his latest work, *Das Weltbild der Primitiven*.[37] In the following paragraphs I quote from the last-named book, citing the former only for necessary supplements or explanations.

Speaking of Australian thought, Graebner declares these peoples to be ' representatives of a particularly low form of culture ' ; but he opposes Lévy-Bruhl's ideas.   In his opinion, the latter

' has quite missed the mark, at least in so far as entirely primitive men are concerned.   The Australian does not consider the natural to be supernatural, but rather the reverse ; the supernatural is natural to him ' (*Weltbild*, p. 16).

Here I entirely agree.   Theirs is normal causal reasoning, although it has been extended, by false analogies, to illicit fields, and finds causal connexions where none exist.   This is also Graebner's view.   He says (*ibid.*, p. 17) :

' Manifestly, in all these cases we are dealing with unusually fixed associations of ideas, the result of experience, between certain causes and effects—so fixed indeed that they proceed *to go beyond experience* ' (the italics are mine), ' and on the occurrence of certain effects, to recall certain relevant causes to the consciousness.'

For the rest, I must emphasize, in opposition to Graebner, as I have done in dealing with Foy (see above, p. 242), that he has not paid sufficient attention to the fact that, the nearer we get to the oldest and most primitive peoples, the less (not more) practice of magic we find.   Consequently, Graebner's treatment of all the Australians as one whole does not fit the facts, indeed is utterly misleading.   The profound difference between the different cultures which he has himself made out for Australia can no more be neglected in this

[35] See further my *Ursprung*, Vol. I, ed. 2, p. 772 *sqq.*, and Vols. II, III and IV, *passim*.
[36] See p. 238, note 33, above.
[37] [' The World as Primitive Man sees it '], Munich, 1924.

connexion than in any other. He does indeed draw some distinctions here and there (as *op. cit.*, p. 19), but should have made far more of them. If he had, it would have been clear that as we approach the south-east of Australia, we find the belief in magic progressively on the downgrade ; a phenomenon the significance of which he has himself called attention to in his *Methode der Ethnologie*, pp. 133 and 163. For this reason, and also because, as Graebner himself admits (*Weltbild*, p. 14), the belief in one god plays no inconsiderable part in the primitive view of the universe, making as it does for generalizing and causal reasoning, I regret it and think it wholly inadequate of Graebner to entitle this whole section of his work simply ' The savage's magical view of the world '.[38]

Passing to a positive description of the religion of primitive peoples, Graebner very properly grasps its widely universal character, which seems to contrast very markedly with the pettiness of primitive thought in other respects.

' It has hitherto been the result of our investigations ', he says (*Weltbild*, p. 24), ' that the savage looks on the world with something like an insect's eye. As a rule he can see only particular associations, which find their unity only in the circumstance that they impinge upon the same centre of perception. This appears to be contradicted by the fact that even primitive peoples know of superior beings which in some sense include in their sphere of activity the whole universe or at least considerable portions of it.'

This as a matter of fact is a point of great importance.[39]

The apparent contradiction which Graebner establishes in this passage and does not attempt to clear up, so far as I can see, can surely be reconciled only by assuming that this divine figure dates from an age in which human thought was not yet so broken up and reduced to pettiness by the development of magic and by other causes, but still functioned on a larger and more inclusive scale.

Graebner's further remarks on the dualism of Tasmanian religion are unsatisfactory, in my opinion ; I have gone into the matter in my *Ursprung der Gottesidee* at some length (Vol. I, ed. 2, p. 263 *sqq.*). On the other hand, his description of South-East Australian religion is so admirable, apart from his estimate of its age,[40] that I cannot refrain from citing the passage at full length (*Weltbild*, pp. 25–7).

[38] [' Die magische Weltanschuung der Primitiven '], *op. cit.*, p. 14.
[39] See *Ursprung der Gottesidee*, Vol. I, ed. 2, p. 641.
[40] Note that he calls this ' the oldest culture next to that of Tasmania ' ; cf., on this point, *Ursprung*, Vol. I, ed. 2, p. 466 *sqq.*

'The nature of the All-Father, the great creative god of the Australians, is yet more all-inclusive than that of the two Tasmanian deities. We find this deity especially in the south-eastern portion of the continent, that is to say, in the seat of the oldest culture, next to that of Tasmania ; he is variously called Mungan ngaua, Bunjil, Baiame, Nurrundere, and so forth. Generally there exists beside him another figure, powerful but subordinate, most frequently considered to be his son, but often as the primeval ancestor of mankind. Sometimes, for instance among the Kurnai, the great god has no wife, or only an invisible one ; occasionally he has produced his son without having a consort. His principal attribute is that of creator, or first cause of, at least, everything which is important for men ; he is the first maker of the most important implements, as the boomerang ; he is a magician whose power knows no bounds ; he is the celestial chief. Knowledge of him is imparted to the youths at their initiation, when they are received into the status of men ; it is given them by the elders. These ceremonies are often celebrated by several neighbouring tribes in common. These are invited to the place of the festival by messengers, and a truce of God prevails during the entire time of the celebration. We see here the most primitive form of amphiktyony. It is moreover very important that the great god is considered not only as creator and maker of all things, but also as guardian of the tribal morality. It is of him that the legend is told how in old days, when men had forgotten their good habits, he sent the conflagration and the flood to punish them. I have already said that the Kurnai fear to this day that the like will happen again when the Aurora Australis appears. It is not improbable that the fire-ceremony of the Central Australian Warramunga is intended to impress a similar event and a similar fear upon the minds of their young men. As regards the nature and meaning of the great god, it must first be said that his existence completely satisfies the lively desire of the natives to know the cause of things. But Preuss is perhaps right in doubting that so abstract an idea as a first cause could have been capable, among primitive men, of producing a figure which is always so full of life. The god is of course also supposed to be the originator of the rites and magical practices by which man rules nature ; and to this extent his existence ensures the continuance of the human race even now. I have already mentioned, moreover, that the idea of a first cause has connected itself with that very concrete phenomenon, the sun, which every morning makes all things clearly visible once more, and thus in a way re-creates them every time it rises. In North-West Australia it is the sun which cast from him his boomerang, the moon, which naturally comes back to him again. But it is also the sun, in Victoria, which begot the moon from himself, without (quite rightly) needing the intervention of any third being. Thus the play of associations is clear enough in the genesis of this divine figure. Nevertheless, his pre-eminent significance and the vividness with which he has been developed are due, in this ancient culture, to another factor still, I mean the ethical. This god is the preserver, not only of the psychical, but above all of the social existence of man, and thus of his very essence.'

Here certainly Graebner does full justice to the all-embracing character of the Supreme Being among the South-East Australians, his nature, not only as creator, but also as guardian of the whole world, and his close connexion, not only with the physical, but also with the social and ethical side of being, which is also traced to him. Likewise, his connexion with astral myths is set forth in a way which scarcely leaves room for any objection on principle.

But it is regrettable and hard to understand why Graebner has completely left out of sight the facts of Pygmy religion. This is one of the worst defects in his whole account. Even if he is not willing to admit the existence of a separate Pygmy culture, or if he considers it later than that of the Tasmanians,[41] still the following few lines are lamentably inadequate to deal with it (p. 15):

' However, these ' (the Pygmy races of Central Africa) ' and still more the Asiatic Pygmies, have already been imbedded in or engrafted upon the areas of later cultures. For instance, none, or almost none of them, have a language peculiar to their own culture.' [42]

It is a manifest fact that it is just the religious phenomena observable among the Pygmies which cannot be derived from the intimate ' imbedding or engrafting of their culture in the areas of later ones ', because those later cultures present no such phenomena.

The above defect is in large measure compensated, at the very end of Graebner's work (op. cit., pp. 128–30), where he suggests that the effects of this old primitive monotheism have persisted even down to the highest civilizations. In ascribing to this conception of God such profound influence and wide-reaching power, he shows clearly how great is the importance with which he is obliged to credit it in general, and consequently even on its first appearance.

[41] I deal fully with this question in *Ursprung*, Vol. III, pp. 9–49.
[42] This dictum can already be shown wrong with regard to the Andamanese and to some extent the Semang ; it probably will soon need revision for the Filippino Negritos. Quite recently, by the discoveries of Father Schebesta (see *Anthropos*, XXV, 1930, p. 312 *sqq.*, 581), it has been proved erroneous for the Pygmies of Central Africa, viz. the Wambutti tribes of the Ituri.

' In general it appears that the growth, already referred to, of the beginnings of higher views of the universe, the tendency to monotheistic and pantheistic conceptions and likewise to the propounding of moral problems, is explicable from the historical phenomena of culture already mentioned, namely the production of a high civilization from the union of the two principal movements of patrilineal and matrilineal cultures. But it is doubtful if this explanation says the last word regarding the original relationships. I have remarked earlier that in ancient cultures of the Australian type, the myth of the Deluge plays a part in conjunction with a highly developed conception of God.[43] We find the same myth again in the ancient culture of Babylon. In the ancient Oriental civilizations, moreover, we find the art of painting, with representations of figures, and the closely related art of sculpture in low relief, neither of which is to be found in the patrilineal or the matrilineal culture, but which can be paralleled from Australia and from the Bushmen. In the field of material culture, Egypt and Mesopotamia both possess the boomerang. We may therefore fairly ask the question whether a strain of extremely old human culture is not to be found, perhaps not in all civilizations, but certainly in some of them. If so, then of course not only the monotheistic tendencies and all the phenomena resulting therefrom, but also the ethical conception of these divine figures, and in general the decided fondness for ethical problems which appears in these civilizations, have at least one of their roots in the strain of ancient culture' (*Weltbild*, pp. 128–30).

These are valuable and far-reaching reflections, well worth thorough consideration and pursuing to their logical conclusions.

(d) W. SCHMIDT

As has been already stated (above, p. 241), of all the members of the historical school it is the present writer who has been most extensively busied with the study of the religious facts and especially those relating to high gods.

As a result of these studies, there has appeared a large and comprehensive work, dealing with the whole field from the point of view of historical criticism. Its title is *Die Ursprung der Gottesidee* [' The Origin of the Idea of God ']; the first edition was published at Münster in 1912, the second in 1926 (both of Vol. I only). Contained in it are also detailed special studies of the South-East Australian Supreme Beings (pp. 334–483 of the second edition) and the religion of the Tasmanians (*ibid.*, pp. 236–73). Earlier there appeared a monograph on the religion of the Pygmies, *Die Stellung der Pygmäenvölker in der Entwicklungsgeschichte der Menschen* [' The

---

[43] He also says, speaking of the Israelites, that ' monotheistic ideas prevailed among them before any of their literature was written '.

Place of the Pygmy Peoples in the History of Human Development '], Stuttgart 1910 ; see above, p. 222 ; and another work, *Grundlinien einer Vergleichung der Religionen und Mythologien der austronesischen Völker* [' Outlines of a Comparative Religion and Mythology of the Austronesian Peoples '], in the Records [*Denkschriften*] of the Imperial Academy of Sciences, Vienna, 1910, Philological and Historical Section, Vol. LIII, article iii. (A shorter sketch of the same subject will be found in *Mitteilungen der Anthropologischen Gesellschaft in Wien* [' Transactions of the Viennese Anthropological Society '], Vol. XXXIX, 1909, under the title, *Mythologie der austronesischen Völker* [' Mythology of the South Sea Peoples '].) But neither of these fulfils the requirements of the historical method with sufficient thoroughness.

The remaining volumes of *Ursprung der Gottesidee* will contain, firstly and foremostly, an extensive series of further monographs on the religions of sundry cultures, and then will pass on to a long and exhaustive synthesis.[44] The second volume is especially devoted to the religions of primitive cultures. But in the meantime, so much material has accumulated and preparatory work has been done on it so thoroughly and on so wide a scale that this one volume is obliged to swell into three. The first of these, Vol. II of the whole work, has already appeared (Münster, 1929) ; it extends to 1065 pages and deals with the religions of the primitive peoples of America, *i.e.* the Central Californian Indians, the Indian tribes of the North-West, the Algonkins and the Tierra del Fuegians. The second, Vol. III of the whole, which deals with the primitive peoples of Asia and Australia, the Asiatic Pygmies, the Arctic primitives (Samoyeds, Koryaks, Ainu and primitive Eskimo) and the South-East Australians, is now (1930) appearing and will contain about 1,000 pages. The third, Vol. IV of the whole, treating of the African primitives, the Central Californian Pygmies and the Bushmen, and adding the synthesis of the religions of primitive peoples, will probably be published in 1931.

I think therefore that I have some claim to being sufficiently prepared to give an account of the ' high gods of low races '. The following chapter presents a short anticipatory synopsis thereof.

[44] See Vol. I, ed. 2, of the work in question, p. 764.

CHAPTER XV

THE DATE AND DISTRIBUTION OF THE PRIMITIVE HIGH GODS

W E have now adduced and examined in order all the theories which have been put forward in the course of centuries concerning the origin of religion. Our examination has taken us further and further into the past history of the races and cultures to which the different religions belonged. We have passed the most recent cultures, then others still comparatively modern, next the older cultures, the tertiary, secondary and primary, till at length we have arrived at the primitive cultures, the oldest which our present means and methods allow us to reach. In sharp contrast to all the theories, however, whose acquaintance we have made, we do not intend to erect a theory, still less a hypothesis, upon the facts which we shall now meet with. It will be enough for us if we can examine these facts with the greatest possible completeness and in the widest possible extent, and set them in their true light, especially that one which at this stage stands commandingly in the foreground, the ethical belief in a Supreme Being and the characteristic form of worship connected therewith.

First of all, we proceed to show briefly that the peoples and races which we reckon as belonging to the primitive culture really are in all cases the most ancient, ethnologically speaking, in the regions where they appear ; and that in consequence they are, taken all together, ethnologically the oldest of ¡ eoples.[1]

1. THE ETHNOLOGICAL PRIORITY IN AGE OF THE PRIMITIVE PEOPLES

Those who have been specially trained in ethnology hardly need any further detailed proof of the fact ; for they have already fully recognized and acknowledged that these are

[1] See above, pp. 235, 238.

ethnologically the oldest of peoples, or at all events the peoples in question are individually admitted to be of higher ethnological antiquity than those around them. However, the matter is so important that a formal proof seems called for.

It is not now a single, self-contained culture that we have to deal with, but a group of cultures which between them make up the primitive culture; see above, p. 239. Their mutual historical relations we do not at present know; but we are certain that each of them, taken singly, is older than the remaining cultures of the later, primary stage. This common quality of higher antiquity in itself constitutes a proof that they are closely related to each other.[2] The general proof of the fact that all these peoples belong, ethnologically speaking, to a higher antiquity than any others rests mainly on three positive considerations and one negative.

(a) THE GEOGRAPHICAL RELATIONS OF THE PRIMITIVE CULTURES

The first positive argument, and this alone is sufficient in itself, is the geographical relations of the areas occupied by the primitive peoples. Their habitats are extremely remote. We find them, in all cases, on the farthest verge, or in other such isolated regions which betray their character as the last refuges of fugitives. In these regions we find them to be the earliest and the only inhabitants, and no traces of a population earlier still are to be found.[3] Furthermore, in the several divisions of the earth these peoples occupy such areas as are hardest of access and exercise the least attraction for the later and more advanced peoples.

Thus, the Pygmies and Pygmoids of Asia occupy the extreme south and south-east of that continent and the islands lying off it; and even here, they are confined to districts which are difficult to approach by reason of mountains or forests. The same is true of the oldest tribes in Australia, those of the extreme south-east; the Kulin group, who live in Victoria, south of the Murray River, and their relations, the Kurnai, who have been driven right over the South Australian Alps to the coast, and their neighbours to the north, the Yuin and the Wiradyuri-Kamilaroi; the latter are very mixed, but still preserve enough of their primitive culture to be recognizable. Farther still to the south-east, the

[2] For the names and sequence of the different cultures, see above, p. 238.

[3] See Graebner, *Methode der Ethnologie*, Heidelberg, 1911, p. 141 *sqq*.

Tasmanians, confined to their remote island, had been already exterminated by the Europeans before we could attain to a competent knowledge of them.

In Africa, the various Negrillo tribes inhabit the impenetrable primeval forest which fills the centre of the southern half of the continent. The advance of the Bantu and Hamitic peoples stopped at its borders. Farther south, the Bushmen, who were already confined of themselves to the extreme south and south-east of Africa, have been driven by these later peoples from more desirable dwelling-places farther still into the Kalahari desert.

In Northern Asia we find a similar series of races, the Samoyeds, Kamchadalas and Koryaks, and Ainu, who have been driven to the extreme north-east by the advance of the great pastoral and agricultural races of the centre and east. From their present habitat the way leads to the Eskimo, whose oldest group, the Caribou Eskimo, west of Hudson's Bay, also belongs to the Arctic culture.

In North America, the Algonkin tribes have been driven by the matrilineal and totemic invasions from the west and south, partly to the extreme north-east and the islands lying off the north-east coast, partly to the prairies; while the Old Californian stocks, Hoka, Penuti and Yuki, are squeezed into the narrow corner of the west coast between the Rocky Mountains and the sea.

For Mexico, Central America and the northern part of South America, we may conjecture that primitive tribes exist, but have no clear proof thereof in the present state of our investigations. South of the Amazon, on the other hand, all ethnologists admit that the Gez-Tapuya tribes form a group which has been driven by the later peoples, the Arawaks, Caribs and Tupi, into the eastern half of the continent, and originally to the east coast, only to be thrust back into the interior again by the quite recent encroachments of certain Guarani-Tupi tribes. Unfortunately, we know next to nothing about the religion of these Gez-Tapuyas. The extreme south of the continent, Tierra del Fuego, is marked by the presence there of two primitive tribes, the Halakwulup or Alakaluf and the Yamana or Yagan, with whom the more northerly Selknam or Ona have also much in common.

Thus we can sum up by saying that every one of these areas of primitive culture, taken by itself in relation to its larger environment, shows by its very position that it is the oldest in the region, *i.e.* the continent, to which it belongs. It is thus older than the culture-areas which have totemism, mother-right, or the patriarchal undivided family, in other words the primary stage. Consequently, these primitive cultures, taken all together, must be credited with a higher antiquity than the rest, cf. above, p. 235.

(b) ECONOMIC AND SOCIOLOGICAL CONDITION OF THE PRIMITIVE PEOPLES

(a) The second positive evidence for the high ethnological antiquity of the primitive peoples corroborates the first. It consists of the fact that with a few small exceptions, whose superficial and circumferential character and recent origin are generally easy to recognize, these peoples, one and all, are still in the initial stage of economic development ; in other words, they are food-gatherers. At this stage there is as yet no exploiting of nature by breeding cattle, tilling the soil, or the more advanced ways of hunting, in order to increase and ensure her productivity.

(β) The third positive evidence, which further corroborates the first two,[4] is the generally primitive state of the housing, clothing, tools and weapons of these peoples, and the simplicity of their social arrangements, in which the individual family plays throughout the fundamental and decisive part. In the abstract, this primitiveness might possibly be of a secondary nature, and the simplicity might, rather less possibly, be so likewise. But in this case there is no such possibility, partly because the primitiveness is of so universal and consistent a nature, partly also because there is, here as elsewhere, no positive indication that in earlier times a richer and higher state of affairs existed.

(γ) We have still to consider the negative fact which makes for the general proof of these peoples being ethnologically the most ancient. This is, that among all of them, the characteristics of the primary cultures are not to be found, or exist at best only in a sporadic, superficial, circumferential and late form—to say nothing of the secondary cultures. Thus, in the sociological and economic spheres, they have neither the higher hunting nor totemism, neither agriculture nor mother-right, neither cattle-breeding nor the undivided family ; in industry, they lack the more developed forms of house, pottery, weaving, and of course metallurgy.

Taken together, all these general proofs are enough to show

---

[4] Graebner, *op. cit.*, p. 160 *sq*.

that these peoples, and therefore their religion, belong ethnologically to the most ancient period.

2. THE METHODOLOGICAL IMPORTANCE OF THE PRIMITIVE
PEOPLES' RELIGION

By primitive peoples, we mean those who belong to the
primitive culture, and therefore are to be considered as the
most ancient races of mankind which we can at present make
acquaintance with.   It is self-evident how interesting a knowledge of their religions must be ; for in them we meet, naturally,
with the oldest forms of religion we can hope to find.   The
importance of these forms extends in two directions.

(a) First, so to speak, it extends further back still.   These
religions are our principal base for attacking the problem of
the origin of religion, for they are comparatively nearest to
that origin and therefore preserve still more of its peculiarities
than any other.   That they are nearest to the origin is certain ;
for they have passed through none of the later phases of
development, but remained in the earliest.

However, this statement needs correction and supplement,
and that in two ways.   First, the very fact that these religions
have never developed any further, and therefore have stood
still, means that they have undergone that fossilization and
loss of inner vitality which is inseparably connected with
such a state of rest, and is especially fatal to anything so
essentially spiritual as religion.   For this reason alone, therefore, it is out of the question to expect now from these forms
all the warmth and richness which belonged to the first
beginnings of religion.   Secondly, even in this, the earliest
stage of culture, we find at least three and perhaps four completely different cultures, with different religions.   If we
assume that mankind originally sprang from one source, it
is obvious that the breaking up into different cultures and
religions which we now find even at the primitive stage must
have taken a long time, which must have elapsed between
the real origin and the date of these differentiated cultures.
It cannot but be that in this period religions, like other things,
underwent very considerable changes.   We may therefore be
certain that the religious forms of the primitive cultures now
available do not immediately and without more ado show us
the primitive form of religion.   However, we do come a long
step nearer this ultimate form if we work out the common
element in these primitive religions and put the results together
into a living synthesis.

But the later religions may also have preserved elements which originated, not in later times, but at the beginning, and have retained, more or less faithfully, their old form. We may even admit the possibility that these include elements which are no longer to be found in the primitive cultures. For these causes alone, the sketch of the religions of the primitive culture which we are now giving cannot be taken unchanged as a sketch of primitive religion proper. It may even be that considerable additions could be made to it from later stages.

This possibility becomes a probability when we learn that the peoples of the primitive culture which still exist are all of them no more than small and insignificant fragments of peoples, which have never played any important part in the world. Even accounting for their smallness and insignificance by the purely external factors of an unhappy history and restriction to uncomfortable outward conditions of life, the question remains open whether we are not dealing with groups of human beings who have never reached any considerable importance because they themselves lacked capability more or less completely. No answer, one way or the other, can be given *a priori* to this question ; that must be done by positive investigation. But however the results of this investigation turn out, there is also the possibility on the other side that those races which have attained to greatness and importance in the course of human history, and more especially those who have in many ways made this history, so to speak, have been fitted for their success not only by a favourable outward environment, but also by the power of their own talents. We must, it is true, not lose sight of the fact that personal mental endowments may be of very different kinds ; but it can hardly be doubted that such talents are somehow reflected in the religion of the people concerned and make it, from the very start, notable in one direction or another. That these important elements must be introduced into the complete picture of the primitive religion, and that they may under certain circumstances modify it considerably, is obvious.

Thus we must keep our picture of the primitive religion in a somewhat fluid state, recognizing that it may be eventually enriched from later stages. A similar necessity exists also on the negative side ; it may be that certain parts must be taken away, on production of proof that they are contaminations of later origin. The primitive religion has travelled a long and adventurous road, the longest indeed of any ; on it there must have been opportunities for such contaminations, superpositions and transpositions. Much can already be shown, when it comes to a positive description, to be such comparatively modern additions. Other circumstances, however, may have affected it in so subtle or so complicated a manner that it must be left for future research to seize upon them, when they must of course be subtracted from our picture of the primitive religion.

(β) Now that we have seen the great importance of these primitive peoples for religion, in connexion with the backward extension of it into its first beginnings, we turn to their yet greater significance for its forward development, its subsequent history. For here we have a *terminus a quo*, the starting-point, or, to speak more exactly, that phase of development which so far as our knowledge takes us lies nearest the starting-point, and a part of the ancient development which attaches itself thereto, given us at once. Here also we can, to a certain extent, determine the course which development took ; a course full of significance and of influence on all further stages of religion. It is this very acquaintance with the primitive peoples, grown so much more exact during the last few decades, which has put out of court, without more ado and at no great cost of reflection, a whole series of hypotheses concerning the origin of religion, which without such knowledge had long preserved a misleading appearance of justification.

3. THE DISTRIBUTION OF THE SUPREME BEING IN THE PRIMITIVE CULTURES [5]

Comparing the primitive cultures with the later ones we may lay down the general principle that in none of the latter is the Supreme Being to be found in so clear, so definite, vivid and direct a form as among the peoples belonging to the former. We may now proceed to supplement this by another, of no less importance. This Supreme Being is to be found among all the peoples of the primitive culture, not indeed everywhere in the same form or the same vigour, but still everywhere prominent enough to make his dominant position indubitable.

[5] Evidence of the facts cited in this and the following sections is all to be found in the author's *Ursprung der Gottesidee*, Vols. II, III and IV.

(a) The Central or Pygmy Primitive Culture

Thus, we can establish his existence among all the Pygmy tribes of the central culture, in so far as we have anything like thorough knowledge of them, both in the Asiatic and in the African groups.

(i) To begin with Africa, we find him among the Boni Negrillos of the east, the Ajongo and Nkule of the west, the Batwa in Urundi, the Bagielli of the Cameroons, the Batwa of Ruanda and the Bambutti (Efe and Bakango) of the Ituri. Till a short time ago, our information concerning these African Pygmies in particular was but scanty; but thanks to the investigations of Trilles in the Gabon district, Schumacher in Ruanda and Schebesta in the Congo, we know to-day that the Supreme Being is present clearly and abundantly among the Negrillos of that continent.

(ii) Among the Asiatic Pygmies, E. H. Man's results concerning Puluga, the Supreme Being of the Andamanese, held the field for some time. Then A. R. Brown believed for a while that his expedition to those parts had quite discredited Man. But in my article *Die religiösen Verhältnisse der Andamanesen-Pygmäen* [6] ['Religious Conditions among the Pygmies of the Andaman Islands'], I have demonstrated what is shown at still greater length in the third volume of my *Ursprung*, pp. 50–154, that Brown really did come across a matrilineal religion in the northern and central districts of the Andaman Islands, and that this religion includes no Supreme Being; but that so far as the south is concerned, Man's results are entirely unimpaired. Indeed, Brown's correct data have actually supported and extended them. With regard to the Semang Pygmies, Father Schebesta's expedition had supplied new light in abundance concerning their Supreme Being, Kari (see *op. cit.*, pp. 246–79). But it must be admitted that both on the Andamans and among the Semang the situation is much more complicated than previously appeared. However, we know for certain that this complication is in very large measure due to crossing with later, matrilineal cultures from Farther India. For the Negritos of the Philippine Islands, Father Vanoverbergh's expeditions have opened really surprising perspectives to us; he has discovered a nocturnal liturgy addressed to the Supreme Being and couched in a sacred language no longer intelligible to the natives themselves (see *op. cit.*, pp. 280–317). In the last twenty years

[6] In *Anthropos*, Vols. XVI–XVII, 1921–2, pp. 978–1005.

Pygmies have been discovered in the interior of New Guinea and of the New Hebrides, but not much is known of them so far; whether we may expect to hear of them being in possession of a primitive culture appears doubtful, for all the tribes of these islands hitherto known are already far enough advanced to practise fairly intensive agriculture, and therefore must have been greatly influenced by later cultures.

(b) THE SOUTHERN PRIMITIVE CULTURE

The ubiquity of the Supreme Being can be established for the groups belonging to the Southern Primitive Culture likewise. Some doubt could formerly be felt regarding (i) the Bushmen, whether or not they really still had a Supreme Being; but the matter has now been made quite certain by the investigations of Vedder and Dornan and the expedition of Dr. Lebzelter. The same applies to (ii) Tierra del Fuego, thanks to the discoveries made at the eleventh hour, just before these races become finally extinct, by the expeditions of M. Gusinde and W. Koppers (see *Ursprung*, Vol. III, pp. 873–1007).

(iii) The first volume of my *Ursprung* gives, founded upon the facts collected by Howitt, Mrs. Langloh Parker and others, an account of the existence of true Supreme Beings in South-East Australia, and also of the various crosses between many of them and sundry later creations (see pp. 334–476). In the third volume of that work I carry on the proof already given in the first in a decidedly more lucid manner; I there rely upon fresh old material and an exhaustive examination of the initiation ceremonies of the young men.

(c) THE ARCTIC PRIMITIVE CULTURE

I have also examined the religions of those tribes which Graebner includes in his new division, the primitive culture of the Arctic regions. In the third volume of my *Ursprung* I show that in this area the Supreme Being is everywhere recognized and worshipped, and certainly that his nature is conceived as so wide, indeed so illimitable, as to make it quite characteristic of these cultures. The peoples in question are (i) the Samoyeds, whom indeed we find already in the transitional stage to the nomadic culture, but still showing plentiful traces of the primitive state. (ii) The Koryaks are likewise in a transitional state, and are in addition much influenced by the matrilineal movement which has passed over all the peoples between Kamchatka and the Behring Straits, leaving a deep impress on (iii) the Eskimo peoples without exception, so much so that these, although originally they all belonged to the primitive culture, now show but slight traces of it, save for the Caribou Eskimo who live in the secluded region of the Barren Grounds west of Hudson's Bay, and whose religion has been made known to us by Rasmussen. (iv) The Ainu again have been strongly influenced by animism ; nevertheless in their religion we find a Supreme Being who is wholly unaffected by it, and preserves, so to speak, the character of a high god in a complete state of concentration. (See *Ursprung*, Vol. III, pp. 340–84, 427 *sqq.*)

(*d*) Among the North American Primitives

Here we find the Supreme Being moving on an astonishingly high plane. He appears among the three groups of primitives whose culture is related to that of the Arctic regions, for all of whom we have data in many ways remarkably good, collected by leading Americanists such as Kroeber, Dixon, Spier, Skinner, Grinnell, Dorsey and others. In particular, the idea of creative activity is in force here in its highest form, amounting even to definite creation *ex nihilo*.

The groups in question are (i) the North Central Californians. These consist principally of the Hoka and Penuti tribes and the Yuki, to which must be added some of the smaller Dene and Algonkin tribes (see *Ursprung*, Vol. III, pp. 21–326). (ii) Certain tribes of the interior of the North-West, the Joshua and Inland Salish (*ibid.*, pp. 328–90). (iii) The Algonkin tribes, including the Eastern Algonkin or Lenape, the Central Algonkin (Cree, Ojibwa, Potawatomi, Menomini, Foxes, Sauk), and the Western Algonkin (Blackfeet, Atsina [or Gros Ventres], Arapaho, Cheyenne), with the addition of certain Sioux tribes under Algonkin influence (Winnebago, Iowa, Dacota). All of these show the belief in a high god in various ways (*ibid.*, pp. 391–872).

(*e*) General Survey

If now we review the distribution of the primitive cultures and with them that of the Supreme Beings belonging to them, it is sufficiently plain that we have no narrow or insecure basis for our discussion. First, the extent of these primitive cultures and the distribution of their Supreme Being is almost like a girdle around the south central part of, at least, the Old World ; while for the New, there is at least a sort of representative in the Gez-Tapuya. All these peoples testify by their present relegation to their last refuges, whether distant islands, extreme verges of continents or inaccessible woods and wooded mountains, that they once had a thicker and more continuous distribution in this area. But besides this belt, there is so to speak a lateral extension reaching to the very ends of the earth, for the northern and southern primitive cultures everywhere occupy the most distant extremities, north, north-east and south, of their respective continents. We may therefore claim that no later culture can boast of a distribution which encircles the whole earth so completely. But if it is clear that wherever remnants of the primitive peoples are still discoverable over this huge area, they show belief in a Supreme Being, then it is likewise manifest that such a belief is an essential property of this, the most ancient of human cultures, which must have been deeply and strongly rooted in it at the very dawn of time, before the individual groups had separated from one another.

CHAPTER XVI

THE NATURE, ATTRIBUTES AND WORSHIP OF THE PRIMITIVE HIGH GOD

1. THE PRIMITIVE RELIGION OF A HIGH GOD A TRUE MONOTHEISM

THAT the Supreme Being of the primitive culture is really the god of a monotheism, and that the religion which includes him is genuinely monotheistic— this is the position which is most attacked by a number of authors. To this attack we may reply that there is a sufficient number of tribes among whom the really monotheistic character of their Supreme Being is clear even to a cursory examination. This is true of the Supreme Being of most Pygmy tribes, so far as we know them; also of the Tierra del Fuegians, the primitive Bushmen, the Kurnai, Kulin and Yuin of South-East Australia, the peoples of the Arctic culture, except the Koryaks, and well-nigh all the primitives of North America.

Among other races, the fact of their monotheistic belief has been obscured. This is partly due to crosses with later forms, partly to differentiation, partly to other causes, all of which can be discovered only by exact historical analysis.

(a) FORMS RESULTING FROM DIFFERENTIATION

(a) It is particularly characteristic of the Arctic primitives to differentiate a divine protector of beasts, both wild and tame. Originally it was none other than the Supreme Being who was lord of the beasts they hunted, these being one of their most important sources of food. But the process by which this differentiation took place can no longer be made out in much detail. Owing to the remarkable breadth which the concept of the Supreme Being has among them (for he includes in his sphere the sky, air, water and often the whole

262

of nature) other differentiations, corresponding to different parts of the universe, have also taken place.

(β) In nearly every separate area of the primitive culture the First Father plays an important part, especially in the initiation ceremonies; originally, he and the First Mother were the parents of the race. Owing to the later influence of the matrilineal cultures, he develops a lunar character, is brought into connexion with the moon and not uncommonly obscures the Supreme Being or blends with him. Where contact has been established with the solar mythology of the totemistic and patrilineal culture, the young and powerful morning sun is represented as the child of the Supreme Being, who later becomes identified with the ageing evening sun and is obscured by the morning sun.

(γ) Another pluralizing of superior beings is brought about by the problem of the origin of evil, with which even these men of primeval days wrestled. The Supreme Being is everywhere represented among them as absolutely good, having nothing to do with evil either in conduct or in the outer world. Evil therefore must have another vehicle or originator; and he, especially in the mythology of the North American primitives and of those of the Arctic, is opposed to the Supreme Being; his origin, however, remains darkly mysterious.

(δ) Yet another source of a multiplicity of superior beings is the family relationships of the Supreme Being, when he appears with a wife and children. But here we must make the following observations. In the first place, there is a number of the peoples of the primitive culture who give their Supreme Being neither wife nor children, and even think it shocking or absurd to inquire if he has them. Such peoples are to be found in each of the several primitive circles and generally are the most ancient races of those circles; this is sufficient to make it probable in a high degree that this is the more nearly original state of things. Among these peoples are the Negrillos of Africa, the Negritos of the Philippines, the Kurnai in South-East Australia, the Samoyeds, the primitive Eskimo, the Ainu—the last three belong to the Arctic culture —and practically all the North American primitives. But in the case of the Supreme Being having acquired a wife and children, we can prove that these are later accretions from solar or lunar myths, and to some extent also from older sources than these. This is true of the Bushman Supreme Being, those of the Southern Andamanese and the Semang, of the Kulin, Yuin and Wiradyuri-Kamilaroi in South-East

Australia, and, in the Arctic culture, of the Koryaks. Thus the high probability already mentioned, that the Supreme Being of the primitive culture had originally neither wife nor child, rises to certainty.

(b) TRUE MONOTHEISM WITH A PLURALITY OF SUPERIOR BEINGS

If we wish to estimate at its real value the objection which has been raised against the existence of a true monotheism, we must also inquire in what relation to the Supreme Being the other superior beings stand, when we find any such. If they are more or less clearly stated to have been created by him, and consequently have acquired their attributes and powers from him ; or, still more, if their occupations and positions are assigned to them by him ; but most of all if the Supreme Being still oversees and regulates the exercise of these functions, then we must declare such a religion to be still completely monotheistic. Such superior beings do not deserve the title of gods. If we add the cases in which there are almost no superior beings of any importance at all, as among the Central African Negrillos, the Negritos of the Philippines, the South Australian Kurnai and others, we find that for the primitive epoch, even supposing that there were numerous superior beings, the Supreme Being was in nature and in activities so much above them that the existence of a monotheism, as such, must be recognized. This is true of the Wiradyuri-Kamilaroi of South-East Australia, the Ainu and the Algonkin tribes.

2. THE HABITATION, FORM AND NAME OF THE PRIMITIVE SUPREME BEING

(a) HABITATION OF THE SUPREME BEING

(a) The Supreme Being of the primitive culture is not nearly so indissolubly connected with the sky as he is in the later cultures, especially that of the pastoral nomads. Among most peoples it is said that he used formerly to live on earth with men, whom he taught all manner of good and instructed in their social and moral laws. That alone is enough to show the close connexion between this being and mankind. Such is, as we know, the case with the Southern Andamanese Supreme Being, Puluga, with that of the Semang, Kari, and those of the South-East Australians, North Central Californians, the Indians of the North-West and of many Algonkin tribes. However, another story is often told among North American primitives, namely that he came down to this earth from the sky, while among practically all peoples of the primitive culture the important doctrine is propounded that he left the earth, generally because of some sin of mankind, and went up to heaven, where he now lives. Among the West-Central Algonkin, the Ainu and the Samoyeds it is believed that he lives in a higher heaven, the fourth, seventh, eighth or even twelfth. Frequently, for instance among the North Central Californians, and in South-East Australia, it is specified that in his departure from earth he went eastward.

(β) While the connexion of the primitive Supreme Being with the sky is undoubtedly clear, it is equally manifest that he is an independent and separate personality; there can be no possible identification of him with the material sky itself. As to the immediate reason for this connexion with the sky and the sources to which that connexion is due, that is a question we cannot answer until our available material is better put together and more narrowly examined than hitherto; no good purpose would be served by more or less ingenious hypotheses.

(γ) Closely associated with the heavenly habitation of the Supreme Being is the fact that lightning is very often represented as his weapon, thunder or the roaring and whistling of storm as the expression of his anger. However, in the whole Arctic culture-area and among nearly all North American primitives, these functions are transferred to the thunder-bird. In the latter region there are usually four thunder-birds, one for each cardinal point; in North America the Supreme Being is himself a thunder-god only among the Kato and, most ancient of all, the Yuki. Very close connexions are to be found between thunder and lightning and the Supreme Beings of the very ancient Bushmen, the Yuin god Daramulun, the Wiradyuri-Kamilaroi deity Baiame (the last two are South-East Australian), the Andamanese Puluga and particularly Kari among the Semang Pygmies, who whenever it thunders and lightens make their sin-offering by throwing their own blood towards the sky.

(δ) Less frequent and less clearly expressed is the connexion which we find the primitive Supreme Being to have with rain, as the source of fruitfulness in the vegetable kingdom and incidentally in the animal also. This exists among the Pygmies of Central Africa, the Bushmen and the Yuin and Wiradyuri-Kamilaroi of South-East Australia. It is therefore doubtful if we may count this among the oldest attributes of the Supreme Being, especially if we are to suppose that the idea of such a being first took shape in the tropics. The connexion between rain and the fertility of plants probably was not a subject of very close observation until the agrarian, matrilineal culture; that between rain and animal fertility, not till the nomadic, patrilineal culture.

(b) THE FORM OF THE SUPREME BEING

The information we have concerning the form of the Supreme Being may be divided into two groups. In the first, we are assured that he cannot be perceived by the senses ; the second amount to this, that he has human form, but also something remarkable in addition ; from which it is clear that the point emphasized is not his humanity but his personality, a personality transcending all experience.

(a) To the first class belong such statements as that of the Kamilaroi man who said that Baiame, their Supreme Being, could not be seen but only heard or felt ; or that of those Tierra del Fuegians who declared that their deity was like the wind and could not be grasped. Here then the Supreme Being is credited with a sort of invisibility. The same statement is distinctly made by the Boni Negrillos of East Africa, the Kalinga Negritos of Luzon, the Batwa of Ruanda and the Andamanese ; while the Samoyeds declare that he, like the sky, has no shape.

(β) The other class of testimonies assure us that the Supreme Being is ' like a man ' ; often his reverend age, marked by a long beard, is emphasized, for instance, among the Pučikwar of the Andaman Islands. If the race in question is dark-skinned, the same is of course said to be the colour of the deity, as among some of the Semang tribes. But even there, on the other hand, his white colour is insisted upon ; thus certain other Semang tribes say he is ' like cotton ' ; or his name is Keto ('Light'), for example among the South-Eastern Semang, or Batek Nogn.

(γ) This leads us to a whole series of other races, among whom the Supreme Being is described as ' shining white ' or ' like fire ' ; for example, among the North-Western Semang, the Southern Andamanese, the Wiyot and Patwin of North Central California, the Lenape, an Algonkin tribe, and the Winnebago, a Sioux tribe influenced by the Algonkins. Among the Maidu of North Central California we are assured that the whole form of the Supreme Being shines

like the light of the sun, but that his face is always covered
and no one has ever seen it, except the Evil Spirit, who did
so once. The Kurnai and Wiradyuri teach that the Supreme
Being is surrounded by an aureole of sunrays. Among the
Samoyeds a shaman saw him blazing with so bright a light
that he could not look at him.

Baiame, the god of the Wiradyuri and Euahlayi, has also
an apocalyptic vastness and majesty. He and his consort
sit in heaven on thrones of transparent rock-crystal ; the
lower part of his body has become one with the crystal, and
crystal pillars rise about him, shining with rainbow hues.
Among the Samoyeds, the rainbow is the hem of the mantle
worn by their Supreme Being, Num ; the Gabon Pygmies
say that it is a hunter's bow with which their deity chases
away the storm-clouds.

(δ) No image of the primitive Supreme Being is made
anywhere, save in those places where (as among the Yuin)
he has coalesced with the First Father, or, as among the
Wiradyuri-Kamilaroi, with the child of the sun.

(c) The Name of the Supreme Being

The names by which the Supreme Being is called are various
and expressive. Almost everywhere they are uttered only
with reverence, and that but seldom and not without necessity ;
in many cases periphrases are substituted, or else gestures,
such as pointing to the sky, as with the Yuin god Daramulun
or the Kulin Bundjil. The most widely distributed names
fall into three groups, denoting respectively fatherhood,
creative power and residence in the sky.

(a) The name ' father ' is applied to the Supreme Being in
every single area of the primitive culture when he is addressed
or appealed to. It seems, therefore, that we may consider
it primeval and proper to the oldest primitive culture. We
find it in the form ' father ' simply, also in the individual
form (' my father ') and the collective (' our father '). So
far, this name has not been discovered among the Central
African Pygmies, but it exists among the Bushmen and the
Mountain Dama. It is lacking also among the Andamanese
and the Philippine Negritos, but is found, although not commonly, among the Semang. Among the Samoyeds we find
the formula ' my Num-father ', i.e., sky-father. In North
Central California, the name occurs among the Pomo and
the Patwin ; all three forms of it are widely distributed among
the Algonkins. It is also widely current among the two

oldest Tierra del Fuegian tribes, the Yamana and the Halakwulup, who use the form 'my father'. Among all the tribes
of South-East Australia it is in common use, in the form
'our father'. There it is the oldest name of all, and even
the women and children know it; the oldest of the tribes,
the Kurnai, have no other name for him. There is no doubt
possible that the name 'father' is intended in this connexion
to denote, not physiological paternity (save in cases where
the figures of the Supreme Being and of the First Father
have coalesced), but an attitude of the greatest reverence,
of tender affection and steadfast trust on the part of man
towards his god.

(β) The name 'creator' is not so widely distributed; for
the power to create is, as we shall see later, not predicated
of all primitive Supreme Beings, or at least not in so many
words of all. When creation is relegated to a subordinate
being, usually the First Father, as the task of a sort of demiur-
gus, this being is fairly often styled 'creator', as amongst
the Koryaks. The Supreme Being is not, it would appear,
called creator anywhere among the Pygmies, nor in the Arctic
culture, with the exception of the Ainu, where he also is known
as 'divine maker of the world'; nor among the greater
part of the groups belonging to the southern primitive culture,
Bushmen, Tierra del Fuegians, and most South-East Australians; among the last, however, we do find it in one place,
for the Wiradyuri-Kamilaroi call Baiame 'the creator'.
The name of creator is most widely distributed among the
Supreme Beings of the North American Primitives, where
it takes the forms of 'maker', 'creator', 'creator of the
earth' and 'creator of the world'; among the Samoyeds
he is known as 'creator of life'.

(γ) More widely distributed names are those derived from
his place of abode, or at least his present dwelling. Only
the Samoyeds actually call the Supreme Being simply 'Sky'
(*Num*), however, and they are already in a state of transition
from the primitive culture to that of pastoral nomads.[1] The
commonest forms are 'He that is above' or 'that lives above'
(North Central Californians, American North-West, Tierra
del Fuego, and, doubtfully, Negritos, Bushmen, Koryaks),
or 'He that is in the sky', *Mirirul* (Yuin).

(δ) We must not omit a certain number of other names,
less widely distributed, but often of a very characteristic
kind. One that is fairly common is that which indicates

[1] Cf. above, p. 259.

his continuance from of old, or from eternity. Among the
primitive tribes of the American North-West he is styled
' the old one ' or ' the old one above '. The Yamana of
Tierra del Fuego call him Watauinewa, *i.e.*, ' the primeval '.
Among the Koryaks he is ' the one above ' or ' the master
above ', while his Ainu name is ' the divine sky-lord '. In
the Andaman Islands, the name of the Supreme Being, Puluga,
is connected with the word meaning storm, especially thunder-
storm ; the name of the Semang deity, Kari, means ' thunder ',
which is also the appellation of the Supreme Being among
the Kato and the Coast Yuki in North Central California.
Among the Yoshua Indians of the American North-West
he has a beautiful name, ' the Giver '. The Supreme Being
of the primitive Eskimo is Sila, whose name reflects excellently the indefiniteness and vastness of the deity of the
Arctic primitives (cf. above, p. 262), for it means, among other
things, ' sky ', ' weather ' and ' power '. The Ainu Supreme
Being has three names, all of them beautiful ; they are
' Upholder ' (of the universe), ' Cradle ' (of the child) and
' Inspirer and Protector '. Among many Algonkin tribes
the Supreme Being is called the Great Manitu, signifying
great and supreme spirit, or, more exactly, personality ; in
like manner Gauab or Gawab, the corresponding name among
the Bushmen, applied to their ancient Supreme Being, does
not mean ' spirit ' in any animistic sense, but ' (invisible)
personality '. Among the Yamana of Tierra del Fuego the
Supreme Being has many names, ' the Primeval ', ' the good
Old One ', ' the Most High ', ' the Most Mighty ', but also
' the Slayer in the sky ', because he remorselessly sends death.
The commonest name is, however, ' my Father '. We also
find among the North Central Californian Maidu the appellation ' Slayer ' ; this signifies supreme and sole power over
death (and life). The Koryaks too have a long string of
names for their Supreme Being, besides that already mentioned ; they call him Master, He who Is, Overseer, Power,
He who is Outside, and Universe.

3. ATTRIBUTES OF THE SUPREME BEING

The names of the Supreme Being which we have made the
acquaintance of are enough to disclose a number of his attributes. However, we have in addition much definite information on the subject.

(a) ETERNITY

A sort of eternity is ascribed to all these Supreme Beings more or less clearly, whenever we have anything like detailed information. The form of the statements is that they existed before all other beings, have always been and always will be, or that they never die ; examples are the Andamanese Puluga and the Semang Kari. In two or three instances the death of the Supreme Being is spoken of, as in the case of Daramulun among the Ngarigo ; but here we may be sure that a crossing with the First Father has taken place, he being of course mortal. The Wiradyuri of South-East Australia actually apply expressly to their Supreme Being, Baiame, a word, *Burrambian*, which come from *burrambin*, ' eternity '.

(b) OMNISCIENCE

Omniscience is often ascribed to the Supreme Being, mostly in the interests of morality ; it is a function of his eminently ethical character. The Supreme Being uses this omniscience especially to supervise the commissions and omissions of mankind. Thus the youths of the South-East Australian tribes are taught his omniscience in emphatic terms, with the added information that he also can punish. Among the Batwa of Ruanda it is emphatically said, ' There is nothing which Imana does not know about, he knows everything ' ; he perceives even secret sins of thought. Among the Wiradyuri-Kamilaroi the omniscience of Baiame extends even to the thoughts of the heart. Puluga, in the Andamans, sees everything in the daytime ; but among the Semang Batek Nogn, Keto's eyes are the sun and moon and so also among the Samoyeds, who believe, moreover, that the stars are God's ears ; he therefore can see by night as well as by day. For the Halakwulup, the stars are the eyes of God, with which he views the whole earth. The Kensiu Semang believe in a sort of omnipresence of their Kari, who is near even to the most distant things ; a similar statement is made concerning Gawab, the Supreme Being of the Mountain Dama, ' he is everywhere and knows everything '. In the Wiradyuri-Kamilaroi deity Baiame we find a beginning of inactivity, for he must learn from an all-seeing spirit what happens on earth ; this spirit, however, is of his own creation. So also among the West Central Algonkin we find such intermediaries, while among some tribes of Bushmen the birds tell the Supreme Being everything.

(c) BENEFICENCE

A quite typical attribute of the primitive Supreme Being is that he is altogether good ; all good that men enjoy, and only good, comes from him.   Among the North Central Californians he wishes men to live in a sort of paradise, with the least possible effort and the greatest possible pleasure. There, and also among the Algonkin, he did not want sickness or death to exist among men ; when they grew old they were to bathe or plunge in the water of life, and come forth young again.   When death came in spite of all, the Supreme Being of the West Central Algonkin instituted the life-ceremony, in order to make life last as long as possible.   The Andamanese Puluga is characterized by sympathy and readiness to help ; so also is the Wiradyuri-Kamilaroi Baiame, who likewise is glad to forgive sins and remit the punishment of them, on penitence and reformation.   Among the Wiyot-Maidu of North Central California, the Old One Above bids men pray trustfully to him in all their troubles, for he will help them. Among the Wintun, He who lives Above makes careful preparation for the men who are to come into the world.   The Supreme Being of the Yamana likewise is helpful and kind to those who pray to him.   His strict insistence on sending death does, it is true, earn for him and also for the Kari of the Semang Pygmies the accusation of being ' hard and cruel ' ; but this petulant reproach is at once set right for both these deities by the admission that they punish none but the wicked.

(d) MORALITY

As regards morality, the primitive Supreme Being is without exception unalterably righteous ; his only connexion with anything morally bad is to abhor and punish it.   The true source of this deeply moral character of the Supreme Being is the fact that he is the first and highest, the giver of the moral law, and consequently its origin ; a point on which we shall have more to say later.   For the very reason that all evil is kept far from the Supreme Being, those peoples which lay especially great emphasis on his moral character oppose to him another being who is the representative of evil, who meets all his endeavours for good with protests and hindrances. We cannot properly call this dualism, for the good Supreme Being is represented as far the stronger and more important ; but the origin and continuance of the evil being is often shrouded in a dim twilight which our present knowledge does not allow us to brighten. This is the state of the case among Arctic primitives, the Samoyeds and the Ainu, and the most part of the primitive peoples of North America, for instance the North Central Californians, the tribes of the North-West and both the Western and Eastern Algonkin.

(e) Omnipotence

An attribute which is especially characteristic of the primitive Supreme Being is his enormous power, which indeed is often said to be boundless. This we must throughout consider to be omnipotence. Several tribes of South-East Australia say of him that he can go everywhere and do everything. For the Semang Pygmies he is mightier than all other beings, and this is tacitly implied of all other primitive Supreme Beings ; there is no other being who can even distantly approach him in power, to say nothing of excelling him. Among North American tribes this idea is frequently expressed in legends to the effect that the Supreme Being engages in trials of strength with other superior beings, generally the First Father, for instance, to move a mountain or alter the course of a stream, to split a rock, to walk on the water, and so forth. In these contests the Supreme Being always wins. Examples may be found among the Kato, the Yuki, the Atsugewi, the Thompson River Indians, perhaps the Arapaho also. Even the strongest medicine-man acknowledges that he is powerless against a mortal disease which is sent by the Supreme Being.

(f) Creative Power

(a) The Supreme Being shows his power at its highest in creation. No primitive Supreme Being is definitely said to lack this power, although there are some who are not said in so many words to possess it, or concerning whom the point is obscure and indefinite. But such cases are comparatively few. Among them are a number of Bushman tribes, and in the Arctic culture, the Koryaks and both divisions of the Samoyeds lack the idea of creation in any decided and clear form. In Tierra del Fuego the Yamana and perhaps the Selknam are in like case. On the other hand, the Supreme Being is recognized as creator more or less definitely among all Pygmy peoples concerning whom we have anything like full information ; also among the Ainu, the South-East Australians, the oldest Tierra del Fuegan people (the Halakwulup) and most especially among the primitives of the American North-West, the North Central Californians, the Algonkin, both Eastern and Western, and the Algonkinized Winnebago. In this last group we find the idea of creation in its highest form, that of creation *ex nihilo*, expressed with the greatest definiteness and explicitness. Their myths are concerned above all with creation, and their great national ceremonies are representations and repetitions of the creative process.

(β) The Supreme Being is explicitly recognized as creator of the earth and of the universe among the Asiatic Pygmies (Andamanese, Semang and Negritos) ; also among the Bushmen, the Ainu, the Samoyeds, all the North American primitives, the Halakwulup, and the South-East Australians. The raising of the earth from the primeval deep, in a myth found among the Samoyeds, some North Central Californians and Algonkins, is accomplished by the Supreme Being in the authentic Arapaho creation story, and not by waterfowl. Almost the same peoples acknowledge the Supreme Being as the creator of men also, or of the primal pair, which is the oldest form of the creation of man ; here we must add the Batwa Negrillos of Urundi and the Gabon Pygmies to the list. As to the fashion in which he made the first man or men, that is by no means always explained. In North Central California, where our information on the subject is most complete, three methods are described. In the first, man was made from birds' feathers ; this probably is due to totemic influences. In the second, he was made from sticks, which became human overnight. In the third, his body was formed out of clay, and life was put into the bodies of clay overnight by the Supreme Being sweating amongst them. Amongst the Kulin of South-East Australia, the body is made of clay and the Supreme Being breathes life into it through the nose, mouth and navel. Among the East Kenta Semang also, Kari makes two children out of clay for his wife Manoid ; among the Kensiu Semang he makes them out of fruits, but nothing is said of a separate creation or immission of the soul. Among the Gabon Pygmies the Supreme Being makes the body of the first man of wet clay, and gives it life by his almighty word. Among the Ainu, God makes the skeleton out of a piece of wood and fills in the gaps with earth.

4. RELATION OF THE SUPREME BEING TO MORALITY

We have already shown that the Supreme Being of the primitive period is always ethically good in himself (see above, p. 271), and that this is ultimately due to the fact that he is the creator and source of morality. This alone is enough to show his fundamental relation to it.

(a) THE SUPREME BEING AS GIVER OF THE MORAL CODE

Among the primitive peoples there is a group which does not clearly, emphatically and intensely express the relation of the Supreme Being to morality. This is especially true of the Bushmen, Koryaks and primitive Eskimo. Clearly, not many tribes come under this head. Among all Pygmy peoples of whom we have fairly full information, and also among the Samoyeds, Ainu, North Central Californians, Algonkin, Tierra del Fuegians, and South-East Australians, he is the author of the moral code. The extent of his activities in this respect is not the same among all peoples, but in general his commands extend to the conduct of the ceremonies instituted by him, prayer and sacrifice, obedience to elders, care for the life of man and avoidance of unjustifiable homicide, sexual morality (avoidance of adultery, fornication, unnatural vices, prenuptial unchastity), honesty and readiness to help those who need it (the sick, weak, old, and those with many children). They are especially impressed upon the young men at their initiation or other ceremonies, as celebrated by the Ituri Pygmies, in South-East Australia, North Central California, among the Algonkin and the Algonkinized Sioux, and in Tierra del Fuego. These ceremonies are the creation of the Supreme Being himself, to be a lasting source of instruction in morals, social feeling and piety. In general, the morality of the primitive peoples is by no means low ; a clear proof that they really follow the ethical commands and prohibitions of their Supreme Being. This obedience, this submission of their own wills, is all the more remarkable when we consider that in social and political life their freedom is unbounded, they acknowledge the right of no man to command, save for the authority of parents over minor children, and in particular there is no one who could give orders, positive or negative, to the whole community of his fellow-tribesmen.

That the Supreme Being is also the guardian of morality and uses for this purpose especially his prerogative of omniscience has already been explained above, p. 270.

(b) The Supreme Being as Author of Moral Rewards and Punishments

(a) The Supreme Being, thus exercising oversight on the doings of men, is likewise able to reward morally good action and punish that which is morally bad. A whole series of peoples declare with one voice that the reward is given on earth, in the form principally of long life, and the punishment also, consisting of early death. Among the Wiradyuri this is naïvely followed out to its logical conclusion, in the axiom that all old men are good, for otherwise God would not have let them live so long. The Supreme Being sends death by means of diseases ; Kari for example, the Semang deity, sends them on evil winds, or among other tribes, for instance the Kulin of South-East Australia, the evil spirits of sickness carry them. It accords well with the goodness which many primitive peoples ascribe to the Supreme Being that they do not believe that he ever executes a sentence of death himself, but employs one of the evil spirits whose *raison d'être* this is ; so for example among the Andamanese and the Ainu. Or it may be tigers or other dangerous beasts, as among the Semang ; these creatures are his apparitors and messengers. Elsewhere, however, as also among the Semang, his lightning strikes evil-doers directly.

(β) But a whole array of primitive peoples, the great majority, I think, of those of whom we have fairly detailed knowledge, extend the Supreme Being's rewards and punishments to the other world. All primitive peoples without exception believe in another life. As to what it is like, they cannot all say ; for instance, the Yamana declare that they do not know, and give that as the reason why they are so sad when any of their relatives die. Others hold that in the other world there is no distinction between the good and the bad ; this seems for instance to be the case with the Semang, who hold that all sins have already been atoned for in this world. Similar ideas exist among the Batwa of Ruanda. But the great majority of them recognize such a distinction of good and bad in a future life. Their most definite opinions concern the future lot of the good ; as to the fate of the wicked, they are often uncertain or vague.

(γ) The good usually go, in cases concerning which we have any information, to the sky, where the Supreme Being lives. In many instances they enjoy his own company ; there they live a life free from death, sickness and pain, full of all manner of happiness. This is the belief of the North-Western Maidu in North Central California. Often this after-life is nothing but a more fortunate replica of the present life; there are cases, however, in which gross sensual pleasures are definitely excluded, as among the Wiradyuri, in whose heaven they do not even eat. In many cases it is expressly stated that there will be no more begetting, for instance among the South Andamanese, Semang and Mountain Dama. This is explained by the fact that there is no more dying. The road thither is sometimes said to be the Milky Way, and where that divides, the good are separated from the bad; this is for example the belief of the North-East and Hill Maidu. Often again the rainbow is the bridge leading to the other world, as among the South Andamanese. Among the Wiradyuri-Kamilaroi, the Supreme Being has prepared a stairway on the top of a mountain to the east, and by this the spirits bring men's souls up to heaven. In other cases, as among the most of the Semang Pygmies at present, the dwelling-place of souls is in the west, on Islands of the Blessed in the midst of the sea. Among the Kulin of South-East Australia the soul goes to the west and then climbs up to heaven on the beams of the setting sun. Among the Ainu, the heaven of the good, like the rest of the other world, is under the earth.

(δ) In some cases there is a regular judgement to decide the fate of the good and bad, the souls having to appear before the Supreme Being. This is the belief perhaps of the South Andamanese, certainly of the Halakwulup of Tierra del Fuego, where the soul presents an account of its life. The Wiradyuri hold that Grogoragally, the sun's son, brings the dead every evening to the Supreme Being, Baiame; Baiame then pronounces sentence, Grogoragally often advocating effectively the cause of those who were not altogether bad. The Yuin believe that Mirirul waits for the souls by the great tree of heaven, and judges them. Among the Ainu, the fire-goddess presents an exact picture, drawn by herself, of the whole life of the person on trial to the Supreme Being.

(ε) The lot of the wicked is often described expressly as one of painful punishment, by fire and heat, as among the Ajongo Negrillos and the Southern Wiradyuri; but it may also be by cold, or by wanderings without rest. In other cases it consists simply in exclusion from the happiness of the good, or in an empty shadow-life. Among the Kamilaroi, the bad are annihilated. The place of the wicked is sometimes in the sky, but separate from that of the good. More commonly, however, it is in or under the earth, as among the Batwa of Ruanda and Urundi and the Kalinga Negritos ; or on the western extremity of the earth, as among the Semang.

5. WORSHIP OF THE SUPREME BEING

(a) GENERAL REMARKS

(i) Preuss, Söderblom and others have given it as a characteristic of high gods that they are elevated far above men, have little or no vital connexion with them and also enjoy but scanty worship, if any.   This is true for many high gods of the primary and secondary cultures, but as regards the Supreme Beings of the primitive culture it is wrong from beginning to end.   The lively intercourse between the Supreme Being and men goes back to those primeval times when he himself lived among them on earth, teaching and instructing them.   Even after leaving earth, none of these Supreme Beings has retired into a leisured existence, showing neither activity nor interest in mankind, but still influences this world and its inhabitants by his omnipotence and goodness, his oversight of what men do and leave undone in the moral sphere, the holy festivals and initiations which he founded and at which he is still often present, and finally by the judgement which he passes on the life of a man at its close.   There are also cases, for instance the Halakwulup, the Semang, the Koryaks and the Ainu, in which the Supreme Being sends down each individual human soul into a human body, and so makes the course of each several human life take its start from his own hand.   Not all these relationships to mankind are to be found in every one of the Supreme Beings to an equal extent and with the same intensity ; nevertheless, the number of cases which show a considerable proportion of such attributes is large enough to prohibit us from treating idleness and remoteness from mankind as the characteristic marks of these beings, the high gods of the primitive culture, in particular.

(ii) But men also have from their side lively intercourse with these Supreme Beings, and acknowledge by means thereof the many ways in which they are dependent upon them and their vast importance for human weal or woe.   This results from the fear they feel of their punishments, if from nothing else, for this moves them to avoid what they forbid and to keep their commandments.   It is shown likewise in the reverence and feeling with which they relate the myths which treat of the power and loving-kindness of these Supreme Beings ; in the respect with which they pronounce their names, avoiding unnecessary mention of them ; and finally by the significance of these names themselves, especially the appellations ' Father ' and ' Creator '. All these things are in themselves manifestations of respect, acts of worship, which they bestow on no other beings.

But we find among primitive peoples other ways of approaching the Supreme Being, which amount to actual cult, and are of such a kind as to set up a personal relationship between themselves and him, a relation of ' I ' and ' thou ', and therefore a real and full, because living, religion. This is done by prayer, sacrifice, and formal ceremonies.

(b) Prayer

(a) To establish the existence, among these primitive peoples especially, of the use of prayer is not an easy task ; and we may be sure that many observers have quite missed certain forms of it, with the result that they have declared the peoples in question to have no such usage. This applies to two sorts of prayer in particular, the unspoken petition which has no outward expression at all and that which is expressed purely by gestures ; these, however, may be combined with words, in which case the name of the Supreme Being will be uttered. Such a purely inward prayer, often combined with a strong effort of concentration in the soul, is to be found for instance among the primitive Eskimo, certain Algonkin tribes, and the Semang, whose seers pray on behalf of the rest of them in this fashion, and among the Bushmen. A prayer expressed in gestures, hardly to be recognized as such by others without further instruction, is practised by the Semang, the Yuin and Wiradyuri-Kamilaroi of South-East Australia, and probably also, in the same continent, by the Kurnai and the Kulin.

(β) But there is yet another kind of prayer not easy to discover, without a good knowledge of the native language and without having lived among the people for some time— two qualifications which it is especially rare to find in those who investigate these remote, retiring and shy races. This is the spontaneous, informal prayer, still in use particularly among such peoples, the majority of whom have not yet advanced as far as fixed formulæ. We have definite and beautiful instances of this from the Negritos of the Philippine Islands, the Yamana and Halakwulup in Tierra del Fuego, the Batwa of Ruanda and the Bushmen. We find also, however, even at this stage, long and elaborate liturgies, as that celebrated by night among these same Negritos, and other ceremonious prayers of the Gabon Pygmies and of Algonkin tribes here and there.

(γ) The commonest type of prayer is of course the petitionary. However, we have evidence for prayers of thanksgiving also among the Gabon Pygmies, in North Central California, among several Algonkin tribes, among the Yamana and Halakwulup of Tierra del Fuego and the Wiradyuri-Kamilaroi of South-East Australia. Among the last-named people we likewise find a prayer for the (male) dead, made at their grave, asking that they may be received into *bullimah*, or heaven. The sin-offering of the Semang is accompanied by prayers for the forgiveness of their sins.

(δ) If we survey the distribution of prayer among the primitive peoples, we can show that there is but one people among whom we cannot certainly prove its existence. This is the Andamanese ; and even among them we find certain mysterious ceremonies the fundamental meaning of which we cannot arrive at ; these may possibly represent a sort of prayer, consisting of gestures, not words. The Kurnai and Kulin of South-East Australia are in a very similar position, only the probability that such prayers exist among them is somewhat greater. The practice of prayer alone is uncommon among the Arctic primitives, the Samoyeds and Koryaks, and such prayers as they have are generally but short ; in this region sacrifice is more developed ; this, however, is almost always accompanied by prayer. The Wiradyuri-Kamilaroi also do not pray much, and have public and ceremonial prayers on two occasions only, the burial of men (not women) and at the conclusion of the youths' initiations. They expressly state that, since the Supreme Being is so benevolent and just, so much prayer as they have seen among the whites is not necessary, and can do little good, as may be seen from the life of these same whites. In Tierra del Fuego likewise, the Halakwulup say that petitionary prayer is not needed, for there is no avoiding any punishment inflicted by the Supreme Being, and he sends blessings unasked ; they do, however, thank him for these. In the same region, we can already establish the existence of a comparatively abundant employment of prayer among the Yamana, and the same is true of a number of Algonkin tribes, also of the Gabon Pygmies and the Batwa of Ruanda. Probably better equipped investigators will be able to discover it in other places as well.

(c) SACRIFICE

(a) Sacrifice appears to be entirely lacking among the South-East Australian primitives, except perhaps for certain offerings of leaves in some tribes, but they have developed the initiation ritual for their young men instead. It is also lacking among the two oldest tribes of Tierra del Fuego, the Yamana and the Halakwulup. In North Central California, also, it is hard to prove its existence, unless the feather-sticks of the Maidu and some others deserve the name ; a view not without difficulties, if only because of their ethnological age. It is found, however, among the Arctic primitives, a considerable number of Algonkin peoples, the Asiatic and African Pygmies, the Bushmen, the Selknam of Tierra del Fuego, and the Veddas.

(β) The dominant form of sacrifice, the only one indeed among the Pygmies and Bushmen, is the offering of first-fruits, presented by hunters and plant-gatherers, and of some small portions of food, offered before the people themselves eat of it. Such an offering is found also among the peoples of the Arctic culture, the Algonkins, and the Selknam. In all these cases the thing offered is nutriment, means of sustaining life, for according to the belief of these tribes, all such means are the absolute property of the Supreme Being. He gave man life to begin with ; now he has given them the means to support and continue it, on certain conditions, which are that they shall own and use them within proper bounds, sparingly and respectfully. In this connexion it is especially noteworthy that a similar offering of skulls and long bones of game (bears and reindeer), unopened and still retaining their precious contents, the brains and marrow, is found in the Arctic culture, and that we meet with it again in the older (premousterian) palæolithic culture, as may be seen from the finds in the Drachenhöhle * in the Tamina valley in Switzerland and that of the Petershöhle * near Velden, Mittelfranhen, in Bavaria. The offering of first-fruits is nothing but the recognition of the Supreme Being's sovranty over the means of life, and therefore over life and death themselves. Outwardly, this type of offering is simple and natural ; in content, it is high. Since we find it so widely distributed in these oldest culture-areas (it is the only form known among the Pygmies), we may rule out, as false from beginning to end,

* [The names mean respectively ' serpent's cave ' and ' Peter's cave '.]

that theory of the origin of sacrifice which derives it from the feeding of the dead ; especially as such feeding is practically unknown in any tribe of the primitive culture.

(γ) One Pygmy tribe, the Semang of Malacca, has no offering of first-fruits, but has on the other hand a sin-offering of a sort unparalleled in the whole world. When the thunder rolls—this is the voice of their Supreme Being, Kari—they take a bamboo knife, make a little cut with it at the knee, mix the blood that comes from the wound with water in a vessel and throw the mixture skywards, praying at the same time for pardon for their sins and also, if the storm lasts a long while, making a detailed confession of their sins.

(d) FORMAL CEREMONIES

Particularly among those tribes of the primitive culture who have no sacrifices, and to some extent also among those who seldom pray, we find solemn ceremonies especially well developed. They may last weeks and months, are regarded as having been founded by the Supreme Being himself, and are celebrated at his behest.

(a) Of special importance are the formal initiations of the youths, which are held among the Tierra del Fuegian tribes, the South-East Australians and the Andamanese with extraordinary rejoicing and devotion and with the most conscientious exactitude. Among the oldest of these tribes, the Kurnai for instance, also the Kulin, the Andamanese and the Tierra del Fuegians, the youth of both sexes are initiated and the ceremony has nothing secret about it. The object is to prepare the young people and make them capable of founding families (which are more or less monogamous), an institution of which the Supreme Being is himself the author. At the same time they are to be filled with all their tribe's wisdom and virtue, social, moral and religious. Among many of these peoples, in South-East Australia for instance, the ceremonial is accompanied by invocations of the name of the Supreme Being, with or without accompanying gestures.

(β) In North Central California and among the Eastern and Western Algonkin these ritual festivities occur almost every year, and have taken the form of grateful, we may even say sacramental, commemorations ; they last four, eight, nine or twelve days and enact the creation of the world and of men. Thus they seek to bring the help and grace of God upon the family, tribe and the world at large, indeed in a manner of speaking to create the world anew.

(γ) In the Arctic culture, prayer, sacrifice and ceremonies belonging to certain important seasons of the year have developed into elaborate festivals, in which thanks are given for help received and fresh help besought. The nocturnal litany of the Philippine Negritos, the Pano ceremony of the Semang, the rainbow ritual of the Gabon Pygmies, the ceremonial prayers for rain among the Khung Bushmen and the arrow-rite and other ceremonies of the Veddas should probably be included in the same category.

(e) Recapitulation

If now we briefly review the data, we find that, while this or that form of worship may be wanting in a particular tribe, no tribe is known in which there is not some form in use. As we might expect, prayer has the widest distribution ; but even here we may be sure that there is still much to discover, and that much will be discovered. The wide distribution of the offering of first-fruits in this, the oldest culture, is of great importance as a matter of principle. The cult of the Supreme Being has already reached a very high level among several Pygmy races, also in the Arctic culture, among the Algonkin, and in North Central California, in the combination of prayer and sacrifice in a solemn, expressive ceremonial. But it is to be noted that these are the areas where the best and most thoroughly trained observers have been employed. Perhaps equally competent researches in South-East Australia, for instance, might have discovered yet more ; and it may be that the Pygmy races of Africa still have many surprises in store for us.

CHAPTER XVII

ORIGIN AND HISTORY OF THE PRIMITIVE HIGH GOD

1. ORIGIN OF THE IDEA OF A SUPREME BEING IN PRIMITIVE CULTURE

(a) THE ORGANIC UNITY OF THE DATA

W E have already shown twice over that the goal of all work on the lines of the historical method is not to set up theories or hypotheses, but to arrive at scientific certainty. Here we mean by 'scientific certainty' the facts which make up our picture of primitive religion, not indeed as separate atoms, but as an organic and mutually interdependent whole.

(a) If we apply that criterion to the abundant mass of data which we can now produce regarding the primitive Supreme Being, the first thing to notice is that the total sum of the facts is of a nature to satisfy the total sum of human needs. Man needs to find a rational cause ; this is satisfied by the concept of a Supreme Being who created the world and those that dwell therein. He had social needs ; these find their support in belief in a Supreme Being who is also the Father of mankind, who founded the family and to whom, therefore, man and wife, parents and children, brothers and sisters and kinsfolk owe allegiance. Man has moral needs ; and these too find their stay and support in a Supreme Being who is lawgiver, overseer and judge of the good and the bad, and is himself free from all moral taint. Man's emotional wants, trust, love, thankfulness, are satisfied by such a being, a Father from whom comes all good and nothing but good. Man needs a protector to whom he can resign himself ; this need is supplied in this Being, who is supreme and great above all others. Thus in all these attributes this exalted figure furnished primitive man with the ability and the power to live and to love, to trust and to work, the prospect of becoming the master of the world and not its slave, and the aspiration

283

to attain to yet higher, supra-mundane goals beyond. Only through this conception of deity can we explain the power of our earliest ancestors to struggle onwards ; and the most precious of human energies—labour, responsibility, aspirations upward, feeling for the unity of all mankind—still trace their origin to those primeval days. We thus find, among a whole series of primitive races, a notable religion, many-branched and thoroughly effective.

(β) The second unity into which all the individual traits of the primitive Supreme Being combine and, as it were, stand shoulder to shoulder, is that of time ; for he fills all time. From his eternal heaven he invades Nothingness, and begins the time-series with his creative activity. Throughout all the periods of creation and all successive periods he is lord of man's history, although he does not always actively interpose. He stands, moreover, at the beginning of each human life, accompanies it through all its length of days, awaits its appearance before his tribunal and determines the nature of its eternity. For such a unity as this primitive man has no model and no corroboration in what he sees and experiences in his own time.

(γ) The third unity, which also combines all the separate facts concerning the primitive Supreme Being, is that of space ; for he dominates all space. There is but one Supreme Being, and he fills this universe ; there is but one sovran and one power extending over these distances and joining them one to another. For the God of these primitive men is not the god merely of one tribe and its environment ; if only because he is the creator of the whole world and of all men, he has no neighbour whose realm could limit his. The thoughts and feelings of these men have no room for more than one Supreme Being. The personal experience of primitive man did not show him unity of time ; still less did he find unity of space therein, and least of all in his social conditions.

Primitive monotheism is founded upon the sovranty over these two unities ; this high god is so great that he alone suffices for everything and for all—for all men and all times, all ideals, longings and needs. And therefore he has no peer, for his greatness knows no bounds and thus leaves no room for any neighbour.

(b) THE ORIGIN OF THESE DATA AND OF THEIR UNITY

But the modern historical method has for its aim, not merely the investigation of individual facts, nor of their interrelations in larger wholes, but also to examine the sources from which the unity and the diversity alike are sprung. The problem is all the more urgent and imperative because of this very all-pervading unity with which we have here to deal.

Let us therefore admit immediately that we are in no position to solve it as yet. To say nothing of the multitude of details whereof we have not yet such clear perception as is desirable if so difficult and delicate a question is to be answered, there are also two major difficulties in our way.

(*a*) The first is, that in dealing with the primitive culture we have still to treat a number of separate cultures, whose historical connexions with each other we can indeed make out in some points and conjecture in some others, but know, on the whole, nothing of as yet. Even though we can say, with practical certainty, that of all these cultures that of the Pygmies is the oldest, we perceive with equal certainty that the Pygmies do not possess all the characteristics of the primitive culture as a whole, and therefore cannot give us the entire solution of the problem concerning the Supreme Being; on the contrary, the other primitives have carried away with them important parts of that culture. The true primitive culture therefore must be reconstructed by combining data from all the separate primitive areas—not a mere mechanical addition of their components, but a methodical and exact investigation of their historical relations; which done, we shall be able to fix the relative date of the several religious elements of the primitive culture.

(*β*) The second hindrance is that the historical investigation of the later culture-areas has not yet gone far enough to furnish a side-light on the great and difficult problems confronting us. For as already stated (see above, p. 256), while it is true that the primitive cultures can furnish the most and the most valuable data for establishing the oldest form of religion, since they are chronologically nearest to it, yet it is not impossible that we may still get important factors for our solution from the later cultures, especially those of the primary stage. And of the primary cultures this is especially true of that of the pastoral nomads, since this has kept the most of the primitive culture, in religion as in many other things. But it is just the religion of this culture which is worst off, even as regards collection of material; a point which became clear when we were discussing the sky-god whose cult is characteristic of it. So far, historical investigation of this field has not even begun.

Outwardly, that is geographically, the individual areas of primitive culture are the widest removed from one another ; since the newer cultures which came after have driven them into inaccessible corners, and especially to the northern and southern fringes of the habitable world. For this very reason, research into the areas of the later cultures which lie between them may often show us lingering remnants of the oldest cultures ; and by the help of the Criterion of Continuity (see above, p. 232) these will enable us to build bridges over the gaps and so establish the historical connexions between the several primitive cultures. This in turn will furnish the means to win through to the oldest and most primitive culture of all.

(γ) Hence we are not yet in a position to answer, positively and with scientific accuracy and certainty, the question how the primitive high god and the religion of which he is the centre originated. But we can give a negative answer to many parts of it ; that is, we can say definitely of a whole series of elements that primitive religion did *not* arise from them. These comprise all the elements on which the theories concerning the origin of religion have been founded, those theories which we have been introduced to, one after another, in the course of this work, nature-myths, fetishism, ghost-worship, animism, totemism and magic. That the religion of the high god should owe its origin to any of these is impossible, as appears from two considerations. First, as all these theories teach, these elements could produce such a religion only as the last and highest stage of a long, complicated process of evolutionary advance. But so far from being the latest of religions, this one is characteristic of the oldest peoples. Secondly, such elements either are not to be found at all among these earliest peoples (they know neither totemism, fetish-worship nor animism) or only in a feeble form, as in the case of magic and ghost-worship ; so weak a form that the powerful and conspicuous religion of the high god could not have been derived from them ; while the fully-developed forms of these elements do not appear, as we have seen, until later cultures, those of the primary and secondary stages.

2. THE FURTHER HISTORY OF THE RELIGION OF THE HIGH GOD IN LATER CULTURES

We have already (above, p. 180) found an attempt to trace the after-history of the religion of a high god in later periods of culture made by Andrew Lang. Standing, as he did, still under the influence of unilinear Evolution, he supposed this history to have been more entirely the result of animism than is really the case. To-day, it is one of the results of historical investigation that the primitive culture developed along three independent and parallel lines. These were the three primary cultures, the matrilineal and agricultural, the patrilineal and totemic and the patriarchal and nomadic ; and each of them developed its own habit of mind and its own outlook on the world. According to the particular influences exercised by each of these three cultures, the religion of the high god took various forms. All this we can already trace in its main outlines, indeed the first thirteen chapters of this book are devoted to that purpose. But for the details, it must be admitted, we must wait for special investigations to be made.

(a) IN THE MATRILINEAL AGRARIAN CULTURE

In the matrilineal agrarian culture the position of women rose both economically and socially, for the cultivation of plants was first undertaken by women. Hence there came into being on the one hand a cult of Mother Earth, on the other hand a religious form of lunar myth, in which the moon was itself conceived of as female, and the two figures, moon and earth, soon came into connexion with each other. Under the influence of this, the Supreme Being was often thought of as female, or else the earth was associated with him as daughter, sister or wife. The Moon-woman had for her children a pair of twins, the bright moon and the dark moon. The bright moon, which was the representative of all that is good and beautiful, became the rival of the Supreme Being, in the so-called Boomerang culture, or amalgamated with him, or displaced him. But the dark moon represented all that was stupid, ugly and bad, and became the lord of the under-world and the dead. In the ghost-worship which the men developed within the secret societies in which they now organized themselves, the ideas of spirit and animism generally arose, and these thrust the religion of the high god still further into the background. The offering of first-fruits, now consisting of food-plants, was given to Mother Earth. The offering of food and drink which was laid on the graves of the dead developed into a new kind of sacrifice, often including a sacrificial meal. As the vital force of blood was often used for fertility-magic, blood-sacrifice arose, including the extraction of the heart while still beating, head-hunting and so forth.

(Cf. in general Chapter VII of this book.)

(b) In the Patrilineal Totemic Culture

In the patrilineal totemic culture, the self-confidence of the man and of the tribe increased, owing to the progress made in improved forms of weapons and the perfection of communal hunting, into a belief in active magic, which found its own proper development in this stage.

In some way as yet imperfectly clear the idea arose that the human male was especially associated with the sun; and as a result, various forms of solar mythology developed. The sun was represented as the source of all natural powers, all beauty and everlasting life. As such, he generally had the form of the young and lusty morning sun, and the initiation ceremonies of the youths (in this culture, boys only) aimed at making them like him.

The morning sun, at first subordinated to the Supreme Being, his father, gradually thrust itself into the foreground; the Supreme Being was represented as the evening sun, weak with age and tired of life, and having no direct connexion with mankind any more. Sacrifice was smothered under the mass of magical rites, backed by the strengthening of man's self-confidence.

(Cf. in general Chapters IX and X of this work.)

(c) The Supreme Being in the Patriarchal Cattle-breeding Culture

The races of the patriarchal culture, nomads and breeders of cattle, retained more of the primitive religion than any others. In their wide deserts and steppes, under the high and limitless vault of heaven, the Supreme Being became for them more than ever a sky-god, to such an extent that he even seemed to amalgamate with the material sky itself. The introduction of a social hierarchy, the beginnings of which were already present in the patriarchal undivided family characteristic of this culture, often resulted in exalting the Supreme Being above immediate and living intercourse with mankind and setting up several orders of superior beings subordinate to him, by whom alone man could reach the Supreme Being himself. His dwelling-place was transferred to the higher levels of the sky.

But also the cult of heroes and ancestors generally reaches its most complete development in this culture, while at the same time nature-myths, especially astral, begin to evolve.

(Cf. in general Chapters IV, VI, VIII and XI of the present work.)

(d) IN THE SECONDARY AND TERTIARY CULTURES

All the above developments were completed in the most disparate parts of the earth, in differing degrees of vigour and with various crossings. The manifold forms which the high gods took as a result were made yet more numerous by the crossings of the primary cultures with one another and with the primitive culture, in various ways and to varying extents. From these crossings arose the secondary and tertiary cultures. All this naturally reacted upon the religion of the sky-god, plunging it deeper and deeper into the spheres of the various astral mythologies, of fetishism, animism, ghost-worship and magic, and often almost annihilating it in consequence.

(See here Chapters V, VI, VII and VIII of this work.)

(e) IN HISTORICAL TIMES

Thereafter, as external civilization increased in splendour and wealth, so religion came to be expressed in forms of ever-increasing magnificence and opulence. Images of gods and daimones multiplied to an extent which defies all classification. Wealthy temples, shrines and groves arose ; more priests and servants, more sacrifices and ceremonies were instituted. But all this cannot blind us to the fact that despite the glory and wealth of the outward form, the inner kernel of religion often disappeared and its essential strength was weakened. The results of this, both moral and social, were anything but desirable, leading to extreme degradation and even to the deification of the immoral and antisocial. The principal cause of this corruption was that the figure of the Supreme Being was sinking further and further into the background, hidden behind the impenetrable phalanx of the thousand new gods and daimones.

But all the while, the ancient primitive religion still continued among the few remainders of the primitive culture, preserved by fragmentary peoples driven into the most distant regions. Yet in their condition of stagnation, poverty and insignificance, even there it must necessarily have lost much of its power and greatness, so that even among such peoples it is much too late to find a true image of the faith of really primitive men. It remains for us, by dint of laborious research, to put gradually together from many faded fragments a life-like picture of this religion.

(In the following indexes particularly important references are in bold-faced type. When the abbreviation n. is not followed by any figure, the reference is to the only foot-note on the page).

INDEX A: SUBJECTS

AÇVINS, 49
Âdityas, 43–4
Africa, 66, 69, 70, 100, 225, 234, 239, 242, 253, 258, 263 ; Central, 190, 248 n. 42, 265 ; East, 239, 266 ; South, 184, 239
Agni, 51
Ahuramazda, 44, 48, 51
Ainu, 64, 113, 157, 253, 260, 263, 265, 267, 269, 272 *sqq.*
Ajongo, 258, 276
Albigensians, 22
Albiorix, 45
Algonkins, 60, 64, 88, 113, 114, 132, 137, 139, 157, 164, 239, 253, 260, 264 *sqq.*
Allah, 192–5
allegory, 79 *sqq.*
Alps, S. Australian, 252
Altai, 69
Amazon, 253
America, 70, 100, **188** *sqq.*, 234 ; Central, 99, 253 ; North, 60, 66, 84, 116, 175, 184, 228, 253, 260–4 ; South, 66, 84, 225, 239, 242, 253
Amesha Çpeñtas, 43–4
ancestors, cult of, 42, 54, **62** *sqq.*, 106, 180, 207, 244, 289
Andamanese, 64, 175, 201, 205, 211, 248 n. 42, 258, 263 *sqq.*, 269 *sqq.*, 273, 275, 276, 279, 281
andria-manitra, 160
angeli fornicatores, 20 *sqq.*
animals, lower, 65 ; god of, 262 ; solar, 66

animism, 11, 31, **73** *sqq.*, 106, 118, 121, 155, 164, 170, **174** *sqq.*, 201, 215, 217, 244, 260, 286, 289 ; origin of, 85–6, 205, 209
anthropomorphism, 58
Aphrodite, 50
Apollo, 48, 51–2
Apollonios of Tyana, 21
Arabs, 192 *sqq.*
Arapaho, 260, 272, 273
Arawaks, 253
Arctic peoples, 88, 114 ; *see also* cultures, Eskimo
Argonauts, 48
Artemis, 50
arungquiltha, 132, 160
Arunta, 116, 117, 124, 141
Ârvakrr and Alsvidhr, 48
Aryans, 91, 187
Asia, 66, 69, 222, 234, 239, 241, 252, 253, 258
Assyrians, 91
Atheism, 58
Atsina (Gros Ventres), 260
Atsugewi, 272
Aurora, 48
Australia, 69, 105, 127, 210, 220, 228, 242, 245–9 ; Central, 12, 104, 109, 116, 124, 130, 132, 139, 160, 247 ; East, 66 ; North-west, 247 ; South, 66 ; South-east, 14, 16, 87, 88, 97, 113, 116, 128, 146, 157, 201, 239, 242, 246, 252, 259, 262 *sqq.*
Aztecs, 70

BABYLONIANS, 11, 69, **91** *sqq.*, 249 ; *see also* Panbabylonians

291

INDEX B: AUTHORS